Hispanic Arizona,
1536-1856

Tucson woman washing clothes in the Santa Cruz River below the ruins of the Convent of San Agustín del Pueblito, 1891 (Arizona Historical Society)

Hispanic Arizona, 1536-1856

James E. Officer

The University of Arizona Press
Tucson

The University of Arizona Press

Second printing 1989

Copyright © 1987
The Arizona Board of Regents
All Rights Reserved

This book was set in 11/13 Linotron 202 Plantin.
Manufactured in the U.S.A.

Library of Congress Cataloging-in-Publication Data

Officer, James E.
Hispanic Arizona, 1536–1856 / James E. Officer.
p.   cm.
Bibliography: p.
Includes index.
ISBN 0-8165-0981-6 (alk. paper) : $45.00 (est.)
1. Hispanic Americans—Arizona—History.   2. Hispanic Americans—
Arizona—Genealogy.   3. Arizona—History.   4. Arizona—Genealogy.
I. Title.
F820.S75033   1987   87-18783
979.1'00468—dc19   CIP

British Library Cataloguing in Publication data are available.

For Jim who kept the footnotes straight,
and for Roberta and Sarah who endured.

Contents

Illustrations

Figures

Maps

Prologue

Juan Bojórquez was a corporal in the military garrison of Tucson when Mexican soldiers finally left that post in March, 1856, nearly two years after ratification of the Gadsden Purchase Treaty. Like many of the soldiers and most of the civilians who returned to Mexico at that time, Juan lingered only briefly in his native country, then came back to Tucson where he established a business, reared a family, and spent the remainder of what turned out to be a very long life. On December 11th, 1920, they buried him in Tucson's Holy Hope Cemetery.

A score or more years after he returned to Tucson, Juan fell to reminiscing about his military adventures with two good friends, Sam Hughes and Hiram S. Stevens. Recounting some of the problems encountered in transferring the garrison from Tucson to Imuris in 1856, he observed that when the soldiers reached their destination, they resolved to get rid of everything they had brought along that did not appear to be of use. The civil and military archives were among the items they decided to discard. Juan and his companions sorted through these documents, took out the papers that could serve for rolling cigarettes, and burned everything else.*

The disaster, fortunately, was not as complete as Juan's story

*Atanacia Santa Cruz (Mrs. Samuel Hughes) told this story to Donald W. Page in 1929. Page's transcript entitled "The Mexican troops' departure from Tucson, as recalled by Doña Atanacia Santa Cruz de Hughes" is at the Arizona Historical Society in Tucson.

implied. More than twenty years later, M. Alphonse Louis Pinart
found some of the military records in a closet located in the sacristy
of the Magdalena church. However, many of the remaining military documents and the bulk of the civil records have never been
located.

A similar situation exists with respect to the sacramental registers
kept by the chaplains who served the Tucson garrison and the
priests, both Jesuit and Franciscan, who labored through the years
at San Xavier. Were these documents available, many of the questions concerning relationships among the early Hispanic families of
the region could be definitively answered. In their absence, we have
relied heavily on the old Guevavi and Tumacácori registers in the
archive of the Tucson Diocese, microfilmed materials from various
Sonoran parishes that are available in the University of Arizona
Library, and items in the Pinart collection of the Bancroft Library.

In part, at least, because records have been hard to come by,
historians have touched rather lightly on the Hispanic periods in
Arizona's history. Bancroft was about the only general reference
available until after World War II. In more recent times, we have
profited from the work of such scholars as DiPeso, Ezell, Dobyns,
McCarty, Kessell, Polzer, Naylor and Fontana. No one, however,
has yet attempted a comprehensive chronicle of the area covering
both the Spanish and Mexican years.

Although much less complete than I would like it to be, this
modest volume is, nonetheless, a product of nearly thirty years of
digging through basic source material from a variety of public archives and private collections, published works, and transcribed
comments of members of old Sonoran families who today live on
both sides of the border between the United States and Mexico. In
one particular—that of the family ties that are so important to a
society integrated by kinship principles—the present book does
offer more information that is both reliable and pertinent to an
understanding of events than one usually finds in chronicles of this
kind. Anthropologists have long emphasized the importance of real
and ritual kinship ties in influencing the destinies of the members of
Hispanic-American societies; recently several, among them Carlos
Vélez-Ibáñez and Larissa Adler Lomnitz, have illuminated the relationship between survival strategies and kinship networks in modern urban Mexico. Lomnitz, along with Marisol Pérez Lizaur, has

also shown that such networks play important economic roles in the lives of contemporary upper-class Mexicans.

Some historians dealing with northern Mexico have also stressed the importance of kinship ties among the elite. D. A. Brading gives special attention to these relationships in his history of eighteenth century mining in Mexico's Bajío. The same is true of Hector Aguilar Camín and Stuart F. Voss in their recent political histories of Sonora. Richard Griswold del Castillo has made the Hispanic family a special focus of his research on the Mexican-Americans of the Southwest.

Having been so many years on the trail, I have acquired numerous companions whose aid merits acknowledgement. Foremost among these is the Franciscan historian, Father Kieran McCarty, at present a research associate with the University of Arizona Library. His contributions are so numerous as to defy memory. He has loaned me microfilm, pointed out sources I had not considered, argued (and sometimes agreed) with me about the value of wild goose chases I was preparing to undertake, and always been willing to share documents and manuscripts with me. Without the help of a partial copy of his manuscript for "Desert Documentary II," I would not likely have identified many of the original materials upon which chapters 6 through 9 are based.

Dr. Henry F. Dobyns is another individual to whom I am deeply indebted. In addition to providing encouragement, he has directed me to critical source materials and shared the fruits of his own research, both published and unpublished, with me. His book *Spanish Colonial Tucson* provided both references and themes for Chapter IV, and his monumental unpublished work on Tubac was an inspiration throughout my endeavors. I am grateful to him, also, for the detailed reading that he gave an earlier copy of my manuscript and for the dozens of worthwhile suggestions and corrections he offered.

Carmen Pellat Sotomayor, municipal archivist at Arizpe, has supplied help and guidance of singular import. I have long admired her encyclopedic knowledge of Sonoran family relationships. We have exchanged information about many people and events, with the flow usually much heavier in my direction than in hers.

David J. Weber struggled through one of the previous versions of this work and took the time to offer many helpful comments and criticisms. I hope he will recognize some of the improvements in it that derive from his kindness and interest.

Another good samaritan is Jack S. Williams, who repeatedly came up with references to critical documents I had not consulted and helped me to lay my hands on copies. He has also been most generous in providing me copies of manuscripts he has prepared on important topics in the history of the U.S.-Mexico borderlands.

With respect to relationships within the large Elías family, I have relied heavily on Armando Elías Chomina, an individual who, for many years, has been helping other members of his illustrious lineage unravel snarls in their ancestral skein. Carmen Pellat and Alberto Suárez Barnett were also of great assistance in this regard, as were Mr. and Mrs. Fred Douglass, and Spanish anthropologist Luis Vicente Elías.

For information about Juan Crisóstomo Ramírez of Tubac and his descendants in Tucson—as well as in Florence and Eloy—I must first thank Chonita Sweeney Burrel. A retired school teacher with an abiding interest in family histories, she has given me numerous clues that have helped to solve mysteries about her prominent ancestor, Teodoro, and his immediate family. Sharing the load of informing me about the Ramírez lineage have been Manuel Ramírez of Eloy, owner of Teodoro's notebook, his son (also Manuel), and his daughter-in-law, Carolina Calvo Ramírez as well as Dr. Edgar Varela Romo and his wife, Irene León Romo, María Urquides, Ann Rainsford Brady Padilla and Carol Brady Gamino.

Much information about the Comadurán family reached me through descendants of Tucson's longtime commanding officer. More than twenty-five years ago, I became acquainted with the late Anita Coenen de Maldonado, who told me about her great-grandfather and, later, I learned more about him from Anita's daughter, Ana Maldonado de Fimbres, who in 1987 was retired and living in Green Valley. They informed me, too, about the Oteros, from whom they are also descended. More recently, Martha Soto Green of Gilbert, Arizona, also of the Comadurán lineage, has enlightened me concerning her ancestors. Helpful, too, have been Dina Díaz Almazán of Tucson, and members of the family of Alberto Comadurán of Benson.

So many other persons have provided me kinship information that it would be impossible to remember and mention them all.

Coming quickly to mind, however, are Richard Willey, who helped with genealogies of the Pachecos and the Ainzas; María Sabori, who did the same for the Telles family; and Ed Ronstadt, who provided information about the Redondos and other Altar Valley lineages.

Although I have for many years had close friendships with Sonoran scholars, including the late Eduardo W. Villa, the number of such associations has grown appreciably since the University of Sonora began its annual history symposium. I am grateful to such persons as Juan Antonio Ruibal and Armando Quijada Hernández for extending me invitations to take part in these affairs, and to Drs. Michael Meyer and Susan Deeds of the Latin-American Area Center of the University of Arizona for facilitating my acceptance of their invitations.

Bernard L. Fontana and Charles Polzer of the Southwestern Mission Research Center have given me good counsel and encouragement, and have made many documents, including their own publications, available to me. I appreciate, too, the suggestions of persons such as John Kessell, Tom Sheridan, Tom Naylor, Nick Bleser, Jim Griffith and Joe Park. David P. Robrock of the Special Collections Department of the University of Arizona Library supplied many new references concerning the Forty-Niners that have strengthened Chapter 12. Shirley and Bill Griffin provided a generous financial gift that has helped to meet the cost of illustrations for the manuscript. I am grateful also to A. Tracy Row who has been a patient and helpful editor.

I have been honored through these many years with excellent company for the trips I have made to locations of importance in the Hispanic periods of Arizona history. Those who have joined me at various times for such pleasant travel include the late George B. Eckhart, Bernard L. Fontana, Jim Griffith, Ed Ronstadt, the late Bob Torrance, Jack S. Williams, Leo Salazar, Don Bufkin, the late Bill Wasley, Armando Elías Chomina, Richard Willey, Jan Hannon and my wife, Roberta.

It has been my privilege also to serve as one of the historians on the Sonoran tours sponsored by the Southwestern Mission Research Center. This involvement has made it possible for me to spend many pleasant hours with those who plan and conduct these trips. They, too, have contributed to the creation of this book and I am pleased to thank them—one and all. To names already mentioned, let me add those of Lea and Oscar Ward, Mary and George Malaby, Carmen and Tom Prezelski, Marjorie and Frank Gould, Mary Catherine Ronstadt, Julieta and Ernesto Portillo, Roberta Stabel, Loma Griffith, and Mardith Schuetz.

Hispanic Arizona, 1536-1856

I

Myth and Reality in the Upper Pimería

In 1889, only thirty-five years after the Gadsden Purchase brought all of the area since known as Arizona under American control, Hubert Howe Bancroft published a history of the region covering more than three and a half centuries of its past.[1] Based heavily on Spanish and Mexican documents, this work might well have buried once and for all the exotic tales and fanciful interpretations of past events that circulated during and after the United States-Mexico War. According to these myths, Tucson was one of the oldest cities in the United States founded by Europeans; the whole of southern Arizona was once covered with prosperous Spanish missions and settlements abandoned because of Apache raids; and the Jesuit and Franciscan priests mined large quantities of gold and silver using Indian slave labor.[2]

Although Bancroft and his associates put the lie to much of this nonsense, the public predilection for a more romantic rendering of events assured the old tales of continued vigor. In 1928, when the Arizona state historian's office began publishing a new journal entitled *Arizona Historical Review*, the editors reprinted without critical comment an item by Patrick Hamilton[3] that included many of the romantic notions that had gained currency during the first quarter century after Americans began to occupy the area. As late as 1958, a well-regarded world atlas placed the date of Tucson's founding at 1580.[4] And in 1968, a Jesuit historian at the University of Arizona was still trying to set the record straight regarding the mining activities of the priests.[5]

Few of Arizona's pioneer historians consulted Spanish language documents, but even after the more scholarly ones began quoting Bancroft and, thus, improving their accuracy with regard to the Hispanic past of the region, they continued to write of the territorial and early statehood eras as further sagas in the Anglo-American conquest of the frontier, managing in the process to ignore the contributions of other groups. Native Americans were represented as simple creatures of nature or as pesky savages unwilling to step aside for the advance of civilization; and the Mexican settlers, when mentioned at all, were pictured as passive bystanders in the development of the frontier, as rustic immigrants, or as treacherous *bandidos* and, later, as potentially dangerous revolutionaries. The many contributions of Mexicans to building Arizona's economy in the territorial period sometimes peep through, but only in the 1960s did any scholar devote a whole volume to the subject. That excellent work, twenty years after its completion, remained unpublished in thesis form.[6]

The tendency of many Anglo-American popular writers to distort what might be referred to as "Arizona's Hispanic perspective"—whether through ignoring, glamorizing, or villainizing it—is not a unique phenomenon. Other regions of the Southwest have been subjected to similar, if not worse, treatment. In California especially, separating truth from fiction has plagued conscientious historians such as Leonard Pitt who, in his book on the *Californios*, remarks that many of his data "were submerged in a veritable quagmire of sentimentality and myth."[7] Furthermore, stereotypes developed in one region of the Hispanic Southwest—even in remote parts of Mexico—have been indiscriminately passed on to other areas without regard for the fact that each of the regions along the U.S.-Mexico border has a distinct history that has given it a flavor all its own.

At its pre-Anglo peak, probably reached around 1820, Arizona's Hispanic population was barely over 1,000 and, thus, was substantially smaller than that of California, Texas and New Mexico.[8] Additionally, that limited presence was confined to a relatively small area in the southeast quarter of the state, being concentrated in or near the settlements of Tucson and Tubac, both of which began life as military establishments and continued to function in that capacity during the entire period of Spanish-Mexican rule. Outside the range of these forts, a handful of frontiersmen lived a precarious, often interrupted, existence on land grants or in the vicinity of a few Indian missions.[9]

Arizona shared with New Mexico and Texas prolonged conflict between Hispanic settlers and native Americans, yet in neither of these areas was the "Indian problem" so conclusive a force in determining the extent and character of Hispanic occupation as was true in Arizona. In this respect, the region perhaps most resembled that of southern Chile, another outpost of the Spanish realm that experienced unremitting Indian warfare, the outcome of which was seldom conclusively to the advantage of the Spaniards.[10]

By comparison with California, New Mexico and Texas, Arizona was almost unknown to Anglo-Americans until the visit of the Mormon battalion in 1846. Sonorans called the southern part of the region Pimería Alta ("Land of the Upper Pimas"), and the word "Arizona" was applied to a specific location southwest of the modern twin cities of Nogales, Arizona and Nogales, Sonora. Many Forty-Niners on their way to California passed through the Pimería Alta, which they regarded simply as part of the Sonoran frontier; most, however, were not particularly interested in the local residents. Their diaries often include detailed information about features of the landscape, including plants and animals, but little about the people. California beckoned, and whatever the Forty-Niners encountered along the way captured their attention primarily if it hastened or delayed their arrival in the promised land.

When, Where, and How It Began

Although Arizona's Hispanic history lacks the depth and breadth associated with that of New Mexico, it was from the latter area that the Spaniards first launched their effort to gain a foothold on Arizona soil. Three decades after establishing the New Mexico colony, Franciscan missionaries initiated a Christianizing program among the Hopi Indians with the assignment of three priests to the mesatop villages.[11] From 1629 until the outbreak of the Pueblo Revolt in 1680, the missionaries maintained a presence in Hopi country. Had they not been expelled during that rebellion, never successfully to return, Spanish colonization of Arizona might have proceeded from north to south, rather than in the opposite direction.

Usually credited with paving the way for permanent Spanish occupation of Arizona is the Jesuit Eusebio Francisco Kino, although this attribution obliges one to stretch the point somewhat. Kino did indeed establish missions at Guevavi and Bac around 1700, but resident priests were at each location for only a matter of months in 1701–1702 and, thereafter, the Indians of these and nearby communities depended upon the occasional visits of Jesuits from San Ignacio and other missions many miles distant. It was not until the 1730s that resident missionaries returned to Arizona soil and although a few Europeans were in the area from then on, the first priests to man the missions after 1730 were not Spaniards, but Jesuits recruited from the German states.[12]

Both directly and indirectly, the most important stimulus to Hispanic settlement in southern Arizona probably came in 1736 with the discovery of silver at a location about seventy miles south of Tucson which the Spaniards called "Arizonac." Its direct influence was to bring large numbers of prospectors into the region, some of whom pushed on northward to become colonists.[13] Its indirect influence was to heighten Indian fears about a Spanish invasion of their territory and, thus, contribute to the Pima Revolt that broke out in 1751. The year after that uprising the Spaniards placed a fort, or presidio, at Tubac. This action attracted other Hispanic settlers and by 1757, several hundred were residing in the area.[14]

For all of the Spanish period, even after transfer of the presidio from Tubac to Tucson in 1776, the Hispanic population of southern Arizona led a dangerous and harsh life. The situation rapidly worsened when Mexico obtained its independence in 1821. During the last years of their control, the Spanish had quite literally purchased peace through distributing gratuities to the Apaches and inviting them to make their homes near the presidios where the troops could keep an eye on them.[15] The fledgling Mexican nation could not afford to continue this practice, nor could it supply the soldiers needed to combat the Indians who were annoyed by its termination.[16] After 1830, southern Arizona actually lost population. By 1850, nearly all the Mexicans in the area—fewer than 1,000 of them—were concentrated in Tucson fighting for survival.[17]

Hispanic Place Names in Arizona

Considered in the framework of the greater Hispanic Southwest, place names derived from the Spanish language, especially those of political subdivisions, are comparatively rare in Arizona, and some that do exist are products of the recent Anglo period. The preceding historical summary should make clear why this is so. Only a tiny strip of the southern part of the state ever experienced sustained Hispanic colonization before the United States gained control of the region. When other areas finally were settled after 1860, especially those north of the Gila River, colonists were for the most part Anglo-Americans who sought to make the region as much as possible like the places in the United States that they were familiar with. Early Prescott residents chose street names from the romantic Spanish-Indian past—Montezuma, for example—but Anglo designations were more common.

From the early years of the present century, scholars have generally agreed that the word "Arizona" is of Pima Indian origin. Ethnologist Frederick Webb Hodge supported this view and he was regarded as the leading authority of his day on the subject of Indian names.[18] In his history of Arizona written just before World War I, James McClintock quoted Hodge and concluded with the comment that "little reason exists for further research along this line."[19] Thus, it was established to the satisfaction of most that the name Arizona came from two Pima Indian words—*ali* and *shonak*—which taken together mean "small springs" or "few springs."[20]

Any debate about the matter that may have been silenced by Hodge and McClintock resumed in 1979 when an etymologist from the Center for Basque Studies at the University of Nevada offered a new theory. Using a variety of linguistic and historical data, William A. Douglass came to the conclusion that, although the Pima thesis was plausible, an equally strong case could be made for a Basque origination. He observed that either of the Basque phrases *arritza onac* ("good" or "valuable rocky places") and *aritz onac* ("good" or "valuable oaks") could suit the purpose of explaining the origin of "Arizona." According to Douglass, the location referred to as Arizonac (spelled in various ways: for example, Arissona and Arizona) was one with extensive mineral deposits and also heavy stands of oak. The oak trees were important to Basque frontiersmen because acorns provided a primary source of pig food in the region of Spain from which they came. Finally, Douglass noted, the association of Basques with the North Mexican frontier is well established. Many prominent early residents of the area—among them Juan Bautista de Anza—were Basques. Additionally, the first Hispanic settler of Arizonac—Gabriel de Prudhon Heider Beltrán y Mújica—was of that origin.[21]

The writings of Father Kino do not mention any Pima village called Arizonac, although later Jesuits refer to one in the region where the famous silver strike was made in 1736.[22] If the village was there prior to 1730 when Prudhon founded the Real de Arizonac,[23] then the Pima theory, rather than the Basque, would appear the more likely.

Another Arizona name whose origin has been attributed to both Spanish and Indian sources is Gila. In her revised edition of *Arizona Place Names*, Byrd H. Granger observed that in 1630 a province of New Mexico was named Xila or Gila, "a Spanish word encountered on maps of Spain itself and used in the language as an idiomatic expression: 'de Gila', a steady going to or from a place."[24] Despite Granger's association of the name with New Mexico, the author of that state's standard reference on place names (writing five years later) attributes the word to a Hispanicized version of an Apache term meaning "mountain."[25] According to Bancroft,[26] the name was first applied to a band of Apaches living in the mountains of west central New Mexico and, later, to a New Mexico province.

Edwin Corle, in his popular work in the Rivers of America series, attributed the word Gila to the Yuma Indian language, specifically to the phrase *hah-quah-sa-eel*, which he translated as "running water which is salty."[27] If an Indian origin is to be assumed, the Yuma theory is less tenable than the Apache, since the Spanish seem first to have applied the term to a region inhabited by the latter.

The only Arizona county with a name that is clearly Spanish is Santa Cruz, or Holy Cross. In this instance, the name comes from the river that constitutes one of the county's principal landmarks. Father Kino called this stream the Santa María in honor of the patroness he had assigned to Soamca, an Indian village near its headwaters. During the eighteenth century, sections of it also bore local designations. Following the relocation of the Santa Cruz presidio to Soamca in the 1780s, the river gradually came to be known by the name it still bears.[28]

Testimony to the fact that the Spanish did wander through much of the area, even if they did not establish permanent settlements, is provided by the names given to some of Arizona's principal rivers and mountain ranges. In addition to the Santa Cruz, such streams as the Salt River (Río Salado in Spanish), the Verde (Green), the San Pedro (Saint Peter), and the Colorado (Red) bear names from the Spanish and Mexican periods. All these streams at various times also had other Spanish designations.[29]

Important mountain ranges whose Spanish names have survived from the pre-Anglo period are the Santa Catalina (also, Santa Catarina), the Santa Rita, and the San Francisco, among others. The uplift known as the Mogollon Rim, like the New Mexico mountains similarly designated, was named for Juan Ignacio Flores de Mogollón, Captain-General of New Mexico between 1712 and 1715.[30]

Tucson and Tubac—Arizona's oldest Hispanic communities—both have Indian names, but they once bore saints' names by which they were commonly known to their Spanish-speaking residents. When founded in 1752, the Spanish fort at Tubac was called San Ignacio. A decade later a newly constructed church was dedicated to Santa Gertrudis. In the 1780s, a troop of Indian soldiers stationed at Tubac was designated the San Rafael company.[31]

Tucson, too, experienced name changes during the Spanish period. Kino referred to the Pima village at the foot of A Mountain (Sentinel Peak) as San Cosme. Captain Francisco Elías González, who relocated Sobaipuri Indians there in 1762, called it San José. By 1774, it was known as San Agustín, the name it continued to carry until Arizona became a part of the United States.[32]

Architectural Influences

The limited area of settlement, meager population, and constant threat from hostile Indians all contributed to the fact that Arizona has few architectural monuments today that date from the Spanish colonial and Mexican periods. However, in the area of mission churches, San Xavier and Tumacácori represent two of the finest examples of Spanish frontier architecture to be found anywhere. They cannot, of course, be compared in terms of size or ornateness with the great cathedrals, convents, and monasteries of central Mexico, but they possess a great deal of charm and contribute more than any other cultural items to relating the contemporary population of the state to its Hispanic past.

Construction on the present church at San Xavier began in the early 1780s (1783 by popular tradition, although it may have been earlier) and is known to have been finished by 1797.[33] The Tumacácori church, started in 1802 during the last days of the Spanish empire in the western hemisphere, was dedicated shortly after the beginning of Mexican independence in 1822, when few of the Indians for whose spiritual welfare it was intended were around to gain from its presence.[34]

The oldest visible evidence of Spanish architecture in Arizona is found at the site of the old Hopi town of Awatovi in the northern part of the state. Here, the ruins of a complex of buildings dating from 1629 to 1700 were still to be seen in 1980 when Governor Bruce Babbitt, archaeologist Watson Smith and a small party visited the location in connection with proposed legislation to protect and preserve such antiquities.[35] At that time, the standing walls of the principal church at the site (there seem to have been three in all) rose to a height of nearly ten feet at the far western end of the sanctuary. The Awatovi ruins were excavated by personnel from Harvard University's Peabody Museum during five seasons beginning in 1935,[36] but no preservation or stabilization work was undertaken then or afterward. The Hispanic buildings at the location were razed during the Pueblo Revolt of 1680 and a subsequent uprising in 1700.[37]

Ruins of Spanish structures were also visible in the early 1980s at three other places: Calabazas, near present-day Rio Rico; Guevavi, a short distance northeast of Nogales; and Santa Cruz, north of Fairbank on the San Pedro River. The Calabazas ruin may include portions of a church built in the 1770s. This structure also served various secular functions, that of customs house among them.[38] Guevavi to the south was abandoned about 1773,[39] and the ruins there are of a church built by Jesuits before their ouster in 1767.[40] Remains on the San Pedro are those of the presidio of Santa Cruz de Terrenate which had a resident garrison for about four years between the winter of 1775–76 and 1780.[41]

Ruins of the Guevavi Mission in 1889 (George Roskruge photograph, Arizona Historical Society)

Ruins of the old Gándara hacienda at Calabazas in 1913 (Forbes collection, Arizona Historical Society)

By the early 1980s, there were few architectural remains that could be positively identified with the Mexican period. Outside of Tucson, these consisted primarily of the fortified structure on Babocómari Creek which was completed in 1833 by land grant owner Ignacio Elías González[42] and that became a part of the holdings of the Brophy family in 1936.[43]

Tucson's "old adobes" have been much admired by architecture buffs[44] and, for sentimental reasons, if no others, many Tucsonans have preferred to believe they pre-date the Anglo beginnings of the city. The fact remains, however, that the extent of Mexican-period architectural survivals in the community is questionable. Prior to freeway and urban renewal projects beginning in the 1950s, there may have been some downtown structures built in Mexican times, and it is even possible that portions of buildings surviving into the 1980s have such origins. On the other hand, historians have thus far failed to turn up the documentation needed to confirm this antiquity. Even the numerous renovation projects in the old presidial area have produced disappointing results. The restored Córdova house, originally thought to have been built before 1850, was later determined through use of the tree-ring dating method to be somewhat younger.[45]

Early in 1849, following a major attack by the Apaches, Tubac residents fled to Tucson for protection.[46] A few of the refugees may have constructed homes in the area that later came to be known as Barrio Libre.[47] Dates in the 1850s are certainly reasonable for buildings in this neighborhood, but many of them disappeared under the impact of urban renewal.

The first Anglos to come to Tucson were, with few exceptions, taken aback by the architecture they encountered in the community, as well as by the generally run-down appearance of the place. The many groups of gold seekers passing through the area between 1849 and 1854 wasted no compliments on the physical aspects of the town. Things had improved little, if any, when journalist J. Ross Browne visited there in 1864. Approaching from the northwest, he wrote:

Passing the Point of the Mountain, eighteen miles below, he [the traveler] is refreshed during the remainder of the way by scraggy thickets of mesquit, bunches of sage and grease-wood, beds of sand and thorny cactus; from which he emerges to find himself on the verge of the most wonderful scatteration of human habitations his eye ever beheld—a city of mud-boxes, dingy and delapidated, cracked and baked into a composite of dust and filth; littered about with broken corrals, sheds, bake-ovens, carcasses of dead animals, and broken pottery; barren of verdure, parched, naked, and grimly desolate in the glare of a southern sun. Adobe walls without whitewash, inside or out, hard-earth floors, baked and dried Mexicans, sore-backed burros, coyote dogs, and terra-cotta children. . . .[48]

Except for its sarcastic tone, Browne's description of Tucson's appearance corresponds quite closely with what others had to say about the town. Indian fighter John Gregory Bourke, who ultimately succumbed to Tucson's Hispanic charm and who was always a more serious and sympathetic observer than Browne, first cast his eyes upon Tucson in 1870. Approaching it from the western end of the Santa Catalina mountain range, he remembered:

That fringe of emerald green in the "bottom" is the barley land surrounding Tucson; those gently waving cottonwoods outline the shrivelled course of the Santa Cruz; those trees with the dark, waxy-green foliage are the pomegranates behind Juan Fernández's corral. There is the massive wall of the church of San Antonio now; we see streets and houses, singly or in clusters, buried in the shade or unsheltered from the vertical glare of the most merciless of suns. Here are pigs staked out to wallow in the congenial mire. . . . Here are "burros" browsing upon tin cans . . . and here are the hens and chickens, and the houses of mud, of one story, flat, cheerless, and monotonous were it not for the crimson "rastras" of chile which, like medieval banners, are flung to the outer wall. . . .[49]

The type of architecture that Tucson's first Anglos encountered was one widespread throughout the regions of Spanish colonization, although it has in recent years been referred to locally as "Sonoran."[50] Buildings were usually located at the front property line, and often joined to adjacent structures. They were one story high with walls made of adobe, often covered with stucco. Roofs were flat with parapets, doors were set deep, and windows were commonly located at the exterior face of the thick walls.[51] Such construction is still typical of many small towns in Sonora and other

Modern skyscrapers provide a backdrop for old adobe houses on Convent Street in Tucson (author's photograph taken in 1987)

parts of Mexico, and the Mexican sections of Tucson provide abundant examples as well. In fact, the persistence of this style in some Tucson neighborhoods has contributed to a false impression of the antiquity of both the structures and the neighborhoods, or barrios, in which they are found. On the other hand, the style is unquestionably old and Hispanic-Moorish in origin, even if the structures themselves are new.

With an increased Anglo population, a transformation in building occurred that combined lightweight construction technology and Anglo site planning with selected elements of the earlier tradition. The changes produced by these and later modifications were documented for Tucson and Florence during the 1970s and early 1980s by faculty members and students from the College of Architecture at the University of Arizona.[52]

In addition to the Sonoran tradition, two other Arizona architectural styles have Hispanic origins, although both were introduced to the area by Anglo architects long after Arizona ceased to belong to Mexico. These are often referred to as "mission revival" and

"Spanish colonial revival." The former is said to have been brought to Tucson by Henry Trost and David Holmes shortly before the beginning of the twentieth century. Both architects had been influenced by the California building at the Columbian Exposition in Chicago in 1893, and both appreciated its possibilities for an area which, like California, had a Spanish-Mexican past. The first Tucson building designed in this style was the Owls' Club on Main Street which was later purchased by Albert Steinfeld and has since been known as the Steinfeld Mansion.[53] Trost was designer of this structure, but when he left Tucson in 1904 the fashion was continued in the work of David Holmes. By 1910 Main Street was becoming well known throughout the state for its private homes based on mission revival designs.

The Spanish colonial form attained popularity in the west following the San Diego World's Fair in 1915. It, too, affected Arizona architecture in a variety of ways. Some buildings of monumental size, such as the Veterans' Hospital, the Pima County Courthouse, and the Benedictine Sanctuary of Perpetual Adoration—all in Tucson—were what might be called "pure" Spanish colonial because they relied primarily on elements associated with that style. On the other hand, many other structures, both public and private, simply borrowed a few features of the style and mixed them with elements taken from other traditions, thus giving a slightly Hispanic touch to the final product. One Tucson critic commented in 1982 that "such touches hinted at the architecture of Renaissance Spain as fleas suggest eagles."[54]

Phoenix architect Bennie González and Tucson architectural engineer E. D. Herreras are two Hispanic Arizonans of the post World War II period with widespread reputations for their successful use of Spanish and Mexican materials and styles. González has specialized in adapting certain features from these traditions to contemporary construction. Herreras has enjoyed a longstanding reputation for his success at restoring or reconstructing older buildings. In 1979, at age eighty-two, he and a close friend, seventy-three-year-old Al Hubbard (also a Hispanic in spite of the Anglo surname), did the necessary work to stabilize the historic Edward Nye Fish house, one of Tucson's most distinguished old adobes.[55] Herreras, who for many years was Tucson's building inspector, also enjoys fame locally for helping with the upkeep of Saint Augustine Cathedral and San Xavier del Bac Mission Church.

Ranching, Farming, and Mining

Hopis and Navajos were the first Arizonans to raise sheep, and the Jesuits established cattle herds among the Indians of the Pimería Alta at the end of the seventeenth century.[56] Some settlers may have run cattle within the present boundaries of Arizona even before Kino's arrival. Certainly by the 1730s, a few families had herds in the region immediately south of Guevavi, a location known as the San Luis Valley, and to the west at Arivaca and Sópori.[57] Later, in Mexican times, Hispanic ranchers raised cattle on granted lands (*mercedes*) along the Santa Cruz and San Pedro rivers, on Babocómari Creek, and in the San Rafael Valley.[58] These operations did not survive the Apache raids of the 1830s and 1840s, and when the first large numbers of Anglo-Americans came into the region, they encountered many wild cattle wandering unattended across the landscape.[59]

Although a few Anglos tried ranching in the 1850s and early 1860s,[60] they were also inhibited by the Apache threat, and except for small herds maintained by Indians and others, the cattle industry did not come into its own until the 1870s and 1880s. As was the case in Texas, which was the place of origin of many Anglo stockmen, ranch owners, especially those south of the Gila River, depended heavily on Mexican cowboys.

Despite the interference of raids by hostile Indians, Spaniards and Mexicans continued to raise livestock, and contemporary Arizona ranchers—like those elsewhere in the region—owe much to Hispanic traditions. The late historian/folklorist J. Frank Dobie once observed that everything that served to characterize the American cowboy was taken over from the Mexican *vaquero*, including utensils and language, methods, and equipment.[61] The horned saddle, as distinguished from the English type, was a Spanish modification of a Moorish invention. From the *vaquero*, also, the cowboy got his lasso or lariat, cinch, halter, chaps, spurs, bridle and bit.

The cowboy lexicon includes many terms borrowed from the lingo (*lengua*) of the buckaroo (*vaquero*). Among the most common are ranch (*rancho*), bronco (*bronco*—rough or coarse), mustang (*mesteño*—stray or wild), lariat (*la reata*—rope for tying horses), lasso (*lazo*—loop), quirt (*cuerda*—cord or rope), stampede (*estampida*), cinch (*cincha*), and calaboose (*calabozo*—dungeon).

Some of the Hispanic ranchers who helped rebuild the cattle

industry after many Apaches were first placed on reservations were descendants of pioneers with deep roots in the Pimería Alta. They boasted family names such as Otero, Pacheco, Elías, Ruelas, León, Ortiz, Ramírez, Amado, Telles and Romero. Joining them were newcomers named Carrillo, Aguirre, Robles, and Samaniego.[62]

The isolation of the Pimería Alta and its limited population provided little inspiration for major agricultural development, and during Spanish and Mexican times the biggest producers of both native and introduced crops were the village-dwelling Indians of the Gila and Santa Cruz river valleys. Hispanic settlers at Tubac and Tucson planted corn, wheat, barley, and vegetable crops, in addition to fruit trees and grape vines. When there was a surplus, they disposed of it through sale to the *comandante* or his representative. The soldiers, when not chasing Apaches, did some gardening, and during the latter part of the Mexican period were expected to cultivate forage crops to provide food for their horses and other draught animals. During a part of both Spanish and Mexican times, Tucson settlers planted and harvested crops on the San Pedro River at Tres Alamos, near modern Benson. Because of the Apache menace, they were escorted to and from their fields by presidial soldiers.

Limited though their agricultural operations were, many of the Mexicans in the Pimería Alta gained farming skills that led to wage work after Anglo-Americans began to dominate the region's economy. By the end of the territorial period, Hispanic laborers enjoyed a near monopoly on this kind of work.[63] A few of the old Mexican families, especially those who came to reside in newly settled areas where irrigation was possible (Florence and Yuma among them), had moderate success as farm entrepreneurs during the 1870s and 1880s.[64]

Just as Apache raids restricted farming and ranching, they also interfered with the establishment of a firm foundation for mining, even though the presence of precious metals had drawn Spaniards to the area in the first place. Gold and silver mines were operated at various locations beginning in the years preceding the establishment of the Tubac presidio, but all seem to have been small-scale enterprises. When the Anglos first entered the region in numbers, the only deposits apparently being worked were near Guevavi and to the west in Papago country. The gold mines of Guevavi were developed during the Jesuit period and operated intermittently thereafter.[65]

In 1854, the year in which the Gadsden Purchase was ratified, an

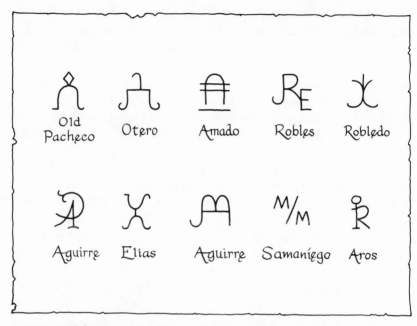

Cattle brands of old Spanish-Mexican families of Southern Arizona (Arizona Historical Society)

American party that included Charles Poston explored the area of the Santa Rita Mountains looking for minerals, and this venture led to a resumption of mining two years later. Poston and his companions were doubtless attracted to the region by stories of the Arizonac discovery and other tales of mineral wealth that circulated after publication in 1829 of a book written by a British naval officer who had been in Sonora a few years before. In this volume, the author stated that "Near Tubac and Toison [Tucson] is the mine of Santa Rita, once very famous for its riches."[66]

The resumption of mining in the Tubac area after 1856 brought back former Hispanic inhabitants who had earlier abandoned it because of the Apache threat. It also attracted other Mexicans who can be considered the first "immigrants" from that country to settle in Arizona (as some were now calling the area) after political control reverted to the United States. Among the newcomers and former residents were experienced miners familiar with the technology developed by their Spanish forbears. From this point on, Hispanic miners would play an indispensable role in the development of Arizona's mineral industry.[67]

Politics in the Pimería Alta

Relatively little that the Hispanic residents of the Pimería Alta experienced during the years of Spanish and Mexican rule prepared them for participation in the political life of the region after it became a part of the United States. In this respect, they differed somewhat from certain of their neighbors in California and New Mexico, where the Spanish founded towns with civil governments. On the Sonoran frontier, leaders established only missions and presidios in which the priests and *comandantes* were the principal authorities. Tucson and Tubac became eligible for civil governments (*ayuntamientos*) in 1813, but the following year this privilege was withdrawn by King Fernando when he outlawed the Constitution of Cádiz promulgated two years before.[68]

Civil government finally arrived at the two Arizona presidios in January of 1825 when officials chosen in local elections two weeks earlier were installed. Being small communities, Tucson and Tubac were not authorized to create town councils, but they could elect a mayor (*alcalde de policía*) and a combination treasurer-attorney, or *síndico-procurador*. These officials and the *comandantes* shared responsibility for keeping the peace and dealing with other matters of concern to the expanding civilian population of the presidios. The title of the principal official at the two villages was changed in December of 1831. Throughout the remainder of the Mexican period, he was known as the first justice of the peace (*primer juez de paz*), and he had an elected assistant. In addition, the position of treasurer-attorney was continued.

Record keeping was a responsibility of the first justice of the peace and the treasurer-attorney, meaning they had to be literate, a requirement that severely limited the pool of candidates. The result was circulation of these offices among a handful of individuals from the elite families of the region. Such persons were closely bound by kinship and the godparent system, or *compadrazco*, to the *comandantes* and to civil and military officials at higher levels. These relationships helped limit the civil-military strife that divided spheres of authority might have produced within the presidios after 1825.

Tucson's first three *alcaldes* were members of pioneer families of the Pimería Alta—families that had intimate connections with the Sonoran military elite. First to serve was José León, who was related to Manuel de León, *comandante* at Tucson during both the Spanish and Mexican periods. He was succeeded in 1826 by Ygnacio Pacheco, descended on his mother's side from Captain Juan Crisóstomo Ramírez, veteran officer of the Tubac presidio. Pacheco was also a cousin of the wife of Captain Antonio Comadurán, Tucson's *comandante* in later years. Next in line was Juan Romero, son of Captain Pablo Romero, and brother of Captain José Romero, both Tucson *comandantes*. Occupying the principal civil office in Tubac were such individuals as Juan Bautista Elías, member of Sonora's most prominent nineteenth century family, one that produced both governors and military commanders of the state between 1825 and 1850.

In January of 1849 Tucson officially became a *colonia militar* (military colony) rather than a presidio. The change brought new people into the area, especially new military officers, and the close bond between civil and military officials began to deteriorate.

The status of Tucson and Tubac on the broader canvas of Mexico's political and military affairs changed frequently during both Spanish and Mexican rule. After 1776, the northern tier of Mexican states made up a politico-military unit called the *Provincias Internas*. This name translates as either "Interior" or "Internal" Provinces, although "Frontier" Provinces would have been more appropriate. Initially, the Internal Provinces were independent of the viceroy's control but their autonomy was short-lived. The first capital was Arizpe, Sonora. Later, other towns, among them the Villa de Chihuahua (Chihuahua City), enjoyed this distinction.

In 1823, the *Provincias* were disbanded and regional government was placed in the hands of the individual states. As far as the residents of Pimería Alta were concerned, this did little, if anything, to stabilize matters. Sonora and Sinaloa, previously united as a single state, were separated, then rejoined as the State of Occidente; and finally separated permanently. In the first decade following independence, the capital shifted among Arizpe and Alamos in Sonora and El Fuerte and Cosalá in Sinaloa. It moved to Ures in 1837, the same year that Sonora was divided into political districts which would later be called prefectures. Tucson and Tubac were initially in the Arizpe district, and town officials reported to a superior with the impressive title of *jefe político*, or political chief. By the end of the Mexican period, however, the Arizona towns were in the San Ignacio Prefecture.

Militarily, during the 1830s Tucson and Tubac joined Santa Cruz in a defensive group known as the "Second Section of the Northern Line." Tucson commanding officers, among them Antonio Comadurán and Hilarión García, often headed this unit.

Women in the Pimería Alta

Even after civil governments were set up in Tucson and Tubac, women remained outside the formal political process. They could not vote, nor hold office. Furthermore, regardless of the social status of their families, they were rarely taught to read and write.[69] The civil records from Tucson and Tubac, so critical to an understanding of other aspects of women's statuses on the Sonoran frontier, have never been found; even without them, however, a few observations are possible.[70]

Women did own real estate. Doña Rita Sosa was a major landholder in Tucson by the end of the Spanish period. Eulalia Elías González was co-owner of the Babocómari land grant; at the time the first Americans began settling in Tucson, widows Ursula Solares and Guadalupe Santa Cruz were property owners to be dealt with.

So long as priests were around, marriage, rather than cohabitation, prevailed; after the friars' departure in 1828, however, liaisons became more casual, and illegitimacy, more common. Women did commit adultery but do not seem to have been punished for it more severely than were men; a marriage was not doomed because a wife strayed.[71]

Although women did not regularly tend the livestock and cultivate the fields, they contributed in ways other than cooking, cleaning and caring for children. They undoubtedly made the rag dolls that were traded to Indians for food during the Mexican period, and they may also have cast bullets for the soldiers.[72]

The fact that the important political and protective statuses were held exclusively by men may well mean that Sonoran frontier so-

Guadalupe Santa Cruz in 1870 with nieces Atanacia and Petra (Arizona Historical Society)

ciety was male dominated. Yet, women seem to have had considerable freedom. Anglo males found them uninhibited compared with the females they had known and often referred to them as "bold" in their behavior. Many chose them as marriage partners or lovers.[73]

On the basis of his demographic analysis of the Tucson presidio in the late colonial period, Henry Dobyns concludes that in spite of high death rates from warfare and disease, the Hispanic women were prolific enough to maintain population levels.[74] Given this fecundity, the European-derived population of the Pimería Alta would certainly have increased markedly, even without further immigration, had frontier conditions been less rigorous.

Contacts with New Mexico and California

The Spanish made two attempts late in the eighteenth century to promote closer relationships between the people of Sonora and the Upper Rio Grande Valley. New Mexico Governor Juan Bautista de

Anza personally led the first of these, departing from Santa Fe on November 9th, 1780, and reaching Arizpe on December 18th. His men defeated a large force of Apaches along the way, capturing more than 200 of their pack animals.[75]

The second expedition came in 1795 and was directed by Captain José Zúñiga, commanding officer of the Tucson presidio. Accompanied by soldiers from his own garrison and five other posts, Zúñiga departed Tucson on April 9th, and was back on May 29th, less than two months later. This time, the troopers found their route relatively free of Apaches, thanks to a new Spanish Indian policy introduced shortly before.[76]

The intrepid Anza was also involved in the first significant effort at linking the people of Sonora and California. In 1772, while serving as *comandante* of the Tubac presidio, he suggested to Viceroy Antonio María Bucareli that he be permitted to lead an expedition to the Colorado River and, he hoped, beyond into Alta California. Receiving no response, he repeated the proposal the following year and, on the second try, received the needed authorization. He and his party left Tubac in January of 1774 and returned in May, having gone as far as present-day Monterey. Convinced that the route they had explored could be used to conduct colonists to the San Francisco Bay area, Anza persuaded the viceroy to approve a second expedition that would include settlers from communities in Sonora and Sinaloa. Among those accompanying him on the journey of colonization were Tubac residents whose relocation created the first of many kinship ties between *Californios* and *Sonorenses*.[77]

Not long after the second Anza expedition, the Spanish attempted to establish an Indian mission and military colony among the Yumans, or Quechans, of the Colorado River. Had this effort succeeded, it would have assured more intense and continuing relationships between the Hispanic populations of California and Sonora. It failed in the summer of 1781, however, when the Indians rebelled against the missionaries and Spanish settlers, killing or capturing many, and driving the others away.[78] Although the Yumans were later subdued, Anza's route, over which an estimated 300 colonists had traveled, remained closed.[79]

In the early years after Mexican independence, new enthusiasm developed for opening a permanent mail route between Tucson and the Hispanic settlements in the area between San Diego and Santa Barbara. In September, 1822, Sonora's governor, Lieutenant Colonel Antonio Narbona, directed Captain José Romero, Tucson's *comandante*, to lead an expedition across northern Baja California to pioneer a new mail road south of the territory controlled by the Quechans. Romero finally got the expedition underway in early June, 1823, and slightly over a month later he and his party reached the mission of Santa Catalina. They had found the Indians of the lower Colorado less trustworthy than expected, however, raising serious doubts about maintaining a trail through the area. Tucson's commanding officer remained in California until the end of 1825, while friendly Indians carried the mail back and forth between Sonora and California over other routes known to them.[80]

The Quechan Indians were at peace with the Mexicans during the late 1820s and early 1830s and some traffic passed back and forth across the Colorado River through their territory. A few Sonorans even migrated to California during these years, although their numbers were never large.[81] The big migration from Sonora to California would await the end of the war between Mexico and the United States, and the discovery of gold at Sutter's Mill.

Because of the difficulty of keeping roads open between Sonora and neighboring regions to the east and west, the average *Sonorense* knew little about California and New Mexico. On the other hand, military and political officials did serve in posts throughout the region. Captain Zúñiga came to Tucson from San Diego, for example. Anza was military commander in Sonora and later governor of New Mexico. Pedro Fages, a California governor, commanded the presidial garrison of Santa Cruz de Terrenate. Antonio Narbona was governor of Sonora and, later, of New Mexico. Ignacio Elías González, Tubac's *comandante* at the time of Mexican independence, received his promotion to lieutenant while serving in the Santa Fe garrison.

Religion in the Pimería Alta

Until 1779, Sonora was part of the Diocese of Durango. Thereafter, it boasted its own bishop whose jurisdiction also included Sinaloa and the Californias. Although the bishops commanded great respect among the Indian and Hispanic Catholics of the Pimería Alta, they were almost as removed from the everyday lives of the people as if they resided in the Vatican. Friar Antonio de los Reyes, the first bishop of Sonora, had worked as a missionary in the San

Miguel River Valley between 1768 and 1771, but after being named to the highest post in the new diocese a decade later, he stayed as far away from the frontier as he could get, locating his headquarters in Alamos, 250 miles south of the designated site of Arizpe.[82] Not until 1820, more than forty years after establishment of the diocese, did a Sonoran bishop enter what would later become Arizona.[83]

The critical links between the church and the people were the Jesuit missionaries, who served the region until 1767, and their Franciscan counterparts, who began arriving in 1768. A true secular clergy did not develop in the northern reaches of the Pimería Alta, although priests from San Ignacio and other Sonoran parishes did visit Tucson and its environs in the 1840s and 1850s.

The primary goal of the missionaries was converting and ministering to the Indians, but they also attended to the spiritual needs of the settlers. The priests stationed at Guevavi and, later, at Tumacácori played major roles in the lives of the soldiers and their families living in Tubac. It is not clear that this presidio ever had a chaplain who was a secular priest, but shortly after establishment of the post, the Bishop of Durango began appointing Jesuit missionaries to serve as chaplains on an interim basis.[84] Similar arrangements were made in the case of the Franciscans.

Tucson, which came into existence during the Franciscan years, had its own military chaplain throughout most of the remainder of the colonial period. The first individual to hold the post was Father Francisco Perdigón who met his death at the hands of the Apaches in 1780 while on his way to Arizpe after having rested for several days in Bacanuchi.[85] Father Pedro de Arriquibar, a Franciscan missionary who had been stationed at Tubac, San Ignacio, and Bacoachi, came to Tucson as military chaplain about 1796, and remained until his death in 1820 at the age of seventy-five.[86] He was not replaced and Franciscans from San Xavier del Bac and San Ignacio served *Tucsonenses* for the next two decades. After the early 1840s, secular priests from San Ignacio and Altar administered the sacraments to both Mexican and Indian Catholics of the region. A military chaplain from Santa Cruz took over these responsibilities in the early 1850s.[87]

Even in the most difficult of times, the people of the Pimería Alta celebrated the major events of their religious calendar with enthusiasm. Two occasions in particular attracted large crowds. One was the feast day of San Agustín, patron of Tucson, which fell on

August 28. The other, the most important of all, was the celebration honoring Saint Francis which was held in Magdalena early in October.[88] Both Indian and Hispanic pilgrims came from far and wide to attend, but it was an event of special significance for the Papagos.

Whether dealing with Indian or Hispanic residents of the Pimería Alta, those missioners who lived and worked in the area quickly became familiar with death, and administering last rites was a common duty. Ethnic conflict was an important contributor to the mortality rate, but even if one sets aside catastrophic events such as the Pima Revolt of 1751, the Yuma uprising of 1781, and Whetstone Mountains massacre of 1848, the priests did not lack occasions for consoling families whose ranks had been diminished by death.

Epidemics took a greater toll than warfare and the Indian populations were highly vulnerable to diseases brought into the area by Europeans.[89] However, the Hispanic settlers did not go unscathed. A major cholera epidemic in 1851 carried away over a thousand residents of the Altar Valley and nearly a quarter of Tucson's total population.[90]

Historians depend heavily on the writings of the priests for their knowledge of Arizona's Hispanic pioneers, as well as on documents prepared by civil and military officials. Meager though this information may be, it clearly reveals that a small handful of people had the resolution, the strength, and the wisdom to survive for a remarkably long time against odds that can only be described as extreme.

2

Early Exploration and Settlement

A North African whom the Spaniards called Estevanico—Little Steven—is the leading contender for the title of first non-Indian to tread the soil of what was to become Arizona. Whether he accomplished this feat initially on his trek with Cabeza de Vaca and his men in 1536 or whether it was on the trip with Fray Marcos de Niza in 1539 is uncertain and will remain so.[1]

Tales of the adventures of the Cabeza de Vaca party and Fray Marcos inspired the Vázquez de Coronado expedition of 1540–1542 that resulted in exploration of the lower Colorado River, the Grand Canyon and portions of eastern Arizona. Various members of Coronado's army passed through Arizona on no fewer than twelve separate occasions, six of them in 1540 alone.[2] Since nine of these passages followed a single route, one might reasonably expect the question of its location to be free of controversy. However, nearly four and a half centuries after Coronado's journey, his trail through Arizona is still a subject for speculation.[3] The route favored by most historians lies along the San Pedro River.

The failure of the Coronado party to find the riches they were seeking diminished the ardor of most Spaniards to continue exploration in northern New Spain. Franciscan missionaries retained an interest in the area, however, because of its large Indian population and because two of their number who stayed behind after Coronado's return experienced martyrdom at the hands of the natives.[4]

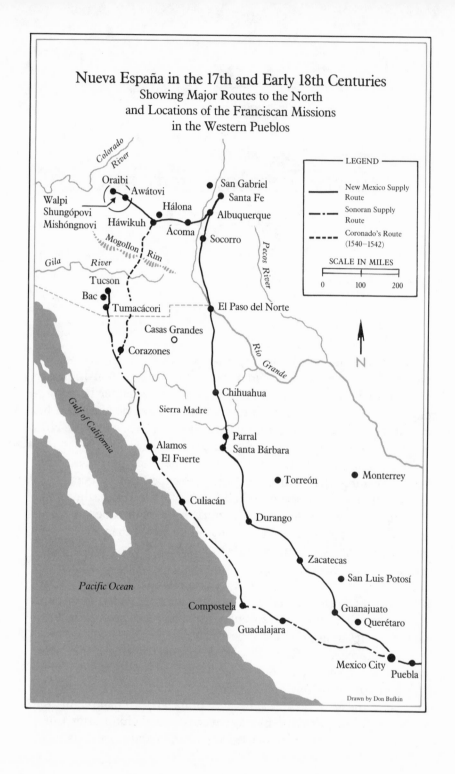

Nueva España in the 17th and Early 18th Centuries
Showing Major Routes to the North
and Locations of the Franciscan Missions
in the Western Pueblos

Colorado River

Oraibi
Awátovi
Walpi
Shungópovi
Mishóngnovi
Hálona
Háwikuh
Ácoma

San Gabriel
Santa Fe
Albuquerque
Socorro

Mogollon Rim

Gila River

Pecos River

Tucson
Bac
Tumacácori

El Paso del Norte

Casas Grandes
Corazones

Río Grande

Chihuahua

Sierra Madre

Parral
Santa Bárbara

Alamos
El Fuerte

Torreón
Monterrey

Gulf of California

Culiacán

Durango

Zacatecas
San Luis Potosí

Pacific Ocean

Compostela
Guadalajara

Guanajuato
Querétaro

Mexico City
Puebla

LEGEND

New Mexico Supply Route

Sonoran Supply Route

Coronado's Route (1540–1542)

SCALE IN MILES

0   100   200

N

Drawn by Don Bufkin

Their interest was finally translated into action in 1581 with an expedition from Chihuahua that reached the upper Rio Grande Valley and ended in the death of three more priests.[5]

A second mission to northern New Mexico late in 1582 also produced a new entry into Arizona. Responding to stories from Mexican Indians left behind by Coronado, Antonio Espejo, financier and leader of the expedition, traveled westward in search of rich mines. Somewhere in the area of present-day Jerome, he and his companions found silver deposits. Espejo carried samples with him on his return trip to Chihuahua,[6] an action that kindled new interest in the region on the part of other Spaniards. King Felipe II instructed his viceroy in New Spain to find a leader who could pacify and settle New Mexico.[7] Finally winning out in a competition that came to include several wealthy Spaniards was Juan de Oñate whose father had been a founder of the town of Zacatecas and who was one of the richest men in the realm. After many delays, Oñate and his colonists finally got underway early in 1598, the year from which permanent European settlement of New Mexico is commonly dated.[8]

After planting a colony in the San Juan area, Oñate took a party westward to the Hopi region in the fall of 1598. From there he dispatched Captain Marcos Farfán to search for the mines Espejo had discovered. The Farfán expedition traveled to an area west of Prescott, where they found promising veins of ore.[9]

On October 7th, 1604, Oñate led a group of thirty soldiers on a journey into Arizona that exposed more of the region to the Spaniards than any other taken before or until long afterward. They went through the Hopi villages along Farfán's route. When they reached the Bill Williams River, they followed it downstream until they struck the Colorado. Then they turned southward, exploring the country as far as the Gulf of California and returning to New Mexico in late April, 1605.[10]

Beginning with the establishment of the San Bernardo Mission at the village of Awatovi in 1629, the Spanish Franciscan friars spent many frustrating years attempting to convert the Hopis. In the process they accumulated additional martyrs, among them Father Francisco de Porras, who apparently was poisoned in 1633.

In spite of the shaky start at Awatovi, by 1641 the priests also had missions at Shongopovi and Oraibi, and *visitas* (visiting places) at Walpi and Mishongnovi. The degree of their success at winning true converts, however, appears to have been limited. When the Indians rose against the Spaniards during the Pueblo Revolt of 1680, the Hopis quickly killed the four Franciscans known to have been in their area at the time. Renewed missionary activity at Awatovi in 1700 prompted Indians from other Hopi towns to destroy that village. Over the next three decades, the Franciscans made at least eight additional attempts to reestablish themselves among the Hopis but all failed.[11]

Jesuit Entries from the South

The unsuccessful efforts by the Spaniards to return to the Hopi villages during the initial decades of the eighteenth century have largely been eclipsed in today's standard histories by the attention paid to the mission-building efforts of the Jesuits in modern southern Arizona. Latecomers to New Spain compared with the Franciscans, the first Jesuits began working among the Indians of Sinaloa in 1591 and by 1607 they had moved northward to make contact with the tribes of southern Sonora.[12] They initiated their mission effort among the Yaquis in 1617[13] and throughout the remainder of the seventeenth century extended their activities to other areas of Sonora. In October, 1686, the superiors of the order decided to assign a missionary to work in the northern reaches of the Pimería Alta. Chosen for this assignmeent was Eusebio Francisco Kino, a native of Segno in the Italian Tyrol, who had been in Baja California.[14]

From his base at Dolores on the headwaters of the San Miguel River, Kino began visiting more remote Indian villages. On one expedition in 1691, he travelled as far as the settlement of Tumacácori, his first entry into Arizona. Thereafter, he visited other parts of the area, including the San Pedro River Valley, the Papago desert, Pima and other Indian villages on the Gila, and the region around Yuma.

To Kino belongs the credit for establishing the first Jesuit missions in what is today the state of Arizona. In 1701, he assigned priests to the Pima settlements of Guevavi and Bac, both in the Santa Cruz River Valley. The first missionary to reach his post was Father Francisco Gonsalvo, who arrived at San Xavier during the spring. A little over a year later, he became ill and was carried

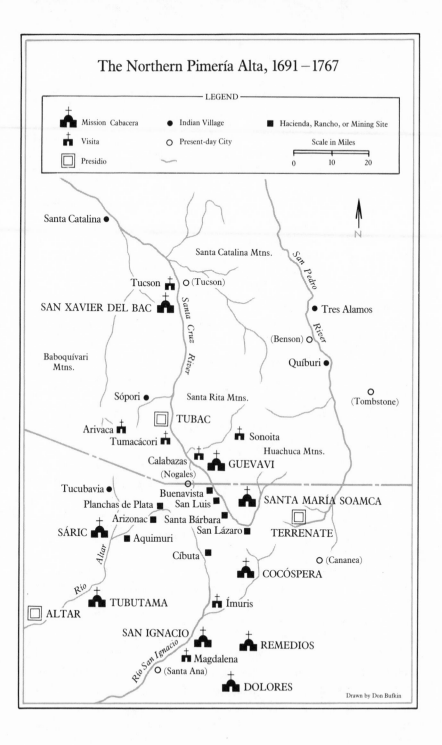

The Northern Pimería Alta, 1691–1767

LEGEND

Mission Cabacera   ● Indian Village   ■ Hacienda, Rancho, or Mining Site

Visita   ○ Present-day City

Presidio

Scale in Miles

0   10   20

N

Santa Catalina ●

Santa Catalina Mtns.

San Pedro River

Tucson ○ (Tucson)

SAN XAVIER DEL BAC

Santa Cruz River

● Tres Alamos

(Benson) ○

Baboquívari Mtns.

Quíburi ●

Sópori ●

Santa Rita Mtns.

○ (Tombstone)

Arivaca

TUBAC

Tumacácori

Sonoita

Calabazas

Huachuca Mtns.

GUEVAVI

Tucubavia ●

Buenavista

(Nogales) ○

Planchas de Plata ■ San Luis

SANTA MARÍA SOAMCA

Arizonac ■ Santa Bárbara

San Lázaro ■

TERRENATE

SÁRIC

Aquimuri ■

Cíbuta ■

○ (Cananea)

Río Altar

COCÓSPERA

Río

TUBUTAMA

Ímuris

ALTAR

SAN IGNACIO

REMEDIOS

Río San Ignacio

Magdalena

○ (Santa Ana)

DOLORES

Drawn by Don Bufkin

southward to San Ignacio where he lingered a few days before dying on August 10th. At Guevavi, his colleague, Juan de San Martín, began work in July, 1701. His first assignment was the construction of a small church, and by October he had it ready for use.[15] Sickness, however, forced Father San Martín to leave the area shortly afterward, and apparently he did not return. In February, 1703, Kino informed the viceroy that no priest was in residence at Guevavi.[16]

In spite of Kino's efforts, the Arizona missions did not thrive. The first priests at Bac and Guevavi were also to be the last during Kino's lifetime and for over two decades thereafter. When the Italian-born missionary died at Magdalena in 1711, the prognosis for San Gabriel and San Xavier was poor at best, and Indians from these and other Arizona *rancherías* were being encouraged to move southward to join their brethren in villages that could be served more easily and regularly by the small cadre of Jesuits who remained in the area.[17]

Although Kino has deservedly received much praise for his explorations of southern Arizona and his attempts to bring Roman Catholicism and European culture to the Indians there, he did not initiate permanent Spanish settlement any more than Vázquez de Coronado, Oñate, or the Franciscans who risked their lives among the Hopis. There were no Spanish colonists in Arizona during Kino's lifetime and for more than a decade after his death. Father Agustín de Campos from San Ignacio kept the candle of Christianity flickering among the Upper Pimas during this period. Jesuit historian Charles W. Polzer has observed that "Kino spent twenty-four years putting the Pimería on the map; Campos spent forty-three . . . keeping it there."[18]

In 1727, Bishop Crespo from the Diocese of Durango visited the Pimería Alta and was impressed with its need for additional missionaries. He encouraged the viceroy to provide three new priests, and when that appeal failed, he wrote directly to King Felipe V. This time he got results. Late in the spring of 1732, priests were installed at Bac, Guevavi and Santa María Soamca, which was located on the headwaters of the Santa Cruz River a few miles south of the present United States-Mexico boundary. Assigned to Bac was a Swiss Jesuit, Father Felipe Segesser von Brunegg. The new priest at Guevavi was Father Johann Grazhofer, a Bavarian; Father Ignacio Keller, a German, was placed in charge of the Soamca Mission.[19]

All were officially established in their posts by Captain Juan Bautista de Anza (the elder), commanding officer at the presidio of Fronteras.

Although it has not been established that there were Spanish settlers in what is now southern Arizona in 1732, there certainly were some nearby and they were not long in coming northward. In testimony that he gave following the Pima Revolt of 1751, don Nicolás Romero stated that he had settled in the San Luis Valley twenty-five miles south of Guevavi in the 1720s. José Romo de Vivar, one of the first Spanish colonists in northern Sonora, probably operated a stock ranch nearby at San Lázaro even before Kino entered Pimería Alta. Romo de Vivar, credited with being the founder of the Sonoran town of Bacanuchi, also had property in Cananea and at the south end of the Huachuca Mountains as early as 1680.[20] Because there were no secular priests in the area, these early Spanish settlers and their families depended upon the Jesuit missionaries in times of spiritual need. Church records relating to births, baptisms, marriages and deaths confirm their presence.

Bolas de Plata

One of the most notable events leading both to Spanish settlement of southern Arizona and to the later naming of the state was a remarkable silver discovery made in October, 1736 by a Yaqui Indian. The site of the discovery was a few miles southwest of present-day Nogales, close to the location of a mining camp (*real de minas*) established a few years earlier by the *alcalde mayor* of the province of Sonora, Captain Gabriel de Prudhon Heider Beltrán y Mújica.[21] The captain called his mine and the small settlement that grew up around it the "Real de Arizonac" (also spelled Arissonac); the name was also applied to the larger region that included the 1736 discovery. The strike was most unusual because some of the silver was found lying on the ground in *bolas* (chunks) and *planchas* (slabs).

Because of the extraordinary nature of the discovery, Captain Juan Bautista de Anza, who by that time was occupying the civil post of *justicia mayor*, or chief justice, under Governor Bernal de Huidobro, raised the question whether the find was that of a mine or of refined silver such as one might expect in the case of buried treasure. If the discovery was a mine, the king's share of the proceeds would be twenty percent; if it was a treasure, his share would be half. The result of this controversy was prolonged litigation, during which the supply of silver was exhausted. Historian John Kessell has commented: "What remained were tenaciously clung-to hopes of new finds, many more *gente de razón* in the Pimería [literally, "people of reason"—a term usually, but not always, reserved for persons of European descent] and the name Arizona, now synonymous with quick wealth."[22]

Before the 1730s ended, the written records of the Guevavi mission had come to include regular references to Spanish families of the region. In addition to the surname Romero, those of Nuñez and Fernández were present, and on St. Valentine's Day in 1740, Father Alexander Rapicani married Tubac residents named Ortega, Barba, Villela and Durán. Other Spaniards living in the vicinity of the Guevavi mission at this time belonged to the Tapia, Grijalva, Bohórquez, Amésquita, Gallego, Samaniego, de Rivera and Covarrubias families. In 1741, when Joseph de Perea, the only Mexican-born Jesuit ever to serve at Guevavi, arrived at his post he found a good supply of native Spanish speakers to share conversation with in idle hours.[23]

Indian Troubles

The first major confrontation between the Spaniards and the native inhabitants of Arizona occurred with the outbreak of the Pueblo Revolt in 1680. During the next twenty years, there were other uprisings on the northern frontier of New Spain that may have involved members of some Arizona tribes. Beginning in 1683, certain of the Indian groups in northwest Chihuahua and northeast Sonora began raiding throughout the region, leading to the founding of Spanish presidios at various locations. El Paso del Norte, the first of these, was established in 1683. Coming later in the seventeenth century were ones at Casas Grandes in 1686, Janos in 1691 and Fronteras (Sonora) in 1692.[24]

In 1695, Pimas in the Magdalena and Altar valleys revolted, frustrating early missionary efforts there. Kino was a principal figure in the peace negotiations that followed. The next year, he extended his ministry into the San Pedro Valley, where he found the Sobaipuris being harrassed by nomads from the east, some of whom were beginning to penetrate more southerly areas of Sonora.[25] These were the Apaches and within a few decades they would prove to be the most persistent and deadly enemies of the Hispanic colonizers of Arizona. Anthropologist Edward Spicer points out that by 1710, the Apache attacks had become so devastating that the warriors had cleared an area 250 miles wide for their exclusive occupation. They now controlled much of western New Mexico and eastern Arizona from the Zuni villages on the north to Casas Grandes, Chihuahua, on the south.

During the first half of the eighteenth century, the Spanish settlements along the Santa Cruz River were protected to a limited degree from Apache devastation by the buffer zone of Sobaipuri villages along the San Pedro. However, the Apaches were able to slip around the Sobaipuri towns and raid farther south—as far as Arizpe and Cumpas in the Moctezuma and Sonora River valleys. Sometimes they also made diversions to the west that took them to communities in the upper reaches of the San Miguel Valley. By the middle of the century, the mission site of Cocóspera had become a favorite target.[26] As the threat to Sonoran villages increased, the Spaniards decided in 1741 to establish another presidio to the west of Fronteras. Although the viceroy had suggested that the new fort be located near Guevavi, it was placed almost fifty miles southeast at a location called Terrenate. This presidio became the first to contribute regularly to the defense of Hispanic residents of Arizona.[27]

Among the victims of the Apaches during the first half of the eighteenth century was the veteran Captain Juan Bautista de Anza, father of a man who a few years later would lead Spanish settlers to the modern-day San Francisco Bay area. Presidial commander at Fronteras and *justicia mayor* of Sonora, Anza was ambushed at a location near the Pima ranchería of Santa María Soamca. The year is said to have been 1739, but there is evidence that he died on May 9th, 1740.[28]

Adding to the Spaniards' woes were European diseases which drastically reduced mission-Indian populations. To repopulate towns during the 1740s, concerned Jesuits tried to persuade other tribesmen to settle where they had constructed churches. On the frontier it was commonly said that "Indians do not come to Christian service when they do not see the maize pot boiling" so the Jesuit fathers considered it indispensable that the mission fields

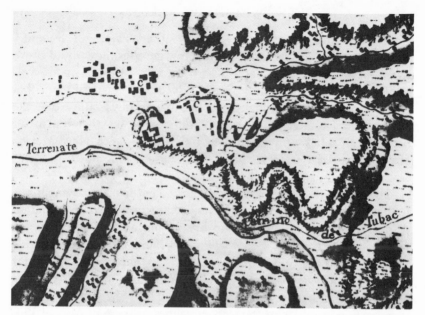

Portion of a map of the presidio of Terrenate, prepared in 1766 by cartographer Joseph de Urrutia (British Museum, courtesy of the Arizona State Museum, University of Arizona)

Aerial photograph of the Terrenate presidio site taken in 1968 (courtesy of Bob Torrance)

produced heavily.[29] Teaching and persuading the Indians to farm and ranch was something of a carrot and stick operation, however, and some Indians came to resent the most demanding priests.

Jesuit attention during the 1740s was by no means exclusively focussed on the chain of missions founded by Kino. As early as 1715, Father Agustín de Campos urged the viceroy to assign to his order the area between the Pimería Alta and the Hopi villages. This issue was pursued by other Sonoran Jesuits and in 1725 viceregal orders granted them what they sought. Although the king gave his approval the following year, well over a decade passed before any missionaries attempted to explore the new territory. Finally in 1743, Father Ignacio Keller, the priest at Santa María Soamca, travelled up the Gila River with the intention of going northward from there to the Hopi country. The Apaches, however, frustrated his efforts. A short time later, Jacobo Sedelmayr left his Tubutama post on a journey to the mouth of the Bill Williams Fork of the Colorado,[30] closing out the explorations of the decade with a trip to the Yuma area in 1749.[31]

Disturbed that the Jesuits were heading into their old stamping grounds, the Franciscans of New Mexico renewed their attempts to return to the Hopi villages during the 1740s. Usually travelling without military escort, Franciscans visited northeastern Arizona converting wherever they could. They also exhorted the Río Grande Puebloans living among the Hopis to return to the fold. In this endeavor, they had some success, especially with persons from the Sandía Pueblo. They also baptized other Indians, some of whom may have been Hopis, but most of whom were undoubtedly Navajos.[32] At mid-century, they were no closer to reestablishing the Hopi missions than in the early years after the Pueblo Revolt.

Meanwhile, the number of Spanish settlers in the Santa Cruz Valley continued to increase. Mining and stock raising began to be important economic pursuits for some. A few individuals may have held formal title to the plots they were using but most did not. A majority, in fact, were squatters on mission lands that legally belonged to the Indians. They lived at such places as Arivaca, Sópori, Tubac, Tumacácori and Guevavi on the basis of informal agreements with the priests who were in many cases glad to have them around.[33] The Indians undoubtedly felt quite differently about it.

Indian resentment was not entirely directed toward the colonists. They regarded some of the priests with hostility as well, especially those inclined to be arrogant in their dealings with the Pimas. Father Garrucho at Guevavi and Keller at Soamca, while liked by some Indians, were viewed as patronizing by others. Both were possessive of their native charges and frowned on outsiders dealing directly with Indians in their jurisdictions. When Governor Ortiz Parrilla conferred special honors and authorities on Luis Oacpicagigua, a resident of Sáric who was captain general of the Pimas, the missionaries were incensed and vented their anger on the Indian leader and some of his close associates.[34]

In November, 1751, the Pimas under Luis' direction revolted and in the course of a few days they killed more than a hundred settlers, miners and herdsmen, as well as two of the Jesuits—Tomás Tello of Caborca and Enrique Ruhen of Sonoita. The rebels caused extensive damage at San Xavier and Guevavi, burned the church and the priest's home at Tubac, and killed eleven Spaniards and some friendly natives in the Arivaca area.[35]

Early in 1752, Governor Ortiz Parrilla placed Captain Joseph Díaz del Carpio in charge of the campaign to subdue the hostile Pimas. After establishing his base of operations at Tubac, Díaz sent an emissary to Luis' camp in the Santa Catalina Mountains. His message for the Pima leader was to surrender or be subject to the full force of Spanish arms. Luis decided to give in. On March 18th, he traveled to Tubac to inform Captain Díaz del Carpio that he would thereafter live in peace with the Spaniards. On March 22nd, Díaz and the Indian leader went south together to confer with Governor Ortiz Parrilla at San Ignacio.[36]

The Pima uprising forced Spanish authorities to consider creating additional forts to protect the missions. During the first few months of 1752, Governor Diego Ortiz Parrilla solicited comments concerning the most strategic locations for new posts. Missionaries Felipe Segesser, Gaspar Stiger and Jacobo Sedelmayr recommended various sites, including two in the Tucson area.[37] Stiger also urged that a temporary post be placed at Guevavi or Tubac. On June 2nd, the Governor announced his decision to establish a permanent presidio at the last location, with a detachment of troops at the Hacienda of Ocuca in the Altar Valley.[38] This action provided the Spanish settlers a firm base of protection and gave Tubac the distinction of being the first permanent Spanish settlement in Arizona.

Luis' surrender in 1752 did not end the unrest among the Indi-

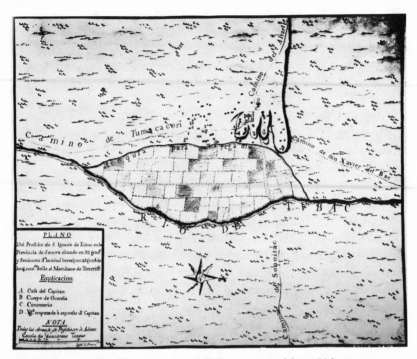

Map of the presidio of San Ignacio del Tubac, prepared in 1766 by
cartographer Joseph de Urrutia (British Museum, courtesy of the Arizona State
Museum, University of Arizona)

ans of the Pimería Alta. Hawani Mo'o (Raven's Head), a Gila River
Indian with a strong aversion to the teachings of the Jesuit missionaries, did his best to convince the natives along the Santa Cruz to
reject them as well. To a degree he was successful with those at San
Xavier and in 1756 he and his warriors, accompanied by Papagos
and some of the mission's own neophytes, pillaged the church and
attempted to capture and kill Father Alonso Espinosa. Ensign Juan
María Oliva of the Tubac garrison led a contingent of fifteen soldiers to the rescue. They overtook the fleeing Indians and killed
fifteen. Luis was already dead when Hawani Mo'o began his cru-
sade, but some of his former followers also continued to cause
trouble for the priests. They broke up the Easter celebration at
Guevavi in 1758, and a year later attacked Sonoita in large numbers, killing a villager and carrying off several horses.

The Apaches, too, were active during the decade of the 1750s.

Their depredations were particularly severe farther south in Sonora, but they also raided the Tubac area, escaping on one occasion with Ignacio Romero's entire horse herd.[39] In half a century, the Apaches had clearly established themselves as the major threat on the frontier and they would continue in this role for over a hundred years more.

Aware of the growing Indian population at Tucson, a village on the west bank of the Santa Cruz River at the foot of Sentinel Peak (today's A Mountain), the Jesuits assigned Father Bernard Middendorff to serve the community as resident priest early in 1757. With ten soldiers as an escort, Middendorff rode into Tucson on January 5th. Although his initial reception was warm, the Indians quickly tired of the restraints on their behavior that his presence imposed. On a May night, Middendorff and his military companions were beseiged by "about five hundred savage heathen." The Spaniards fled to San Xavier to escape the wrath of their attackers and never returned.[40] Tucson resumed its previous status as a *visita* of the San Xavier Mission.

On September 7th, 1759—as the troublesome decade of the 1750s was approaching its close—don Juan Tomás Belderrain, first commanding officer of the Royal Spanish Fort of San Ignacio de Tubac, breathed his last. Like the Anzas and the Urreas, Belderrain was a member of the Basque frontier elite that contributed so much to the colonization of northern Mexico. Father Francisco Pauer saw to it that his friend was appropriately honored in death, interring Belderrain beneath the altar steps of the recently completed Guevavi church.[41]

The fears instilled in the hearts of the Spanish settlers by the apostate Pimas diminished notably after 1760. In that year, the new *comandante* at Tubac, young but experienced Juan Bautista de Anza, pursued a contingent of the rebels to the depopulated ranchería of Arivaca, where he came suddenly upon them in the act of scalping soldier Miguel de la Cruz, whom they had just slain. With a vengeance, Anza and his companions attacked the Indians and killed nine, including their leader Ciprián.

Anza was only twenty-four years old when he took command of the Tubac post and his first year there was eventful for more than the actions he took to quiet the rebellious Pimas. In the early fall of 1760 his widowed mother, doña María Rosa Bezerra Nieto de Anza, died in Juan Bautista's home. She was buried beneath the altar

A leather-jacketed presidial soldier of the late Spanish colonial period. The legend at the top refers to the "condition of the troops who garrison the frontier line of the nine Interior Provinces of New Spain." Translation of key: (N 1) Quilted leather jacket of seven-ply buckskin. (N 2) Pommel and cantle of saddle. (N 3) Carbine. (N 4) Saddlebags for carrying water and provisions. (N 5) Lance. (N 6) Pistols hanging from hooks on saddle skirt. (N 7) Shield. (N 8) Boots and spurs. (N 9) Wooden stirrups. (N 10) Cartridge box. (Archivo General de Indias, Sevilla, courtesy of John L. Kessell)

steps of the Guevavi church next to Captain Belderrain who had been a friend of both her husband and her son. Not long after his mother's death, Juan Bautista was married at Arizpe to Ana María Pérez Serrano, daughter of one of the wealthy merchant families of the province. Parish priest Joseph Manuel Díaz del Carpio, son of the former commanding officer at Terrenate, stood at his side as witness.[42]

During the entire decade of the 1750s, populations at various mission and *visita* rancherías continued to decline. Many people died; others deserted to escape from the authority and influence of the priests; some fled to avoid becoming targets for the Apaches. By the early 1760s, Arizona's Jesuit missions confronted a crisis that threatened their survival. In an effort both to strengthen the capacity of the mission villages to defend themselves and to bring

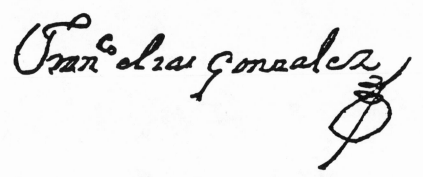

Signature of Francisco Elías González de Zayas, commanding officer at
Terrenate, 1752–1770, and founder of the Elías family of Sonora (Archivo
General de Indias)

more of the wild Indians within the priestly orbit, Interim Governor Joseph Tienda de Cuervo signed an order early in 1762 directing the transfer of the Sobaipuri Indians from their villages along
the San Pedro to Pima communities on the Santa Cruz. The order
was to be carried out under military authority. Before the end of
March, 1762, it was an accomplished fact. Some 250 of the immigrants were settled at Tucson with smaller numbers at Santa María
Soamca and Sonoita. Entrusted with the relocation was Captain
Francisco Elías González de Zayas, by now the veteran *comandante*
of the Terrenate presidio. In addition to delivering Sobaipuris to
the Tucson ranchería, Elías christened it San José, a saint's name
that did not remain long with the community.[43]

At the time of the Sobaipuri relocation, Captain Elías was rounding out twenty-two years of service in the frontier presidios and a
decade as Terrenate's commanding officer. He was married to a
daughter of a fellow captain, Joseph Díaz del Carpio, who had been
his commanding officer at Janos, and the man he succeeded at
Terrenate. A native of the wine producing La Rioja district in
northern Spain, Elías had come to Mexico in the 1720s, settling first
at Alamos. His descendants were destined to be among the most
famous of Sonorans, and one of them would attain the Mexican
presidency.[44]

By the middle of the eighteenth century, affairs on the Sonoran
frontier were firmly in the hands of an elite represented by families
such as that of Captain Elías. Although most members of these

lineages were *criollos* ("creoles"—Mexican-born Spaniards), they maintained close ties with persons still residing in Spain who from time to time joined them in Mexico. They were extremely finicky about marriage partners, and sometimes to assure purity of the family line contracted unions with near relatives.[45]

Prominent though they were, the elite families were few in number. Mixed bloods were the predominant element among the Hispanic-derived population of the Pimería Alta.[46] Father Ignacio (Ignaz) Pfefferkorn, a German Jesuit who served in Sonora between 1756 and 1767, commented that "Besides the governor of Sonora, the officers of the Spanish garrisons, and a few merchants . . . there is hardly a true Spaniard in Sonora."[47] Pfefferkorn also observed that the individuals classified legally as Spaniards in the census records and elsewhere were often *castizos*, persons of predominantly Spanish ancestry, but with a quarter or less mixture of Indian blood. He noted that the children of *castizos* were considered "real" Spaniards and could be admitted to the holy orders and cloisters of the Catholic church, a privilege denied the members of other social classes.

The most numerous group among the *gente de razón* of Sonora in the eighteenth century, according to Pfefferkorn, were the *coyotes* who were offspring of Europeans and Indians. Pfefferkorn apparently considered *coyote* to be a synonym for the more common term *mestizo* which was also used in Sonora.[48] Two classes that included persons of Negro ancestry were also recognized: *mulatos*—those descended from a Spanish father and a Negro mother; and *lobos*— the offspring of a mating between a *negro* and an Indian. Pfefferkorn comments that both *lobos* and *mulatos* were "regarded with contempt by the other classes."[49]

Because of the importance of the presidios, the commanders of these establishments were at or near the top of the power structure. Pfefferkorn describes in considerable detail the various elements that contributed to the high status of the *comandante*. To begin with, it was he who decided which local merchants would be called upon to supply the troops under his command. Not surprisingly, those nominated were usually kinsmen through blood, marriage or godparent relationships (*compadrazco*). Most, if not all, commanders received tidy kickbacks from this arrangement. Furthermore, the food consumed by the soldiers had to be purchased from the *comandante* who, although he was required to sell at prices fixed by Spanish authorities, could buy provisions as cheaply as the market would permit. This same situation prevailed with respect to the troopers' horses. According to Pfefferkorn, buying from or selling animals to the soldiers was a particularly profitable business for presidial commanding officers. Finally, if the captain had any goods left over after making sure the troops were provided for, he could sell them to the settlers for whatever price he chose.

Pfefferkorn, who seemed to have little respect for Spanish officers, implied that their business skills were far superior to their military abilities. He also believed the job of *comandante* was more likely to be purchased than earned, and mentioned a cash payment of 12,000 to 14,000 pesos as the approximate cost.[50]

The wealth of the members of the military elite permitted them to invest in mining and ranching ventures, secure good marriages for their offspring, and obtain political and other favors from representatives of the Crown. They could afford to educate their children and literacy was a distinguishing mark of males (and an occasional female). Their offspring often became clergymen or joined religious orders.[51]

The difference between the lifestyles of members of the elite families and that of the common folk most certainly was very great, even under the frontier conditions that all had to endure. Pfefferkorn observed that the dwellings of the lower classes were of baked or sundried bricks and contained two or at most three rooms. Furnishings were few—a chest for clothes, a bench or a couple of logs for seats, and a bed of raw oxhide over which a woolen cover was spread. By day the oxhide served as a table on which the family meals were served.

Just as they had little in the way of household furnishings, the Sonorans possessed few changes of clothing, although what they did have seems to have been rather colorful. Pfefferkorn wrote that men wore coats of red or scarlet cloth that reached only to about hip level. These were trimmed with copper or silver buttons that served primarily as decoration. Beneath the coats were long-sleeved blue jackets. Trousers were of heavy blue or red plush. Those who could afford to sometimes decorated their clothes additionally with silver trim. Men wore round, stiff hats with silver borders, as well as blue mantles with red decoration. The latter were donned to attend mass and were worn on long journeys to provide protection from the weather and to serve as a cover at night. The Jesuit priest described shoes resembling the sandals or *huaraches* worn by rural Mexicans in more modern times. Men's stockings were footless, but the bare part of the foot was wrapped with red cloth which showed through the straps on the sandals. Deerskin leggings were often used.

Women wore pleated gowns, the upper part of the body being partly covered also by a shirt-waist closed at the neck. On formal occasions, they put on shirt-waists that were elaborately embroidered with silk, over which a silk jacket might also be worn. Pfefferkorn commented that women's gowns, shirt-waists and jackets could be made of expensive materials and wondered how people could afford such finery. The final, indispensable item of female garb was the *rebozo* which, depending upon the occasion and the wealth of the woman, was of cotton, mixed cotton and silk or pure silk.

In spite of the paucity of their possessions, Arizona's Hispanic pioneers were exceedingly fond of fiestas, a trait they inherited from both their Indian and Spanish forbears. According to Pfefferkorn, "They observe weddings, baptisms, and burials of children with particular ceremoniousness. Friends and acquaintances of both sexes assemble on such occasions. The guests are served chocolate and tortillas instead of the customary wheat bread." Dancing and singing were essential aspects of these events, and some drinking took place, although drunkeness was not so common as during Indian celebrations.[52]

The diet of the Hispanic frontiersmen was heavily influenced by that of the Indians although, as the priest observed, it did not include "rats, snakes, and other such Indian delicacies." Pfefferkorn mentioned specifically such dishes as *posole* (hominy soup), *pinole* (a gruel of ground, parched corn), *atole* (a porridge made of the pith extracted from boiled corn kernels) and tortillas. The settlers also used corn as a base for tamales, and for two of their favorite pastries: *puchas*, ring-shaped cakes of corn flour mixed with sugar, cinnamon and egg yolk; and *biscochuelos*, hard rolls made of corn flour, sugar and milk. Chocolate was much favored by the Hispanic pioneers but was expensive and relatively few could afford to serve it regularly. The common people consumed some beef but mutton and chicken were for the tables of the wealthy.[53]

Pfefferkorn considered the Sonorans to be lazy, a trait he felt they shared with the people of Spain. He commented on their unwillingness to walk even the shortest distance and on their lackadaisical approach to both farming and mining. On the other hand, he complimented them for outstanding horsemanship and for their indefatigable dedication to stock raising. It was for their horsemanship, rather than other qualities, that they were recruited into the ranks of the presidial soldiers, according to Pfefferkorn; and they responded readily to recruitment because of the security that military service provided. The German-born priest did not consider them good soldiers, however.[54]

The Hectic Decade of the 1760s

Given the trials and tribulations of the 1750s, the Hispanic settlers of Arizona doubtless breathed a sigh of relief when Captain Anza and his Tubac troopers brought an end to the Pima uprising, and they looked forward to better days with the able young commanding officer nearby. Their hopes were dashed, however, by the actions of the Seri Indians to the south. In some respects, the decade of the 1760s would turn out to be worse, not better.

Although a comparatively small group of Indians, the Seris were much feared by the Spaniards because of their deadly marksmanship and because they poisoned the tips of their arrows with a substance so strong that it caused certain death. The Seris had been in continuous revolt for many years when Governor Ortiz Parrilla sent a major force against them in 1750. Failing to achieve victory after the Indians retreated to Tiburón Island, the governor captured a small number of Seris and deported them to Colima. This action intensified the Indians' hatred for the Spaniards, and when the Seris were joined by some of the hostile Pimas following their revolt, they were able to establish a reign of terror throughout the region.[55]

According to a report he prepared in 1767, Anza and his Tubac forces made five different trips to the Seri frontier in 1760, the year in which these Indians murdered Governor Juan Antonio de Mendoza. Two years later, Anza's men killed thirty Seris; then in 1766 they captured the Indians' horse herd.[56] The situation continued to deteriorate, however, so Spanish authorities recruited a large army of professional soldiers and mercenaries, known as the *Expedición de Sonora*, to send into the region. This force reached Guaymas in May, 1767.[57]

With many of the Tubac soldiers off fighting Seris, the northern frontier was again vulnerable to renewed Apache attacks. The fierce warriors hastened to take advantage of the situation. As early as the spring of 1763, when Father Custodio Ximeno arrived in Guevavi, Apache raids had become so numerous that no one was safe working in the fields or herding livestock. The first two persons buried by Father Custodio, in fact, were victims of an attack on the old ranch settlement of Buenavista.[58]

In October, 1763, colonists from the San Luis Valley south of Tubac came to the presidio seeking Anza's permission to move elsewhere. They brought with them the body of the Captain's sister-in-law so that she might be buried in the Guevavi church. Although later criticized for his action, Anza approved the request, and shortly afterward the ranches of Buenavista, San Luis and Santa Bárbara were abandoned.[59]

In December, 1766, the Sonoran frontier received a visit from the Marqués de Rubí, a high-ranking Spanish nobleman who was conducting an inspection tour of all the northern defenses of New Spain. During his two-week stay in the Tubac area, Rubí was favorably impressed with Anza who was selling items to the soldiers at prices below the ceilings specified by the regulations. The indispensable leather jackets, for example, cost the Tubac troopers twenty percent less than the usual amount. While Anza was undoubtedly pleased with the favorable comments of the Marqués, he may not have agreed with Rubí's recommendation that the Tubac post be moved to the southwest. The Marqués also suggested relocation of the Altar presidio to a site on the Río Concepción near the Gulf of California.[60]

The Expulsion of the Jesuits

By the time of Rubí's visit, a second generation of Jesuits had been at work in Arizona for nearly thirty-five years in spite of the declining population of mission Indians and impressive increases in Apache raiding. The priests who met with the Spanish visitor could not have known how little time was left to them. King Carlos III, whose twenty-nine-year regime (1759–1788) was marked by an unprecedented climate of reform, had decided that one major step in subordinating the Catholic church to the Spanish crown was to expel the highly independent and successful Jesuit order from his realm. Once the monarch made his decision on February 27th, the wheels were set in motion for simultaneous action throughout the Spanish empire. The purge would begin on July 23rd, 1767. Preparations were so secret that Governor Juan Claudio de Pineda of Sonora and Sinaloa did not learn until July 11th that he would direct the expulsion in his region.

Pineda's choice for a military leader to conduct the operation was Captain Bernardo de Urrea of Altar who, though distressed with the assignment, proceeded to carry it out. Gathered first at Tubutama, the padres were marched to Mátape where the official decree was read to them. Ahead lay months of confinement in the port of Guaymas, a disease-ridden voyage on the Gulf of California, and a death march across Mexico. Some did not survive to be placed on a Swedish ship that sailed from Veracruz for Europe on November 10th, 1768.

The aftermath of the expulsion was chaotic on the Sonoran frontier. The agent appointed to inventory mission resources and debts at Guevavi informed the local Pimas that they were the absolute owners of the goods in storage there and gave them the keys to the granaries. In a few days, almost everything on hand had disappeared. A concerned Anza retrieved the keys and held them until he and the agent could work out a better approach.[61]

As Spanish authorities became aware of the frontier situation and of the lack of secular priests who could replace the Jesuits, they decided to entrust the missions to Franciscan friars from the College of Santa Cruz de Querétaro. Assigned to the Arizona posts were Juan Crisóstomo Gil de Bernabé at Guevavi and Francisco Garcés at San Xavier del Bac. Gil arrived in May of 1768;[62] Garcés followed at the end of June. Along the way, Garcés stayed at Anza's Tubac home.[63] A few years later the two would share the trail from Tubac to California.

The Apaches were not long in greeting the new arrivals. Less than a month after Gil reached Guevavi a war party attacked Sonoita, one of the *visitas* of the mission, and two of five Sobaipuris working in their fields were killed. In a letter describing the event, Governor Pineda stated that, "Every day the Apaches extend their raids, because for more than two years it has been impossible to patrol their territory since all the troops of the northern presidios are on the southern front."[64] Riding fresh mounts taken in a raid on

The College of Santa Cruz de Querétaro, headquarters for the Franciscans in Arizona (Englehardt, *Franciscans in Arizona*, courtesy of John L. Kessell)

Captain Elías' horse herd at Terrenate, Apaches hit San Xavier del Bac on the morning of October 2nd. The two soldiers stationed at the mission joined the native governor and Indian residents of the community in pursuing the enemy. Not far from La Cebadilla (present-day Redington Pass) they rode into an ambush. The soldiers and the governor were killed.[65] The following month, the Apaches besieged and burned the mission of Santa María Soamca. In mid-February, 1769, the Indians struck Tumacácori, and three days later were back at San Xavier. In reporting the raid to Governor Pineda, Father Garcés also informed him that Piman-speaking Indians had abandoned two small villages between Tucson and the Gila River, leaving a gap through which the Apaches could sweep into the Altar Valley.[66]

The Hispanic population of southern Arizona at the time the Franciscans entered the region was almost entirely concentrated at Tubac. Apart from members of the garrison, their dependents and their servants, the settlement in 1767 included over two hundred persons belonging to thirty-four households. The total population must have been close to five hundred, the largest it would ever be during the Spanish and Mexican periods.[67]

The attacks to which the Franciscan missions had been subject in

1768 and 1769 continued into the early years of the following decade, and in 1770 the situation was further aggravated by an outbreak of measles that struck the area in March. In one week Father Gil buried eight of the mission's Indians, including the governor of the village of Tumacácori. Two months later the Apaches swept down on the *ranchería* of Calabazas, leaving seven dead Pimas in their wake.

Rumors mounted that to the west the Papagos, disguising themselves as Apaches, were stealing and slaughtering stock. In spite of the high priority placed on the Seri campaign, Governor Pineda ordered Anza and Urrea to withdraw substantial numbers of soldiers from the southern front and to march with them through Papago country to discourage members of that large tribe from joining the rebellious Seri and Pima. The two commanders followed their instructions and the expedition concluded with promises of loyalty from the Papagos.

The attack on San Xavier del Bac in 1768, combined with the abandonment of the Pima towns north of Tucson, had by 1770 heightened the feeling of insecurity among Tucson's Sobaipuri immigrants and many made plans to move to the Gila River. Concerned that such an action would harm all of the Santa Cruz Valley, the Spaniards acted promptly. During the last half of April, 1770, Anza visited Tucson. He was accompanied by the troopers who had been involved in the show of force against the Papagos. The Tubac commander persuaded the Sobaipuris to construct an extensive earthen breastwork for their own protection. The Indians insisted that they should also have their own church. To help with this project, Father Garcés promised wheat to sustain the families of the construction workers.[68]

The church and breastworks constituted the first Spanish building project in what is today the heart of Tucson. The record does not show when the structures were completed, but the work apparently did not take long. The fortifications proved very helpful on February 1st, 1771, when Tucsonans withstood an Apache attack in which two boys were killed. A short time later when the church was completed, Father Garcés began referring to the settlement as San Agustín del Tucson, a name that stuck through the remainder of the Spanish and Mexican periods.[69]

Shortly after Anza left Tucson, his troops engaged in a fourteen-day campaign that ended with the slaying of two Apache men and

two women, plus the capture of seven children. The Indians retaliated with a devastating raid on the Sonoita *visita*. Nineteen
Pimas, including the governor of the village and his wife, were
slain. Among the dead were eleven children.[70]

As the populations of the mission communities continued to
decline through the 1770s, the Franciscans attempted to recruit the
desert Papagos to settle at these locations. They found few who
were interested in doing so. The Papagos could point with pride to
some impressive victories over the Apaches, whereas the accomplishments of the Spanish troops were embarrassingly meager; the
Indians stated frankly that they felt safer in the desert than in the
missions. The situation of the soldiers was so pitiful that they could
not even protect their own horse herds. In mid-October, 1772,
Apaches stole over a hundred of the animals from the Tubac garrison, killing a trooper in the process. And a few weeks later, they
seized 257 head from the herd at Terrenate.[71]

By 1774 the old Indian *rancherías* of Guevavi and Sonoita were
deserted and the Indians gathered at Tumacácori and Calabazas
included refugees from these communities. The total Indian population of Tumacácori was ninety-eight, and there were 138 at
Calabazas. No one classified as a Spaniard was residing at Calabazas
but there were nineteen at Tumacácori. Several of the latter were
descendants of Juan Crisóstomo Ramírez, veteran officer of the
Tubac presidio, who had served under both Belderrain and his
dashing young successor.[72]

In spite of being away from Tubac much of the time, Captain
Anza—in the eyes of both the Spanish authorities and the local
Hispanic settlers—was the most important political or military figure on the Sonoran frontier during the 1770s. Father Francisco
Garcés, absent from his post almost as much as Anza, elicited similar respect in the ecclesiastical sphere. These two individuals stuck
their noses into each other's affairs with impunity, neither having
any particular respect for the exclusivity of the other's domain.
While friction developed between them, they were united by a
common love for the trail.

Garcés roamed over the landscape even more than had Kino,[73]
and Anza was almost as peripatetic as Cabeza de Vaca, who must be
accorded the record among Spaniards for long distance travel. It
was their shared wanderlust that brought these two frontiersmen
together on the first journey from Tubac to the Pacific Coast of

California in 1774. Although that expedition encountered problems in getting underway, including an eleventh hour theft of 130 horses by the Apaches, it met its goals, and Viceroy Antonio María Bucareli in Mexico City was so pleased that he arranged for Anza to be promoted to lieutenant colonel and given a life-long monthly pay raise.[74]

The Founding of Tucson

As a result of recommendations made by the Marqués de Rubí, King Carlos III issued a new set of royal regulations for the presidios in 1772. These called for realignment of the frontier forts to provide more adequately for both offensive and defensive action. The task of determining what the new alignment should be was turned over to Hugo Oconor, an Irish expatriate who had gone to Spain and enlisted in the Regiment of Volunteers of Aragón. In 1763, he was sent to Cuba and later to Texas, where he was a presidial commander and interim governor. Oconor began his review at the eastern end of the presidio line. He sent Adjutant Inspector Antonio Bonilla ahead of him to Tubac in 1774, but did not reach there himself until May of the following year. By that time he had accumulated a trunkful of ideas about where the Sonoran forts should be located. Unfortunately, Anza—whose thoughts would have been the most valuable of all—was not around to express them.

To provide greater protection for Sonorans going to California, Oconor chose to move the Tubac garrison to a point downstream on the Santa Cruz opposite the Indian village of Tucson. With Father Garcés at his side, he marked out the new site on August 20th, 1775. The patronage of St. Agustín, extended by Garcés to the Indian settlement, would serve the fort as well.[75]

The Tubac post was not the only one to be moved. Oconor called also for transferring the Fronteras garrison to San Bernardino and removing the Terrenate presidio to a site on the west bank of the San Pedro River a few miles from the modern town of Tombstone.[76]

Under normal circumstances, the transfer of Tubac's company would have taken place under Anza's direction, but the *comandante* had already been selected to lead an expedition of settlers to the San Francisco Bay area and, in fact, was at San Miguel de Horcasitas recruiting colonists at the time of Oconor's visit. Insofar as Anza and the Viceroy were concerned, the California effort had a higher priority than did relocation of the Tucson garrison. On the other hand, the *comandante* might have preferred to be in Tubac, instead of Horcasitas, when Apaches struck in September, 1775 and ran away with the horse herd he had planned to use for the California trip.[77]

During Anza's frequent absences, the Tubac commander was elderly Lieutenant Juan María de Oliva whom Oconor had recommended for retirement prior to selecting the Tucson site. When the move northward would finally come, however, Oliva would bear that responsibility.[78]

Anza and his colonists left Tubac on October 23rd, 1775, passing through the Tucson area three days later. Since none of the persons who kept diaries of the trip mention any military activity at Tucson, it is reasonable to assume that up to that time no effort had been made to relocate the Tubac garrison. In fact, an undetermined number of months were to pass before the task would be completed. In the absence of any other documentary verification of the move, historians depend on a letter written by Anza to the viceroy in November, 1776, to confirm that the soldiers had by then reached their new destination.[79] Anza never returned to lead the San Agustín company but he was not officially replaced until February, 1777, when Captain Pedro Allande y Saabedra, a veteran Spanish regular army officer of noble birth, became Tucson's first resident commander.[80]

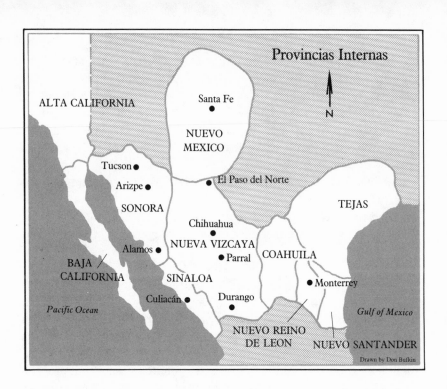

Provincias Internas

ALTA CALIFORNIA

Santa Fe

N

NUEVO
MEXICO

Tucson

Arizpe

El Paso del Norte

SONORA

TEJAS

Chihuahua

Alamos

NUEVA VIZCAYA

Parral

COAHUILA

BAJA
CALIFORNIA

SINALOA

Monterrey

Pacific Ocean

Culiacán

Durango

Gulf of Mexico

NUEVO REINO
DE LEON

NUEVO SANTANDER

Drawn by Don Bufkin

3

The Provincias Internas of New Spain

In July, 1776, at about the time Lieutenant Juan María Oliva was leading members of Tubac's beleagured garrison to Tucson, King Carlos III named José de Gálvez Minister of the Indies in the court of Spain. Gálvez had previously occupied the important post of visitor general, a position in which he had devoted far more attention than his predecessors to the problems of the northern frontier. He would later be accorded the title Marqués de Sonora.

With his new appointment, Gálvez was now in a position to carry out a plan he had long favored—one that called for the establishment of a northern jurisdiction, independent of the viceroy of New Spain. The reorganization could provide more flexibility in dealing with the hostile tribes and, thus, facilitate Hispanic colonization. The new minister moved quickly to secure creation of what he called "La Comandancia General de las Provincias Internas" (The General Command of the Interior or Internal Provinces). The new subdivision included the six northern provinces of New Spain, stretching from Texas to California. Officials of these provinces were to report directly to the general commander of the new jurisdiction who in turn would report to Gálvez and through him to the King of Spain.

For reasons that remain obscure, Arizpe, a small town on the Sonora River, was chosen to be the first capital of the Interior Provinces. It was a community that previously had enjoyed no particular distinction, although some prominent and wealthy Spanish families had property there or nearby. Placing the capital at Arizpe, however, gave administrative officials of Sonora relatively easy access to the most important of the King's appointees on the northern frontier.[1]

The impact of Gálvez' revolutionary change was slow in coming to Sonora. The earliest reverberation to reach the area was a change of governors. A few days after assuming his ministry, Gálvez named former governor Pedro Corbalán to the new office of *gobernador intendente* (intendant governor). Stepping down was Francisco Antonio Crespo, an appointee of the viceroy. It would not be long before this action would raise the question of the relationship between the upstart General Command in the north and the viceroyalty that prevailed throughout the remainder of New Spain.[2]

When Captain Pedro Allande y Saabedra reached his Tucson post in June, 1777, he may well have been thinking about the changes that would result from the creation of the jurisdiction of the Interior Provinces but his mind quickly shifted to other things. His first reaction to what he encountered in his new assignment was one of horror. He wasted no time in writing to Teodoro de la Croix, Gálvez' choice to head the new jurisdiction who had arrived in Mexico City six months earlier. Allande advised Croix that the construction of the presidio walls had scarcely begun and there were no funds with which to continue the building projects. The Papago workers had not been paid and the troopers lacked even the basic necessities. Not sure where the blame fell for the slovenly conditions, he had locked up poor old Brevet Captain Oliva who was still waiting to hear some news about his retirement which had been proposed nearly two years earlier.[3]

Before the year was out, Allande was to learn of the desperate condition of those who remained behind in Tubac. Three Spaniards from that area informed him in November that since the transfer of the presidio they had suffered untold casualties. They reported that the Apaches were openly grazing stolen horses in the Santa Cruz Valley, daily attacking the cornfields of the Indians and *gente de razón*, and taking captive any persons found working in those fields.[4]

To protect themselves the people of the region had formed a militia unit headed by Captain Juan Crisóstomo Ramírez, retired officer of the post. However, Ramírez, who had come to Tubac as an ensign (*alférez*) a quarter of a century earlier, died before he could do much to whip the volunteers into shape. Probably the most highly respected resident of Tubac in his day, Juan Crisóstomo was buried in the Tumacácori church, the construction of which he must have witnessed shortly after taking up his assignment at the presidio. His close friend, Fray Pedro de Arriquibar, performed the last rites. Later, the priest would assist the old soldier's son, Juan Joseph, and his wife with rearing their large family and would become the godfather of one of their sons.[5]

In May, 1777, Anza returned to Sonora following a trip to Mexico City. Chief Palma of the Yumas had accompanied him to the capital and the Indian's presence strengthened Viceroy Bucareli's resolve to establish missions and a colony on the Colorado River. Anza now carried the title of Sonoran military commander and he set up his headquarters at San Miguel de Horcasitas. He quickly advised his superiors of the sad state of the presidios and he strongly protested the relocation of the Tubac, Fronteras and Terrenate garrisons. From Mexico City, Croix authorized him to return the presidios to their old sites if he saw fit to do so. King Carlos III, however, had already decided to appoint Anza governor of New Mexico and he would not remain in Sonora long enough to make any changes.[6]

The government of the new General Command was not physically in place until 1779 and in the meantime the situation on the frontier deteriorated further. The Apaches had killed two commanding officers and many men of the highly exposed Terrenate presidio, now carrying the name Santa Cruz. Members of the Fronteras garrison, in their new location at San Bernardino, were often sick and unable to campaign. At Tucson, Allande had to use personal funds just to build a log palisade.[7]

Croix reached Arizpe on November 13th, 1779. Officially designating it the capital of his jurisdiction, he elevated the political status of the community to that of *ciudad*, or city. He also took steps to attract more residents and to create the institutions necessary for governance. Using revenues from a new tax on mescal, he provided the town with an aqueduct. He set out, also, to establish a mint, but failed at that endeavor.[8]

It was sometime after Croix's arrival before the Spaniards began to gain control of the Apache situation and during the period the frontier death toll mounted. In March, 1780, Brevet Captain Mi-

El Caballero de Croix, first commander of the Provincias Internas (Thomas, *Teodoro de Croix*)

Don José de Gálvez, Minister of the Indes and Marqués de Sonora (José Antonio Calderón Quijada, ed., *Los Virreyes de Nueva España en el reinado de Carlos III*, vol. 1, Sevilla, 1967, courtesy of John L. Kessell)

guel de Urrea, a veteran of service at Tucson, was killed by Apaches near Altar, the post his father had founded. The following month, the Apaches made their most successful attack in history on the Gila River Pima villages. Disguised as soldiers in leather jackets and Spanish-style hats, and carrying muskets, they swooped down on a large party of Pimas. When the dust cleared they had killed or captured at least 120 of their sedentary foes. The Pimas thought that troopers from Santa Cruz were responsible for the attack until advised otherwise by a woman who later escaped from her Apache captors.

In June, 1780, Father Francisco Perdigón, chaplain of the Tucson presidio, came to his death at the hands of Apaches while travelling between Bacanuchi and Arizpe. Perhaps overworked by trying to serve the residents of both Tucson and Santa Cruz, he had fallen ill and was on his way to the capital to seek medical attention.

Father Juan Agustín Morfi, who dressed the corpse, wrote in his diary that there was hardly a spot on it that did not show a wound.[9]

The Yuma Disaster

In spite of the continuing problems with the Apaches, plans for establishing a mission and colony in the Yuma area moved ahead. In August, 1779 Father Garcés and two soldiers went to the Colorado River to spend a few months with the Indians there. In October, Friar Juan Díaz and ten additional troopers joined them. They were still in the region a year later when Ensign Santiago de Islas began recruiting settlers for a Yuma colony. He persuaded a few residents of Tucson and Tubac to accompany him and his wife on a move to the Yuma area that finally came about in December of 1780. By the middle of the following month, the Mission of La Purísima Concepción (across the Colorado River from contemporary Yuma) and the town and mission of San Pedro y San Pablo de Bicuñer, five leagues upstream, were officially established.

Well before the beginning of summer, however, problems began to develop. Indians protested Spanish usurpation of their lands and the destruction of their crops by wandering Spanish livestock. On July 17th, 1781, the dam burst. While Father Garcés was saying mass, the Indians began clubbing the settlers and the other priests. Díaz and Father Joseph Matías Moreno died in the initial onslaught, as did Ensign Islas whose body was thrown into the river. The killing continued for two more days, culminating with the death of Fathers Juan Antonio Joaquín de Barreneche and Garcés. In all more than 100 Spaniards met death at the hands of the Yumas and another seventy-four were captured but later ransomed.

Punitive expeditions against the Yumas later in 1781 and again the following year failed to produce conditions that would have improved the possibility of reestablishing the missions and town. Croix concluded that the effort was not worth the cost. Although failure of the Yuma colony represented a setback to Minister Gálvez' new program, it did not result in abandonment of the concept of a separate northern jurisdiction—that idea was to continue in altered form until Mexico achieved its independence.[10]

The destruction of the settlement and missions on the Colorado River was a serious blow to the few *gente de razón* remaining in the

A group of Yuma Indians
(Arizona Historical Society)

vicinity of Tubac. Among those killed in the massacre was Manuel
Barragán, member of a family that had been prominent in the area
since the establishment of the presidio. His wife, Francisca Olguín,
also lost her life, as did respected citizens Francisco Castro and
Juan Romero. A few Indians were the only residents of Tubac two
years after the Yuma incident and Hispanics would not resettle
there until later in the decade. At Tumacácori, three Spanish families were still hanging on in 1783.[11]

Meanwhile in Tucson work on the adobe walls proceeded at a
snail's pace. They were still not up on May 1st, 1782, when a force
of several hundred Apaches attacked the settlement. Remarkably,
the soldiers drove off the Indians without losing a single man.
Captain Allande and two others were wounded.

The May Day assault probably sped up the construction time-
table and the walls were in place by December, 1783. Still, the
Apaches were not impressed. Five-hundred of them hit Tucson at

Antonio de los Reyes, first
bishop of Sonora (Villa,
Bodas de Plata)

dawn on March 21st, 1784. After slaying five soldiers, the Indians
fled northward with 150 horses. Ensign Juan Carrillo and Lieutenant Tomás Egurrola were among those who pursued them. The
presidial force of soldiers, civilians and Pimas killed at least seventeen warriors. A few months later, the King awarded the two officers increases in rank and reimbursed the soldiers for the value of
their horses.[12]

Farther south in the mining town of Alamos, the first bishop of
the newly created diocese of Sonora arrived just two weeks after
Tucson's desperate May Day battle. He was Father Antonio de los
Reyes, a Spanish Franciscan who earlier had served for a short time
at the Mission of Cucurpe in the San Miguel Valley. Reyes brought
with him two nephews from Spain—José Almada, a fellow priest,
and José's brother Antonio, a mining engineer. Within a few
months after their arrival, Antonio married heiress Luz Alvarado
González de Zayas, thus linking the Almadas to the mining elite of
northern New Spain.[13]

The new bishop attempted from the outset to institute changes in the administration of church affairs in Sonora and in the process alienated himself increasingly from his former Franciscan colleagues of the College of Querétaro. He also attacked the frontier military establishment, in spite of his links to it through kinship ties established by the marriage of his nephew Antonio.[14]

Loath to be separated from his nephews and the comforts provided by his rich in-laws, Bishop Reyes protested the location of his see in the raw frontier town of Arizpe even though the community, in accordance with a direct order from the King,[15] had been officially declared a city. The status change did not, however, result in a population explosion; and Arizpe in 1783 had only about a thousand inhabitants, most of them Indians. In September of that year, Reyes paid his first and only visit to the village that was now the capital of the whole northern region of New Spain. Afterward he lived in Alamos, beginning construction of a cathedral there in 1786. He died a year later.[16]

A New Indian Policy for the Frontier

In 1782, the same year that Bishop Reyes arrived in Alamos, General Commander Croix received orders to take over the viceroyalty of Peru and in August, 1783, he left Sonora. To replace him, Spanish authorities selected Felipe de Neve, a former governor of California, who had served briefly as one of Croix's aides. In the spring of 1784, Neve launched a major offensive against the Gila Apaches, leading almost 800 soldiers into the field. The results were disappointing. Spanish forces managed to kill only sixty-eight of the enemy and to capture seventeen. Shortly after returning from this expedition, Neve became ill. He died on August 21st, 1784.[17]

Filling in after Neve's death was José Antonio Rengel, who had arrived from Spain a few months earlier to occupy the post of adjutant inspector. He inherited from his predecessor problems with both the Comanches and the Apaches; but before he could mount a major campaign against either, he learned that other Indian matters were also of concern to his superiors. In April, 1785, Pedro Galindo Navarro, military judge and legal advisor to Rengel's command, called his attention to previously issued royal and religious decress related to mixing of the races. These decrees were intended to discourage the settlement of *mulatos, negros, coyotes, y semejantes razas* (mulattoes, blacks, half-breeds, and similar races) in the Indian villages. Where such persons were already present local officials were called upon to persuade them to move to nearby "Spanish" communities. Missionaries were directed to do what they could to discourage intermarriage between the Indians and members of these other groups.[18]

The record is not clear whether the Indian population of the Provincias Internas was in greater danger of contamination in 1785 than had been the case earlier, but the number of outsiders in the Pimería Alta had certainly increased as a result of the gold discoveries at La Cieneguilla. Although the boom ended before 1780, some of the newcomers, among them blacks and mulattoes, had remained in the area.[19]

Historians lack reliable data on the number of frontiersmen with Negro ancestry in northern New Spain at the close of the eighteenth century, but the available statistics clearly indicate the presence of some, and their overall representation may have been close to the national average.[20] Twenty-five of the original forty-six settlers of Los Angeles were *negros, mulatos,* or children of the same.[21] The Tubac troop roster of 1775, assembled just before the garrison's transfer to Tucson, included three individuals classified as *moriscos* (children of mulattoes and Europeans) and one as a *mulato.*[22]

The term *lobo*—indicating a mixture of Indian and Negro—was uncommon on the Sonoran frontier during the colonial period, which may mean that the priests of the region were successful in keeping single men of Negro ancestry from fathering the children of Indian women.[23] According to Father Pfefferkorn, *lobos* and *mulatos* were "regarded with contempt" by members of other classes and were "themselves ashamed of their origin."[24]

Rengel, who remained in charge of the affairs of the frontier provinces until April, 1786, accomplished relatively little in bringing the Apaches under control. After securing a peace with the Comanches, he moved against the Apaches during November and December, 1785, but the results were embarrassingly meager. Nearly 350 Opata and Spanish soldiers were in the field for three weeks. They killed just fourteen Apaches and recovered only twenty-seven horses while losing one of their own men and over fifty of their mounts.[25]

Despite his limited resources and the injuries he received in the

Apache attack of 1782, Captain Pedro Allande y Saabedra carried the battle to the enemy. Between 1783 and 1785, he and his troops conducted nearly a dozen major campaigns in addition to limited engagements carried out in behalf of settlers and mission Indians. In sending a report to King Carlos III in 1785, Allande stated that he and his men had successfully repulsed all of the Apache attacks on the presidio and in the process had killed many hostiles whose heads "have crowned the palisades." He wrote of the fatigue he had suffered in the fighting and of the pain he had been forced to endure from his leg wounds. Because of the pain, he wrote, his men had sought to have him turn back, but he had never once done so.[26]

In April, 1786, Rengel turned over his post to the King's appointee, Brigadier General Jacobo Ugarte y Loyola, a man of vast experience whose military career had begun forty-four years earlier when he enlisted in the Royal Infantry Guards. He was under fifteen at the time and had to obtain special dispensation because of his age.[27] Later, he had served as military commander of both Coahuila and Sonora—posts in which he had become familiar with the 1772 Regulations that had resulted from the Marqués de Rubí report, as well as the reforms instituted by Croix in compliance with a royal order of 1782. When he took office, he knew that he would soon be called upon to carry out still another set of directives from the new viceroy. This time, however, they would provide the basis for a frontier Indian policy more effective than any previously adopted.

The instructions prepared by Viceroy Gálvez and dated August 26th, 1786, noted that the hostile Apaches often made peace primarily to obtain through trade and subsidy certain items that they craved—horses, guns, food and ornaments. They noted, too, that the Indians violated the conditions of their agreements whenever it suited them to do so but that they could be weakened by division and induced to fight among themselves. Given this set of conditions, the viceroy called upon Ugarte to exploit the existing discord among the Apaches, form alliances to create further dissension, offer terms of peace to those desiring it, and wage constant warfare upon those who insisted on remaining hostile, or those who broke the peace treaties. Apaches who asked for peace were to be rewarded with "defective firearms, strong liquor, and such other commodities as would render them militarily and economically dependent on the Spaniards."[28]

In southern Arizona the Apaches appear to have adopted an early attitude of cynicism about the new policy. On October 1st, 1786, a small group of them appeared at the Calabazas village stating that they wished to settle down and would like to examine the nearby lands to locate some suitable to their needs. Aware that Chiricahua Apaches had taken up residence near the Bacoachi presidio a short time before, the Pimas lowered their guard long enough to permit the Indians to infiltrate. Taking quick advantage of the situation, the visitors killed two Pimas, wounded another and escaped with considerable booty. Captain Pablo Romero, Tucson's new commander, put his entire troop of fifty-four men into the field in pursuit of the raiders. The outnumbered soldiers trailed the hostiles to their camp in the Sierra de Arizona (southwest of modern Nogales), killed four, captured the stolen stock and chased the Apaches from the area. Nevertheless, the hoax was the last straw for the remaining Indian families at Calabazas which was abandoned shortly thereafter.[29] Tumacácori had become a mission without *visitas*.

Tubac finally got its presidio back in 1787, the year following promulgation of the Gálvez instruction. This time, however, the old fort was garrisoned with Pima Indians under the direction of Spanish officers. They were members of the San Rafael de Buenavista Company, formed five years earlier to be stationed at the old ranch of Buenavista. Initially, however, they served at San Ignacio. The *comandante* was Pedro Villaescusa, a Peninsular-born Spaniard who began his military career with the ill-fated Santa Cruz garrison on the San Pedro River. Destined to attain the rank of colonel,[30] Villaescusa was married to Ignacia Otero, sister of Arizona's first recorded land-grant owner. The Villaescusas were not complete strangers to Tubac when they moved there. A few years before—in 1783—they had lived briefly at Tumacácori, where María Ignacia gave birth to a son they named Juan José.[31]

Shortly after the San Rafael Company was transferred to Tubac, Pedro Sebastián Villaescusa moved on to another assignment and was replaced by his ensign, another Spaniard named Nicolás de la Errán. A year later, Errán received his promotion to lieutenant and was designated permanent commander of the Tubac post.[32]

Early in 1788, the much travelled Juan Bautista de Anza, by now a full colonel and ex-governor of New Mexico, was back in Sonora to return to his former assignment as military commander. In addition to the changes he found at Tubac, he discovered the presence of a new presidio at the site of the former Indian village and mission of Santa María Soamca. The garrison there was the one known as the Santa Cruz Company. It was the same troop that had first been stationed at Terrenate, then moved to the area of the former Sobaipuri villages on the San Pedro River. After his arrival in Arizpe, Croix transferred the Santa Cruz soldiers to Las Nutrias, not far from the original location of the Terrenate presidio. The final move to Soamca came in 1787.[33]

Anza wasted no time in getting underway. He chose Captain Manuel de Echeagaray, *comandante* of the Santa Cruz post, to head an expedition of soldiers from forts in both Sonora and Nueva Vizcaya in a major campaign against the renegade Chiricahua Apaches who had fled from the *establecimiento de paz*, or peace camp, created a year and a half earlier at Bacoachi. Using friendly Apache scouts—a tactic employed nearly a century later by George Crook and other American generals—Captain Echeagaray and his 400 presidial soldiers succeeded far better than previous expeditions. Going almost as far as the Pueblo of Zuni, they killed fifty-four Apaches, captured 125, and persuaded fifty-five to give themselves up to a life of peace. In addition, sixty-one horses and mules stolen from the Spaniards and mission Indians were recovered.

Commander General Ugarte was so impressed with Echeagaray's performance that he recommended him for immediate promotion to lieutenant colonel.[34] The report upon which the recommendation was based had come from Juan Bautista de Anza who died unexpectedly in Arizpe a month later. He was buried in the Arizpe church on December 20th, 1788.[35]

Spanish victories over the Apaches during 1788 were not without cost. Following a successful campaign at the head of a large force of presidial troops during June, Captain Romero of the Tucson garrison headed for Arizpe to report the good news to the authorities there. On the 30th of the month, he was ambushed and killed by Apaches on the hill of San Borja between Chinapa and Bacoachi. His saber was later recovered by Captain Echeagaray who forwarded it to Arizpe for delivery to Romero's heirs. Another officer of the Tucson garrison, Lieutenant Francisco Barrios, was also killed that year.[36]

The reestablishment of the presidio at Tubac encouraged a few Spanish settlers to migrate or return. Lieutenant Errán was in-

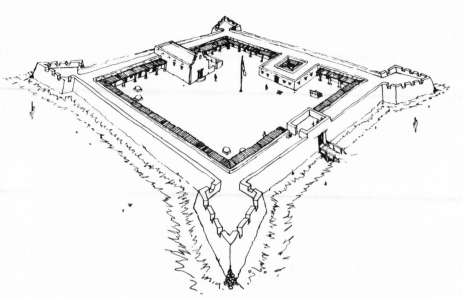

Conjectural sketch of the Tucson presidio in the late 1780s (Jack S. Williams)

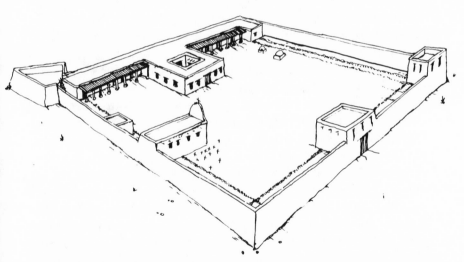

Conjectural sketch of the presidio of Santa Cruz de Terrenate in 1780 (Jack S. Williams)

structed by his superiors to stimulate new colonization, making use of a provision of the Royal Regulations of 1772 whereby those who wished to engage in agriculture could receive title to presidio lands in return for keeping arms and horses available for defense of the country. Apparently the first Spaniard to apply was a young man named Toribio de Otero who had earlier established ties to the area through his sister, doña Ignacia Otero de Villaescusa, wife of the first commander of the San Rafael Company. Otero was twenty-eight years old in 1789 when he approached Lieutenant Errán concerning a grant. The small land base he acquired a short time later would remain in the hands of his descendants until the early 1940s.[37] Doña María Ignacia Salazar of Santa Ana, whom Toribio had married ten years before, joined him in Tubac. The Salazar and Otero families were additionally linked through the marriage of one of Toribio's sisters and a brother of María.[38]

In 1789, the year after Captain Romero met his death at the hands of Apaches, Nicolás Soler received an appointment to head the Tucson presidio. He had previously been adjutant inspector of the peninsula of Lower California but the record does not reveal when he left that post to come to Tucson. Immediately following his appointment, however, and for some time afterward, the Tucson garrison was in fact commanded by Lieutenant José Ignacio Moraga, who had been cited for bravery while serving under Captain Romero.[39] Soler was officially replaced in 1792 by Captain José de Zúñiga, who was not able to report for duty until 1794.[40]

Lieutenant Moraga was in command on January 5th, 1793, when a group of Arivaipa Apaches came to the presidio to establish a peace camp. They were the first of their tribe in Arizona to accept the Spanish terms and the first hostile Indians to reside in the vicinity of the Tucson post. Manuel de Echeagaray, by then the military commander for Sonora, directed Moraga to give the Apaches gifts of raw sugar and to outfit their leader Nautil Nilché with a suit of clothes. To demonstrate his sincerity, the Indian chief presented Moraga with six sets of ears purportedly taken from the heads of enemy Apaches. Two weeks later, Echeagaray purchased fifty head of cattle to provide meat for the new arrivals. Within a short time, the number of Apaches had increased to more than a hundred.[41]

Not long after accommodating the request of the Arivaipas, Lieutenant Moraga moved on to new responsibilities as command-

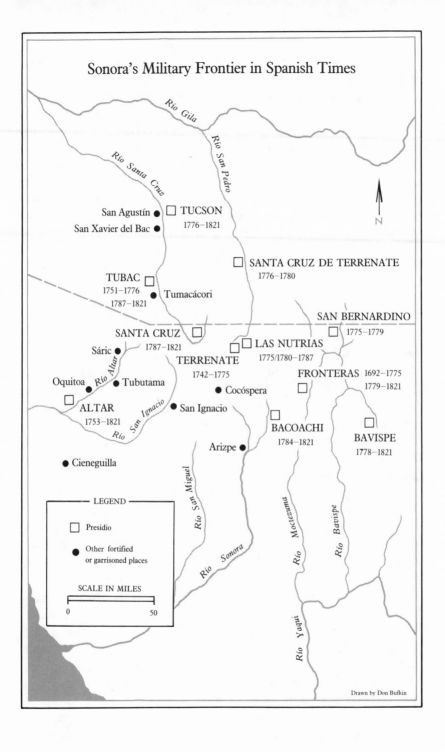

Sonora's Military Frontier in Spanish Times

Río Gila

Río Santa Cruz

Río San Pedro

N

San Agustín ● ☐ TUCSON
San Xavier del Bac ●   1776–1821

☐ SANTA CRUZ DE TERRENATE
1776–1780

TUBAC ☐
1751–1776   ● Tumacácori
1787–1821

SAN BERNARDINO

SANTA CRUZ ☐   ☐ ☐ LAS NUTRIAS   ☐ 1775–1779
Sáric ●   1787–1821   1775/1780–1787
TERRENATE
Río Altar   1742–1775   FRONTERAS 1692–1775
Oquitoa ●   *Río*   ● Tubutama   ● Cocóspera   ☐   1779–1821
San Ignacio
☐ ALTAR   ● San Ignacio   ☐
1753–1821   BACOACHI   ☐
Río   Arizpe ●   1784–1821   BAVISPE
1778–1821

● Cieneguilla

Río San Miguel

Río Sonora

Río Moctezuma

Río Bavispe

Río Yaqui

LEGEND

☐ Presidio

● Other fortified
   or garrisoned places

SCALE IN MILES

0   50

Drawn by Don Bufkin

ing officer at Altar. Replacing him as acting *comandante* at Tucson was Lieutenant Mariano de Urrea, bachelor grandson of veteran presidial captain Bernardo de Urrea, who had died shortly after retiring from active duty in 1777.[42] By the time young Mariano began his service in Tucson, Spain had undertaken another reorganization of the Interior Provinces. Since 1787, they had been divided into eastern and western sectors, with the general commander of each sector reporting to the viceroy in Mexico City. In November, 1792, King Carlos IV reunited the provinces under a single command and restored the autonomy they had previously enjoyed. Pedro de Nava, who a year earlier had taken charge of the western sector, was elevated to the top post and established his headquarters in the Villa de Chihuahua. Arizpe continued as the capital of Sonora and Sinaloa.[43]

One of Nava's most significant acts after taking command of the western sector had been to provide a new set of instructions for presidial commanders concerning the Apache peace settlements. Softer in tone and purpose than the Gálvez pronouncement, Nava's directive of October 14th, 1791, may have contributed more than that of the viceroy in bringing some peace to the northern frontier in the closing years of Spanish rule.[44] Three years after issuing his instructions, Nava outlined a ten-year plan for secularizing the Catholic missions and incorporating the Indians into the colonial system. Thereafter, his actions would be viewed with suspicion by the frontier clergy.[45]

In 1794, the same year Nava forwarded his secularization plan to the Council of the Royal Court, Captain José de Zúñiga took over the Tucson command. His most pressing duty was to lead a military expedition to New Mexico. He departed his post on April 9th, 1795, and at the end of the following day joined his forces with men from other posts at the abandoned Santa Cruz presidio on the San Pedro River. Their journey took them as far as the Zuni villages. Seven weeks after departure, the Tucson troopers were back at their home base. Ten years earlier, such a trip might have failed because of the Apaches, many of whom had moved from their traditional encampments by 1795 to the vicinity of the presidios. On the other hand, enough remained hostile to prevent much use of the trail blazed by Zúñiga and his soldiers.[46]

The expedition to New Mexico was one of the important happenings in 1795. An even more significant event for historians, how-

The parish church at Arizpe, Sonora, whose construction was supervised by Jesuit missionaries (1964 photograph by Elizabeth Keleman, Eckhart collection, Arizona Historical Society)

Ruins of the Provincias Internas military hospital in Arizpe (author's photograph taken in 1982)

ever, was the visit which Father Diego Miguel Bringas de Man-
zaneda y Encinas made to the Pimería Alta six months after Zúñiga
returned to his post. Bringas, a native of Alamos, headed northward from the College of Querétaro at about the time Zúñiga's
forces were approaching New Mexico and spent some time with
General Commander Pedro de Nava in Chihuahua before going to
Tumacácori early in October. His goal was to resolve some of the
differences that divided the Franciscan friars in the Pima missions,
as well as to ascertain just what Nava was up to with the secularization issue. He carried the special credentials of a "Father Visitor"
appointed by the College. Bringas' stay in the Pimería Alta was a
brief one. He spent a few days at Tumacácori, then moved northward to San Xavier and Tucson. Provided a military escort by
Zúñiga, he next visited the Pima villages along the Gila River.

In the two years following his trip, Bringas prepared a number of
recommendations for Commander General Nava; then, when disappointed with the response, put together a comprehensive report
for those with higher authority in Spain. Because of the complicated political position in which Spain found itself in the closing
years of the eighteenth century, Bringas' recommendations had little
effect on frontier policy in New Spain. The friar's description of
Sonora has proved a blessing to historians for more than 100 years,
however. The data contained in his report constitute one of the
primary sources of information about the Yuma massacre and its
aftermath, as well as the growing problems of competition between
Indians and others for land and water on the Sonoran frontier.[47]

Life Settles Down

The combination of the new Indian policy initiated by Viceroy
Gálvez and the reestablishment of the presidio of Tubac improved
the quality of life for the settlers of southern Arizona and their
numbers increased after 1790. At some of the established locations,
newcomers included more Indians from outside the area than persons of Spanish descent. The Tumacácori census of 1796 reveals,
for example, the presence of thirteen "outside" Indians—most of
them Yaquis—but only two Hispanics.[48]

Tucson, on the other hand, had a substantial population of individuals of European extraction. Instructions for a general census of Sonoran Catholic parishes reached the presidio in 1795,[49] shortly before Father Pedro de Arriquibar took over as military chaplain. It was he who then prepared Tucson's most complete early population register.[50] Probably assembled early in 1797, when the priest also prepared an inventory of church property, the register lists 395 individuals: 102 were soldiers, and twenty-five were servants (the latter, undoubtedly Indian). In addition to the military families, there were twenty-one civilian households, some—such as that of Ylario Santa Cruz—headed by men who had formerly been soldiers. Names such as Pacheco, Durán, and Ramírez attest that Tucson had become the home of families formerly residing at Tubac and other locations to the south.

The whereabouts of Captain Zúñiga and his family at the time of the census is not clear from Arriquibar's compilation. Although it is known that he was still assigned to the Tucson post, as he would be for several more years, Zúñiga's name is missing from the register. The highest ranking officer is Lieutenant Mariano de Urrea. He is seconded by Ensigns Phelipe Belderrain, son of the first captain of the Tubac presidio, and José María Sosa. Sosa is usually viewed by his descendants as the founder of the family lineage in southern Arizona, although records exist of other Sosas residing earlier in the Guevavi area.

Among the sergeants listed are Juan Antonio Oliva, *mestizo* son of the man who brought the Tubac troopers to Tucson in 1776, and Domingo Granillo, descendant of one of the early New Mexico colonists who settled in the San Miguel Valley of Sonora in 1637.[51] Also on the roster of military families is that headed by Salvador Gallego, founder of another important Tucson lineage, who by the closing days of Spanish rule would become the first sergeant of the Tucson garrison.[52]

Luisa Bohórquez, widow of former commanding officer Pablo Romero (killed by Apaches in 1788), had remarried and in 1796 was living with her second husband, Simón Maldonado. They shared their household with two servants and six children, three girls and three boys. Some, if not all, these children were from doña Luisa's first marriage. However, José, her oldest son, was a cadet in the Tucson company and was residing elsewhere.

One of the wealthiest households in the presidio was certainly that of Ensign José María Sosa. He and his wife, doña Rita Espinosa, boasted a total of five servants. Four Sosa children, a son and three daughters, were also living in the home.

Although Father Arriquibar shows Lieutenant Mariano de Urrea as a bachelor, the young officer had, in fact, married a short time before. Several months earlier, Captain Zúñiga had granted him a leave of absence to go to Arizpe and marry Gertrudis Elías González, a granddaughter of Captain Francisco Elías González de Zayas.[53]

A year after they were married, Mariano and Gertrudis produced a son they named José Cosme. Historians disagree as to the exact date and place of birth of this boy who would grow up to be one of the most important figures in Mexico during the early independence years. What is not in dispute is the fact that young José Cosme was baptized in the chapel of the Tucson presidio by Father Pedro de Arriquibar on September 30th, 1797. The child's godparents were Captain Zúñiga and his wife Loreto Ortiz, a close relative of doña Gertrudis.[54] The Zúñiga couple had celebrated the arrival of a son of their own a year earlier. Born in Tucson and probably baptized by Father Arriquibar, the boy was given the name Ignacio. He, too, would grow up to be a man of prominence, and his career would be closely linked with that of José Cosme de Urrea.[55]

As early as 1796 there were disputes over water between the Indian and non-Indian populations of the Tucson area. In January of that year, a group of Papagos from the *ranchería* of Aquituni, northwest of the presidio, were persuaded to settle in the old Pima village at the foot of Sentinel Peak. Any advantages they might have expected to gain by virtue of the move were negated by the unwillingness of the *gente de razón* to share the limited water supply with them. Also, livestock belonging to the Spaniards damaged the few crops they were able to grow. Coming to the defense of the Indians was Father Juan Bautista Llorens of San Xavier, who provided the immigrants with both food and clothing. Father Visitor Bringas, following his visit to the Pimería Alta in 1795, wrote General Commander Nava requesting assistance in resolving the water and trespass problems and in supplying the Papagos with oxen and tools.[56]

Upon receiving Father Bringas' various recommendations, Nava asked his legal adviser, Pedro Galindo Navarro, for an opinion.

Galindo responded in December, 1796 with a letter stating that the most critical issues had been settled. He made reference to a set of documents that provided for the apportionment of land and water between the Indians and the settlers of Tucson.[57] He then expressed the opinion that the responsibility for helping the Papagos lay primarily with the Franciscans at San Xavier; he recommended against burdening the Royal Treasury with the expense of providing oxen and tools.[58]

New Mission Construction

In 1797, only a few months after Bringas heard from Nava about the water matter, Father Llorens of San Xavier had the agreeable duty of presiding at the dedication of a magnificent new church. According to popular tradition, construction of this edifice had begun around 1783 under the direction of Fray Juan Bautista Velderrain. A key figure in assuring the completion of the temple was a wealthy Spaniard named Antonio Herreros who loaned Velderrain 7,000 of the 30,000 pesos needed for the project. The new building replaced one constructed sometime after 1756 by Jesuit Father Alonso Espinosa.[59]

Completion of the San Xavier church freed the laborers and artisans to apply their recently acquired construction skills elsewhere, and sometime shortly after 1797, Llorens began directing new projects at the old Indian village across the river from the Tucson presidio. With its immigrant Papagos and a new water allocation, this community—which was popularly known as El Pueblito (The Little Village)—seemed to have a promising future. More than a quarter of a century earlier, Captain Anza had directed the construction of fortifications at the site and shortly afterward Father Garcés had supervised the building of a small church which had begun to deteriorate by 1797.

The building project at El Pueblito probably focused in the beginning on renovation or replacement of the Garcés church, and the resulting structure endured into the closing years of the nineteenth century. Once this work was done, Llorens and his crew turned to something much more ambitious, the construction of a large, two-story structure whose precise purpose remains obscure. Tradition ascribes to it the functions of both convent and industrial school.[60]

Tradition also holds that Apache Indians characterized as "coyoteros" assisted with building it.[61] No information has come to light on when it was begun or finished, but Captain Zúñiga in an 1804 report of major "public works" within his jurisdiction does not mention any such edifice.[62]

Uneasiness Prevails at Century's End

The deteriorating political situation in Spain and central Mexico at the close of the eighteenth century began to have an effect on the Sonoran frontier shortly after Bringas paid his 1795 visit. Late in 1797, General Commander Nava wrote to Friar Rouset, Bishop of Sonora, calling for compliance with a Royal Order instructing all persons travelling the roads of the region or venturing outside the fortified towns and missions to carry arms for defense against robbery, murder and other assaults committed by fugitive Indians and vagabonds.

In his letter, Nava also pointed out that the priests were to cease collecting fees for burials and other sacraments, and to begin paying the Indians for labor and personal services they rendered in support of the missions. The general commander advised Rouset that a public defender for Indians was to be appointed to investigate violations of his order. Earlier in the same year a Royal Decree had been circulated prohibiting churches and parishes from offering privileges of sanctuary to army deserters and revolutionaries.[63]

The gap between the military and the priesthood in Sonora widened additionally in 1799 with a wave of uprisings by Apaches and Seris. The parish priest at Pitic (Hermosillo) accused Nava of inciting these uprisings to increase the dependency of the settlers and sedentary Indians on the soldiers, and to provide a rationale for denying the missionaries support in their plans for carrying the gospel to Pima Indians along the Gila River.[64]

Contributing to the unrest in Sonora at the close of the century was a rumor that England, angry at Spain because of her alliance with France, planned to invade northern Mexico. In August a Portuguese sailor, said to have deserted from a British ship, testified at Pitic that the British planned to sail through the gulf and establish a base on the Colorado River, from which they would enlist Indian allies to help them take over Sonora.[65]

... dho Baptizé solemnem.te y puse los santos
oleos a una Niña de nacion Apacha, como de
edad de doze años a quien puse por nombre M.a
Loreta; fue su padrino Josef Lorea, vecino de
la ciudad de Mexico: y para que conste lo firmé en dho dia, mes, y año.———
                              F. Ignacio Ballmilla

En dho dia, Baptizé solemnem.te y puse los santos oleos a
una Niña de Nacion Apacha, como de edad de siete
años, a quien puse p.r nombre María Soledad:
fue su Madrina María Mora, vecina de
Arizpe, y p.a q.e conste lo firmé, en dho dia, mes, y año.
                              F. Ignacio Ballmilla

En dho Baptizé solemnem.te y puse los santos oleos, a
un Niño de nacion Apache, como de edad de seis
años, a quien puse por nombre Juan Antonio:
fue su Madrina Rita Sudiona, vecina de
Arizpe, y p.a q.e conste lo firmé, en dho dia, mes, ya.o
                              F. Ignacio Ballmilla

En dho. Baptizé solemnem.te y puse los santos oleos
a una Niña de nacion Apacha, como de edad de
Sinco años, a q.n puse p. nom.e Josefa Maria de los ...
fue su madrina maria de los ... vecina de Baconchi.
y p.a q.e conste lo firmé — F. Ignacio Ballmilla

Page from a document in the Arizpe church archive showing baptisms of captured Apache children in 1787

In spite of the growing antagonism between priests and soldiers, it seems likely that they continued to cooperate in distributing women and children captured during forays against the hostile tribes. Since the initiation of the new Indian policy in 1786, the number of such captives had increased many fold. The priests were concerned both with the treatment of the prisoners and with making Christians of them; the presidial captains, as well as their superiors, looked to the missionaries to assure placement of captives in homes where both these goals could be met.

The 1798 Arizpe census shows that the Apache captives in that community were living in the homes of the wealthiest residents. Fifty-two Apaches between the ages of three and twenty—most of them in their teens—were distributed among twenty-five households whose heads were all classified as "Spaniards." The family names of these householders are among the most prominent in northern Mexico: Tresierra y Cano, Pérez, Escalante, Tato, Comadurán, Corella, Elías González, Pesqueira, Zubiria and Morales.[66]

In Tucson, Hispanic families acquired Indian household servants through purchase as well as capture. Gila River Pimas and Maricopas brought Yuma, Yavapai and Apache children to the fort for sale. In his 1796 letter to Pedro de Nava, Father Bringas describes an incident in which a high official from Arizpe appropriated several captives from ten Pimas who were in Tucson but failed to pay the captors anything in return. He expressed concern that such an action might convince the Pimas that slave-taking was not worthwhile and in the future they would simply kill their captives (in this case Apaches). Friar Bringas also noted that the captives living in Tucson households were being taught the catechism.[67]

Sacramental registers from communities in northern Sonora reveal that most, if not all, the Indians who wound up in Hispanic homes during the last dozen years of the eighteenth century became Catholic converts. Remarkable numbers of baptisms are recorded in the Arizpe parish archives beginning in June, 1787, when don Domingo Bergara brought many captive children into Arizpe and Bacanuchi.[68]

4

The Last Years of Spanish Rule

As the nineteenth century began, Franciscan priests in the Pimería Alta were busy responding to new directives from the general command of the Provincias Internas and from their religious superiors. These directives often called upon them to provide information about persons residing in mission communities under their jurisdiction. One such report, prepared in 1801,[1] makes it clear that in spite of royal policy the Indian villages continued to experience settlement by outsiders. Persons identified as *coyotes*, *mestizos*, and Indians of various tribes—along with others classified only as *vecinos* or *gente de razón*—were sharing land and water with the native inhabitants.

The census prepared by Father Llorens of San Xavier in 1801 includes separate lists of the native Indians at Bac and its *visita*, El Pueblito. The priest classified as Pimas and Papagos all 218 of those living at El Pueblito notwithstanding the Sobaipuri ancestry of some. He lumped together the names of the non-natives residing in the two villages without indicating who lived where. Nevertheless, it can be taken for granted that outsiders were present at both locations.

The total of thirty-nine *vecinos* in the two Indian communities includes *españoles*, *coyotes*, *mestizos*, *mulatos* and Yuma Indians. Llorens listed more Spaniards than *vecinos* of any other type, but the sum of fourteen still placed members of this group in the minority. All of the Yumas were children and they were residing with families whose names they had adopted. In five of the eight cases, they were in households headed by persons described as Spaniards. Three were in the home of a twenty-nine-year-old bachelor named Ygnacio Pacheco whom Father Llorens, correctly or not, classified as a *coyote*. Also present in this household was Pacheco's mother María del Carmen Romero, daughter of pioneer Nicolás Romero.[2]

Given the prominence that Pacheco and his descendants in Tucson would later enjoy and the fact that he was literate, it is somewhat unusual that Llorens should have classified him and his mother as *coyotes* rather than *españoles*. Literacy, almost unknown among women on the Sonoran frontier, was largely confined to upper class males, whose racial classification nearly always turned out to be Spanish. Curiously, Father Llorens also listed as *coyotes* members of the León family. Joseph de León, seventeen and unmarried at the time, would be Tucson's first elected mayor in 1825 and he, too, could read and write.[3]

Of the three persons shown as *mulatos*, two were women. One was married to a *mestizo* and the other to a *mulato*. The two children of the *mestizo-mulata* marriage were classified by Llorens as *mestizos*.

From the beginning of Spain's rule in Mexico, the whole system of racial classification had been a highly arbitrary affair and it became increasingly so toward the end of the colonial period. Father Francisco Iturralde of the Tubutama mission did not even attempt to record the origins of individuals in his juridiction that he listed as *gente de razón*, saying that he did not have this information at his disposal. The Tumacácori census provided by Father Gutiérrez was equally vague. He counted twenty-nine persons in the *vecino* category, most of whom were apparently either servants or farm laborers (*peones y agregados*). Eleven of the twelve Yaquis reported living at Tumacácori in 1796 were no longer there but the Cocóspera census includes a sufficient number to make it clear that the Yaquis were still well represented in the region.

Although the combination of the new Indian policy and the assignment of troops to Tubac made things considerably easier for the Hispanic residents and peaceful Indians of the Santa Cruz Valley after about 1790, the Apaches did not give up raiding altogether. In June, 1801, a large number attacked Tumacácori and killed three mission residents who were tending their flocks of sheep close to the village. The villagers were afraid to go outside and retrieve the bodies because the raiders remained in the area. The next afternoon, a small force of Pima soldiers from Tubac came to the rescue.[4]

In 1801, Lieutenant Mariano de Urrea, commanding the presidio in the absence of Captain Zúñiga, made a grant of Tucson land to settler Reyes Pacheco on the same terms as the assignment made earlier to Toribio Otero at Tubac. Pacheco, one of few survivors of the Yuma massacre, was listed in the 1797 census as a civilian settler of Tucson and also appeared on a 1767 register of Tubac males. The earlier record reported him to be a teenage boy whose full name was Joseph Reies. He was almost certainly a son of Juan Joseph Pacheco and his first wife, María de los Santos Gómez, possibly a daughter of the original commander of the Terrenate fort.[5] (She died in 1764.)

Sometime prior to 1803, Father Narciso Gutiérrez began work on a new church at Tumacácori to replace the crumbling ruin built by the Jesuits in 1757. He was hard pressed to sustain the effort, however, for there were few wealthy benefactors nearby. Furthermore, while he might have raised money through the sale of cattle, which were plentiful at that time, livestock prices were down. Getting the church ready became a long drawn-out affair and Father Gutiérrez died before that day came.[6]

On August 4th, 1803, the Bishop of Sonora dispatched a circular letter to the chaplains of the Pimería Alta presidios informing them that it would be their responsibility to see to the education of the children in their communities. The emphasis was primarily on religious and secular law and obedience to their fathers. Teaching would take place on Sundays and religious holidays; on Saturdays, family heads would be required to send their servants and slaves, as well as their children, to learn Christian doctrine.[7]

While the more peaceful conditions that prevailed in northern Sonora with the advent of the *establecimientos de paz* contributed to an increase in the *vecino* population, there were other factors that attracted settlers to the region. Early in October, 1803, new gold discoveries were reported a few miles north of Cieneguilla, where the great strike of the 1770s had caused so much excitement. Father José María Paz y Goicochea reported in a letter to Bishop Rouset that Cieneguilla itself was all but abandoned. The miners were not returning to the town to attend mass, so the priest journeyed to the placer fields to carry the faith to them.[8]

In June, 1802, King Carlos IV of Spain had ordered an evaluation of the worth of the colonial outposts, such as those on the Sonoran frontier. It was late in the spring of 1804, however, before instructions for conducting this appraisal reached the Pimería Alta. Captain José de Zúñiga prepared the report for Tucson; Second Ensign Manuel de León did the same for Tubac.[9]

Zúñiga, with a full decade of Tucson service behind him, provided a detailed description of the presidio and its surroundings, including a statement about San Xavier mission. According to him, "The only public work here that is truly worthy of this report is the church at San Xavier del Bac. . . . Other missions here in the north should really be called chapels, but San Xavier is truly a church." Tucson's *comandante* provided a head count of all persons at the presidio and in the surrounding area (including San Xavier). The total came to 1,015. León, who had replaced Errán as the commanding officer at Tubac, reported that his post included eighty-eight soldiers and their families, eight civilian Hispanic households and twenty Indian families. The count of *gente de razón* at Tumacácori, although down somewhat from two years before, stood at eighty-two, equal to the population of Pimas and Papagos.[10]

Southern Arizona was beginning to enjoy a measure of prosperity in 1804, at least compared to previous years. León noted that the Tubac district annually harvested about 600 bushels of corn and 1,000 of wheat. The presidio cattle herd consisted of 1,000 head, and there were 5,000 sheep.

Tucson's corn crop was about the same size as that of Tubac, but the wheat harvest was larger—2,800 bushels. Tucsonenses grew about 300 bushels of beans and other vegetables and the Indians of the Tucson district produced cotton for their own use. Tucsonans were raising more cattle than their southern neighbors, about 3,500, but they had only about half as many sheep. Captain Zúñiga reported some occupational diversity at his presidio: four individuals were operating pack trains and an unspecified number were engaged in making soap. The *comandante* lamented the absence of weavers, leather tanners, tailors and saddlemakers and also felt that the opportunity for cultivating grapes was being lost.

The larger sheep flock at Tubac had contributed to a weaving industry there. León observed that some 600 woolen blankets had been produced and sold at a price of slightly more than 5 pesos each. Over 1,000 yards of coarse serge had also been woven, and the sale price for this material was around half a peso per yard.

Both León and Zúñiga noted that the settlers did not pay any sales or personal taxes. At Tubac, no tobacco taxes were collected either but the Tucson *comandante* reported that individuals within his jurisdiction had paid out more than 2,000 pesos for this purpose. Soldiers and settlers bought their tobacco directly from the presidio paymaster, who was responsible for collecting the tobacco tax, or at the company store.

Prominently mentioned in both reports is the dependence of Tucsonans on the Sonoran capital of Arizpe, which had become the principal supply point for the northern presidios. León noted that there was no company store in Tubac and that merchandise from Spain was all brought in through Arizpe. According to him, both soldiers and settlers travelled frequently to the capital to make purchases. Zúñiga observed in his report that the paymaster, with a military escort, visited Arizpe in connection with his duties of delivering and picking up the mail. León mentioned that goods from Asia and China—even southern Mexico—did not reach his post. Zúñiga, on the other hand, stated that 500 pesos were spent each year on merchandise from the orient—presumably brought in from Arizpe. He commented that no products were received directly from Veracruz, Acapulco or San Blas. Both commanding officers insisted that there were no smuggled goods within their jurisdictions.

In spite of the more peaceful situation throughout the region, it does not appear from either report that mining activities had been resumed to any significant degree by 1804. Zúñiga states quite positively that "we have no gold, silver, lead, tin, quicksilver, copper mines, or marble quarries." He continues that there is an outcropping of lime twenty-five miles from the presidio that supplies local construction needs, but "we have no salt beds."[11] León does not mention the subject of mining at all.

In appraising the work habits of the local gentry, Zúñiga is almost as critical as Father Pfefferkorn had been nearly half a century earlier. Noting that the privileged settlers are exempt from all personal taxes, he questions why they are not more prosperous. He then goes on to speculate that since so few demands are made on them, they have lost all ambition. It is in this context that he laments the absence of more industry in the community.

More Early Land Grants

The *vecino* population associated with the Tumacácori mission declined slightly after about 1802, but the number of *gente de razón* at Tubac increased substantially. As the possibility became ever greater that some of the settlers might try to establish ranches and farms on the lands of the long abandoned Guevavi and Calabazas communities, Father Narciso Gutiérrez decided the time had come to encourage the residents of Tumacácori and its environs to petition for a formal grant, or regrant, of mission lands and any other property that the original Jesuit missionaries might have acquired for raising livestock.

Tumacácori Governor Juan Legarra headed a small delegation that travelled to Arizpe late in 1806 to confer with an attorney about obtaining title to lands the Indians were occupying and using. The attorney helped them draw up a petition which they presented to Intendant Governor Alejo García Conde. A short time later, on December 17th, 1806, the governor responded favorably. Manuel de León, who by this time had received his promotion to lieutenant, was instructed to make the required survey. When he completed this work, the Indians had title to a long strip of land beginning just south of Tubac and following the Santa Cruz River approximately to the present Mexican border. It included areas previously associated with all three mission communities: Tumacácori, Calabazas and Guevavi (see map, page 295).

The formal deed to the Tumacácori-Calabazas grant, dated April 2nd, 1807, included three special conditions. The first provided that claims by any other persons to lands within the grant would be considered if they were presented "in due time and form." The second stated that the lands of the grant were to be cultivated, protected and inhabited; if they should lie totally abandoned for three consecutive years, they would become subject to the claims of others. Finally, the document specified that if Calabazas were to be

Arivaca (*Sonora Silver Mining Company Report*, courtesy of John L. Kessell)

resettled by its former Indian inhabitants, that part of the grant would be segregated from the remainder.[12]

Five years after the award of the Tumacácori grant, another abandoned *ranchería* that had once been a *visita* of Guevavi became the object of a petition from one of the wealthy Spanish settlers of the area—don Agustín Ortiz, a member of the same Arizpe family to which the wives of Mariano de Urrea and José de Zúñiga belonged. About 1800, if not slightly before, Agustín came to southern Arizona with his wife María Reyes Peña[13] and a son Tomás. Not long after arriving in their new home, they had another boy named Ignacio.

Sometime in 1812, while living in Tucson, Agustín Ortiz applied for a grant at the site of Arivaca, one of the oldest mining and ranching locations in the region. In accordance with the usual procedures, the petition was posted and persons opposing the grant were given an opportunity to be heard. When no objections were raised, the property was offered for sale at public auction. Don Agustín was the highest bidder and, according to testimony offered later, paid 747 pesos and three *reales* to the treasury at Arizpe. The Ortiz family lived and ranched on the grant for a generation thereafter.[14]

Arizona and the Independence Movement

In his history of Sonora, Professor Eduardo W. Villa has observed that because of the general ignorance about outside events resulting from the isolation of the northern frontier, the area was not caught up in the developments leading to the Mexican independence movement of 1810. When Father Miguel Hidalgo y Costilla initiated the revolution against Spanish rule with his famous *grito*, or shout, of independence, the civil, military and religious authorities of Sonora and Sinaloa were shocked. They moved quickly to affirm their loyalties to the Crown, as well as to encourage others within their jurisdictions to oppose the revolt.[15]

Had it not been for the presence of the presidios in their midst, the Hispanic residents of southern Arizona might have escaped the independence movement altogether since the fighting took place deeper inside Mexico. As it was, however, the soldiers of the presidial garrisons were among the most experienced troops Spain could call upon and these units were deemed of critical importance in putting down the revolt. The intendant-governor of Sonora when the rebellion began was Alejo García Conde, the same man who had assisted the Pimas and Papagos of Tumacácori with obtaining title to their lands a few years before. Born in North Africa, García Conde began his military career at the age of twelve, then rose through the ranks to become a colonel. He was fifty-nine years old when the independence movement got underway in 1810.

Noting the early successes of Hidalgo's followers in central Mexico, García Conde took steps to keep the rebellion from spreading into areas under his jurisdiction. He chose Lieutenant Colonel Pedro Sebastián de Villaescusa, *comandante* at Buenavista (the southernmost presidio), to lead the first contingent of troops southward. In the years following his service at Tubac, Villaescusa had moved slowly up the ranks, while acquiring considerable fame as an Indian fighter. By 1794, he had been wounded four times by lances and twice by arrows.[16]

Villaescusa's forces consisted primarily of troops from his own post, but soldiers from both Tucson and Altar were included.[17] The orders from García Conde called for the Sonorans to take up positions in the plaza of the important Sinaloa mining town of El

Father Miguel Hidalgo y
Costilla (Library of
Congress)

Rosario, where they were to await the arrival of an insurgent army
headed northward from Guadalajara.[18]

Leader of the revolutionary force for campaigns in Sinaloa and
Sonora was José María González de Hermosillo, a native of Jalisco,
whom Father Hidalgo had anointed with the rank of lieutenant
colonel. He set out from Guadalajara on December 1st, 1810, with a
small force; by the time he reached Rosario it had increased to
several thousand. Heavily outnumbered, Villaescusa was unable to
defend the plaza which fell to the insurgents before the end of the
first day of battle. The Sonoran commander himself was captured
but Hermosillo allowed him his freedom, along with a small escort,
and promised him safe conduct in returning to his home. Villaescusa took advantage of this situation to dispatch messengers to
García Conde to inform him of the defeat and to request reinforcements.[19]

Convinced that the situation was more serious than he had first
thought, García Conde decided to assume personal command of the

presidial forces. Ordering several units southward to slow the advance of Hermosillo, he assembled the remaining forces and began his march. Toward the end of the first week of February, 1811, García Conde reached a spot on the outskirts of the Sinaloan town of San Ignacio Piaxtla.[20] Villaescusa had arrived there earlier and had taken up a defensive position opposite the troops of González de Hermosillo which were deployed on the other side of town. The soldiers under Villaescusa's command included a few who had been with him at Rosario but most were reinforcements from the presidios sent ahead by García Conde.

Sharing the direction of the Royalist forces with Villaescusa was Captain Manuel Ignacio Arvizu who, following his service on the southern front, would become the *comandante* of the Tucson presidio. In command of the Royalist artillery under Arvizu's direction was Antonio Leyva, ensign of the Tucson post.

García Conde arrived on February 5th and after taking a quick look at the situation decided to initiate a major offensive against the enemy troops. He chose the morning of February 9th for the attack. Meanwhile, however, González de Hermosillo was making similar plans. Perhaps aware of García Conde's intentions, Hermosillo decided to send his forces into action on the morning of the 8th. The insurgent commander might have been better off to wait. The result was a disastrous defeat. More than 500 were killed and the number of wounded exceeded 1,000. The survivors fled in disorder. Contributing importantly to the Royalist victory were Opata soldiers from Sonora who ambushed 400 of the rebels.

In March, 1811, just a month after the Battle of San Ignacio, Father Miguel Hidalgo was captured and brought before a military court which ordered his execution. One member of that court was Captain Simón Elías González, then commander of military forces at the Villa de Chihuahua (Chihuahua City). A few years before, he had served in the garrisons of both Tucson and Tubac.[21]

On July 31st, 1811, Father Hidalgo was put to death in Chihuahua. In spite of his execution, however, and the defeat suffered by González de Hermosillo,[22] the revolutionary effort continued. Troops from Tucson and Tubac were tied up in the south until about 1818.[23]

Tucson-born Ignacio Zúñiga,[24] writing in 1835, asserted that the beginning of the Mexican independence movement sounded the death knell of the *establecimientos de paz* created around the presidios by the Indian policy initiated in 1786.[25] Transfer of troops to the south, plus the drain on the Royal Treasury to fight the insurgents, set in motion a chain of conditions and events that weakened the capacity of the frontier forts to subjugate and control the hostile Indians. The impact of these developments was slow, however, in reaching its full effect on Tucson and Tubac. While Apache raids and forays against the raiders continued to be regular events for the troopers between 1812 and 1820, these were small-scale affairs compared with those of thirty years before. The sacramental registers do not assign the Apaches responsibility for many deaths, Hispanic or Indian, during this period.[26]

The fact that the *establecimientos de paz* were still functioning institutions in the Pimería Alta at the close of the colonial era is demonstrated to some extent by the decision of Pinal Apache chief Chilitipage and seventy-eight of his followers to settle near the Tucson post early in 1819. Because of the enmity between members of this Pinal band and other Apaches already at the post, Antonio Narbona, overall military commander for Sonora, arranged to transfer some of the original group to Santa Cruz.[27]

More deadly than the Apaches in the early years of the nineteenth century were epidemics that periodically swept through the area. Father Gutiérrez of Tumacácori buried twenty-five Indians from his jurisdiction during the final two months of 1816, fifteen of them children. The pestilence had struck first at San Ignacio in August, then spread northward. Its impact was probably heavy among the Indians of Tucson and San Xavier, as well as among those at Tumacácori, for ethnohistorian Henry Dobyns reports that the Native American population at those locations declined by 209 between 1804 and 1818.[28]

The *vecinos* fared somewhat better than the mission Indians in maintaining their numbers during the final two decades of Spanish control over southern Arizona. Father Arriquibar's 1797 census of Tucson included seventy-nine civilians (counting children, but not household servants); in 1819 the total was sixty-eight. At Tumacácori Father Gutiérrez reported seventy-five *gente de razón* in 1820, compared with eighty-two counted by the same priest sixteen years before.[29]

The relative peace that prevailed on the northern frontier in the early 1800s resulted in some increase of the *vecino* population in mining and ranching areas away from the presidios and missions.

By 1808 some *gente de razón* families were back in the Calabazas area; others were living at Arivaca; still others were grazing stock in the San Pedro and San Rafael valleys.

Probably no better evidence of the generally peaceful conditions prevailing on the frontier can be offered than the fact that gold mining in the Guevavi area was resumed in 1814 after a lapse of more than fifty years. The principal labor supply for this effort was Yaqui, and Father Narciso Gutiérrez of Tumacácori recorded many Yaqui baptisms, marriages and burials at Guevavi prior to his death in 1820. The mines were on land included within the 1807 grant to the Pimas and Papagos and it may be presumed that the Franciscans dedicated some of the proceeds to construction of the Tumacácori church.[30]

With the presence of Hispanic settlers again in the Arivaca region, mining likely was resumed there also. The Arivaca mines are known to have been worked from the 1730s to the time of the transfer of the presidio from Tubac to Tucson, but they may have been abandoned shortly thereafter.[31] El Salero mine in the Santa Rita Mountains was back in production shortly before the end of the colonial period. Tomás Ojeda was killed there by Apaches in December of 1820.[32]

Something of the status of Tucson and Tubac as frontier settlements in the last decade of Spanish rule can be inferred from the fact that both were among sixteen Sonoran communities said to qualify for the establishment of town governments, or *ayuntamientos* under the terms of the Constitution of Cádiz imposed on Spain by France in 1812. Article 310 of that document provided for the creation of such municipal bodies in all communities with populations of "more than a thousand souls." Neither settlement had anything like a thousand Hispanic residents, but Tucson could have qualified if the population count included mission Indians, *vecino* Indians and tame Apaches. Professor Francisco Almada states that the organization of councils got underway in 1813 and implies that town government in Arizona began at that time. There does not appear to be any documentary evidence to sustain such a claim, however. The Constitution of Cádiz was suspended in 1814 and Sonoran communities today consider the origin of their town councils to be the Occidente Constitution of 1825, although the first municipal elections in the state took place on December 19th, 1824.[33]

Changes in Command

When the first fighting of the Mexican independence movement began in the fall of 1810, the Tucson presidio was commanded by Captain Antonio Narbona, a veteran frontier officer born in Mobile, Alabama in 1773 when that city was a part of Spanish Louisiana. Narbona had been one of the junior officers under Zúñiga's command during the 1795 trek to New Mexico and later served in other Sonoran posts.[34]

Narbona may have been the first Tucson commander to recognize that the presidio's food supply could be supplemented through cultivation of the San Pedro River floodplain at Tres Alamos. Peaceful Apaches, protected by fifteen or more soldiers from the garrison, lived at the site and did most of the work. In 1814 their leaders appealed to Fray Juan Bautista de Cevallos, *comisario prefecto* of the Querétaro missions, to provide them a priest. Although Father Cevallos favored doing so, nothing ever came of the request.[35]

At various times during his Tucson assignment, Narbona seems to have been called to duty elsewhere and his command taken over temporarily by Lieutenant Manuel de León, who had earlier earned his spurs at Tubac. León was a member of the large family of that surname who came from the Arizpe vicinity.[36] Although the exact relationship is not clear, he was undoubtedly a kinsman of José de León, Tucson's first mayor during the Mexican period, who appears in Father Llorens' 1801 census.

The last decade of the Spanish colony is a confusing one for the historian interested in the changes of command at Tucson, and the situation at Tubac is not much better. Between about 1812 and 1816, Lieutenant León alternated at intervals with both Antonio Narbona and Lieutenant Colonel Manuel Ignacio Arvizu.[37] Although the Apaches were not as troublesome during this period as they had been twenty years before, the absence of many soldiers who were on duty in southern Mexico and the frequent shifts in commanding officers contributed to a certain deterioration in the quality of life at the frontier villages.[38]

Just when Arvizu ceased to be the *comandante* at Tucson is another element in the puzzle. Almada states that he was not assigned to the post until 1818,[39] an assertion that documentary evidence

El Teniente Comandante Don José Romero. Su edad: 41 años; su país: el valle de Oposura; su calidad: Español; su salud: robusto; sus servicios y circunstancias los que expresa.

Tiempo en que empesó a servir los empleos				Tiempo que ha que sirve y quanto en cada empleo			
Empleos	*días*	*meses*	*años*	*Empleos*	*años*	*meses*	*días*
Cadete	1	marzo	1790	de cadete	10	3	6
Alférez	6	junio	1800	de alférez	9	—	29
Teniente	5	julio	1809	de teniente	2	11	25
Teniente comandante	1	julio	1812	de teniente comandante	5	6	0
				en campaña contra los insurgentes	1	11	—

Regimientos y compañías donde ha servido

En el presidio de Orcasitas, Tucson, y Altar. En la de Opatas de Bacoachi donde continua.

Campañas y Acciones de Guerra

En 18 campañas y 12 mariscadas que ha hecho, una de estas mandada por si, se han logrado dar muerte a 69 enemigos de ambos sexos y edades. En una de las mariscadas que ha hecho recibió una herida grave. Teniendo el mando provicionalmente en el presidio de Altar, se consiguieron las pases y amistades con la numerosa Nación Yuma que havía en el Río Colorado, punto divisorio de la provincia con la California.

José María Tresierras
(rubric)

Informe del Inspector	Notas	
Buen oficial para la guerra Alexo García Conde (rubric)	valor: aplicación: capacidad: conducta: estado:	se manifiesta poca regular buena casado

Edited transcript of the 1817 service record of don José Romero who soon afterward became the commanding officer of the Tucson presidio. This document mentions Romero's success in promoting peace with the Colorado River Indians, an accomplishment that led to his later assignment as the head of an expedition to open a new mail route between Sonora and California (Archivo General de la Nación, Provincias Internas 233).

contradicts, and implies that Arvizu was still at Tucson in 1821 when he swore allegiance to the Plan of Iguala which established Mexico's independence. However, Ensign Juan Alexo Carrillo was acting commander at Tucson early in 1819 and by May of that year Lieutenant José Romero was in charge.[40] It was Romero, not Arvizu, who must have taken the oath of allegiance to an independent Mexico.

Before coming to Tucson to join the *comandante* rotation, Manuel de León had spent at least three years heading the Pima Indian garrison at Tubac, having arrived as an ensign in 1804. Although he was officially replaced by Captain Simón Elías González on the first of April, 1807, León may have continued to direct the garrison while his superior officer was elsewhere. He was apparently still at Tubac in December, 1808 when he and his wife were godparents of a child baptized at Tumacácori.[41] He was already fifty and had been a soldier for twenty-two years.[42]

León's assignment to Tucson probably came at about the time Elías González was replaced by Lieutenant Ygnacio Sotelo, perhaps in 1812 or 1813. Although Sotelo remained in Tubac until his death in 1816,[43] and members of his family stayed on thereafter, he does not seem to have been the *comandante* after December, 1814, when Lieutenant Ignacio Elías González, a first cousin of Simón, was officially assigned to the post.[44] Elías would be the last commander of the San Rafael Company in Spanish times.[45]

The role that the Sonoran presidios played during the independence movement involved the region more broadly in the affairs of the rest of New Spain than had been the case previously. After independence the communities at the farthest northern extremity of the frontier, including those in Arizona, would return to their former status of isolation. The military officers who had commanded these outposts would, however, move on to political careers that would bring them both fame and notoriety in the young Mexican nation.[46] Meanwhile, in the closing years of Spanish rule, the families of these officers continued to provide the frontier with its aristocracy.

Most military posts were in the north of Sonora and both commissioned and non-commissioned officers were rotated among these establishments. The result was a remarkably similar elite throughout the region. As headquarters for the command of the Provincias Internas and later as capital of the combined states of Sonora and

Sinaloa, Arizpe became a nest of Sonoran political and military elitism during the late eighteenth and early nineteenth centuries. The church archives of the Arizpe parish have, therefore, become a primary source of information about kinship connections within the ranking families of northwest Mexico prior to and for some years after Mexican independence.

With rare exceptions, the service records of military officers show them to be *españoles*, indicating wholly or predominantly European ancestry. In some cases those of highest rank are classified as members of the nobility. Certain to be identified as *noble* (noble) were members of the Elías González, Comadurán, Urrea, Zúñiga and Pesqueira families. Classified simply as *españoles* were such persons as Ensign Juan Bautista Romero, who served at both Tucson and Tubac; Brevet Captain José Romero, Tucson's *comandante* in the 1820s; and Lieutenant Manuel de León. One non-commissioned officer classified also as an *español* was red-headed Salvador Gallegos, veteran first sergeant of the Tucson company, who fought against the insurgents during the war of Mexican independence.

Because of the shortage of eligible marriage partners, members of the frontier elite often wed close relatives, but sometimes they also selected spouses from families of somewhat lower social station. Commissioned officers at the presidios occasionally chose wives from among the daughters of their non-commissioned colleagues, as well as the long established landholding civilian families of European descent. Upward mobility was thus possible to a limited degree and by the time of Mexican independence a certain leveling of the social classes had taken place.

Even some Indian families found it possible to move up the social ladder. Following the death of her father, the daughter of Tubac officer Ygnacio Sotelo married the Indian lieutenant of the Pima company.[47] By 1817 an Opata named José Soto had become a lieutenant in the Santa Cruz company, where he was second in command behind Captain Simón Elías González. In his service record, he is accorded the title of *don*, usually reserved for those of purportedly pure Spanish descent.[48]

The non-commissioned officers of the lowest ranks and the common soldiers did not move from post to post as their superiors did, and it was the families of these men who provided the backbone of the settler population. Although a few were classified as *españoles*, the majority are shown on military rosters as *mestizos*, *coyotes* and, occasionally, as *mulatos*. Sacramental registers prepared by the priests in the last days of Spanish rule do not include sufficient information to inform us how often members of these families inter-married with the Indian population. Through military service, however, Pimas and Opatas gained in social stature on the frontier, and marriages with *mestizo* and *coyote* families are likely. The Ocoboas, a Yaqui family from the Tubac area, may have gained *vecino* status at the end of the colonial era and moved upward socially through intermarriage.[49]

One of the notable features of southern Arizona's Hispanic popu-lation on the eve of Mexican independence is the extent to which it included families whose roots in the region were put down before the establishment of the Tucson presidio in 1776. In spite of all the pressures exerted by the Indians to drive them out, members of these families hung on, moving to Tucson or Tubac when they could no longer reside safely at Sópori, Calabazas or Arivaca, but returning to those and other villages when the situation grew calmer and they felt secure.[50] While life in these small settlements was exceedingly harsh and dangerous, with little time for activities not directly related to survival, between campaigns the men of the presidios engaged in pursuits that were not part of their military roles. Many obtained small plots of land for temporary use where they could plant gardens and maintain livestock. As the years passed, they came to think of the acreage as theirs.

In the Tucson region, where the Indian population dwindled notably through the last years of the colonial period, military fam-ilies often took over Indian fields and after retirement the soldiers continued to cultivate them. This produced controversy and made the Indian settlements even more dependent on the military posts. One aspect of this dependency was increasing influence of the *gente de razón* over the behavior of mission Indians, a development much deplored by Father Llorens at San Xavier prior to his death in 1815. He blamed Father Arriquibar, Tucson chaplain, for encour-aging Spaniards and *mestizos* to undermine his authority with the Indians of his jurisdiction. The quarrel between the two priests began at least as early as 1808 when Llorens intervened in a dispute between Arriquibar and Antonio Narbona, then commander of the fort.[51]

In 1803, Father Arriquibar had been charged with educating the youngsters of the presidio in religious and secular law and obedience to their elders.[52] Whether he succeeded with the children is not known, but he apparently had problems in getting morality messages across to the parents during the last two decades of his ministry.

While some of the troopers were off campaigning, others remaining behind were not averse to occasional dalliance with the wives of their departed comrades-in-arms. In 1803, José María Syqueiros, armorer of the Tucson company, informed the priest of adultery on the part of his wife during one of his absences. There was no question about commission of the offense since the couple had been caught in the act. Arriquibar reported the incident to the bishop of Sonora, explaining further that he had been successful in persuading the distraught soldier to forgive his spouse and resume living with her.[53]

Three years later, in 1806, he had another serious problem to confront. A young officer, not identified by the priest, had become involved with the widow of a recently deceased soldier, and had impregnated her. According to Arriquibar, the couple did not then marry as he might have hoped they would, because "he was an officer and she was poor." Sometime later, the brother of the offending male proposed to legitimize the child by marrying the woman. In the process of consoling her, however, he too succeeded in making her pregnant. Determined not to let the brother off the hook, Arriquibar wrote the bishop seeking a dispensation to permit the couple to marry.

In his correspondence with his superior, Arriquibar was less than candid. The two brothers involved in this curious triangle were José and Juan Romero, sons of Captain Pablo Romero. The widow was María Gabriela Ramírez, then thirty-two years old, who was the daughter of Juan Joseph Ramírez and granddaughter of Tubac officer Juan Crisóstomo Ramírez.[54] Father Arriquibar had been a close friend of María Gabriela's grandfather and was the godfather of her brother.[55] The priest's assertion that the elder Romero brother could not marry María Gabriela because "he is an officer and she is poor" was also a slight misrepresentation of the situation. Perhaps she was in difficult financial straits at the time, but the widow was of good family—at least equal to that of the young officer. The real problem may have been that José was engaged to María del Carmen Rodríguez of Arizpe and their wedding date was not far off.[56]

Last page of the Tucson troop roster of August 1, 1818, showing the signatures of Lt. Colonel Arvizu, Ensign Comadurán, and Chaplain Arriquibar (Archivo General de la Nación, Provincias Internas 233)

Regrettably, the archive does not reveal the outcome of this colonial soap opera. Juan Romero, for whom the marriage dispensation was sought by Arriquibar, is probably the same man who was later elected mayor of Tucson. María Gabriela Ramírez was still alive in 1820 when Father Arriquibar mentioned her in his will, but whether she was married to Juan at that time is unknown.[57]

In 1811, just a month after the defeat of González de Hermosillo by presidial troops, Father Arriquibar again wrote the bishop about a matter that was of great concern to him. Young José Sosa, son of the former ensign of the Tucson garrison, wanted to marry a woman with whose sister he had already been intimate. Eager to see the couple wed, Arriquibar made light of the relationship, advising his superior that the girl previously involved with Sosa was really only a half-sister of the bride-to-be, a daughter of the same mother but a different father. Furthermore, wrote the priest, they had never lived together.

The aging Franciscan was in the middle of still another crisis in 1813 when settler Francisco Xavier Díaz, a cowboy employed by the San Xavier mission, was charged with killing his wife, María Ignacia Castelo, whom he accused of committing adultery with an Indian from the Tucson pueblito. Arriquibar granted the accused sanctuary in the military chapel, but released him to the authorities after being promised that Díaz would receive a proper civil trial. The defendant admitted his guilt and was sentenced to death for the offense.[58]

Although murders seem to have been uncommon in Spanish-colonial Tucson, another took place in 1817. The victim was one of the community's tame Apaches. A military court wasted no time in sentencing three soldiers to prison for this crime.[59]

As Mexican independence drew nearer, a condition he neither desired nor considered imminent, Father Arriquibar closed out more than four decades of service in the Pimería Alta. To the south at Tumacácori, the other distinguished veteran of the missionary wars, Father Narciso Gutiérrez, was finishing a quarter century of similar labor. Neither lived to see the changes in the political and religious atmosphere that independence brought, for both expired in the closing months of 1820. Arriquibar went first in September and Gutiérrez followed him in December. The old Basque chaplain was seventy-five at the time of his demise. Gutiérrez was twenty years younger.[60]

5

The Sonoran Frontier
After Independence

Between 1817 and 1820, the Mexican independence movement lagged notably and planning for self-government came to a halt. The insurgency gained new vigor in 1820, however, when King Fernando VII declared the Constitution of Cádiz, which he had previously suspended, back in force. Strongly opposed to the liberal provisions of this document, the conservative forces in New Spain shifted their support to the side of the revolutionaries.[1] Colonel Agustín Iturbide, long a dedicated Royalist, took over the leadership of the independence movement. Together with his old foe, General Vicente Guerrero, Iturbide published the Plan of Iguala on February 14th, 1821, proclaiming freedom from Spanish rule, equality under the law regardless of place of birth, and supremacy of the Roman Catholic Church over all others. Following promulgation of this declaration, which was carefully designed to appease all factions of Mexican public opinion, Iturbide and Guerrero began rallying support for a triumphal march on Mexico City.

The few troops remaining loyal to the Spanish Crown put up meager resistance but more than six months passed before Iturbide took the capital. Meanwhile, political and military officials throughout the provinces proclaimed their adherence to the Plan of Iguala. Don Alejo García Conde, then the general commander of the Provincias Internas, swore his allegiance on August 24th, 1821, and urged the men serving under him to do likewise.[2] Among those responding was Lieutenant Colonel Manuel Ignacio Arvizu, Tucson's former commanding officer who had fought with García Conde against the insurgents in Sinaloa a decade earlier. On September 3rd, 1821, he seconded the action of his commander.[3]

Communication between García Conde and his military subordinates was apparently better than that between the commander general and officials of the civil government of the Intendance of Sonora and Sinaloa. Unaware of García Conde's oath of allegiance to the Plan of Iguala, Governor Antonio Cordero and his associates met on September 6th at Arizpe to decide what action to take. The outcome of the meeting was an almost unanimous decision to support Iturbide and Guerrero, the lone dissenting vote coming from Cordero himself. Cordero immediately set out for the Villa de Chihuahua to inform García Conde about his colleagues' action. His surprise must have been great when he learned that García had also thrown his support to the revolution.[4] A few days later, on September 27th, 1821, Iturbide and his victorious forces swept into Mexico City. Independence was at last a reality.

Governor Cordero's departure from Arizpe thrust into prominence Colonel Antonio Narbona, former commander of the Tucson garrison, who had pledged allegiance to the Plan of Iguala at the September meeting. He moved up in rank to succeed Cordero as governor and military commander of Sonora and Sinaloa. (For much of the next decade veterans of service in the Arizona presidios would occupy the most important civil and military posts in northwest Mexico.) One of Narbona's first acts was to send troops to Guaymas where wealthy local citizens, headed by Father Pedro Leyva, were holding out against independence. Narbona also took military action against certain Yaqui and Opata leaders who appeared to be planning a general uprising.[5]

Also favored with a governorship in the early period of independence was Colonel Mariano de Urrea who had been Tucson's second-in-command between 1793 and 1804. On September 17th, 1821, Iturbide named him to head the government of Nueva Vizcaya which at that time included Chihuahua, most of Durango and part of Coahuila. He remained in that position until the following summer when Iturbide, then calling himself Emperor Agustín I, removed him because of his liberal views. Not long afterward Urrea joined the conspiracy against Iturbide, known as the Plan de Casa Mata, that was led by Antonio López de Santa Anna.[6]

Late in 1822, Emperor Iturbide decreed the separation of Sonora and Sinaloa, leaving Governor Narbona with half of his former jurisdiction.[7] When the emperor was deposed a few months later, Santa Anna asked Narbona to step down. His replacement was Colonel Urrea, who arrived at Arizpe in 1823 during the hottest part of the summer. At the time of his return to his native state, Urrea was under the impression that it would be reunited with Sinaloa, but he learned shortly afterward that Mexico's provisional congress had decided to leave them as separate jurisdictions.

Three months after his arrival in Arizpe, Urrea was directed by the central government to turn the military responsibilities of his post back over to Narbona. He refused to obey the order, however, and continued occupying both offices.[8] The following February the national congress named Simón Elías González, a veteran of military service at both Tubac and Tucson, to replace Urrea. Again Urrea refused to step down, reminding the central government that under the newly drafted Mexican constitution, the Sonora legislature—not the national congress—was responsible for naming the provisional governor.[9]

The same new constitution that Urrea cited provided that Sonora and Sinaloa would be rejoined and would be known as the state of Occidente ("West"). Provisional legislators from the new jurisdiction met in September, 1824, and selected Juan Manuel Riesgo temporary governor. He replaced Urrea in October, but his authority was limited to civil affairs. Urrea remained as military commander. Between October, 1824, and installation of Occidente's first constitutional governor in March, 1826, political stewardship was in the hands of four provisional governors, among them Simón Elías González.[10] During part of the time, Elías also held the title of military commander. Urrea was forced from the post by the central government which sent General José Figueroa to oust him in 1825. When Urrea resisted, he was arrested and taken to Mexico City under armed guard. (Two years later he would be exiled to Ecuador for the remainder of his life because of his role in a rebellion against the central government.)[11]

Occidente's first constitutionally elected governor took office on April 1st, 1826. Not surprisingly, the man chosen for the position was Colonel Simón Elías González, the most respected and popular figure in Sonora at that time in spite of the role he had played with the military tribunal that sentenced Father Hidalgo to death. By his own choice, Elías did not remain in office long. Faced with another bitter legislative battle over dividing Occidente, he opted to accept election to the governorship of the newly formed state of Chihuahua. He resigned in August, 1826, and a month later became the only person in Mexican history to serve as the first constitutional governor of two different states.[12]

Arizona Under Mexican Rule

As a result of their deaths in the fall of 1820, neither Father Arriquibar at Tucson nor Father Gutiérrez at Tumacácori was around to celebrate or lament—as the case might have been—the independent status of Mexico. Their departure from the scene also deprived them of the opportunity to be present when a bishop of Sonora finally made his way to the frontier of the Pimería Alta to observe the state of affairs among his remote emissaries and parishioners.

On New Year's Day, 1821, just six weeks before promulgation of the Plan of Iguala and a month after the death of Father Gutiérrez, Bishop Bernardo de Espíritu Santo was greeted at Tumacácori by Father Juan Bautista Estelric, Gutiérrez' newly arrived successor.[13] The first bit of business that Estelric presented to his superior was an affair of heart—two affairs of heart, in fact. A pair of young frontiersmen from elite families had fallen in love with two young ladies from equally distinguished lineages and wanted to marry. The problem was that the lovers were closely related and they needed special dispensation from the Bishop to permit them to wed. One of the couples was Teodoro Ramírez, grandson of the old Tubac militia captain, and his cousin Serafina Quixada. They were related through the Peña family of Arizpe.[14] The other included Tomás Ortiz, son of the owner of the land grant at Arivaca,[15] and Josefa Clementa Elías González, daughter of the commanding officer at Tubac.[16] The couples were closely allied because Tomás Ortiz and Serafina Quixada had been reared in the same household. They were children of the same mother, but different fathers.[17]

With the Bishop present, Teodoro and Tomás were able to obtain the required dispensations without delay and shortly after they gave up their bachelor status. Teodoro, the godson and heir of

Bishop Bernardo del Espíritu Santo who visited the Pimería Alta in 1820–1821 (Villa, *Bodas de Plata*)

Agustín de Iturbide, liberator and first emperor of Mexico (*Gobernantes de México, 1325–1911*)

Father Arriquibar, was married to Serafina on January 7th, 1821. Father Estelric performed the ceremony.[18] The following month, Tomás became the husband of Josefa Clementa.

Another marriage between members of old Pimería Alta families of Tubac took place not long after. The principals were José Romero, grandson of pioneer settler Nicolás Romero,[19] and María Soledad Sais. Later the couple would have a son named Francisco for whom a street in Tucson and a famous ranch near town would be named.[20]

One of the most important developments in Arizona in the aftermath of independence was the decision to reopen communications between the Arizona presidios and those in California. Anza had pioneered this route almost half a century before, but it had been little used for more than a decade. Responding to a directive from Iturbide and a related inquiry from the governor of California, Lieutenant Colonel Narbona ordered Captain José de Romero of the Tucson presidio to lead an expedition to California for the purpose of establishing a safe, new mail route. The Romero party set out on June 8th, 1823, accompanied by Father Félix Caballero, a priest from Santa Catalina, who had made the journey from California to Arizpe the preceding month. The expedition reached its California destination in mid-July.[21]

Not long after Captain Romero left Tucson, the residents of the presidio became alarmed when rumors reached them that all members of the California expedition had been killed by Yuma Indians. Young 1st Ensign Antonio Comadurán, acting post commander while Romero was away, wrote the California governor in September, 1823 requesting permission to lead a detachment of soldiers to the California side of the Colorado River to punish the Indians responsible. A short time later, he learned that the rumors were false.

Comadurán, who figured importantly in the history of the Pimería Alta between 1830 and 1851, was the son of the royal surgeon of the military hospital in Arizpe. The elder Comadurán, also called Antonio, was a native of Barcelona. Following his arrival in Mexico, he married into the Díaz del Carpio family,[22] also tying him to the large and prominent Elías González clan.[23] With the departure of Romero, Comadurán received his first experience at running the Tucson post. He was the acting commander from the early summer of 1823 until September, 1825, when Lieutenant Colonel Manuel Ignacio Arvizu began his final tour of duty at the fort.[24]

One of Arvizu's first responsibilities was to welcome to Tucson the largest military force the community had ever seen. Heading this force was General José Figueroa who, having accomplished the task of removing Mariano de Urrea from the post of Occidente military commander, now occupied that position himself under orders from Mexico City. Figueroa came to Tucson after visiting the Arizonac region where the famous silver discovery had been made nearly 100 years earlier.

The general was in Tucson for only a few days—long enough to add Lieutenant Colonel Arvizu and some of the presidial soldiers to his contingent of troops. Early in October, they set out for the Yuma area to rendezvous with Romero and his men returning from California. On November 19th, while at the Colorado River, Figueroa learned that the Yaquis were staging a major uprising in southern Sonora. He did an immediate about face, making a forced march in the direction of Tucson which he reached on November 29th.[25] Twenty-five of the men who had accompanied Figueroa remained at Agua Caliente on the Gila to await the arrival of the

Romero party, which was nearly a month in coming. On December 19th, Romero crossed the Colorado River and the following day learned of Figueroa's hasty departure.[26] He continued on toward Tucson which he probably reached sometime in January.[27]

One of the most significant events to occur during Romero's absence was the election of Tucson's first mayor of record. Pursuant to an action by the Occidente legislature, Sonoran and Sinaloan towns chose their *alcaldes* on December 19th, 1824. José de León was the successful candidate in Tucson and he took office on January 1st.[28]

Another important event for Tucsonans in 1824 was the departure of Father Juan Vaño, the Franciscan priest at San Xavier, who, since the death of Father Arriquibar four years earlier, had been serving as the presidial chaplain. He was replaced by Fray Rafael Díaz.[29]

There were changes at Tumacácori also during the early years of Mexican independence. In 1822, Father Juan Bautista Estelric, who had replaced Father Gutiérrez, was reassigned to Santa Cruz and Father Ramón Liberós took over. Estelric's health was given as a reason for the change,[30] but later in the year Father Faustino González reported to the Bishop of Sonora that the real reason for the transfer was that the priest had become involved with a woman. According to González, Estelric continued the behavior after arriving at Santa Cruz and was also discovered to have taken from his previous post more than 1,000 pesos worth of gold and other valuables.[31]

Following his arrival at Tumacácori, Liberós set a hectic pace in getting Father Gutiérrez' church ready for use. In December of 1822 he conducted his first mass there and interred a recently deceased member of the community in the new walled cemetery behind the structure.[32]

Sometime after the inauguration of Tumacácori's new church, Ignacio Elías González left Tubac where he had been commander for nearly a decade.[33] At no time during the remainder of the Mexican period would the small presidio be manned by a full complement of troops under a high-ranking officer. On a temporary basis following the departure of Elías, Teodoro Aros filled in as *comandante*. On All Saints' Day, November 1st, 1824, Apaches ran off a bunch of horses at Tumacácori. Aros and his men were unable to pursue them because there were no mounts for the three soldiers and four militiamen who constituted the entire military force of the garrison.[34]

Although the hostile Apaches did not renew large-scale raiding until the end of the decade, the attack on the Tumacácori horse herd was a sign of things to come. Not long after, Apaches were seen throughout the area in numbers larger than during the last days of Spanish rule. Worried by this development, Tucson Mayor José de León protested vigorously when the legislature of Occidente, in March of 1825, exempted civilian settlers of the presidios from paying certain taxes that had previously been used for the support of militias. At the time he wrote the letter, the mayor was well aware that the Tucson garrison was undermanned because some of its members were in California with Romero.[35]

Shortly before Romero returned to Tucson in January, 1826, Lieutenant Colonel Arvizu, who had been assigned as his replacement, went south to the Yaqui country with General Figueroa. Stepping in for him was an old soldier who had spent much of his military career in Tubac and Tucson: Manuel de León, now in his late sixties with almost forty years service behind him. He would conclude his military career, and possibly his life, in Tucson. By the time a complete census of Tucson residents was taken in 1831, he was gone from the scene.[36]

Anglo-Americans in Arizona

The first Anglo-Americans to enter what later became Arizona were the so-called mountain men and some of the most famous—including Kit Carson, Bill Williams, Pauline Weaver, Ewing Young, Michel Robidoux and James Ohio Pattie—reached the area shortly after Mexican independence. Sometime in late December, 1825, or early January, 1826, Pattie and a small party of men crossed what is today the Arizona-New Mexico border and travelled along the Gila River to its confluence with the Salt south of present-day Phoenix. They then returned to New Mexico, arriving at their point of departure early in April, 1826.[37]

The intrusion of Americans into Mexican territory did not go unnoticed by officials of the Occidente government. In May, 1826, Governor Simón Elías González sent a circular to the mayors of the frontier presidios reminding them of an earlier directive to provide monthly reports of any activities involving the entry of foreigners onto Mexican soil.[38] The Pima Indians who resided on the Gila served the Mexicans well in providing information about the American trespassers. Furthermore, they were well instructed by the presidio commanders about the advice they should give the invaders. When a party of Americans came down the Gila early in the fall of 1826, the Pimas informed them that they should provide identification papers or proceed to Tucson to report their destination. The leader of the group responded that the Americans came only to acquire mules and horses from the Indians.[39]

Information about contact between the Pimas and the Yankee visitors was provided to Tucson Commanding Officer Manuel de León by a delegation of Indians who reached the presidio on October 28th, 1826. Shortly thereafter, Mayor Ygnacio Pacheco wrote the governor of Occidente to inform him of these incidents.[40] According to Pacheco, León sent Brevet Lieutenant Antonio Comadurán with a detachment of seven men, including the mayor, to investigate the presence of the Americans. When they arrived at the Gila, they were told by the Pimas that the trappers had left three days earlier. They also learned that the Americans were friendly and supplied the Indians with many gifts. Furthermore, the Pimas reported, the visitors informed them that Antonio Narbona, now the governor of New Mexico, had advised them that beaver trapping was good along the Gila.

Two months after Pacheco wrote his letter to the governor, his replacement, Mayor Juan Romero,[41] sent a message of his own to the Occidente chief executive. His purpose was to let the governor know that on New Year's Eve, 1826, three Americans had suddenly appeared at the presidio to show their passports to the *comandante*. This was probably the first time that most of the Mexican residents of Tucson had ever seen Anglo-Americans.

In his letter to the governor, Romero also mentioned that on December 26th, 1826—shortly before the strangers appeared at the presidio gates—a delegation of visiting Pimas had informed León that two parties of foreigners were trapping beavers.[42] However, except for the three who showed up on New Year's Eve, none of the other Americans put in an appearance at Tucson.

Not long after the unidentified Americans visited Tucson, James O. Pattie was back on the Gila with a group of trappers headed by Michel Robidoux. In January, 1827, all the members of this expedition—except Robidoux, Pattie and an unnamed Frenchman—were killed by Indians somewhere in the vicinity of modern Phoenix. A few days later, the three survivors joined another group of trappers led by Ewing Young.[43]

The Arizona Land Grants

The early years of Mexican independence produced a great increase in the number of land grants to Hispanic settlers of southern Arizona (see map, p. 295). The first of these, actually sought while Arizona was still under Spanish rule, was known as San Ignacio de la Canoa. Petitioners for the grant were Tomás and Ignacio Ortiz, sons of Agustín Ortiz, who had died a short time before,[44] and María Reyes Peña. The Ortiz brothers requested a total of four *sitios* (four square leagues or about 17,000 acres) along the Santa Cruz River stretching from the northern limits of the Tubac presidio to about the present location of Sahuarita. Although the original application was filed in September, 1820, the actual survey of the property did not take place until the following year. By that time, Tomás Ortiz had become the son-in-law of Tubac Comandante Captain Ignacio Elías González, who was charged with conducting the survey.[45] Following the conclusion of the complicated proceedings associated with the granting of lands, the Ortiz petition was approved in December, 1821.[46]

Another grant made under circumstances similar to that of La Canoa was known as San José de Sonoita. Don León Herreros (also spelled Herreras and Herrera) applied for the land early in 1821 and it was surveyed in June of that year. In November, Herreros paid for the property but he did not receive title until May, 1825. When the title was issued, the authority cited was a Spanish law of 1754. Very shortly afterward, the state of Occidente adopted a law of its own to regulate land-grant awards.[47]

Other holdings sought at the end of the Spanish period or the beginning of Mexican rule were the San Bernardino and San Rafael de la Zanja grants. The former, located in the southeast corner of what is today Arizona and extending far down into Sonora, was sought in December, 1820, by Lieutenant Ignacio Pérez, member of a prominent mining family that like so many others of its class was related to the Elías González clan.[48] In May, 1822, Pérez paid for

Cover page of the title to the San Ignacio de la Canoa land grant issued at Ures, Sonora, to the Ortiz brothers (Willey, "La Canoa: A Spanish Land Grant Lost and Found")

the land—more than 73,000 acres—but no formal title was ever issued. To stock his large ranch, *Teniente* Pérez contracted with Father Estelric of the Tumacácori Mission for the purchase of 4,000 cattle. When Pérez did not pay, Estelric and his replacement, Father Liberós, were obliged to seek help from Rafael Elías González, who had kinship ties with the lieutenant. More than two-and-a-half years later, Elías guaranteed payment of the outstanding balance.[49]

The San Rafael de la Zanja grant was unusual in two respects. First, the man who originally applied for the land, a Santa Cruz resident by the name of Manuel Bustillo, was outbid at the public auction that constituted the final step in the granting process. Then, the title that was issued on May 15th, 1825, was in the name of "Ramón Romero and other shareholders (*parcioneros*), their children, heirs and successors." A problem that later arose, quite understandably, was how to establish the identity of the "other shareholders" whose names do not appear in the title document.[50]

Located in the San Rafael Valley north of the presidio of Santa Cruz, the San Rafael de la Zanja grant was for approximately the same amount of land as the Canoa property. It included what continues to be regarded as some of the finest grassland in Arizona and at least since the beginning of the Mexican period has been extensively grazed except when Indian attacks made ranching impossible.

These four grants are the only ones for which application was made during the first half of the 1820s when the Apache situation was still more or less under control. By the late 1820s, when several other petitions were filed, the Indians were raiding consistently throughout the area, although not in such large numbers as would later be the case.

Between 1826 and 1831, residents of the Pimería Alta submitted applications for five grants. The first came on September 30th, 1826, from Francisco José de Juvera,[51] a citizen of Arizpe. He sought the abandoned ranch of Buenavista, originally the home of the Nicolás Romero family, which lay along the Santa Cruz River south of Guevavi Mission. Juvera died before the long grant process was finished and it was his widow, Josefa Morales, who was finally awarded title to four *sitios* in 1831.

The year 1827 was important for members of the large Elías González family, several of whom petitioned for land along the San Pedro River and a tributary called the Babocómari that flowed into it from the west. The locations sought were farther away from the presidios than had been the case with earlier petitions.

One of the first of the family to seek a grant in 1827 was Ignacio, the former commanding officer of the Tubac presidio, who by now held the rank of captain. On May 12th, he and a partner named Nepomuceno Félix requested four *sitios* of land along both sides of the San Pedro River between the modern locations of St. David and Charleston. Although officials processed the petition rapidly, they did not award title to the grantees until May 8th, 1833. Elías and his partner called their ranch San Juan de las Boquillas y Nogales.

Also in May, 1827, Joaquín Elías, who identified himself as the agent of his brother Rafael,[52] petitioned the treasurer general of Occidente for an assignment of four *sitios* lining the banks of the San Pedro upstream from the southern boundary of the land sought by Ignacio. Just over a year later, on April 18th, 1828, Rafael Elías paid for the grant which he called San Rafael del Valle. Like his cousin Ignacio, he had to wait for the title which was not issued until September, 1832.

Another Ignacio Elías González, the brother of Rafael, was also a petitioner in 1827. Together with his sister Eulalia, he applied on July 1st for a large grant of eight *sitios* stretching along Babocómari Creek from about the vicinity of modern Elgin to the San Pedro River. This Ignacio, who had also had a brief military career in his youth, was a resident of Rayón in 1827, apparently having gone there from the Altar Valley where he had previously lived.[53] His sister resided in Arizpe, which for more than fifty years had been the family headquarters.

The Babocómari grant, officially known as San Ignacio del Babocómari, was surveyed in the fall of 1827 and purchased in December of that year.[54] It included more land within the present-day boundaries of Arizona than any other made during the Spanish and Mexican periods.[55]

In 1831, the newly created Congress of Sonora authorized Leonardo Escalante, acting governor of the state, to represent eight different promoters (*empresarios*) in stimulating the occupation and development of fifty-eight *sitios* along the lower San Pedro from north of the San Juan de las Boquillas y Nogales grant to the Gila River and stretching eastward all the way to the present Arizona-New Mexico border. The old farming site of Tres Alamos, apparently not being used by Tucson residents at that time, was included and the entire acreage was later called the Tres Alamos grant. Because of a major Apache onslaught that got underway early in the decade, extensive plans for development of this area did not materialize.[56] Later, the hungry residents of the Tucson presidio, at great personal risk, returned to grow crops at Tres Alamos.

The lengthy delays that petitioners often encountered in securing titles did not deter them from developing and stocking their ranges. In spite of the growing threat of Apache raids, the largest of the ranching operations were those of the Babocómari-San Pedro drainage and the San Rafael Valley, where there was more room to expand than in the more densely populated Santa Cruz Valley. The owners of the former grants were not much concerned with exactly where the boundaries of their lands lay and those who eventually acquired their interests would claim so-called "overplus" lands outside those boundaries.

The major Arizona grants were controlled to a remarkable extent during the 1830s by members of the Elías González family, or families with which they were closely linked through marriage such as Ortiz and Pérez. Their combined landholdings included many thousands of acres. Because of the Apache threat, however, they were able to live on their ranches for no more than a dozen years, but during that time they apparently built large cattle herds upon which the settlers of the region depended long after the landowners sought safety elsewhere. Many of the Anglo-Americans entering the region during the California gold rush would also dine on beef from the descendants of the first cattle grown on the land grants.

Politics in the State of Occidente

From the beginning Occidente was plagued with problems, and the outbreak of the Yaqui wars in 1825 made the situation even worse. The original plan was for the old town of El Fuerte in northern Sinaloa to serve as the state capital but the Yaqui uprising led to its transfer in August, 1826, to Cosalá, south of Culiacán. This satisfied the wealthy residents of the southern part of Occidente, but did not please those in the north. Pressure for division of the state became intense.

In response to a survey of the town councils sponsored by the Occidente legislature, nearly three-quarters of the local elected offi-

cials called for separation. The residents of Alamos, most prominent town in the state, straddled the fence.[57] In January, 1827, two
legislators from Culiacán succeeded in having a petition for division
of the state presented to the national congress in Mexico City. That
body discovered, however, that it could not act on the petition.
Occidente owed its existence to the Constitution of 1824, which, by
its terms, could not be modified until 1830.

Frustrated by their inability to resolve the issue, the deputies
from Culiacán sought to have the capital transferred to their community. Sonorans, backed by the representative from El Fuerte,
opposed the move and boycotted the session in which it was to be
considered, leaving the legislature without a quorum. In the fall of
1827, they returned to their seats and voted with the majority to
have the capital moved from Cosalá to Alamos. Acting Governor
Francisco Iriarte, whose home was in Cosalá, vetoed this action,
whereupon Occidente's military commander intervened and forced
him to accept the change.

After being overruled by the military, Iriarte stepped down and
was replaced by José María Gaxiola who favored keeping Sonora
and Sinaloa united. In January, 1828, Gaxiola signed a decree of the
Occidente legislature to implement the federal order of December
20th, 1827, expelling all peninsular-born Spaniards from Mexican
territory.

From the point of view of the Arizona presidios, the decision to
send the *peninsulares* back to Spain was a serious blow. It meant the
departure of the priests at Tumacácori and San Xavier who had
long served the religious needs of the civilian and military families
of the Pimería Alta. Occidente's military chief, Mariano Paredes
Arrillaga, who had forced the resignation of Iriarte and supported
his replacement by Gaxiola, issued orders to Tucson's commanding
officer, Captain Pedro Villaescusa,[58] to proceed with the expulsion
of Fray Rafael Díaz from San Xavier and Fray Ramón Liberós from
Tumacácori. Before the middle of April, 1828, Liberós was gone
and shortly after Díaz left San Xavier.[59] During the remainder of
the Mexican period only one other priest resided in Arizona, and
his tenure lasted but three years.

While the legislature was haggling over the location of the capital
and the division of the state, conditions everywhere deteriorated.
The troops from the presidios were off fighting Yaquis in the south,
leaving residents of the frontier settlements without protection

from Apaches who had stepped up their raiding. The rations that the Spanish had provided the peaceful Apaches were no longer available, contributing to restlessness among those Indians.

Early in 1827, Mayor Juan Romero prepared a report for Acting Governor Iriarte stating that Tucson was threatened on all sides. Apaches, purportedly in alliance with Papagos and Yumas, were rumored to be preparing for an attack on the fort which was now without troops.[60]

Throughout the remainder of 1827 and well into the following year, the Apaches ravaged the countryside, striking with particular force in the Altar Valley. Some of the residents of Tubutama and Sáric lost their lives to the raiders and by April, 1828, Sáric was abandoned.[61] A month later, Tucson's fourth mayor, Ygnacio Sardina,[62] wrote Governor Gaxiola that an Apache war party had besieged a group of miners in the Sierrita Mountains, killing three of them. Over the next several days, they raided cattle herds in the Tucson area, taking mother cows but leaving the calves behind.[63]

The severity of the situation forced the Occidente legislature to enact a series of regulations in June, 1828, establishing a state militia. Within a few years the militia units, known colloquially as *los cívicos* (the civilians), became the first line of defense against the Apaches as the presidial troops were drawn increasingly into the political squabbles that divided Sonora for the next forty years.[64]

Late in November, 1828, Manuel Escalante y Arvizu, political chief, or *jefe político*, of the Arizpe district, wrote to Acting Governor Gaxiola requesting 100 muskets to arm the civilians of Tucson and Santa Cruz so that they might more successfully defend themselves against the Apaches.[65] Escalante's letter may have been intended as a partial response to a request Gaxiola sent him the previous month for comment on a communication from Mayor Sardina regarding the situation in Tucson.[66] On December 9th, Escalante prepared a lengthier reply for the governor which makes clear how truly desperate the state of affairs in Tucson had become.[67]

The Arizpe political chief began with the observation that Tucson was the most isolated outpost of the Mexican frontier. He went on to inform the governor that attacks on the presidio livestock herds had so reduced the number of cattle that none of the settlers could boast as many as twenty-five head. Some horses were available, he noted, but only because the soldiers kept these animals under constant surveillance. Bulls and oxen were pastured outside the fort during the day, but guarded inside at night. These conditions, Escalante reported, were driving presidio residents to despair.

Tucson was having water problems as well. Agreements made with the Pima residents of El Pueblito during the Spanish era apportioned three-quarters of the Santa Cruz flow at that point to the Pimas and one-quarter to the residents of the presidio. In the years that had passed since negotiation of this agreement, the fort's population had expanded notably, whereas the Indian village had lost many of its inhabitants. The original apportionment was outdated, and the *jefe político* recommended that legal steps be taken to give the presidial residents at least half the water.

Escalante observed also that Tucson settlers and soldiers were no longer cultivating the Tres Alamos area, which had made them self-sufficient in grains and vegetables. Instead, they were importing the needed food items from the people of the Magdalena River Valley near San Ignacio. To make matters worse, Tucson's military commanders refused to buy other supplies from the limited local sources that were available, preferring to obtain them at cheaper prices from the merchants of Arizpe who, in the opinion of Escalante, did not always give full value. As Father Pfefferkorn had done many years before, Escalante implied that the officers were often guilty of black market dealings and kickbacks. He recommended the death penalty for persons convicted of such dealings. Escalante, perhaps unfairly, placed much of the blame for the deterioration in Tucson's situation on Manuel Ignacio Arvizu, the veteran campaigner who served as Tucson's presidial commander in the last years of Spanish rule. It is difficult for the historian to assess the validity of this attack on Arvizu, whom Escalante chooses not to mention by name. Two years earlier, at the age of sixty-six, the old soldier had won an important battle with the Yaquis at Cócorit. Charged with desertion shortly thereafter, he successfully defended himself and was named presidial commander at San Buenaventura.[68]

In concluding his letter, Escalante expressed concern that the settlers might abandon Tucson entirely, and made some recommendations for preventing such an action. He stressed especially the importance of keeping a full complement of well-supplied and well-armed soldiers on hand at all times. He also suggested assignment to the post of a *comandante* who would rather "sleep with his gun than with his wife"; who had enough political sense to understand the civilians and get along with them.

Following preparation of his letter, Escalante went into the field to review the manner in which the mission properties of the Franciscans were being administered. At Tumacácori, he found don Tomás Ortiz in charge of this effort but was apparently not fully satisfied with the way in which the co-owner of the Canoa land grant was going about it. Escalante called upon him to remedy certain inequities and later in the year replaced him with Buenaventura López. A year later, when the church properties were turned back to the Franciscans for management, they had declined greatly in value. This may in part have been because of the attacks of the Apaches, who had frightened off the Pimas hired to tend the cattle. By 1830, the 400 animals of the Tumacácori herd were running wild in the desert and much of the mission's farmland lay idle. The church itself and adjacent convent were reported still in good condition.[69]

The Tucson Fields

Departure of Father Rafael Díaz in 1828 left the Indians of El Pueblito without protection against usurpation of their resources by local Hispanics, who soon began appropriating both land and water.[70] In some cases, the Mexicans paid individual Indians for parcels of land, but in others they simply took what they wanted. Don Fernando Grande, the civil administrator appointed to look after Franciscan properties, attempted to protect the interests of the eight remaining Indian families at El Pueblito—an effort resented by the local Hispanic population and one that apparently had little long-term effect.[71]

One of the largest land transactions of 1828 that involved Indians and Mexicans took place before Father Díaz left San Xavier; it involved Apaches rather than Papagos. On January 18th, Lieutenant Antonio Comadurán and Mayor Ygnacio Sardina conferred with chiefs Antuna, Benito and "others of their rank" concerning the desire of the tame Apaches to sell a tract of land granted to them in 1796 by Adjutant Inspector Roque de Medina. The prospective buyer was Teodoro Ramírez, brother-in-law of the *comandante*. After convincing themselves that the Indians had chosen of their own free will to make the sale, Comadurán and Sardina gave their approval.

Payment to the Indians consisted of two muskets, four zarapes, a horse, 16 pesos worth of tobacco, and 10 pesos in cash to be used for purchasing powder—all told, an estimated value of 100 pesos. The *comandante* delivered a short sermon to the Indians, advising them that since they had entered into the agreement voluntarily, they had no right to attempt to recover the land. "They understood what I said and were convinced by it," Comadurán noted in the sale document. Juan Romero and Ygnacio Saenz witnessed the transaction.[72]

A map of the Tucson fields prepared in 1876 makes clear that the Apache land acquired by Ramírez was located north of present St. Mary's Road between the Santa Cruz River and Main Avenue. It included much of what later came to be known to Tucson's Mexican population as Barrio Anita.[73]

6

Sonora Becomes a Separate State

After the Yaqui situation settled down somewhat in 1827, those in Sonora and Sinaloa who favored division of the state of Occidente again asserted themselves. They were opposed primarily by Governor Gaxiola, one of few top officials who continued to support the union. The separationists extended the political arena to Mexico City, and in 1829 succeeded in persuading the national congress to call for Gaxiola's removal.

Confident of support by General José Figueroa, Occidente military commander, the governor refused to step down. However, Figueroa, who had returned to his post just a short time before the ouster vote of the congress, cast his lot with those who favored division. In August, 1829, he called upon the Occidente legislature, in whose hands the matter rested, to take the necessary steps to remove the governor. Both out of respect for Figueroa, whom the legislators admired, and because they could see the handwriting on the wall, the lawmakers removed Gaxiola and replaced him with Francisco Iriarte. They also agreed to take up the question of dividing the state.[1]

By early 1830, it was evident to all that sentiment throughout Occidente strongly favored separation and the national congress, now safely past the six-year restriction on amending the 1824 constitution, resumed consideration of the issue. In a decree dated October 13th, 1830, the lawmakers made public their decision to create the separate states of Sonora and Sinaloa; and they named March 14th of the following year as the day the division would take effect.[2]

The publication of the decree did not completely resolve the matter. For a full year afterward, Sinaloans did their best to have Alamos, Occidente's most important town, included within their jurisdiction although Alamos residents had expressed a strong preference for becoming Sonorans. The difference of opinion almost led to bloodshed before the national congress intervened in January, 1832 to settle the issue once and for all. The *Alamences* would have their wish.[3]

Ironically, once the question of separation was decided Sonorans began fighting among themselves over the location of the capital. The federal decree had named Hermosillo, fastest growing town in the state, as the seat of government and the constituent legislative assembly had approved that selection. But Arizpe residents were not happy with the decision. Their community, long the political nerve center of the region, had declined economically and getting back the capital was considered essential to its welfare. In the spring of 1831, the citizens of Arizpe and its neighboring villages petitioned the national congress to amend its earlier decree and return the capital to its old location. Provisional Governor Leonardo Escalante, long a resident of Hermosillo, opposed the petition, observing in a statement that Hermosillo was growing, whereas the population of Arizpe had decreased; further, Hermosillo was close to the center of the new state, while Arizpe was at its northern extremity.[4]

Among those who most strongly favored returning the capital to Arizpe were several members of the Elías González family. Colonel Simón Elías González was Sonora's commanding general just before the first Sonoran legislature convened in 1831 and he did what he could to influence the decision in favor of the town where he and his ancestors had long been prominent. It was his brother, Lieutenant Colonel José María Elías González, however, who brought the greatest pressure to bear on the lawmakers. From his position as adjutant inspector of the general command, he solicited petitions from the presidios in support of moving the capital to Arizpe, where he had been born on February 2nd, 1792.[5] For this action, he almost certainly had the backing of Colonel Ramón Morales, who would replace Colonel Simón Elías González as commander general. Morales was from a family that had been in Arizpe at least as long as that of José María and Simón.[6]

As a result of Elias' solicitation, the residents of Tucson and Tubac became involved in the capital controversy. Getting their support for moving the capital to Arizpe was probably not difficult, since the veteran soldiers of the frontier posts were accustomed to receiving their orders from that direction.[7] Antonio Comadurán, commanding officer at Tucson, was also a native of the former capital of the Provincias Internas.

Governor Escalante responded to the petitions from the presidios by asserting that all decisions about the mattter would have to be made by constitutionally elected legislators. They could not be chosen, however, until the constitution itself was written. For much of the remainder of 1831, the members of the provisional legislature worked on preparation of that document, completing their labors in December.

Once the constitution was drafted, the legislators issued regulations on December 15th, 1831, for internal government in Sonoran towns. Of all the communities in the northern part of the state, only Arizpe and Altar had sufficient populations to be considered "major" towns. Tucson and Tubac were classified in a lesser category, one that did not provide for municipal governments (*ayuntamientos*) or mayors (*alcaldes*). For the remainder of the Mexican period, the chief civil officer of both settlements would be a *juez de paz*, or justice of the peace, assisted by a deputy and another official with the combined functions of treasurer and attorney. The 1831 regulations also provided that municipal elections would take place on December 3rd of each year, with the installation of officers on January 1st.[8]

Sonora's first constitutional legislature convened at Hermosillo in April, 1832. Almost immediately the members received a petition from residents of Arizpe and neighboring towns requesting transfer of the capital to their area. In spite of strong opposition from Governor Escalante, the lawmakers voted to make the change promptly. May 25th, 1832, was set for the move and it took place on schedule. To make sure that no problems developed, the legislators were escorted to Arizpe by twenty-five soldiers from the Buenavista garrison.[9]

While all the political maneuvering was taking place to the south, the residents of the Pimería Alta were defending themselves against

increasing Apache raids. In January, 1830, the hostile Indians attacked Calabazas, where they burned buildings and raided the San
Pedro ranch, stealing large numbers of livestock. Governor Iriarte
wrote his commander general that "because of the absolute lack of
funds . . . we are unable to respond to the communications . . .
seeking help for the presidial troops in punishing the Apaches."[10]

Two months after Iriarte's letter, Tucson Mayor Francisco Ortega
wrote to the Arizpe political chief[11] to inform him of the readiness of
Tucsonenses to aid in defending the frontier. With the letter he
included two lists, one containing the names of able-bodied adult
males who were willing to campaign against the Apaches, the other
including the names of persons disposed to contribute to provisioning the troops while they were in the field. Among those volunteering
to fight were Teodoro Ramírez and two of his brothers—Antonio and
Pedro—both of whom had experience as presidial soldiers. Former
mayors Juan Romero and José León also offered their services, as did
prominent residents José Herreras, Clemente Telles and Saturnino
Castro. In all, twenty-eight settlers agreed to campaign against the
hostile Indians. Twenty Pimas from the Tucson *pueblito* and eighteen from Bac also volunteered.

The list of those willing to contribute to the support of the others
was much shorter. It included only former mayor Ignacio Pacheco,
Vitor Aros, José Bejarrano, Juan José Orozco, Tomás Ortiz and
Juan Acuña. The poverty of Tucsonans is reflected not only in the
shortness of the list, but in the nature and extent of the goods
offered. Ygnacio Pacheco promised two *fanegas* (3.2 bushels) of
wheat; José Bejarrano, a musket; Juan José Orozco, a saddle; and
Tomás Ortiz, probably the wealthiest of the group, a horse and a
mule.[12]

The decline of the Franciscan missions after the expulsion of the
peninsular-born priests was evident by 1830 according to a report
on San Xavier prepared in May by Fernando Grande, who had the
responsibility for looking after the missions. Grande noted that San
Xavier had no judges of its own and was obliged to rely on those of
the presidio for the administration of justice. Since the last Franciscan had departed, the priest's residence had been locked up with all
tools and furnishings inside. For a time Tucson citizens Juan González and Ignacio Sardina were the caretakers of these items but the
key had later been turned over to Juan Ignacio Zapata, native governor at San Xavier.

One of Grande's comments confirmed an observation made nearly two years earlier by Manuel Escalante y Arvizu.[13] He stated that
many of the fertile fields of San Xavier lay uncultivated because of
the sad state of the presidios whose residents had previously purchased all the surplus grain the Indians could produce. He also
observed that, in spite of decreased farming, San Xavier was still
visited by Papagos from the villages of Santa Ana and Santa Rosa,
who helped the San Xavier Indians with their harvests; and by
Pimas from the Gila River towns, who came in the winter when
their own food supplies were low.[14]

In the same month that Grande prepared his report, Tucson
troopers, civilians and friendly Indians began a campaign into the
territory of the Western Apaches that continued for nearly two
weeks. Somewhere in the area of Pinal Creek, they encountered a
large encampment of Apaches who were employing a rudimentary
irrigation system to raise corn and who had more than 2,000 horses
grazing on nearby ranges. Antuna, chief of the friendly Apaches
accompanying the Tucson party, reported to Captain Comadurán
that the Pinal Creek Indians wanted peace and would return the
Mexican captives in their possession if satisfactory terms could be
arranged. Comadurán promised to carry the message back to his
commanding officer, Colonel Simón Elías González, and to solicit
his reaction. If it was favorable, he would send word to them by one
of the peaceful Apaches and they could come to Tucson to confer
with him and to surrender the Mexican prisoners.

During their exchange, Comadurán learned that the Apaches
were well armed, having obtained their weapons by trading horses
and mules to Anglo-Americans in New Mexico. The Indians proposed to Militia Captain Ignacio Ortiz that the Tucsonans and their
allies remain in the area for three days to continue treaty discussions. Captain Comadurán declined the invitation, however, pointing out that his party was short of provisions and still had far to go.[15]

Sonora's 1831 Census

Although Escalante had pessimistically predicted in 1828 that
Tucson might soon be abandoned, the population held steady over
the next few years. A census taken in 1831 reveals that 465 persons

were residing in Tucson (not counting friendly Apaches) and 303 were living at Tubac.

The compiler of the Tubac census did not distinguish between military and civilian households, but later events make it clear that there were a few soldiers manning the San Rafael company at the time. Some civilian families, such as that of José María Sosa, had formerly lived in Tucson. Along with three other adult males of the community, Sosa was accorded the title *don*, attesting his high social status. The census taker similarly identified Atanasio Otero, Tomás Ortiz and Pedro Quijada. The wives of three of these men— Carmen Quijada de Otero, Gregoria Nuñez de Sosa and Josefa Elías de Ortiz—were referred to as *doña*, a title also bestowed on María Reyes Peña, mother of Tomás and Ignacio Ortiz, and of Pedro and Carmen Quijada.

Newcomers to Tubac during the 1820s were members of Juan Elías' family. He had been a soldier in the Tucson garrison in 1818, as was his father Cornelio. Later, when Americans came to control the area, Juan's sons, Jesús María and Juan, Jr., would serve in the Arizona territorial legislature.[16]

In addition to Tomás Ortiz, Tubac's residents included two other land grantees: León Herreros, owner of the San José de Sonoita ranch; and Toribio Otero, who more than fifty years earlier had settled on Arizona's first presidial grant at Tubac. Toribio, well into his seventies by 1831, was living in the household of his son Atanasio. Herreros, considerably younger, headed a household of his own that included his wife Peregrina Valencia and four of his children.

The family name Jácome, which would later become well known in southern Arizona, appears for the first time in an Arizona community in the census of 1831.[17] Rafael Jácome and his wife Gregoria Grijalva were at Tubac that year.[18]

The ranking military officer in Tucson was apparently José María Villaescusa, younger brother of the man who had shared command of the fort two years before. Antonio Comadurán, who as early as 1828 had listed himself as Tucson's *comandante*, is missing from the 1831 count, as are members of his immediate family.

Another of the officers of the Tucson garrison was Ensign José Loreto Ramírez, brother of Teodoro, whose military service had begun in the presidio in 1797. The other members of Loreto's household were his grown son, Rafael, another adult named Antonio who may also have been a son, and a female child named Josefa, who could have been a daughter. Teodoro is listed as a civilian whose household included adult relatives, probably nephews, named Pedro and Juan Antonio.[19]

Not long after the count of frontier residents had been completed, Teodoro Ramírez responded to a circular from Governor Leonardo Escalante requesting information about resources in the Tucson area. The preceding year, the central government in Mexico City had created an industrial bank to stimulate economic development, and the bank's managing board had requested information from all regions to assist it with planning. On July 19th, Ramírez prepared a report for Governor Escalante in which he noted that Tucsonans grew some cotton, but that the Gila River Pimas produced much more. The area was suitable for raising sheep, he observed, but the citizens could not protect their flocks from the Apaches. Ramírez commented that the hostile Indians also prevented the search for gold deposits known to be in the vicinity of the Salt River.[20]

Several events of the late summer and early fall of 1831 generated excitement for the residents of the Tucson presidio. The first occurred in September when the Pinal Apaches made overtures of peace to the Apaches who resided on Tucson's outskirts, probably with the intention of getting them to join a general uprising being planned by Apaches at the presidio of Janos in Chihuahua. Chief Antuna of the Tucson Apaches sent two warriors and three women to discuss the matter with their longtime enemies. Perhaps because the Indians from Tucson were unwilling to join them, the Pinals killed one of the visiting warriors. The other warrior retaliated by killing a war captain of the Pinals. Less than a month later, fifty friends and relatives of the slain Apache captain rode their horses around the outside of the fort in a mock attack to frighten the residents.[21]

As if the Apache threat was not enough, October also produced a new visit to Tucson by a party of Americans. They had marched to the presidio along the course of what later would become the main highway between Tucson and Lordsburg, New Mexico.[22] David E. Jackson headed a group of eleven Americans who entered the walled town seeking guides to conduct them over Romero's road to California. None of the Tucsonenses volunteered to accompany them.

Tubac's first justice of the peace under the 1831 regulations was prominent citizen Trinidad Irigoyen who took office shortly before Apaches from the peace establishment at Janos resumed hostilities against the frontier settlements. Tubac was too far away to be raided by the Janos Indians, but some Apaches from Sonoran presidios also defected.[23] More important than the uprising's influence on the other tame Apaches, however, was the stimulus it gave to new efforts by the hostile bands to drive the Mexicans from the northwest frontier.

The handful of soldiers stationed at Tubac in 1832 was too small to provide any protection at all for the local people. Furthermore, those few who were assigned to the post spent most of their time in the south helping to guard against violence stemming from political differences related to the question of where the Sonoran capital would be located.[24] During the summer, José María Villaescusa, now the commanding officer at Tubac, tried to obtain help from the settlers of Imuris, but was told that no one in that community had either a horse or a gun. Villaescusa was alone at the presidio with three retired soldiers, one aide and the families of the absent troopers. In June, Justice of the Peace Irigoyen advised the *comandante* that only twelve civilians remained in the fort and even they were about ready to leave.[25] In view of the relatively large civilian population reported at Tubac in the census of 1831, Irigoyen's comment implies a mass exodus of families, most of whom probably went to Tucson.

A month after Villaescusa's futile appeal to the citizens of Imuris, Sergeant Julián Zubia arrived in Tubac at the head of a militia company of twenty-four auxiliaries recruited at Oposura (Moctezuma) for short-term service in Tucson. Captain Comadurán, satisfied that Tubac needed help more than his own post, sent the volunteers southward. Within a matter of days, seven had deserted. Those who stayed were so homesick and frightened that, according to Zubia, they were "not fit to contribute anything . . . actively or passively."[26]

Shortly before the unhappy volunteers arrived in Tubac, settlers of other towns threatened by the new Apache uprising decided to get together and organize a strong militia unit that would provide them greater protection than they were receiving from the presidial garrisons. Meeting at the home of Father Rafael Díaz in Cocóspera, they organized a force which they called *La Sección Patriótica* ("The

Watercolor painting of an Apache warrior (Arizona Historical Society)

Patriotic Section").[27] Lieutenant Colonel Ignacio Elías González, former commanding officer at Tubac, came from his home in Arizpe to serve as chairman of the meeting. When it concluded, Joaquín Vicente Elías, kinsman of Ignacio, emerged as the elected leader.[28]

Members of the Patriotic Section marched into Tubac on the afternoon of May 23rd, 1832, ready to do battle with the Apaches. At the fort, they encountered Antonio Comadurán who was leading a contingent of Tucson soldiers in pursuit of Indians headed for the Santa Rita mountains. Unable to replace their tired horses in Tubac, the troopers were prepared to give up the chase. Elías volunteered his eager militiamen and Comadurán accepted the offer. A hundred men under Elías' command began the pursuit anew; although they did not catch or kill any Apaches on that occasion, they did whet their appetites for further action.

Ten days later, on June 4th, Elías and his volunteers attacked a party of Apaches—some of them former residents of Tucson and Santa Cruz—in the canyon of Arivaipa Creek. The Mexicans fought to an overwhelming victory, one of the greatest in the history of frontier warfare between the two groups. Elías claimed seventy-one braves killed, thirteen children captured, and 216 horses and mules recovered. Later, Elías returned the branded livestock to their owners. He also permitted the Mexicans to keep the Apache children they had captured. Just one militiamen was killed; twelve others suffered wounds.[29]

Apache actions against the frontier towns and forts continued throughout 1832 and, had it not been for the militia, the already desperate situation might have become much worse. In August, Yaquis led by Juan Ignacio Jusacamea (better known as Juan Banderas) revolted again. This time they were allied with a group of Opatas directed by Dolores Gutiérrez.[30] Civilian volunteers, as well as soldiers, from central and southern Sonora were tied up the remainder of the year battling the Yaquis and Opatas. In December, the Mexicans won a major victory at Soyopa, capturing both Jusacamea and Gutiérrez, whom they executed at Arizpe in January, 1833.

In the same month that the Yaquis and their Opata allies were defeated, a change of profound importance took place in Mexico City. Antonio López de Santa Anna toppled the government of President Anastasio Bustamante and backed General Gómez Pedraza for the presidency.[31] The leaders of the revolt then scheduled new elections for state and federal legislators for April, 1833. Sonora's first constitutional legislature dissolved itself in January, leaving the government in the hands of elected Governor Manuel Escalante y Arvizu.[32]

In the state of confusion that followed, the residents of Hermosillo and nearby towns mounted another effort to have the capital brought back. Exceeding its authority, the elections committee (a majority of whose members favored Hermosillo over Arizpe) chose representatives to a new legislature and attempted to install Manuel María Gándara as governor and Leonardo Escalante as lieutenant governor. The spurious new legislature convened at Arizpe in April amid rumors that its members planned to move the capital south. They adjourned in July with the announcement that they would meet again "however, wherever, and whenever" they might wish.[33] To the people of Arizpe that meant an imminent change in the capital location.

In an effort to settle the issue peaceably, some of Arizpe's most prominent citizens sought a meeting with men of comparable stature from Hermosillo, and a conference took place on July 31st at the Barrio del Ranchito in Hermosillo. Those present were unable to reach an accord and the Arizpe representatives returned home to develop a new strategy. On August 12th, the municipal council met with individuals from surrounding communities and drafted a proclamation refusing to recognize the legitimacy of the legislature. They also appealed to Escalante to continue as Sonora's chief executive no matter what the members of the legislature might try to do.

Three days later, the legislators reconvened in Hermosillo in defiance of the action taken by the people of the Sonora River Valley. Residents of the state then took sides and a civil war appeared to be on the horizon. Concerned about the gravity of the situation and perhaps feeling that his side was outnumbered, Gándara dissolved the legislature on September 3rd, bringing the dispute to a peaceful conclusion.[34] For the time being, so long as the scope of Gándara's power was limited, the capital would remain at Arizpe.

As the politicians were fighting over the question of the capital site, trouble was brewing among members of the military establishment as well. For many months, the presidial troops had gone without sufficient rations and equipment—even without clothing. Now that the Apaches were back on the warpath and again decimating the frontier towns, the situation could no longer be tolerated. In the same month Gándara dissolved the legislature, the principal commanding officers of the presidios gathered in Arizpe where they found veteran Ignacio Elías González sympathetic to their problem. The old Tubac *comandante* led them in a barracks revolt against Colonel Francisco Xavier Arregui, Sonora's commanding officer. Elías assumed temporary leadership over the Sonoran military, passing the command a month later to his first cousin, Lieutenant Colonel José María.[35]

Appeals for a Major Offensive

As the tumultuous year of 1833 came to a close, the residents of Tubac, many of whom had apparently returned to the community once the *Sección Patriótica* began campaigning, held an election to choose a new justice of the peace. Juan Bautista Elías was selected to head the village's civil government during 1834. Married to Jesús Orozco, he was the father of two children when he took office.

Shortly after assuming his duties, Elías presided at the trial of

José María Sosa, administrator of Tumacácori mission lands, who had been charged by the Pima Indians with "embezzlement and other offenses no less serious." Although the documents concerning the trial do not indicate the outcome, they do make clear that the state of affairs between the Indians and the settlers was strained at best. The native population of the Tumacácori area had dwindled to a mere handful by this time and there were no priests at the community to protect the Pimas against usurpation of their land and water by local Mexicans. Elías summoned six witnesses for the trial, none of them Indians. Of the six, only two—Ignacio Ortiz and Tiburcio Campa—knew how to sign their names.[36]

At about the same time that Justice of the Peace Elías was engaged with the Sosa trial, Ensign Antonio Ramírez wrote to Lieutenant Colonel Elías González to inform him of some of the difficulties he was having in converting civilians into soldiers—his militia command had been seriously depleted by desertions, mostly by men from Arizpe and Chinapa. Elías González forwarded Ramírez' letter to Governor Escalante.[37]

In April, Juan Elías sent more news to the governor, telling him that Tubac would supply the four men requested of it by Captain Leonardo León, whom Escalante had called upon several months earlier to coordinate a major campaign against the Apaches.[38] He also reported, however, that as the men selected were about to march from the fort, they received word that 600 well-armed Apaches had attacked the Babocómari Ranch. The people of Tubac feared they would be next.[39] Less than a week later, Tucson Justice of the Peace Juan Nepomuceno González wrote Escalante to tell him that an Indian man and five women, who had been captured by Apaches in the Babocómari raid, had escaped and come to Tucson. The escapees had apparently been employees of the ranch owners.[40]

Later that month, González, backed by the residents of the presidio, drafted a proclamation supporting a plan proposed earlier by settlers of Santa Cruz to appeal directly to the central government in Mexico City for maintenance of the frontier forts. They were satisfied that only in this fashion could the garrisons be restored to professional status. Clearly, the residents of the Pimería Alta were frustrated by all the political maneuvering that had gone on in Occidente and Sonora during the last ten years.[41]

The frustration showed at Tubac also. On April 21st, 1834, Justice of the Peace Elías again took pen in hand to write the

Babocómari Ranch in the 1850s (Gray, *Report*)

governor about the desperate situation there. He reported that the settlers were ready to leave the place because of the lack of interest in their welfare that the *comandante* displayed. He appealed to Escalante to give them a commanding officer who would be more "active" against the enemy Apache.[42]

On July 3rd, 1834, the Sonoran legislature authorized Governor Escalante to undertake a major campaign against the raiders. On that same date, Ensign José Loreto Ramírez, brother of Teodoro and Antonio, wrote to José María Elías González, adjutant inspector of the northern line, about the possibility of a massive renewal of raiding by the Apaches. Ramírez had obtained information about the matter from a peaceful Apache woman who had been captured during the March 30th raid on the Babocómari Ranch. She had been falsely told by the hostile Indians that the members of her band at Tucson had either been wiped out or had joined the rebels. Consequently, she had been careful about approaching the presidio and had wandered through the nearby countryside looking for friends and relatives. During this time, she had gathered much information about those Apaches who had deserted the presidios. She reported they were living in the Chiricahua mountains and preparing to attack Tubac and Tucson. They had not joined forces at that time with the Pinal and White Mountain Apaches who were planning the big raiding venture.[43]

The day after Ramírez prepared his letter, Justice of the Peace Elías of Tubac was back at his desk. His communication was again directed to the governor. He began by noting that the fort was without a wall and that the rains of the previous winter season had been so heavy that they had caused severe flooding which changed the course of the Santa Cruz River, moving it so far away from the presidio that it was almost beyond reach in the event of Apache attack. He commented also that Tubac boasted only a single piece of artillery, and the settlers, by and large, were without arms altogether. There were fewer than a dozen soldiers. He included with his letter a copy of a circular prepared the preceding day at Tucson, probably by Ensign Ramírez, warning of an imminent Indian attack.[44]

Late in the summer of 1834, the frontier settlers prepared for the major campaign authorized shortly before by the Sonora legislature. On September 1st, Justice of the Peace González of Tucson wrote Governor Escalante, who was to lead the campaign, that residents of Tucson, San Ignacio and Tubutama were prepared to contribute forty militiamen, provided that munitions could be supplied for all.[45]

By the end of September, Escalante had established his headquarters at the Elías hacienda on Babocómari Creek, an ideal location from which to move against several different bands of hostile Apaches. On September 27th, he sent a detachment of men under the command of Antonio Narbona and Ramón Urrea[46] into the field with instructions to remain there, harrying the Apaches for twenty-four days. The detachment included six companies of cavalry and infantry—a total of 442 men.

The governor stayed behind with a small force of 100 men, guarding 200 loads of provisions and 1,800 horses. His plan was to move the supplies and the herd to Willcox Playa (then known as La Playa de los Pimas), and from there to San Simón. In a letter written to Vice-Governor José Ignacio Bustamante on September 29th, Escalante stated that he was sending word to Tucson to provide him some Papago allies. He also reported that he would inform the people of Santa Cruz and the San Ignacio Valley that he was ready to receive the volunteers they had been recruiting.[47]

As Governor Escalante prepared to send his first detachment into the field, Tucsonan Juan Nepomuceno González led a force of his own into the territory of the Pinal Apaches. Accompanied by fifty-six Pimas and peaceful Apaches, as well as twenty-seven settlers, Justice of the Peace González left Tucson on September 16th. Along the way, he was joined by more than 200 Papagos and Gila River Pimas. With the assistance of their Apache scouts, the contingent penetrated the most remote areas of the Pinals, going almost to the Salt River Canyon. In four different battles, they killed twenty braves, six women and twelve children.[48] They also recovered eighty-seven horses and eighty-six cows, the Papagos sharing in the booty. They cut the ears from the warriors, but took none from women and children.

In his report of the expedition, González praised the contribution of the peaceful Apaches. He observed that at no point did they demonstrate any evidence whatsoever of an intention to desert, and remarked that they could serve the state with great usefulness. Commanding General José María Elías González transmitted a copy of González' letter to Vice-Governor Bustamante, calling attention to the remarks about the faithfulness of the *Apaches mansos.*

A few days after González' return, Escalante dispatched a second detachment against the Apaches. This one had the Mogollon Mountains of New Mexico as its ultimate destination. They proceeded generally along the route followed in modern times by the highway between Willcox and Lordsburg, New Mexico. The strategy was to surprise the Indians of the Mogollon area, who were headed by Tutijé, principal leader of the Apaches who had formerly resided at Janos. They were detected, however, and unable to gain the major victory they had hoped to achieve. They did capture Tutijé, kill a pair of warriors, and recover a few stolen horses, however.[49]

The great offensive of 1834, for which the residents of the frontier towns had waited so long, ended with relatively little accomplished. The most successful part of the operation was the victory gained by the handful of Tucsonans and their Indian allies over the Pinal Apaches who sued for peace soon after. Given the condition of Sonoran politics, though, it is a wonder that any large-scale action took place at all.[50]

Problems with the Papagos

As the campaign against the Apaches slowed late in 1834, a new threat to some of the Hispanic communities of the Pimería Alta began to emerge. Barely perceptible at first, this threat would grow into what later came to be known as the Papago war. Early evidence of what might lie ahead is found in a letter written on the last day of February, 1835, by the governors of the Papago communities of Caborca and Pitiquito, and the captain general of the Pimas and Papagos, an appointee of the Sonoran government headquartered at Caborca.

Directed to the president of the Franciscan missions of the Pimería Alta, this document set forth grievances of the native inhabitants of towns in the Magdalena and Altar river watersheds. The writers noted that since the introduction of liberal ideas about Indian administration in the closing years of Spanish rule,[51] the missionaries had been without power to help the indigenous people maintain themselves in the face of invasions of their land and usurpation of their water by incoming Hispanics. They lamented that the Indians had been driven entirely from San Ignacio, and were rapidly disappearing from Sáric, Tubutama and Oquitoa. They forecast that the Papagos would be forced to adopt the tactics of the Apaches and subsist through raiding the Mexican towns in the fertile river valleys.[52]

Four days after the Papago leaders prepared their letter, members of the Altar *ayuntamiento* (town council) wrote Governor Escalante to tell him of new developments. Retaliating for the death of three of their number the preceding December, a band of Papagos had stolen the horseherd of José García. A hundred armed Altar residents chased some of the Indians into the Quijotoa mountains. In the discussion that followed, the Papagos stated that they had no intention of returning García's horses until the persons responsible for the murders were turned over to them. Their hostility and determination convinced the outnumbered citizens of Altar that it might be dangerous to continue the parley. The *vecinos* turned their horses around and rode back to their homes.[53]

On June 1st, 1835, the Altar town council again wrote the governor about Indian matters, but this time they forwarded Papago complaints against the peaceful Apaches of Tucson who, they claimed, were entering their territory and causing damage. Acting Governor Ignacio Bustamante sought the advice of José María Elías González who a short time before had been named general commander of Sonora.

In response to the governor, Elías first stated his belief that it was of critical importance to prevent the outbreak of hostilities between Papagos and *Apaches mansos*. He went on to observe that, in his opinion, the Apaches could never become "sociable human beings and useful citizens" unless they were permitted to settle down in a town of their own, cultivate the soil, and become private property owners "as nature intended." He proposed that a new Sonoran town be established in the vicinity of the presidios where the Apaches could settle. And he offered to assume some of the responsibility for providing them with oxen and farming equipment, as well as aiding them in other ways.[54]

On June 23rd, 1835, Acting Governor Bustamante forwarded Elías's proposal to the Sonoran Congress with the request that the deputies provide the necessary authorization for the project because it was not within the jurisdiction of the executive department to do so.[55] The legislators responded on July 10th with Decree Number 71 endorsing the commander general's plan and calling upon the governor to make a recommendation about lands most appropriate for the Tucson Apaches.[56]

Colonel Elías was in the field when the legislators took their action, but in anticipation of a favorable response, he met with the leaders of the *Apaches mansos* during a visit to the Santa Cruz presidio. After informing them of the plan, he asked them where they would like to establish a village. They answered immediately that they favored the site of El Pueblito across the river from the Tucson presidio. Elías explained that this was impossible since Pimas were still living there. As an alternative he recommended the abandoned site of Sáric, but the Apaches were not interested. They opted, instead, for the old Pima village of Sonoita which more than a decade earlier had been included in the land grant awarded to Don León Herreros.[57]

By the time Elías returned to Arizpe, Governor Escalante y Arvizu was back at his desk and it was he who recommended to the legislators that an Apache town be created at Sonoita. The deputies responded favorably, but postponed final action until the governor could inform them about the estimated value of the property. On September 7th, 1835, Governor Escalante replied that he could not locate even two persons in Arizpe who were familiar with the Sonoita site, but that its current owner, Joaquín Vicente Elías, was reported to have paid 600 pesos for it.[58] He proposed that Elías be offered the same sum and if he refused to sell, the government could use the expropriation authority provided it by the Sonora constitution.[59]

At no time during these negotiations did the legislators request information concerning the number of Apaches at the Tucson presidio, although by September such information was available. Perhaps stimulated by Colonel Elías, with whom he was in close communication, Captain Comadurán in July prepared a complete census of *Apaches mansos* receiving rations at his post. His tally showed 486 of them, twenty-one more than the number of *gente de razón* reported at the presidio four years earlier.[60]

The legislators apparently did not pursue the matter of authorizing a village for the peaceful Apaches. Although the descendants of these Indians would later tell the Americans of a reservation provided them at Sonoita, they never established a settlement there and Joaquín Vicente Elías remained in possession of the title to the Sonoita grant. In 1857 he sold the property to Antonio Crespo for 1,950 pesos.[61] By that time the Apache population of Tucson had declined to a handful of Indians who were about to undertake another unsuccessful effort to obtain a land base. In the bargain, they would find American bureaucrats and politicians just as difficult to deal with as their Mexican counterparts had been in 1835.

7

Power Struggles
Leave the Frontier Helpless

As Colonel Elías González formulated plans for dealing with the Papagos and *Apaches mansos* in the summer of 1835, he and other Sonorans anxiously awaited news from Mexico City where a new conservative government was plotting significant changes in the political structure of the country. A little over a year earlier, in April, 1834, General Antonio López de Santa Anna had overturned the government of Valentín Gómez Farías, which the general himself had installed the preceding year. Unhappy with the liberal reforms being urged by Gómez Farías, conservatives appealed to Santa Anna to return to the presidency and he agreed. His first act was to dissolve the congress and install a new, more conservative one. When this body refused to follow his directions, he left the capital and returned to his Veracruz estate.

With no chief executive to interfere, the congressional delegates were free to do as they pleased, and they moved quickly to centralize the political affairs of the country. On October 3rd and October 20th, 1835, they decreed the elimination of the sovereign states of Mexico and their replacement with governmental units known as "departments." Each state legislature was called upon to appoint six individuals to a departmental *junta* and turn the reins of local government over to that body.[1]

Sonora's second constitutional legislature ceased to function on November 21st, 1835, after installing a *junta* that included the

parish priest of Arizpe, Juan Chrisóstomo Elías González, brother
of José María, Rafael, Simón and Ignacio. Temporarily, Governor
Escalante y Arvizu was permitted to continue in his post, but he
could no longer operate against the Apaches without permission
from the central government whose attention was increasingly di-
verted to the situation shaping up in Texas.[2]

Greatly distressed over the change from a federalist to a centralist
government, many Texans by early 1835 were eager for independence. Santa Anna responded to the threat by calling upon his
brother-in-law, General Martín Perfecto de Cos, to restore order to
the region. In September, Cos moved toward San Antonio but the
fired-up Texans were more than a match for his soldiers, dealing
them severe defeats early in October.[3] When Congress later that
month issued its decrees eliminating the sovereignty of the states
and dissolving their legislatures, the Texans assembled on November 7th, affirmed their adherence to the federalist constitution, and
declared that "the present authorities of the nominal Mexican republic" had no right to govern them.

Early in March, 1836, the Texans met again, abandoned their
previous position and opted for independence. They also chose a
president and vice-president. A few days later, Santa Anna—now
back in the picture—began his siege of the Alamo.[4]

Although the Battle of the Alamo is undoubtedly the most famous encounter of the Texas war for independence, more significant was the confrontation that took place two weeks later at the
town of Goliad. In that battle, Colonel James E. Fannin and his
party of Texans were surrounded by a larger force under the command of General José de Urrea, Tucson's most famous native son.
Considering his situation hopeless, Fannin surrendered to his ad-
versary. Leaving the prisoners in the custody of Lieutenant Colonel
Nicolás de la Portilla, Urrea moved on to another battlefield. Before
doing so, however, he wrote Santa Anna urging clemency for Fannin and his men. Santa Anna ignored the plea and directed Portilla
to execute the prisoners. After agonizing about the matter through
the night of March 26th, Portilla carried out Santa Anna's order the
following day and 365 Texans were put to death.[5]

Less than a month after the events at Goliad, Sam Houston and
his army of Texans soundly defeated Santa Anna's forces at the San
Jacinto River. Two days later, on April 23, Santa Anna himself was
taken into custody. General Filisola then ordered the evacuation of

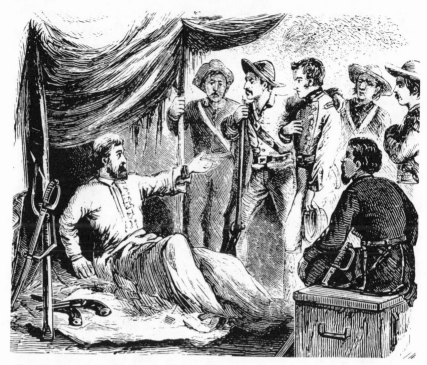

General Antonio López de Santa Anna being taken prisoner by the soldiers of
Sam Houston (Bancroft Library)

Mexican troops from Texas, a decision strongly disputed by Urrea.
A month and a half later, President José Justo Corro removed
Filisola and put General Urrea in charge of the Texas campaign,
but it was too late to recover what had been lost. Texas was independent.[6]

A Peace Treaty for the Pinals

On March 5th, 1836, the day before Santa Anna began his siege
of the Alamo, Tucson was headquarters for the largest peace parley
ever held between the presidials and their perennial enemies, the
Pinal Apaches. The latter, who had become a primary target of
Escalante's wrath, had begun to feel they were taking the brunt of a
war kicked off by the peaceful Apaches of the Janos presidio, and

they were eager to work out a truce that would take some of the pressure off them.

Among the signers of the peace treaty was Tucson's *comandante*, Captain Antonio Comadurán. Except for brief assignments at near-by posts, Comadurán had been in Tucson eighteen years—half his lifetime. Signing, too, for the presidial forces were Ensign José Loreto Ramírez, a veteran of nearly forty years of frontier service, and Ensign José Saenz Rico. The other two Mexican signatures were those of Lieutenant Colonel José María Martínez and José María Elías González, who the preceding September had received his promotion to full colonel.[7]

Included in the treaty were provisions that the Indians would settle temporarily at the juncture of Arivaipa Creek and the San Pedro River and would travel to Tucson only with the permission of the presidial commander. The document provided further that every two weeks the Pinal chiefs would report to the *comandante* on what was taking place in their settlement, including any information they might have about impending actions by the more hostile Apaches.[8]

Shortly after assisting his commanding officer in negotiating with the Pinal Apaches, Captain Comadurán took a temporary assignment as commander of the Santa Cruz presidio. Replacing him both as *comandante* at Tucson and as overall commander of the combined troops of the garrisons of Tucson, Tubac, Altar and Santa Cruz (a unit known as the Second Section of the Northern Line) was Lieutenant Colonel José María Martínez, who seems to have enjoyed unusual recognition for his abilities as an Apache fighter. His antecedents are obscure but he may have been a member of the family of Ensign Juan M. Martínez who was assigned to the presidio of Tubac in 1801, after previously serving as a sergeant in the Altar company.[9] Ensign Martínez is probably the individual shown on the 1818 presidial register as a retired Tucson soldier and he may have been the father of the Juan Martínez who was still on active duty with the Tucson garrison in that year.[10]

Arizona territorial censuses of 1860 and 1864 list José María Martínez, but are in conflict concerning his age. The 1860 compilation shows him as a forty-nine-year-old resident of the Santa Cruz settlements, whereas the special census of 1864 reports him to be fifty-eight at that time. In either case, he was certainly a very young man in 1836 when he became Tucson's *comandante*. That he should have reached the rank of lieutenant colonel while still so young is truly remarkable. Martínez remained in Tucson as the post commander until 1838; then he took up residence in Tubac until driven out by the Apaches a decade later.[11]

Problems with the Apaches were not the only ones the new commander faced when he came to Tucson in 1836. By that time relations between the local Papagos and the *vecinos* were at one of their lowest points. Poor Father Antonio González, last of the Franciscans, had tried unsuccessfully during his tenure at San Xavier to persuade Tucson's justices of the peace to enforce trespass laws against settlers whose horses and dairy cows trampled and ate grain raised by the Indians at San Xavier and at El Pueblito.

In April, 1836, just a month after conclusion of the Pinal treaty, González wrote a desperate letter to Sonora's governor. He set forth a series of complaints stemming from incidents that occurred during the two years he had served at the mission. To emphasize his point that the Papagos were as frustrated as he, the priest mentioned a case in which one of the Indians struck and apparently killed an animal that had invaded a San Xavier field. González found himself obligated to compensate the unhappy owner of the animal. He turned over a yoke of oxen worth 20 pesos.

Adding to the friar's unhappiness was the difficulty he had in finding Indians to work in the fields on which he and the mission staff depended for subsistence. He informed the governor that the *alcaldes* were advising the Papagos that since the secularization of Indian missions they were now citizens and *vecinos*. As a result, the priest wrote, the Papagos "do not want to do communal labor, as has always been the custom in the missions." González pleaded for some relief from the application of new laws regarding the status of former mission Indians. He asked, also, that the governor instruct the justices of the peace to enforce the laws against livestock trespass.

The friar closed his letter with an ultimatum that the governor may have regarded as impertinent. "If," González wrote,

> your excellency does not take the measures that justice demands to end these damages that I am experiencing . . . I shall be forced to inform my prelate that I can no longer endure the

discomfort stemming from these causes, and regretfully abandon these settlements and retire to my college to rest and recuperate. . . .[12]

The Pinal peace treaty paid its first dividends in July, three months after Father González composed his message to Governor Escalante y Arvizu. True to their promise to report any events they considered newsworthy, the Apaches informed Lieutenant Colonel Martínez of a new party of Americans on the Gila. To find out more about the foreigners, the *comandante* sent two peaceful Apaches to investigate. His Indian spies returned with the news that a large group of Americans—forty in all—had constructed and fortified a small house near the Gila River and planted a field of corn. While the Apaches watched, the foreigners packed up and left. They returned early in the fall, however, and after harvesting their crop in November permanently abandoned the site.[13]

Given the potential significance of such a large party of Americans in Mexican territory—especially in view of the events that had taken place shortly before in Texas—it seems surprising that Martínez should not immediately have reported the intrusion to his superiors. In fact, however, neither he nor Tucson's justice of the peace supplied any details to higher authorities until autumn of the following year after merchant Teodoro Ramírez, on one of his frequent trips to Arizpe, told people there that the Americans were building a fort on the Gila River. Sonora's governor then wrote José Grijalva, Tucson justice of the peace, for information about the matter, and Grijalva responded, explaining that the events in question had all taken place the preceding year. A month later, Martínez sent a more detailed letter to the interim military commander.

In December, 1836, shortly after the Americans had left the Gila, Mexico's conservative national congress promulgated a new organic document for the country which, because of its division into seven main parts, came to be known as *las siete leyes constitucionales*, or "the seven constitutional laws." Designed to centralize the government further, the document was also highly autocratic in nature. It specified, for example, that no one with an annual income of less than 4,000 pesos per year could aspire to the presidency, and no one with an income of less than 1,500 pesos could sit in the chamber of deputies.[14] In January, 1837, former president Busta-

Rafael Elías González, governor of Sonora and owner of the San Rafael del Valle land grant (Corella collection, courtesy of Carmen Pellat Sotomayor)

mante was persuaded to move into the post that Santa Anna had vacated in 1835, but he was now subject to a five-man ruling clique known as the *poder conservador* ("conserving authority").

In keeping with provisions of the new constitution, the Sonorans early in 1837 reorganized their old system of political districts into one composed of prefectures. The Santa Cruz Valley, previously a part of the Arizpe district, remained within the jurisdiction of what now became the Arizpe Prefecture (although the term "district" continued to be used). Tucson and Tubac were also under the *partido* (now the sub-prefecture) of San Ignacio.[15]

In June, 1837, Sonora's first constitutional governor, Manuel Escalante y Arvizu—surely a man highly respected in Tucson and other frontier communities—stepped down to permit the central government, under the 1836 constitution, to appoint a new chief executive. On a temporary basis, his position was filled by Rafael

Elías González on whose San Pedro Ranch Escalante had maintained headquarters in the closing days of the 1834 Apache campaign. At the time he took over, Elías was chairman of the *junta* that
had replaced the Sonoran legislature.[16]

As political changes were taking place in Mexico City and in
Sonora, the peace treaty with the Pinal Apaches continued to provide information critical to the survival of the frontier communities
of the region. Late in January, 1837, three members of the Pinal
band appeared at the Tucson presidio to seek an audience with
Lieutenant Colonel Martínez. Through their White Mountain
Apache friends, they had learned that the Janos Indians, still seeking revenge for the death of their great war chief Tutijé, were
plotting the assassination of Colonel José María Elías González. The
scheme included killing the commanding officer of the Fronteras
presidio as well. Afterward the Janos Apaches planned to surprise
the garrison at Santa Cruz and murder Captain Comadurán. Their
campaign of revenge would then conclude with destruction of the
peaceful Apache camp at Tucson.[17]

The rumor of possible new depredations by the Janos Apaches
deeply disturbed Sonoran authorities, for they despaired of counting on any help from their counterparts in Chihuahua, who they felt
would rather negotiate peace with the Indians than deal with them
strongly.[18] They could not be certain either that the central government in Mexico City would come to their aid, so representatives to
Sonora's ruling *junta* conferred about the matter with prominent
citizens, then petitioned President Bustamante in September seeking the right to govern their own internal affairs. Uppermost in
their minds was the use of departmental revenues to finance war
with the Apaches.[19]

By the time of the Arizpe petition, Lieutenant Colonel José
María Martínez was forced to deal with a new kind of Indian problem within his jurisdiction. Although he now considered the members of the Pinal band to be his allies, these Indians were not viewed
as friends by the Pimas and Papagos. To them, an Apache was an
Apache.

Shortly after taking command at Tucson, Martínez had promised Chief Azul, leader of the Gila River Pimas, that he would
reward him with a new suit of clothes for every campaign he made
against the hostiles. Unfortunately, the *comandante* had not distin-

guished one Apache band from another and as far as Azul was concerned raids against the Pinals camped at the Arivaipa-San Pedro junction were worthy of reward.

Late in the summer of 1837, Chief Azul confronted Martínez with fifteen pairs of Apache ears, but was told the new garb would not be granted since the *comandante* considered it highly probable that the ears had been attached to Pinal heads shortly before. The Pima leader repaired to the home of his old friend Teodoro Ramírez to complain both about the failure of Martínez to live up to his side of the bargain, and his unwillingness to provide the Pimas with ammunition or with help to repair some of their weapons.

Ramírez, who probably spoke Piman as well as any of the Indians, comiserated with Azul and gave his friend cartridges and ammunition from his own supplies. He then wrote Governor Elías González of the incident—an action that combined with Ramírez' description in Arizpe of the American threat on the Gila might have perturbed Martínez, but did not destroy their friendship.[20]

In his letter to the governor, Ramírez mentioned that some weeks before he had secured Azul's support in trying to recover from the Apaches some oxen and cows stolen from the presidio. He called the Gila River Pimas "loyal allies" and urged that they be rewarded with firearms and ammunition, bolts of cloth and clothing. With such encouragement, he speculated that the Pimas might be persuaded to take the offensive against the Janos Apaches, "our real enemies to the east." Evidently impressed with his letter, Governor Elías forwarded a copy of it with a favorable recommendation to the central government.[21]

Sometime late in 1837, the Tucson area lost the last resident Catholic priest it would have during the Mexican period. Father Antonio González took his frustrations with him to a new assignment at the mission church in Oquitoa. Four years later he would return briefly to serve the spiritual needs of southern Arizonans from headquarters in San Ignacio.

During the time González was at Oquitoa, Father Rafael Díaz rode the circuit from San Ignacio to Tubac, Tucson and vicinity.[22] His visits were infrequent, however, and sometimes members of his Arizona congregations took their children south for baptism. A few even made the long journey to get married, among them Teodoro Ramírez, who became the husband of María de los Angeles Salazar in Santa Ana on June 26, 1838. The Tucson merchant was forty-seven years old at the time. María, a niece of his first wife, was twenty years younger.[23]

Politics and Papagos

At the time the Sonorans petitioned the national government for more autonomy in managing their own affairs, sentiment for some kind of separate status was strong in such places as Arizpe. At the very least, the people longed for a return to the federalist constitution of 1824, which had given them the right to select their own state officials. Proponents of this position began to publish and circulate a semi-official weekly newspaper called *El Restaurador Oficial* that urged support for a retreat from centralism.

As they waited impatiently for a response from Mexico City to their petition of September 6th, 1837, members of the departmental *junta* turned again to Manuel Escalante y Arvizu to direct another campaign against the Janos Apaches. They reinstalled him in the office of governor on October 12th.[24] Before he could get started with a new offensive, however, the *poder conservador* and President Bustamante finally appointed a new chief executive. Manuel María Gándara, a figure of rising political importance who five years earlier had cast his lot with those who favored placing the capital in Hermosillo, was selected for the post.[25]

Oldest son of a peninsular-born Spaniard who had been expelled from Sonora in 1828, Gándara from the early days of his political career seems to have enjoyed the backing of powerful commercial interests in Guaymas and Hermosillo. Foremost among his supporters was Manuel Iñigo, a native of San Miguel de Horcasitas, who had become the most successful and wealthy businessman in the department of Sonora during the 1830s.[26] Gándara also could count on help from prominent citizens of Ures, where he had lived from 1829 to 1833, and such important Altar Valley families as the Redondos, to whom he was related through his mother, doña Antonia de Gortari.[27] In short, by 1837, when Gándara became governor he already had a strong power base.

Escalante y Arvizu stepped down for the second time on November 26th, 1837, and Gándara became the official governor of the department. Shortly afterward, President Bustamante named General José de Urrea, in the eyes of many the only Mexican hero of the

War of the Texas Rebellion, as military commander of Sonora. The stage was now set for a confrontation between two powerful personalities: Urrea—closely linked with the aristocratic old families of Arizpe and Alamos; and Gándara—strongly tied to the powerful business interests of the fast-growing towns of Guaymas, Ures and Hermosillo.

The Sonoran faction that favored greater autonomy for the region regarded Gándara as the representative of the centralism they despised and viewed Urrea as a possible champion of their cause. Those close to him knew that the general felt restoration of the federal system was the only way in which Mexico could avoid future rebellions such as the one which had resulted in the loss of Texas. Additionally, Urrea had an eye on the governorship. Members of Sonora's *junta* had named him their second choice behind his mother's first cousin, Colonel Simón Elías González (who was named governor of Chihuahua instead), but the central government had passed over him in favor of Gándara, the *junta's* third choice.[28]

Late in December, 1837, Urrea met with his supporters in Arizpe and issued a proclamation calling upon President Bustamante to convene an extraordinary national congress to reform the liberal constitution of 1824. While this was taking place, the separate states would organize provisional governments of their own. In many respects, the document prepared by Urrea constituted a declaration of rebellion by the Sonorans against the central government in Mexico City. Perhaps because he felt that federalism had more appeal for Sonorans than centralism, Gándara decided to back the proclamation and resign his post.

On May 14th, 1838, the Sonorans installed a special congress whose duties included choosing a governor and a vice-governor. Heading the congress was Manuel Escalante y Arvizu. When the votes were counted, Urrea emerged as the choice for governor and Leonardo Escalante for vice-governor. Gándara, dismayed that he was not chosen for one of the offices, disavowed the special congress and returned to the centralist fold.[29]

Urrea, who was determined to gain support for his proclamation in other parts of Mexico—by force if necessary—stayed in Arizpe only long enough to satisfy himself that the situation in Sonora was under control. He then turned the governorship over to Escalante and, after appointing his cousin José María Elías González military

Manuel María Gándara (Villa,   José Cosme de Urrea (Villa, *Galería*)
Galería)

commander of the state, marched off to Sinaloa to continue his
political revolution in that area.[30]

Early in May, Urrea seized Culiacán with the intention of establishing an independent government there. However, he had seriously miscalculated the strength of both the conservative movement and the armies supporting it. Driven from Culiacán by the
forces of Teófilo Romero, military commander of Sinaloa, Urrea
returned to Sonora in the summer of 1838, only to find that during
his short absence Gándara had rallied the forces of centralism, put
together a strong army, and reassumed the office of governor. The
luckless general attempted to negotiate; he failed, however, and
touched off a six-year civil war in Sonora. Urrea left the state but
his followers, including Antonio Narbona and José María Martínez,
continued fighting during the remainder of 1838.[31] With politics
taking over, hostile Apaches encountered less and less resistance
from the presidial forces.

As the initial phase of the Urrea-Gándara feud heated up, gold
strikes in the Altar Valley added to the tension between Papagos
and their Mexican neighbors. Little distracted by political events,
prospectors moved into the area, most with no regard for the Indians' rights or for their property. In April and May, 1838, Santiago

Redondo, sub-prefect at Altar, wrote to Urrea providing information about events within his jurisdiction, and warning the governor
of serious problems with the Papagos.[32] With one of his communications, he included the diary of Rafael Moraga, commanding
officer of a militia unit attempting to deal with the situation.

Moraga's diary makes it clear that arrogant Mexican trespassers
had contributed to the deteriorating state of affairs. Singled out
specifically was Diego Celaya, the same man who more than three
years before had attempted to recover from the Indians a horseherd
they were holding hostage to gain custody of Mexicans from Altar
who had killed three of their number.[33] Governor Tonolic of the
village of Carricito reported that Celaya had come to his community
with a crew of workmen instructed to deepen the Papago village
well to accommodate the needs of incoming Mexicans. The Papagos
offered to help with the project but protested when Celaya decided
to use dirt from the excavation to channel all water collected in the
entire area to a site of his choice. The Indians pointed out that this
would force them to abandon another water hole upon which they
depended. When Celaya refused to listen, they pushed him away
and confiscated his tools. Later he falsely reported to the justice of
the peace at San Perfecto that the Papagos had restrained him from
deepening the well and the incident was widely publicized as an
Indian revolt.

By the time Redondo's communications reached Arizpe, Gándara had taken over the government. Not long afterward, he would
begin to plot with Indians of the Altar Valley against supporters of
Urrea and, thus, exploit the already existing tension.[34]

The Frontier Situation Grows More Desperate

Even before the outbreak of open warfare between the Gándara
and Urrea factions, life at the frontier forts had become a desperate
struggle for survival. Removing Francisco Xavier Arregui from the
general command in 1832 did little to improve the situation. The
Sonoran treasury, with meager resources at best, was depleted by
the groups competing for political power and no money could be
found to pay and provision the presidial soldiers. Both the barracks
revolt of 1832 and the 1834 appeal of the Santa Cruz and Tucson
garrisons for direct help from the central government[35] resulted

from the serious plight of the soldiers and their families. Troopers even resorted to selling their arms and other equipment to civilians to get money for food. This practice had become so common by 1835 that the Sonoran government felt obliged to impose penalties on those making such purchases.[36] Two years later, Acting Governor Rafael Elías González again warned his fellow citizens of what lay in store for any who bought arms from members of the presidial forces.[37]

The harsh conditions under which Tucson Mexicans lived during the 1830s and 1840s would be recalled many years later by some of those who survived into the period of American rule. The danger of Apache attack made it necessary for people to crowd together inside the walled compound which they shared at night with considerable livestock. Houses were single-roomed adobe structures, some of them built directly against the walls of the fort. Being lower than the rampart, the roofs formed a parapet used by soldiers in firing at Apache raiders. Few houses had windows and doors were of saguaro ribs.[38]

Clothing, including the soldiers', was extremely simple. During summer, Mexican males wore as little as the Indians. Their homemade shoes, called *taguas*, were of leather. Women garbed themselves more elegantly—wearing blouses and long skirts of unbleached cotton cloth. They also wore shawls and scarves.[39]

In spite of the Apache menace, the Mexicans enjoyed a limited social life. They visited Magdalena for the San Francisco fiesta in October and held dances on other Saints' days such as those dedicated to San Juan (June 24) and San Agustín (August 28). Gambling was popular, especially betting on horse races or footraces involving community members.[40]

Tucsonenses in the 1830s lived on foods similar to those described earlier by Father Pfefferkorn. Desert plants such as tender prickly pear pads (*nopalitos*) and fruits were favored. The beans of mesquite were ground to make *pinole*. Since the soldiers were not paid regularly and cash was scarce, it is unlikely that imported delicacies such as tropical fruits and chocolate were available. Apparently coffee was unknown.[41]

Mescal, the alcoholic beverage made from the *agave* (century plant), was one item that always seems to have been plentiful.[42] It was almost certainly supplemented by *tesguino*, a drink made from fermented corn, when supplies of that plant were sufficient to per-

Magdalena, Sonora, site of the October pilgrimage (Bartlett, *Personal Narrative*, volume 1)

mit its preparation. In the summer, Papago wine prepared from the juice of saguaro cactus fruit may have added to the store of intoxicating liquor.

Sometime in the late 1830s, as more of the people from the countryside moved into Tucson, residents of the pueblo may have resumed farming at the old Tres Alamos site on the San Pedro River. Those who cultivated and harvested the crops were escorted by presidial troops who remained with them while they were at work.[43] Escorts were also provided for women from the presidio who left the walled compound to wash clothing in the irrigation ditches,[44] as well as for men who went to the ranches to obtain cattle and sheep for meat.

Abandonment of the Land Grants

The land grants approved in southern Arizona by the Mexican government during the 1820s and early 1830s had scarcely been awarded to their owners when the major Apache offensive began. Although between raids they were able to attend their herds, most of the grantees had ceased to reside on their ranches by 1840.[45] Exactly when they moved to more protected jurisdictions such as those of the frontier forts is unknown, but according to testimony taken by Surveyor General John Wasson and his associates in the 1880s, it occurred quite early for some.[46]

Rosa Ortiz, daughter of Canoa grantee Tomás Ortiz, told Wasson that the members of her family abandoned the Arivaca ranch when she was thirteen years old. That would have been in 1835, a likely year for Apache attacks throughout the region.[47] It may have been about that same time, according to other witnesses, when Ignacio and Eulalia Elías abandoned the Babocómari grant, which had been attacked in March of the previous year.[48]

The Ortiz family apparently did not actually live on their Canoa grant after the early 1830s, although they continued to run cattle there. Rosa testified that Indians burned their ranch house "when I was a little girl" and the family then moved into Tubac. Later, the Apaches also burned the house they occupied within the presidio. The title papers for the grant were apparently destroyed in that raid.

Another ranch said by witnesses to have been abandoned during the 1830s was the San Juan de las Boquillas y Nogales grant on the San Pedro River. Other testimony, for the most part, indicates simply that the grantees had ceased to reside on their property "sometime before the beginning of the war between the United States and Mexico in 1846."

The fact that the first Americans to enter the region at the time of the war found cattle in very large numbers grazing on grant lands suggests that the owners did not totally neglect their properties. The Ortiz brothers living at Tubac, for instance, were able to make occasional visits to their ranches at Canoa and Arivaca, even when Apache raiding was at its height. Other owners could venture out when the Indian situation was relatively quiet and round up a few animals for food. On the other hand, none could regularly perform such basic ranching chores as castrating the young male animals, and the Americans who began coming into the area in 1846 found herds composed almost exclusively of fierce, wild bulls.

8

Sonoran Politics and Indian Affairs

Although the treaties negotiated with the Apaches in 1836 might have brought Sonora a stretch of much needed peace, the internal political battles of the period so weakened the military forces of the state that the Indians had an open invitation to continue hostilities. Furthermore, an incident that took place in southwestern New Mexico in the spring of 1837 created new animosities that the presidial garrisons could not likely have controlled even if they had been at full strength and properly outfitted with ammunition and other supplies.

Figuring prominently in the New Mexico incident was John Johnson, an American merchant who had married a Mexican woman several years before and settled at the old town of Oposura (known as Moctezuma since 1828). In March, 1837, Apaches raided the small nearby settlement of Noria and Johnson headed a party that went after those responsible. Some accounts of the subsequent events maintain that Johnson's primary motive was to collect Apache scalps, which the Sonoran government was then paying bounties for. However, he may have been more interested in obtaining mules from the Apaches, whose herds were glutted with animals stolen from the Mexicans. The force he put together included seventeen other Americans, several of whom were also residents of Sonora, and five Mexican mule drivers.

Encountering a band of Apaches led by Chief Juan José Compá,

Johnson offered to trade them goods in return for safe conduct to Santa Rita del Cobre. Informed by a captive Mexican girl that the Indians planned to accept the trade items, then guide the Johnson party into an ambush, the Americans decided to strike first. On the morning of April 22nd, as the Indians examined the trade goods, Johnson and his men opened fire. When the battle was over, nineteen Indians were dead, among them Chief Juan José Compá and his brother Juan Diego.[1]

Following the incident, Chihuahua Governor José Joaquín Calvo encouraged professional scalp hunters by offering bounties for Apache forelocks. An American soldier-of-fortune named James Kirker was one of those who responded, and until Calvo's departure from office early in 1838, did well by his trade. However, Calvo's successor, José María Irigoyen, favored another approach to scalp-taking. Irigoyen thought the Mexican cause would be best served by turning the Indians against each other, so he negotiated a treaty with the Mogollon Apaches whereby they would be compensated for bringing in scalps of their old enemies, the Comanches. The plan, however, did not work out as Irigoyen had expected it to; by the summer of 1839, he was back to doing business with Kirker who had become a Mexican citizen in the meantime.[2]

The bounty policy—including compensation for the scalps of women and children, as well as warriors—kindled a hatred in the minds of the Apaches that would endure for the remainder of the century and perhaps longer. From this time on, it would be uncompromising warfare between the two groups.

While these events took place on the frontier, the struggle between the followers of Gándara and Urrea competed for attention. From the time he initiated his campaign in May, 1838, Gándara considered himself to have been restored to the office of governor. At times between May and November, however, Manuel Escalante y Arvizu also claimed the office.[3]

By the late summer of 1838, Gándara's forces, swelled in number by the Indian allies he had recruited, were gaining the upper hand. In November, with Manuel María himself leading them, the centralists won the decisive battle of the year against troops commanded by Antonio Narbona. Shortly thereafter, on November 20th, Escalante withdrew any claim he might have to the governorship and Gándara was undisputedly back on top.

At roughly the same time Narbona and Gándara were engaged

James Kirker, scalp hunter
(Newberry Library)

in battle, Urrea was miles away in Tampico where a part of that garrison had rebelled against the central government. With Gándara firmly established as chief executive of Sonora, Urrea's chances of returning to Sonora were greatly diminished and he spent much of the next two-and-a-half years fighting for the federalist cause in other parts of Mexico. From time to time, he would be captured and imprisoned by the centralists, but with help from his many friends in Durango he would gain his freedom and return to the fray.[4]

Well aware that Arizpe was the enemy stronghold, Gándara wasted no time in transferring the departmental capital elsewhere. The two largest cities in the state at that time were Hermosillo and Alamos. The latter was as much out of the question as Arizpe, for it was the home of the Almadas, relatives of Urrea who had financed much of his effort to hold on to the governorship. Gándara had friends among the wealthy businessmen of Hermosillo and nearby Guaymas, but he apparently felt more secure close to his devoted followers in San Miguel de Horcasitas. So he chose Ures, an important town near the site where the Sonora River bends southwestward in its course toward the Gulf of California, as his capital. By the end of 1838, Arizpe's long, if sometimes interrupted, tenure as the political heart of Sonora was over. During the next decade, the town's population would drop from more than 7,000 to barely over a thousand.

New Difficulties in the Papaguería

Although the people of the frontier continued to be occupied with keeping the Apaches at bay, the Indian battlefront was relatively calm during much of the first year of Gándara's administration. In part this situation may have been due to the alliances that the governor had previously made with the Yaquis and other native groups. Gándara did announce in August, 1839, that there would be a new general campaign against the Apaches led by Colonel Francisco Duque but little seems to have come from plans made at that time.[5]

Meanwhile, relationships between the Papagos and the local Mexicans continued to deteriorate in the Altar Valley and surrounding areas to the north and west. In the spring of 1840, a pitched battle took place between Mexican auxiliaries and Papagos from the Tecolote Valley, southwest of modern Sells near the present international boundary. At least twelve Indians and one Mexican lost their lives.

Leading up to the unfortunate encounter was a decision by Dionisio González, political chief at Altar, to intimidate Papago leaders with a major show of military strength. Accompanied by Rafael Moraga and 150 militiamen, as well as Father Antonio González (then stationed at Oquitoa), the Altar *jefe* confronted Tecolote leaders at a location known as Cóbota. In his initial dealings with the Indians, Señor González made little, if any, attempt to be diplomatic. Instead, he recited a series of complaints against the Papagos, who, having many complaints of their own, responding by attacking. The fight did not last long since the Indians were badly outgunned and outnumbered.[6] Angered by this event and perhaps considering the Altar civil and military officials to be federalist sympathizers, Gándara replaced both González and Moraga and instructed their successors to deal kindly with the Indians and seek peaceful relations with them. In spite of these good intentions, the situation improved little and early in the summer of 1840, the Mexicans learned that Yaqui Indians who had been working in the mines near Altar were preparing to join the militant Papagos in attacks on Mexican towns. By mid-July, the Indian uprising was in full swing, its principal fury directed against settlements in the Tubutama-Sáric section of the Altar Valley.

Although a special military force known as the "Permanent Section of Western Operations" had been formed at Altar to deal with the problem, the Indian campaigns were largely unsuccessful and a number of Mexicans lost their lives. Late in November, Gándara decided to confront the situation personally. Shortly after the middle of December, he was at Altar heading a large expeditionary force that included men drawn from the Sonora, San Miguel and San Ignacio river valleys.

The final battle of the 1840–1841 struggle occurred on January 14th in a canyon at the foot of Baboquívari Peak. The Mexican forces killed more than forty Papagos and recovered over a thousand head of livestock. They lost two men killed and thirty-one were wounded. That night, following burial of their dead, four Papago representatives met with the Mexican leaders to ratify a promise made earlier to maintain the peace thereafter.[7]

The Papago-Yaqui outbreak brought a new personality to Pimería Alta, a man who would figure importantly in military events throughout the remainder of the Mexican period in Arizona and whose efforts in 1860 to overthrow Governor Pesqueira would cost him his life. That man was Hilarión García who had directed the auxiliary infantry at the battle of Baboquívari and was appointed commander of the Permanent Section of Western Operations in May, 1841. One of his first acts after taking over the Altar post was to meet with the various rebel groups. In the course of these parleys, García learned of the discovery of three new gold placers in Papago country and that Chief Azul of the Gila River Pimas was conferring with the Papagos about a peace plan of his own.[8]

The Urrea-Gándara Feud Heats Up

While Gándara was playing the battlefield commander in the Altar region, two significant events took place that rekindled the Sonoran civil war. The first occurred on December 21st, 1840, when a group of citizens in the Arizpe area openly voiced their defiance of the Gándara regime and called for reinstatement of the federalist system.[9] The second came about a month later when General Urrea slipped back into Sonora from Durango and at the mining camp of Gavilanes, not far from Ures, issued a pronouncement against Gándara.

Lieutenant Colonel Ignacio Elías González was caught in the middle during the initial revival of Urrea sentiment. Despite being Urrea's uncle,[10] Elías had earlier secured an appointment as adjutant inspector to Colonel Francisco Duque, general commander of the military forces of Sonora and Sinaloa. Shortly before the Arizpe incident, Duque had written Elías that he was prepared to turn over the military command in Sonora to Governor Gándara whenever the governor indicated that he wanted it. By the time Gándara heard of Duque's offer he was already in the field, commanding the forces fighting the Papagos. From that point on, he apparently regarded himself as both governor and military commander.

Toward the end of December, Elías wrote Duque of the Arizpe affair. His letter and one written by Duque crossed in the mail. Duque's contained a piece of news that thickened the plot considerably. He informed his subordinate that Elías was now the Sonoran *comandante*, appointed to the position by the central government—on his recommendation. Elías received Duque's letter on February 5th and the following day went to Gándara, who was just back from the Altar front, to tell him about it. By this time, of course, the governor was aware that Urrea had returned and was trying to incite an uprising. He must also have known that Urrea and Elías were close kinsmen; and he certainly did not relish the thought of having his army under the control of any such individual. After a week had elapsed without Gándara informing Elías whether he would recognize him as the general commander, the old frontier veteran wrote the governor again. He informed Gándara that Duque had instructed him to put down the revolt in Sonora and to encourage any who felt they had grievances against the Sonoran administration to take them up with representatives of the central government.

Within a few days, Gándara responded that he regarded himself the Sonoran military commander, that the post had been turned over to him before Elías' appointment, and that he did not intend to step down. Furthermore, he asserted that he would rather be military commander than governor. Gándara accused Elías of having been present when the Arizpe incident occurred and of having done nothing about it.

The governor did not mention in his letter that two weeks before he had publicly branded Elías a traitor and had sent Lieutenant Colonel Fernando Cuesta to apprehend him. However, that fact would certainly have been known to Elías by the time he received Gándara's letter, for he and Cuesta were already trying to reach a settlement about their respective roles. Before they could reach an agreement, however, Cuesta was transferred to Michoacan on a temporary assignment.[11]

During the spring of 1841, Urrea and Gándara partisans squared off in a series of confrontations that turned out favorably for the Gandaristas. Once more, General Urrea sought refuge in Durango. Then in August, he and Santa Anna joined forces to initiate still another revolt against the central government. Conditions were favorable for such an insurrection, and the Tucson-born Urrea was about to see his star rise another time.

With help from his Sonoran comrade, Santa Anna returned to power in late October, 1841, and reappointed Colonel Duque to the military command of Sonora and Sinaloa. On November 3rd, he informed Gándara that he was no longer in charge of the Sonoran army. Believing that he would soon be removed from the governor's office as well, Gándara resigned. Within a week, he was replaced temporarily by José Lucas Picó, senior member of the new *junta*, who was one of the ex-governor's most implacable foes.[12]

Early in 1842, Urrea, whose rebellious exploits had cost him his official commission, was restored by Santa Anna to the rank of brigadier general.[13] A month later, on March 15th, Sonora's official press announced the general's appointment as governor and military commander of the state.[14] On May 6th, Urrea took charge of Sonora's military establishment and on the 1st of June he reoccupied the governor's chair.[15]

While the events were shaping up in Mexico City that would bring Urrea back to Sonora, the Apache situation on the frontier continued to deteriorate. The Indians of northern Chihuahua and western New Mexico were raiding farther south in Sonora than ever before. There was no money in the Sonoran treasury with which to pay the presidial soldiers or to supply them and their families with food; desertions were becoming commonplace. *El Voto de Sonora*, the official newspaper of Acting Governor José Lucas Picó, pub-

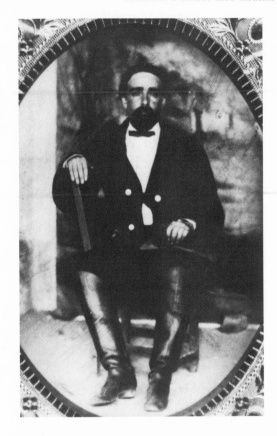

Ignacio Elías González, Tubac commander and owner of the San Juan de las Boquillas y Nogales land grant (Corella collection, courtesy of Carmen Pellat Sotomayor)

lished an article in January, 1842, stating that members of the Santa Cruz garrison were talking of deserting in mass and heading south to safer locations where they could make a living.[16] Picó commented that conditions were little, if any, different in the other presidios.

The boldness of the Apaches was well demonstrated in late February, 1842, when they rampaged through the Sonora River Valley, killing eight or nine people, most of them at Bacoachi where a garrison of Opatas had long been stationed. They were not halted until they reached the outskirts of Ures, the capital city.[17]

Following the announcement of Urrea's appointment, Gándara and his associates began conspiring with their confederates to frustrate once more the efforts of the Sonoran general. Not long after Urrea's arrival in Guaymas, they met with Yaquis at Gándara's Topahue hacienda to offer them arms and to encourage them to return to the battlefield against Urrea and his followers. Leader of the Indian delegation was a Yaqui known to the Mexicans as General Tomás who, only a few months before, had been a man with a price on his head—a price placed there by Manuel María Gándara himself.[18]

One of Urrea's first actions after assuming office was to announce that Indians aiding the *Gandaristas* would be deprived of the village lands previously given them.[19] Far from frightening the Yaquis, this announcement may have sparked a new uprising. On July 24th, a force of more than 600 warriors, commanded by Juan Bautista Gándara, stormed Hermosillo causing damage and casualties before they were repulsed.[20]

The action at Hermosillo officially began what is known in Sonoran history as the Rebellion of 1842. Over the next several months, forces under Gándara and Urrea would meet on many battlefields throughout the state, usually with unhappy consequences for the Gandaristas. Still, they kept fighting and in mid-December even made an attempt to overpower the garrison protecting Ures.[21]

Controlling the Indians

In spite of the civil war, Urrea wasted no time in making plans for an offensive against the Apaches. Much of the responsibility for this effort fell on the shoulders of Colonel José María Elías González, who had been fighting Apaches longer than any of his fellow officers.[22] Aiding him as field commander was veteran Antonio Narbona, son of Tucson's old presidio *comandante* who had died a dozen years before.

The initial effort against the Apaches was to begin October 26th from Tres Alamos.[23] Lieutenant Roque Ibarra, acting commanding officer at Tubac, was to lead a combined force of men from Tucson, Santa Cruz, and his own garrison to a rendezvous with Colonel Narbona at the San Pedro River location. The problems Ibarra encountered in getting underway demonstrate clearly the pitiful condition of the presidios in 1842. On October 28th, two days after the scheduled rendezvous, he wrote Elías González to explain why he was getting a late start.

After receiving his instructions from the general command, Ibarra had contacted the *comandantes* of the other presidios to make sure they knew what was expected of them. Comadurán at Tucson was to supply forty men, some cattle, and 100 *fanegas* (160 bushels) of *pinole*, as well as a quantity of salt. Saturnino Limón, commander at Santa Cruz, was to furnish as many men as he could spare and march with them to Tubac. Ibarra, meanwhile, would muster whatever troops and supplies he could. When Limón reached Tubac, they would march together to Tucson.

On October 17th, Comadurán informed Ibarra that he needed at least thirty cattle hides to make bags for carrying the *pinole*. Furthermore, he could not provide 100 *fanegas* without leaving the presidial residents destitute; he could spare only sixty. The presidio was entirely out of salt but Comadurán sent a trooper to Santa Cruz to borrow some. His messenger was also able to buy twenty cattle hides from private parties.

On October 20th, Limón pulled into Tubac with twenty men. Four were ill, however, and were allowed to return home. Fourteen of the others had disabled weapons and two had none at all. Ibarra gave them 570 cartridges, forty flints and two muskets from the Tubac supply. On the following day they departed for Tucson but Ibarra was able to take only one man from his own garrison. Of the seven other soldiers on the post, three were sick and four were needed to look after the arms and ammunition left behind for the residents' self-defense.

At Tucson more bad luck awaited them. They had so few serviceable arms that they dared not go into battle. It was necessary, therefore, to call upon the Tucson armorer to make repairs before they could leave. Furthermore, the cattle they had planned to take along for meat had not been rounded up, and the number of available hides was not sufficient to make all the needed bags. On October 25th, Ibarra sent a hurried message to Narbona to explain their delay. The situation was additionally complicated because Limón had brought along only thirty pack mules, not enough to carry the *pinole*. There were ten mules at Tucson but the troopers needed these to transport other supplies.

In spite of all the obstacles mentioned by Ibarra in his letter, the soldiers finally did get away from Tucson on October 28th and presumably joined forces with Narbona either late that day or early the next.

The following month, Captain Comadurán had his own set of Apache problems that he would surely have preferred to do without. On the last day of November, Papagos from the villages of Santa Ana, Santa Rosa and Lojia—accompanied by their governors—appeared at the captain's quarters. They were all armed and had somehow managed to get by the presidial guards who usually confiscated weapons from Indians planning to enter the fort. The Papagos presented charges to Comadurán against the peaceful Apaches living on Tucson's outskirts, maintaining that the Apaches had stolen horses from San Xavier del Bac and turned them over to hostile kinsmen.

Convinced of the innocence of the *Apache mansos*, Comadurán informed the visitors that they were mistaken. He pointed out that five of the Tucson Apaches had, a short time before, been hunting in the Santa Rita Mountains and had encountered two horses hobbled and hidden in a box canyon. They recognized these as animals stolen from one of the settlements and brought them to the Tucson *comandante*. The following day, hostile Apaches did raid the San Xavier horse herd and retreated through the same area where they had previously hidden the stolen horses. Papagos chasing the raiders into the mountains had uncovered the tracks made by the peaceful Apaches and, thinking they were the culprits, followed them to the presidio.

Comadurán told the Papagos that if they could prove their version of the story he would take appropriate action against the Tucson Apaches and try to recover the property the Papagos had lost. Refusing to believe him, the Indians dashed from his quarters and prepared to attack the Apaches. Comadurán ran after them and placed himself between the two groups. Ignoring his presence, the Papagos hurled themselves upon the Apaches who refused to fight back. The captain called for help and soldiers and *vecinos* poured from the fort to bring the situation under control. Remarkably, no one was hurt.

The next day, the Papago governors returned to the presidio— this time unarmed—and apologized. Comadurán accepted their apology, but warned them against ever again trying to enter the fort carrying their arms. He told them they should thereafter leave all weapons at El Pueblito or he would regard them as enemies.

In reporting these events to Colonel José María Elías González, the Tucson *comandante* expressed concern that what was taking place might be simply a prelude to more serious confrontations between the Papagos and the Mexicans. He pleaded with his superior to send more men and supplies to the fort, pointing out that the handful of settlers who remained in Tucson were without weapons to resist Indian attacks. Furthermore, he observed, the other nearby presidios (Santa Cruz, Altar and Tubac) had no men of their own to send to Tucson's defense.[24] The ink was scarcely dry on Comadurán's report when Papagos placed the mines at Quitovac under siege. Lorenzo Martínez, chief civil officer of the Altar subprefecture, reported this development to Urrea on December 21st, 1842.[25] He wrote that the Papagos had been in communication with hostile Yaquis concerning a joint offensive against the Mexicans. Noting that Urrea had now succeeded in bringing the Yaquis under control, Martínez suggested the governor give his full attention to the Papagos.

Shortly before Urrea received the message about the Papagos, three of his friends serving in the national legislature in Mexico City informed their colleagues about events in Sonora, placing heavy emphasis on Gándara's actions in starting a "racial" war. Two of the men—Ignacio and Anselmo Zúñiga—had, like Urrea, spent some of their childhood years in Tucson.[26] Joining them in praising Urrea and condemning Gándara was Manuel María Gaxiola, kinsman of the former governor of Occidente. They began their campaign in October when they met with high officials of the Mexican government to plead with them to leave Urrea in office. A month later, they wrote the minister of war to urge him to send Urrea 500 men and enough military supplies to bring the situation in Sonora under control.[27]

Comadurán in the Eye of the Whirlwind

For Captain Antonio Comadurán of the Tucson presidio, the first six months of 1843 were among the busiest of his life. He began the year by making another plea to his cousin Colonel José María Elías González. "The soldiers have no cartridge boxes or saddles," he wrote, "and we have but twenty horses [up from ten three months earlier] for eighty-eight men. The next time the Apaches attack we may have to defend ourselves with lances, something we cannot do very effectively because we have so few of those weapons also." He concluded by noting that the presidial company was short eleven men and nineteen muskets.[28]

By 1843, don José Antonio Comadurán had been in Tucson for a quarter of a century. Approaching his forty-sixth birthday, he could claim more experience fighting Apaches than any other active presidial commander. Frustrated as he was at the time he wrote Elías, he would not likely have predicted that the situation would soon grow much worse.

Captain Comadurán was married to Ana María Ramírez, sister of merchant Teodoro Ramírez who so frequently came to the rescue of the *comandante* when there was a shortage of food for the troops, or when someone was needed to translate during a meeting with the Pimas or Papagos. From his father, who served many years as Fray Arriquibar's translator, Teodoro had learned the Indian dialects. Comadurán's brother-in-law and ally would often take part in the events that captured the captain's attention during 1843.

Early in February, the Tucson *comandante* saddled up and rode southward to Tubac. Accompanying him were a corporal and eight privates from his troop, plus four peaceful Apaches who had by now become an indispensable part of his military force. Their immediate purpose was to escort Father Antonio González to Tubac and Tumacácori, so that he might perform his sacramental duties for the Indians ahd *vecinos* in the area. This was to be González' last round. Sometime after his February visit to Tucson and Tubac, the old Franciscan, last of his order in Pimería Alta, would pass to his reward.[29]

After conferring with Lieutenant Roque Ibarra, still at Tubac on detached service from his post at Pitic, Comadurán and his small force headed for Arizpe where they hoped to obtain the arms and ammunition they desperately needed.[30] During the three weeks that they were away, the Apaches swooped down on the Sópori ranch and absconded with a drove of mares and other livestock. Fourteen of the civilians from the surrounding area took to the field in pursuit. Unsuccessful in their efforts, they called on the Indians at San Xavier for help. The Papagos took up the chase, and at a place known as Amole they overtook the fleeing raiders. All the livestock were recovered and one Apache was killed. On February 28th, a week after the Sópori raid, Captain Comadurán was back at Tubac on his way home from Arizpe.[31]

Hardly out of the saddle at Tucson, Comadurán again wrote to Elías González about the Papago situation. As on other occasions, he sent his commanding officer both official and personal letters.

They were addressed to Elías in his new position as *Segundo Jefe de la Comandancia General*, or Second Chief of the General Command. Urrea had named his kinsman to the post the month before.[32]

Comadurán reported that the restless Papagos of the Altar Valley were finding willing allies among the Pimas along the Gila River. About the only Gila leaders steadfastly refusing to join the proposed new rebellion were Culo Azul[33] of the Pimas and Antonio, the Maricopa chief. There were apparently some Altar Valley Papagos, also, who did not want to be involved in a war with the Mexicans, and Comadurán stated that they were settling in among the Indians at Tubac, Santa Cruz and San Ignacio. As a result, both they and their hosts were subjected to a good deal of pressure from the more militant Papagos who advocated a general rebellion.

The Tucson *comandante* made reference again to the sad state of his garrison and called upon Elías to send him a small cannon, fifty muskets, ammunition and lances. He also mentioned the importance of providing weapons for the civilians and the peaceful Apaches.

Less than a week after sending the letters, Comadurán discovered some of the Papago arm-twisting taking place under his very nose. On March 10th, a man deemed to be an emissary of the hostile group was arrested at El Pueblito. When the captain asked him what he was doing in that village, the Papago responded that he had come to attend a scalp dance being held to celebrate the slaying of an enemy Apache two weeks earlier (following the Sópori raid). Highly skeptical of the story, Comadurán jailed the man. The following morning, the Papago asked to see the *comandante* and informed him that he had a different tale to tell. The Indian confirmed that an uprising was under way and that Gila River Pimas, except for Azul, Antonio, and their closest followers, were involved. He told Comadurán of the extensive participation of Papagos in a successful attack on Oquitoa a short time before and said that raiding parties were now going out at regular intervals under the leadership of Pimas and Papagos from different locations. One of the leaders he mentioned appears to have been a man identified earlier as an agent of Manuel María Gándara.

In a letter written to Elías from Tucson on March 12th, Comadurán included all the details.[34] He also informed his cousin that he was undertaking a labor of diplomacy that he hoped would restore peace to the Papaguería. Following the release of the Papago prisoner, the *comandante* had dispatched a messenger from the village of Santa Rosa to inform all the Papago leaders of nearby towns that the Mexican government would not punish those persons who clearly separated themselves from the rebellion. He encouraged them to do so immediately so the troops would make no mistake about their loyalties.

Comadurán also informed Elías that he was planning to send another emissary with a similar message to the Indians of the Gila River and he had hoped to engage the Pima governor of El Pueblito for that task because he was related to them. However, the governor told the captain's interpreter[35] he considered them a bunch of barbarians and would have nothing to do with them. It was the interpreter's opinion that the Indian leader would feel more comfortable among the Apaches.

Comadurán's March 12th letter crossed in the mail with a circular put out the following day by Elías. The purpose of the circular was to inform the presidial commanders that the Apache campaign, which had gotten off to a tentative beginning three months earlier, would have to be postponed until August because Urrea was in Guaymas trying to straighten out the situation there. Gándara's old ally and financial backer, Manuel Iñigo Ruiz, had gained control of the export-import trade over the preceding three years, and Urrea was determined to break up his monopoly.[36] In the process he would make himself even more hated by the Sonoran capitalist, especially after jailing Iñigo for four months without preferring charges or granting him any kind of trial.[37]

In his circular, Elías also stated that it was his intention to strengthen the forces of the Fronteras, Santa Cruz and Tucson presidios so they could protect the populace until the Apache offensive ended successfully. A short time after receiving his copy of the document, Comadurán again wrote his cousin to say that he would do his best "to hold the fort," but that his horses were in poor condition, and he could put together only twenty men for any kind of field campaign.[38]

While all the correspondence was prepared and circulated, Urrea—in spite of other duties—put the final touches on a plan to do away once and for all with the Papago threat.[39] The campaign was to begin early in April under the direction of Lieutenant Colonel Felipe Flores.

Departing from Altar on April 4th with a large force of regulars and auxiliaries, Flores headed for the Baboquívari Mountains, the same general location where Gándara had defeated the Papagos two years earlier. The first skirmish with the Indians took place on April 10th. In spite of encirclement tactics by Flores' troops and those commanded by Lieutenant Colonel José María Martínez (apparently out of retirement from Tubac), the Papagos escaped. However, they left behind a large quantity of stolen livestock that were rounded up and taken to Altar.

A major engagement between Flores and the Indians occurred on April 20th with the Mexicans the victors. Six Papagos were slain in the encounter and the Mexican troops lost their surgeon, an Englishman or American named Charles Grimes. Several of Flores' men were wounded seriously. Singled out for special mention by the commanding officer in his report to Colonel Elías González was Ensign Lorenzo Rodríguez, a veteran of the Tucson garrison, who led a detachment of cavalry that chased the hostiles for fifteen miles.[40]

Documentation about other aspects of the Papago campaign is scanty but it is known that by early May, Flores and his forces had destroyed the will of the Papagos to continue the struggle. Many had fled northward to take refuge with the Gila River Pimas and Maricopas. By that time, those tribes had also lost their taste for warfare with the Mexicans.

Sometime late in April, Captain Comadurán sent Carlos Castro from his garrison to the Gila River with a message for Chief Azul. The Tucson presidial commander, perhaps in response to his March 12th letter concerning his diplomatic plans, had been authorized by Governor Urrea to offer amnesty to the Pima and Papago rebels, provided they were willing to abide by certain conditions. On his arrival, Castro presented himself to the Pima leader and explained the contents of the official letter that he carried. Following their conversation, Azul agreed to send messengers to all the Gila River towns.

When the leaders of the different Pima communities were assembled, Azul passed on the terms of the letter. One by one, they expressed their feelings of shame and regret for all that had occurred, many implying that Gándara's agents had been involved in the conspiracy. Speaking for the Maricopas, Antonio stated that they, too, begged forgiveness and promised never to rise against the Mexicans again. He then told Castro that he or his representatives would come to Tucson for a peace conference, but only after completion of a campaign against the Apaches who shortly before had killed a Maricopa woman. One of the Pima governors then stated that he had in his possession a captive Mexican woman whom he would free as soon as the Mexicans released two sons of his whom they had captured.

Upon receiving the news from Tucson of Castro's successful visit to the Gila, Colonel Elías González ordered Lieutenant Colonel Flores to leave Altar well protected and march with 250 men to Tucson. While there, the commander of the Papago campaign was to coordinate the peace negotiations with Captain Comadurán who "better than anyone else knows the northern region and its tribes."[41]

Sometime in the month of June, 1843, Flores rode into Tucson at the head of one of the largest contingents of soldiers and auxiliaries ever to visit the presidio. The fact that Elías had commanded Flores to bring so many men with him is probably related to a recommendation made earlier in the year by Comadurán, who wrote his superior that the best way to assure permanent peace with the Papagos was to intimidate them with an awesome show of force. Whether the size of the Mexican contingent was a factor in the final peace negotiations is not known, but when Flores marched out of Tucson, warfare between the Mexicans and the Pimas and Papagos permanently ended.[42]

The Condition of the Missions in 1843

When the the 1843 struggle began, the Christian Indians of the Arizona missions had been through fifteen years of neglect from church and state authorities. Two reports on the condition of the missions during the years of conflict reveal such deterioration that it seems indeed remarkable that the mission Indians chose to resist the urgings of their wilder brethren and remain on the sidelines.

The secretary of the Sonora department requested the mission reports in February, 1843, and the following month, the San Ignacio sub-prefect passed the request on to the justices of the peace at Tucson and Tubac. Both local officials responded before the end of May and on the last day of that month, Sub-Prefect Joaquín Quiroga transmitted their replies to the secretary, who was in Guaymas where Governor Urrea had established temporary headquarters.[43]

The Tubac *juez de paz* noted that the Tumacácori church was in a good state of repair but that portions of the adjacent convent, constructed in 1821, had either fallen down or were threatened with imminent ruin. The mission fields were overgrown with mesquite trees and other scrubby vegetation and the one lying most distant from the village was visited only occasionally by a few Indians ("*unos cuantos*") who went there to irrigate small plots. None of the fields was being rented to outsiders and none had been sold. The Calabazas pastures and fields were abandoned, as was the case with those at Guevavi and Sonoita. Only wild cattle (*broncos*) grazed on the hillsides.

The situation at San Xavier was not much better. The church was still in good condition, although the arches were fissured and weatherbeaten from the heavy rains of summer (*las aguas*) and the slow, steady drizzles of winter, or *equipatas*. The humidity had caused the paint to deteriorate, and the Tucson justice of the peace expressed concern that if no priests were appointed to supervise repairs, the ruin of the church might not be far off.

The convent was already well on its way to destruction, according to the reporter. In two of the rooms, the gallerys had collapsed, roof beams were broken, and the matting over the beams was rotting away. The wall surrounding the priests' orchard and garden had fallen, and the ground was littered with branches from fruit trees that were no longer producing. The San Xavier governor was cultivating a part of the garden and about one-eighth of the acreage previously devoted to growing crops for the support of the priests and their projects. The homes of local residents and visitors from Santa Ana village—few of whom planted anything—dotted the landscape.

The report is critical of Father Rafael Díaz, the circuit priest who had died a short time before. According to the Tucson justice of the peace, he had not only neglected the church and other buildings but had carried away the furnishings, some of which he had sold. He had also sold or otherwise disposed of the mission livestock, leaving the Indians with no oxen to plow their fields. Friar Díaz had also appropriated five of the best animals from the wild horses and mules that the Papagos rounded up and placed in corrals, depriving the Indians of the benefits of their labors.

The Tucson official does not provide information in his report about the number of Indians living at San Xavier but he does indicate that few remained at El Pueblito. He notes that "the mis-

Sketch of the ruined mission of Tumacácori in the 1850s (Gray, *Report*)

sion fields with their abundant irrigation water are cultivated by six Indians, the only ones still here, and by residents of this presidio who have not paid any rent since 1840 because they were freed from doing so by the deceased Father Rafael and by his successor Antonio González." The reporter goes on to comment that prior to 1839, the Tucson residents had paid one *fanega* of grain for each *fanega* of seed they planted, although the proceeds seem not to have been used for the benefit "either of the mission or the Indians."

Tucson's justice of the peace supplies a description, also, of the condition of the mission buildings at El Pueblito. The roof of the church had already collapsed due to broken and rotted beams; the adobe walls were full of cracks; and the sacristy and baptistry had lost all doors. Still, the official felt the church could be restored with the aid of a stone buttress and some new woodwork.

The convent or mission house was in somewhat better condition, although the roof was weak with rotten matting and broken drainage channels. The wooden beams were generally in good condition, but without needed repairs, the first-floor roof might collapse, ultimately destroying the building.

The Tucson justice of the peace mentions that one of the convent rooms contained statues of saints, among them a "majestic representation of the miraculous image of Our Savior of Esquipulas."[44] He faulted Father Rafael for having lost the key to the saints' storage room and not having bothered to replace it. He also observed that the priest had taken the clerical robes, sacramental vessels, tabernacle and baptismal font to the church in Imuris. Furthermore, he had sold one of the presbitery doors to a Tucsonan who wanted to use part of it for a saddle tree. (The El Pueblito governor had traded two other doors to a *Tucsonense* for a yoke to use with oxen in plowing his fields.) The Tucson justice also accused Father Díaz of investing some of the rental income from El Pueblito fields in the establishment of a winery[45] and of appropriating copper kettles for his own use. The mission, so far as he could see, received no benefit from all this.

A New Campaign Against the Apaches

Late in May, 1843, at about the time Sub-Prefect Quiroga forwarded the Tucson and Tubac reports to his superior in Guaymas, *El Voto de Sonora*, the state's official newspaper, praised Governor Urrea for his successful campaigns against the Yaquis and Papagos and predicted that extensive cotton farms would soon dot the landscape of the Yaqui and Mayo river valleys. "However," the editor warned, "there are still the Apaches to be dealt with."[46] Threat of Apache raiding from the northeast was considered to be particularly serious. The Mogollon and Gileño bands were willing to work out peaceful arrangements with the government of Chihuahua, but there were many obstacles to doing the same with Sonoran officials. Nevertheless, in June, 1843, while the Papago peace conclave was in progress in Tucson, Governor Urrea met at Guaymas with several of the Mogollon and Gileño chiefs. Although deals were apparently struck, they did not produce an end to the incessant raiding against the frontier towns.[47]

As fearsome as the attacks from the east were, the threat from the Pinal Apaches and their allies was of greater and more immediate concern to the residents of the Santa Cruz and Altar valleys. Early in June, 1843, Francisco Narbona, military commander of the Santa Cruz section of the northern line, began assembling forces to continue the offensive begun the previous autumn. It was his intention to take to the field before the end of the month but as with earlier expeditions, the Mexicans encountered delays.[48]

Narbona and the other presidio commanders had been instructed

to round up cattle on the San Pedro Ranch to supply the troops
with beef. When they set out to do so, they found the cattle too wild
to gather. As on other occasions, Tucsonan Teodoro Ramírez came
to the rescue, making animals available from his private herd. More
than a year later, Captain Antonio Comadurán, Ramírez' brother-
in-law, was still trying to get the general command to repay the
debt.[49]

The offensive got underway on June 29th, not long after the
conclusion of the Papago peace treaty. Colonel Antonio Narbona,
principal commander of the northern line, reported the results to
Colonel Elías González on July 8th.[50] The force he directed had
been comparatively large—241 soldiers, auxiliaries and Indian allies. They came from a wide range of communities, including some
such as Bavispe and Bacerac that had not previously been represented in this part of Sonora. The peaceful Apaches were drawn
from Fronteras, Tucson and Tubac; the professional soldiers on the
expedition were members of the presidial garrisons at Fronteras,
Santa Cruz and Tucson.

Setting out from Tucson late in the afternoon, Narbona's men
marched eastward toward the San Pedro, probably skirting the
south end of Rincon Peak. Twenty-four hours later, they saw their
first Apaches, who stood on ridges high above them and made
insulting gestures. The Indians shouted that they were strong and
rich and had no need for peace. They boasted of the many head of
livestock they possessed and of their arms and ammunition, some of
which they claimed to have obtained from Americans in New Mexico. Narbona sent a small contingent of troops to challenge them
but the Apaches vanished and were not seen again.

On July 1st, Narbona's force camped near Tres Alamos while a
small party explored the region to determine whether it was safe to
proceed. Sighting no Apaches, they moved northward along the
San Pedro River headed for the Gila. The next evening, they were
again the targets of insulting signs and remarks from their enemies.

The battle finally got underway on July 3rd when a large group
of Apaches attacked the Mexicans and their Indian allies head on.
Since frontal assaults of this kind were unusual, one may infer that
the Apaches were supremely confident that their appearance would
send their adversaries fleeing. Narbona's scouts had sighted them,
however, and the colonel was ready. His infantry took the offensive
and isolated fifteen Apaches (including two women and a boy) who

resisted fiercely but were wiped out. Their companions fled into the surrounding mountains. It could hardly be classified as a major victory but Narbona apparently considered it enough to give the enemy pause. He began the march back to Tucson the following day. His losses were two men wounded. One of them was a friendly Apache from Fronteras named Juan, whom the colonel cited for bravery.

Troopers from Tubac were conspicuous for their absence during the campaign of early July, 1843. The reason is quite obvious from the monthly post reports. The entire garrison included only thirty-two men that month and all but ten were on detached service. The post had no permanent commander, the last, veteran Salvador Moraga, having retired on May 1st, 1842. Lieutenant Roque Ibarra of Pitic was still filling in when Colonel Narbona led his troops down the San Pedro, but he would soon depart and leave the presidio in the hands of Sergeant Gerónimo Errán (also spelled Herrán), a member of the Tucson garrison, who was one of the sons of Nicolás de la Errán, commander of the San Rafael Company a half century earlier.

The 1843 post reports[51] clearly establish that the most numerous residents of Tubac at that time were peaceful Apaches. In his first report of 1843, Ibarra counted 169 of them, including forty-nine men, fifty-three women and sixty-seven children. This did not change until November, when Sergeant Errán reported an increase of two children, bringing the total to 171.

Sometime during 1843, the residents of Santa Cruz suffered their most devastating blow from the Apaches. Many ranchers from that community were gathered at the location called La Boca de Noria (present-day Lochiel) when Apaches in great numbers swept down, killing at least thirty and escaping with an exceptionally large quantity of livestock. Concepción Elías, who was a prisoner of the Apaches for two years, testified to Surveyor General John Wasson that most of those who died at La Boca de Noria—including his father—were *parcioneros* ("partners" or "shareholders") in the San Rafael de la Zanja land grant.[52] Ramón Romero, the only *parcionero* whose name appears on the grant's title, escaped the slaughter. The Apaches continued raiding in the San Rafael Valley during 1843 and by the end of that year ranching in the area had ceased.

9

Urrea Wins in Sonora, Gándara in Mexico City

Despite his victories on the battlefield in the months after returning to Sonora, General Urrea was unable to end the feud that had divided the state for so long. Gándara renewed his intrigues with the Indians following the peace treaty with the Pimas and Papagos, and in the late summer of 1843 he persuaded the Yaquis to undertake a new offensive. Early in September a large force of Indians, accompanied by other Gandaristas, launched a furious assault on Guaymas. They were repulsed by units of Urrea's army assisted by local civilians who favored the federalist cause.[1]

Not long after the fight at Guaymas, Gándara's partisans tried to capture the capital city of Ures. During the struggle, Pedro Bautista Aguayo, who had served briefly as governor before the newly appointed Urrea reached Sonora in 1842, was killed by Gándara associates.[2] When they failed to seize the capital, Gandaristas ravaged the countryside. They suffered several defeats during the fall of 1843, including one at Tepupa that cost them more than 200 men. Gándara went into hiding for a short time, then returned with an army of nearly 1,500 and engaged Urrea's forces in a major battle at Mátape on the 21st of November. Losing this battle, also, the frustrated ex-governor and his followers headed northwest into the San Miguel Valley, where they confronted their foes anew at Opodepe in December.

According to some accounts, Gándara had taken seventy-three

hostages at Matape who were to be executed in the event he lost the battle at Opodepe. Lose he did, and the execution apparently took place as scheduled; however, the number surrendering their lives was twelve, rather than seventy-three.[3] The Opodepe defeat was so devastating that the Gándara forces were not able to mount a serious threat on the battlefield thereafter. Instead, they wisely chose to pursue the fighting elsewhere. Mexico City was now their arena of choice.

During the first few months of 1844, while the eastern villages of Sonora were under constant siege from the Apaches, Gándara and Urrea backers confronted each other in the capital. In the process, they managed to convert the Sonoran squabble from a local power struggle into a national nuisance. Both factions had their supporters and neither suffered from a lack of detractors. Spokesmen for Urrea repeatedly condemned their opponents for having touched off a "racial" war in Sonora, whereas the Gándara partisans portrayed Urrea as an unstable revolutionary. As the debate raged, more and more officials of the central government began to draw the conclusion that Sonora was not big enough for both Gándara and Urrea, and that choosing between them was impossible since one was as bad as the other. The growing sentiment was perhaps best summarized by General José María Tornel, Mexican minister of war and the navy, who told the Congress in January, 1844:

> In the Sonoran war, the struggle is not one of causes but of persons; and these persons are selfish and cruel—execrable in all aspects. . . . Might talks, might prevails, and no effort is made even to find excuses that could put a better face on the acts of violence that take place. In Sonora . . . there is a most urgent necessity . . . to reestablish society and afterwards to organize it. Those communities in which the elements of social order do not exist cannot enjoy the benefits of civil government.

Not long after General Tornel's statement, the Urrea-Gándara war came close to spilling over into neighboring Chihuahua. Following the defeats suffered in the late fall of 1843, some of Gándara's closest supporters and advisors, including a Spaniard named Anselmo Larrondo, took refuge in the Chihuahua mining town of Ocampo. The sub-prefect of Sahuaripa, a nearby Sonoran community, attempted to have the Gandaristas extradicted to his jurisdiction. When Ocampo officials turned him down, he threatened to invade Chihuahua and forcibly remove them. The Ocampans then armed themselves and prepared to resist the invasion.[4]

Such incidents finally stimulated the central government to act. On April 1st, the national congress decreed that all who had participated in the Sonoran disturbances would be granted amnesty provided they lay down their arms within a prescribed period; the central government would dictate the measures required to restore order to the state. General Francisco Ponce de León, governor and military commander of Sinaloa, was named to fill both positions in Sonora. He relieved Urrea on May 21st.

Events on the Frontier

In June, 1844, just a month after General Ponce de León took charge of the Sonoran government in Ures, the residents of the Santa Cruz Valley learned that they would soon be hearing the sacraments from a new priest. Trinidad García Rojas had been named parish priest at San Ignacio and he would shortly become the first secular clergyman to attend the spiritual needs of the people at Tucson, Tubac and Santa Cruz, the most northerly and most isolated Sonoran communities.[5]

Escorting the priest on his rounds was one of the important assignments for the frontier presidio soldiers and post commanders sometimes also chose to ride along. García Rojas made his first escorted journey to the Santa Cruz Valley in late August and early September, 1844. He reached Tumacácori on August 28th and paused there long enough to baptize three infant girls, all more than a month old. The initial entry in his register records the name of Paula, daughter of José Sánchez and Carmen Bojórquez. The girl's godparents were Bruno Ríos and María Juana Sandoval. The Sandoval and Sánchez names appear elsewhere on the register, along with Soto, Cruz and Romero. Although the families at Tumacácori may have been few in 1844, the location was by no means abandoned. Nevertheless, the Indians remaining there did not realize that the entire property had been classified as an abandoned mission site and had been sold at public auction in Guaymas four months earlier. The buyer was Francisco Alejandro Aguilar, Manuel María

Gándara's brother-in-law. Gándara would later develop a sheep ranch there.[6]

From Tumacácori, Father García Rojas moved on to Tubac, where on August 29th and 30th, he baptized fifteen infants, among them a tame Apache girl.[7] The family names that the priest recorded in his register included several that had been represented in the region since Spanish times: Sosa, Otero, Orozco, Romero, Ortega, Herreras and Cruz. Also on the list were José María Martínez and his wife Felipa Hirigolla. They were godparents to a daughter of José Corrales and Andrea Irigolla; and they also baptized a daughter of their own named Juana María who had been born six months and twenty days earlier. Manuel Otero and his wife, María Clara Martínez, also baptized a daughter whom they named María Manuela.[8]

García Rojas spent an entire week at Tucson, arriving there on September 1st. One of the first children he baptized at the presidio was a son of Teodoro Ramírez and María de los Angeles Salazar, whom they named José Francisco de Paula Ramón. He had been born nearly five months before on April 2. Teodoro's joy must have been great, for he was almost fifty-three years old and this was his first child.[9] Godparents for the infant boy were Mariano Salazar and Rosa Ortiz Elías, both cousins of María de los Angeles.[10]

The day after the baptism of Teodoro's son, Father García officiated at a similar ceremony for a daughter of one of Teodoro's favorite nephews, Rafael Ramírez.[11] Rafael and his wife, Petra Ocoboa, named their child María Florencia; in later years she would become the wife of Tucson miller James Lee. Also baptized on that day was María Petra Alcantar, infant daughter of Juan María Santa Cruz and Manuela Bórquez. She, too, was destined for marriage to a prominent Anglo-American, Hiram S. Stevens.

During the first week of September, 1844, Father García Rojas baptized a total of twenty-one children in Tucson. He then moved to San Xavier, baptizing three more. He was briefly in Tubac again on September 9th before winding up his tour at Santa Cruz on September 11th. It would be almost a year before he would visit the Santa Cruz Valley settlements again.

Although the priests were always welcome, Father García Rojas was in Tucson at a rather bad time for Captain Comadurán in 1844. On September 5th, while the priest was busy with his sacramental duties, friendly Apaches informed the *comandante* that they had

Baptismal register signed by Father García Rojas in 1844. At the top of the page is a record of the baptism of José Francisco de Paula, first son of Teodoro Ramírez (Magdalena Parish Archive) discovered the tracks of their hostile brethren in the Peña Blanca area. Comadurán wasted no time in gathering a force to investigate. He left the presidio at midafternoon with fifteen soldiers, twenty *vecinos* and twenty friendly Apaches. Tubac's commanding officer, Ensign Gerónimo Errán, who happened to be in Tucson on leave, accompanied the expedition.

At noon on September 7th, the Tucson party encountered the enemy in the Atascosa Mountains and skirmished with them. Four Apaches were slain and three were wounded. Two of Comadurán's men also suffered injuries but none was killed. The leader of the Apaches informed Comadurán of his desire for peace and agreed to accompany the *comandante* on the return trip to Tucson. He also informed the Captain that another Apache war party of about the same size as his was on its way to raid farther south in Sonora.

The day following the battle, Comadurán reached Tubac and hurriedly sent messengers south to the San Ignacio area to warn of possible attacks. He then returned to Tucson, arriving about four in the afternoon with a force of men who were completely exhausted from their ordeal. Two days later, September 11th, Comadurán learned that the second Apache force had raided the Búsani Ranch southwest of modern Nogales and escaped with about sixty horses and mules. His informants reported that the Indians intended to head next for the Babocómari area, passing to the south of Tucson.

Comadurán assembled forty men and proceeded to a point where he thought he could intercept the raiders. They reached their destination on September 12th and waited three days without sighting any hostile Indians. Following his return to Tucson on the 16th, the captain learned that the Apaches had taken another route to the north of the presidio. In reporting these incidents to Colonel Elías González, Captain Comadurán lauded the valor of his men, singling out Ensign Errán for special mention. The Tubac commander, he said, had rescued a peaceful Apache who had been captured by the enemy. Seizing the captor by the hair, Errán dispatched him with a thrust of his lance.[12]

Two weeks after his futile effort to engage the Apaches who had raided the Búsani Ranch, Comadurán had another opportunity to avenge losses suffered by Mexicans of that region. Early in the morning on September 29th, two members of the Tubutama militia (*los cívicos*) rode into the presidio to report that a large body of

Apaches had struck the ranch again, killing eleven of its residents, capturing one woman and escaping with a large herd of cattle and horses.

Within two hours, Comadurán was in the saddle at the head of a force of fifty-nine soldiers, *vecinos* and *Apaches mansos*. They moved this time toward the area the hostile Indians had traversed on their return from the previous Búsani raid. Initially, they were unable to find any sign of the Apaches but late that evening a reconnaissance party uncovered a fresh trail. Before midnight, the captain was on the move again. However, before departure he sent some of the most exhausted men back to the fort. Only forty accompanied him on the second leg of the journey. They had travelled but a short distance when a heavy rain began and continued for over an hour. They pushed on with the greatest difficulty, only to be hit with another shower an hour or so after the first ended.

Shortly before dawn, Captain Comadurán learned from his acting adjutant, Corporal Solano León, that only ten horses were in any condition to go on. León reported that the troopers in the rear were slogging through the mud leading their animals.[13] Since the enemy was nearby, Comadurán decided to take his strongest men and best horses and push ahead. He chose eight cavalrymen and ten foot soldiers to accompany him, ordering those who remained behind to follow as rapidly as their circumstances would permit.

At dawn near present-day Picacho Peak, the *comandante* and his small force overtook a group of nearly fifty Apaches and engaged them in a running battle that continued for more than two leagues (five miles). At least two warriors were killed and, judging from the trail of blood, others were wounded. Comadurán's men recovered more than 140 cattle, four horses (three with saddles), and a mule, plus other booty. They also freed the captive woman. The Apaches dispersed and the *comandante* felt it would be useless to continue the pursuit.

As they rode back toward Tucson, the woman whom the Apaches had taken from the Búsani Ranch told Comadurán that the preceding day the Apaches had fought with the Tubutama militia, defeating the Mexicans and killing six men. One Apache died in the encounter and a second was wounded. When Comadurán and his force got back to Tucson, they found don Benigno Ortiz, commander of the Tubutama militia, waiting for them. He confirmed what the Indian woman had said about his casualties, adding that four others had been wounded.[14]

Colonel Elías Invades Chihuahua

By the time Comadurán's report of the late September campaign reached headquarters of the general command in Arizpe, Colonel Elías González may have been too busy to give it his immediate attention. He was just back from an expedition of his own, one that had carried him across the Sierra Madre into Chihuahua, and brought the two north Mexican states to the verge of open warfare.

For the better part of a decade, officials from Sonora and Chihuahua had disagreed over how to deal with the Apaches. The people of northern Chihuahua had consistently favored signing treaties with the nearby Apachean groups, whereas the Sonoran frontiersmen considered these Indians too treacherous to be trusted and favored exterminating them or driving them elsewhere. Each state separately pursued its own Apache policy—that of the Chihuahuans based on negotiation; that of the Sonorans on warfare. Over the years, the Sonorans had come out losers. Apacheans would sign treaties with Chihuahua authorities and abide by those treaties in Chihuahua, but would continue raiding into Sonora. They would then sell livestock and other booty from their forays to people in Chihuahua and New Mexico from whom, according to the Sonorans, they obtained weapons and ammunition which they used on more raids.[15]

During the winter and spring of 1844, residents of eastern Sonora became progressively more annoyed by this state of affairs and also came more and more to believe that some of the Apaches living near the presidio of Janos were the primary culprits. Feelings were already high when the Apaches made a major raid into the area toward the end of July. Ensign Manuel Villa and a force of Mexican soldiers went in pursuit but were ambushed. Around thirty Mexicans, including Villa, lost their lives.[16] Outraged, Colonel Elías determined to hunt down the guilty parties and punish them, even if doing so involved an invasion of the neighboring state. On August 16th, he personally led a large Mexican force out of the presidio of Fronteras, following as best he could the trail of the Indians who had been responsible for the raid. On September 5th, the government newspaper *El Voto de Sonora* reported that, according to unofficial reports, the Sonorans had killed eighty Apache warriors in attacks on Indian camps and had taken more than thirty prisoners "of all classes."[17]

Janos, Chihuahua in the early 1850s (Bartlett, *Personal Narrative*, volume 2)

On August 23rd, well before any reports had filtered back to Ures, Elías and his men reached the Janos area and fell on the unsuspecting Apaches. At least fifteen Indians were killed in the encounter and many prisoners were taken. Chihuahua authorities protested the invasion and carried their protests to the central government in Mexico City.[18] As far as officials there were concerned, it was another black eye for Sonora, but this one could not be blamed on either Urrea or Gándara.

Whether the Sonorans could justify their action depended in great measure on proving that the Janos Apaches were involved in the raiding that had plagued the eastern part of the state for so long. Early in October, at about the time Comadurán's report would have reached Arizpe, Colonel Elías was busy writing to the civil and military officials of the towns in eastern Sonora asking them to provide him the information that would be needed to answer the inquiries he was already receiving from Mexico City.[19] By October 12th, the first reply was back and others would continue coming in until early December.[20] There would always be doubt, however, and establishing that the raiders were from Janos remained a problem.

One of the December letters to Elías was from Colonel Antonio Narbona, who shortly before had assumed command at Fronteras.

He wrote that Sonorans might soon have more to worry about than the peaceful Apaches at Janos. Mangas Coloradas, the most famous and most feared Apache leader, was planning an invasion of the state with a large force of warriors. He intended to take many captives, including whole families, back with him as slaves.[21]

Urrea Back in Power

History repeated itself in December, 1844, when new political upheavals in Mexico City produced reverberations in Sonora, leading to General Ponce de León's removal from the twin posts that he had occupied since May. Replacing him was his predecessor, General José Cosme de Urrea.[22]

Colonel Elías wasted no time in informing his cousin of the intelligence he had received from Narbona regarding the imminence of an attack by Mangas Coloradas and his braves. Urrea wasted even less time in responding to Elías. He wrote on January 1st, 1845, stating that his major preoccupation of the moment was to put together a large army of Sonorans to go to the aid of the residents of the northern frontier. Furthermore, he pointed out, it was his intention to lead this army into battle against the Apaches. He instructed Elías to issue whatever orders he felt necessary to keep the hostile Indians at bay while he organized the offensive.[23]

Shortly after the middle of January, 1845, Captain Comadurán— who was both the chief justice of the peace and the *comandante* at Tucson—called a meeting to discuss the political events that were taking place to the south. In attendance were both civilians and soldiers. He told them that two months before, General Mariano Paredes y Arrillaga—who had twice served as military commander of Sonora and Sinaloa—had "pronounced" against the central government.[24] President Santa Anna had immediately appealed to military and civil adminstrators at all levels to come to his support. Convinced that Santa Anna's appeal would fail, the Mexican national congress had replaced him with José Joaquín Herrera. Now, Comadurán told his audience, the sub-prefect at San Ignacio was asking for a report on where the Tucsonans stood in this matter.[25]

After listening to the *comandante*, the Tucsonenses enacted three resolutions. The first declared support for the "Plan of Guadalajara" which was the proclamation issued by General Paredes. The second endorsed José de Urrea to serve again as governor and mili-

Colonel José María Elías González, governor and military commander of Sonora (Corella collection, courtesy of Carmen Pellat Sotomayor)

tary commander of Sonora. The third rejected an oath of allegiance to Santa Anna who was cooling his heels in Veracruz waiting for a groundswell of support that would not develop.

Comadurán's report to the sub-prefect is an interesting document, both because it reveals much about the political sophistication of Sonoran frontiersmen, and because it tells about those living in the region at the time. Understandably, Comadurán's own name heads the list of signers. It is followed by the signatures of retired ensigns Loreto Ramírez and Manuel Orozco. Ensign Lorenzo Rodríguez, head of the auxiliary militia of Altar, signed next for those under his command. Then came the signatures of Bautista Romero, representing all the sergeants, and Solano León, representing all the corporals. Last on the list of military signatures is that of Juan Martínez who represented all the common soldiers.

Ignacio Saenz, second justice of the peace, headed the civilian list, followed by Teodoro Ramírez, José Grijalva (Tucson's last elected mayor during the Mexican years), Clemente Telles, Luis Burruel, Gerónimo González, Pascual Cruz, Joaquín Comadurán (the captain's oldest son), Miguel Pacheco, Jesús María Ortiz (son of Tomás and son-in-law of Comadurán), Ramón Castro, Juan María Santa Cruz, Francisco Granillo, Tomás Ortiz, Juan José Azedo, José Paulino Castro, Ramón Pacheco and Manuel Ygnacio Elías. José Grijalva then affixed his signature for the second time in representation of some fifty settlers who did not know how to write. Corporal León signed again, this time in his capacity as secretary for the meeting.

A similar report was prepared at the same time in Tubac by Leonardo Orozco, second justice of the peace. Apart from Orozco, only six persons signed that document reflecting the great drop in *vecino* population. They were Tiburcio Sotelo, Manuel Otero, Valentín Sotelo, José María Martínez, José María Bórques and Trinidad Yrigoyen, who signed for himself and *todo este vecindario que no save firmar*—"all of the people here who do not know how to sign."

By early February, General Urrea was ready with the most ambitious plan ever devised to dominate the Apaches.[26] It involved extensive use of the local militias, as well as troops from the presidial garrisons. Under the command of experienced officers, these forces would operate out of nine temporary camps, as well as out of the presidios.

Among those Urrea called upon to head one of the encampments was Lieutenant Colonel José María Martínez who had been living at Tubac with his family since the late 1830s and who had a small presidial land grant there. Martínez was assigned to the encampment at Agua Caliente, a location between modern Nogales and Imuris just south of the La Casita Ranch. His specific responsibility would be to patrol the east-west trails used by the Apaches in attacking ranches and towns in that area. Assisting him would be Captain Tiburcio Escalante and Ensign Lorenzo Rodríguez, each of whom would lead a different patrol. The total force of the outpost would be fifty men drawn from Altar and twenty-five from towns along the San Ignacio (now the Magdalena) River. Not far south of them would be another encampment at El Alamo to watch the trails between Cucurpe and Magdalena.

Urrea's plans called for similar bases extending across the northern frontier of Sonora and down the western slope of the Sierra Madre as far as Sahuaripa. Figuring importantly as commander of two in the central region was Arizpe native Ignacio Pesqueira, who in a few years would be the most powerful political figure in all of Sonora. Only twenty-four years old, Pesqueira was already a captain of the militia force charged with protection of the lower Sonora River region between Baviácora and Huépac.[27]

While Urrea was wrestling with the logistics of putting his Apache plan into effect, Mexico's president, José Joaquín Herrera, wrestled with the question of whether to give his official blessing to Urrea's reappointment. Although strongly supported by a resolution from the Sonoran legislature, Urrea had not been confirmed by the central government as the state's constitutional governor. Herrera's minister of war, Pedro García Conde, was one of those urging the president to make the appointment official. He was a native of Arizpe and a close friend of Urrea.

For reasons of his own that are not likely ever to be known, Herrera reached the conclusion that peace could never come to the region as long as the Urrea-Gándara feud continued, and that it would be easier to find a way to get Urrea out of Sonora than to try to remove all the Gándaras and their wealthy backers. Late in February, 1845, he issued instructions to General Francisco Duque to return to Sonora and oversee another change in the government.[28]

President Herrera's decision brought a halt to Urrea's plans for reorganizing the frontier defenses. During March, all Sonorans anxiously waited the arrival of Duque. The questions in peoples' minds were whether Urrea would turn over the government without a struggle; and, if he did, would Duque allow power to fall into the hands of the Gandaristas again?[29]

On April 10th, 1845, Urrea surrendered his military post to Duque and his civil office to Francisco Andrade, oldest member of the departmental assembly.[30] The expectation in Mexico City was that Urrea would accept the position of senator from Durango to which he had been elected shortly before. However, he informed Duque that he had a military force ready for an offensive against the Apaches and that he wished to remain in Sonora to lead it.[31]

Named by Herrera as constitutional governor of the state was José María Gaxiola, the same man who seventeen years earlier had decreed the expulsion of the Spaniards from Sonora.[32] He officially took office on June 26th.[33] Duque, believing that his job was finished, left the state.

The general's exit left the military situation in Sonora somewhat up in the air. Late in April, shortly after taking over from Urrea, Duque had appointed Colonel Fernando Cuesta to be his adjutant inspector in Sonora, a post previously held by José María Elías

González, who remained in charge of the forces on the northern frontier.[34] With Duque's departure, the post of Sonoran military commander became vacant and Cuesta assumed the responsibilities of that office.

While various changes occurred above him, Colonel Elías González awaited comment from his superiors on a proposal for Apache warfare that he had forwarded to Duque on April 30th. It was a plan that differed in some very important particulars from Urrea's. First, it called for beefing up the presidial garrisons—none of which was at full strength—and making them the pivotal elements in both defending the frontier and launching assaults against the Apaches. He noted that there had been a time when detachments located away from the forts could be very effective but said he no longer considered this to be the case since the Apache forces had increased greatly in size and strength.

Elías included with his letter to Duque a chart showing the existing and projected staffing situations for the presidios. Only twenty-eight soldiers were assigned to the Tubac garrison; Elías proposed expanding the force to eighty-one. Tucson's existing complement of seventy-eight men would be expanded to ninety-four. Curiously, Elías' plan showed the Tubac garrison headed by a captain, whereas a lieutenant was in charge at Tucson. Other documents of the period indicate that Comadurán, the captain, was still directing the Tucson garrison, while Ensign Gerónimo Errán was commanding at Tubac.

According to Elías, the Fronteras encampment was the only one sufficiently supplied with ammunition to defend against a major attack. Santa Cruz, Tucson, Bavispe and Fronteras all had some artillery pieces, but of the total the only gun worth using was a four-pounder at Tucson. The soldiers were further handicapped because the combined garrisons of Fronteras, Tucson and Santa Cruz had fewer than 200 horses (for nearly 250 men) and none of those could stand up to a journey of more than ten leagues. He recommended that each soldier be furnished with at least three horses.

The Colonel dwelt at length also on questions related to the pay and provisioning of the men. After the fashion of earlier critics, he found fault with the system of middlemen and speculators who got rich supplying the troops, and he recommended that a bidding system be instituted.

Consistent with early Spanish policy and the later strategy of

Escalante y Arvizu, Elías insisted that the Mexican forces should carry the battle to the Apaches in their remotest locations. To begin with he suggested a campaign involving 600 infantrymen and 300 horsemen. He even went so far as to present Duque with a detailed accounting of what a 120–day campaign for such a force would cost and proposed that it begin from three different frontier locations at the end of July.[35]

Colonel Elías González was destined to see his plan suffer the same fate as that of Urrea who was still in Sonora in mid-summer. Cuesta, who had been charged by Duque with the responsibility for making sure that Urrea left the state, was reluctant to take action against the veteran general and, in fact, had joined him in a plot to seize the government from Gaxiola. When President Herrera learned of all this, he ordered Duque to visit Sonora one more time and to forcibly remove Urrea just as his father had been removed by General Figueroa twenty years earlier.[36]

The fuss over Urrea's removal from Sonora would provide the Gandaristas a new excuse to go into action, and, although they would have some difficulty in regaining power at first, they would soon be back, stronger than ever. In Urrea's case, the situation was different. His removal by Duque ended his efforts to control the affairs of his native state and he would never return to it. Four years later, in 1849, he would fall victim to the cholera epidemic sweeping Mexico. Even his exiled father was fated to outlive him.

10

No Matter How Bad, Things Can Always Get Worse

If President Herrera's expectations had been fulfilled, orderly government would have been restored in Sonora following General Urrea's forced departure. Unfortunately, things got off to a very bad start with a revolt by the Gandaristas in late August, 1845. One aim of the rebellion was to force the government to exile Urrea from Mexico just as his father had been exiled seventeen years earlier. The Gándara incident and subsequent conspiracies would keep the political merry-go-round in motion.

Among those most frustrated by the continuing instability of the Sonoran and national governments were Colonel José María Elías González and the presidio captains serving under his command. They perhaps more than other Sonorans could appreciate the seriousness of the Apache threat and the fact that these Indians were becoming bolder and more innovative in their warfare with the Mexicans. In mid-August, 1845, Captain Comadurán reported to Colonel Elías that the Pinaleños had shortly before attempted to place a spy within the Tucson presidio. A young woman who belonged to one of the hostile Apache groups came to the fort and requested sanctuary to escape the wrath of an angry husband. The spouse was nowhere in sight and Comadurán was convinced that she was there to gather information. He wrote Elías that he had taken the precaution of placing her under guard.[1]

Father García's 1845 visit to the Santa Cruz settlements came shortly after the incident involving the Apache woman and coincided with the period of the Gándara revolt. The priest stopped first at Tumacácori where he had baptized three children the year before. On this occasion, he baptized only one.

It is unlikely that the few remaining Indian families at the mission were aware at the time of Father García's second trip that they were now squatters on land belonging to Gándara's brother-in-law. It would be some years before the stormy Sonoran would do anything with the Tumacácori-Calabazas property. What the Indians and other residents of the area did know, however, was that other nearby lands had passed into private hands. A few years before, they had loaned their title to Francisco González so that he could survey the northern boundary of a land grant he was seeking in the area of present-day Ambos Nogales. His application was filed originally in May, 1841, but the grant was not approved until early 1843. The Pimas at Tumacácori were still waiting in 1845 for the return of their title but they would never see it again.[2]

When Father García Rojas had come through Tubac in 1844, he found fifteen sets of anxious parents waiting to have their children baptized. On his 1845 visit, the total was down to eight. Among them were don León Herreros, original owner of the Sonoita land grant, and his wife Peregrina Valencia. Now past middle age and with grown children and grandchildren from his first marriage, Herreros must have been regarded by local residents as one of the patriarchs of the area.[3] Evidence of his progeny is abundant in García's baptismal register, which includes the names of Pedro, María de las Nieves and Nicolasa Herreras (spelling of last name changed) who were either parents or godparents of children baptized in 1845. Nicolasa was especially busy during García Rojas' visit that year. She was *madrina* (godmother) to three of the eight youngsters who received the sacrament.

On August 25th and 26th, the priest was at San Xavier, where he performed seven baptismal ceremonies, more than double the number of the previous year. Between August 27th and September 4th, he brought the sacrament to twenty-seven infants of the Tucson community, the largest number he would baptize on one visit at any Arizona location. His registers provide persuasive evidence of the degree to which the population was beginning to concentrate within the protective orbit of the large Tucson fort.

Church at San Ignacio, Sonora, headquarters for Father Trinidad García Rojas
(Linda Kyle photograph taken in 1978, courtesy of the Southwestern Mission
Research Center)

Among the youngsters baptized at Tucson in 1845 were a son of
Luis Elías and María Ysabel Ruelas, whom they named Jesús
María, and a daughter of Tomás Ortiz and Josefa Clementa Elías,
called María Carmen Esquipulas. Don José María Vásquez and
doña Jesús López were the godparents of record for the Ortiz girl,
but Father García Rojas' register shows they were standing in for
Teodoro Ramírez and María de los Angeles Salazar.

Comadurán on the March Again

Father García was scarcely out of sight when Tucson played host
to a major gathering of Sonora's veteran soldiers. Colonel Elías
González convened the meeting on September 11th to seek the
support of presidial commanders and others for a manifesto he
proposed to send to the officials of the department. The document
called upon Governor Gaxiola and General Commander Cuesta to

put down the Gándara revolt using military forces other than those of the presidios and frontier militias. To do otherwise would result in further postponement of the Apache campaign.

The manifesto was approved unanimously and signed by representatives from Bacoachi, Bavispe, Fronteras, Arizpe, Santa Cruz, Hermosillo and Oposura (Moctezuma)—as well as Tucson and Tubac. Captain Comadurán's name appears near the top of the list and he was one of the principal speakers at the meeting. His son Joaquín signed on behalf of the common soldiers of the Santa Cruz garrison; and Teodoro Marín signed for the common soldiers of Tucson. Bautista Romero represented Tucson's sergeants; and Francisco Solano León, the corporals of the Tucson company. Spokesmen and signers for the Tubac troopers were Luis Frías and Francisco Ortega. Lieutenant Colonel Francisco Narbona was elected secretary of the meeting and it was he who was to carry the manifesto to the governor.[4]

Midway through October, as Elías and his subordinates awaited word from Ures, Chief Antonio Culo Azul of the Gila River villages visited the Tucson presidio where he learned that death sentences had been imposed on several individuals who had deserted during a recent campaign. Captain Comadurán was about to send the prisoners under escort to Elías' headquarters, along with some dispatches for the Colonel. Azul obtained assistance, perhaps from Teodoro Ramírez, in preparing a letter for Elías asking that the deserters be pardoned. His appeal was in the name of Christianity, although Azul himself was apparently not a convert.[5]

The end of the year approached with no word on the grand offensive against the Apaches. Rather than continue waiting, Colonel Elías decided to authorize a modest campaign by the Tucson troopers and their Indian allies. In response to this decision, Captain Comadurán put together a force of 155 men that included sixty professional soldiers from his own garrison and twenty-three from Tubac, twenty civilians from Tucson, thirty-five peaceful Apaches and seventeen Pimas from San Xavier. Departing from the fort on November 29th, they headed northward and arrived at the Gila River on the evening of December 1st. They travelled along the Gila to its intersection with the San Pedro, which they followed as far as the mouth of Arivaipa Creek. They were back at Tucson about noon on the 7th.

Although they saw evidence of many Apaches and engaged some in battle, the results were disappointing—only six Apache warriors slain and three others wounded. Throughout his diary, Captain Comadurán lamented the miserable situation of his cavalry, and in a personal letter to Elías accompanying his official one, he was very candid. He told his cousin that the garrison was limited to defensive measures because of the lack of horses. They were also nearly out of provisions and had no money to purchase the grain they needed. Comadurán reported that he had called the residents of the fort together and begged from them a hundred *fanegas* of wheat; but if the government did not send money to pay for it, the citizens would sell it to the merchants supplying the gold miners of the Papaguería. Finally, the captain said he hoped the political mess would soon be cleared up so that Elías could concentrate on the frontier.[6]

Two months later, on February 3rd, 1846, Comadurán reported to Elías again that the anticipated funds from the government had not arrived. Fortunately, Teodoro Ramírez, had once more come to the rescue. With money Ramírez had received from the sale of tobacco, plus cigarettes from his existing stock, the Tucson merchant bought eighty-eight *fanegas* and promised to try to get more by trading additional cigarettes.[7]

Political Turmoil Continues

Not long after Comadurán's disappointing campaign, Sonora's acting military commander, Colonel Fernando Cuesta, found it expedient to inform his fellow citizens of the reasons for the removal of Urrea. He did so in a document for general circulation that includes more than a hint of hypocrisy.[8] To begin with, Cuesta stated that he had prepared the document as a final report to the people before stepping down from his post. In fact, he was on the verge of taking measures that would assure his retention. Then, he took credit for having carried out the orders of the central government in removing Urrea, when, in fact, his failure to do so had made it necessary for General Duque to undertake that task. Finally, he announced that he would leave Sonora in the hands of his second in command, Elías González, who had "returned to the campaign against the Apaches." Throughout the document, Cuesta portrayed Urrea as a soldier who consistently disobeyed the orders of his superiors and encouraged people to revolt against their duly constituted governments.

The hypocrisy of Cuesta's rhetoric became evident shortly after publication of his report. Early in 1846, General Mariano Paredes, who had staged the revolt against Santa Anna slightly over a year before, ejected President Herrera and installed himself as Mexico's chief executive. Colonel Cuesta wasted no time in endorsing the change, and in ousting Gaxiola, Sonora's constitutional governor. As a result, he soon occupied the top civil and military posts of the department.[9]

Continuing political turmoil could not have come at a worse time for the central government of Mexico. Just a year before General Paredes' second coup, the United States had annexed Texas, a move that many Mexicans bitterly opposed, feeling that it would lead inevitably to a war between the two countries. At issue, among other points, was the question of where the Texas boundary lay. The Texans insisted that the Lone Star Republic included parts of New Mexico, the region later called Colorado, and all of the land between the Nueces River and the Rio Grande. Mexico contended that these areas had never been part of Texas and, therefore, could not become part of the United States through admission of Texas as the twenty-eighth state. President James K. Polk chose to accept the word of the Texans. He also secretly sent an envoy, John Slidell, to Mexico City to negotiate the purchase of California and the part of New Mexico not claimed by Texas.[10]

When news of Polk's plans came to the attention of the Mexican press, the outcry was so great that President Herrera was effectively stopped from conducting any more secret talks on the matter. By the time Paredes took office, public opinion was firmly set against the United States and further negotiation on any aspect of the boundary issue was out of the question.

As the two countries stood poised on the brink of war, the situation along the Sonoran frontier remained much the same. Once again, political intrigue had prevented concerted action against the enemy Apache. In May, 1846, at almost the very time President Polk announced to the American people that the United States was at war with Mexico, Father García Rojas began his long ride north to the Santa Cruz settlements. Perhaps because of his experience of the previous year, he expected to find more work in the Tucson area than elsewhere, so he went there first, arriving May 7th.

In five days at Tucson, the priest performed the baptismal sacrament for nineteen infants, among them two Indian girls, one of whom he identified as an Apache. A woman by the name of María Ramírez, probably the wife of Captain Comadurán,[11] served as godmother for the Apache child. Teodoro Ramírez and his wife were godparents for the other Indian girl.

Among the Mexican settlers of the post, Juan Elías and his wife Jesús Orozco—recently migrated from Tubac—celebrated the baptism of an infant daughter whom they named María Merced Silvestra.[12] Godparent honors were provided by Captain Comadurán and his daughter Encarnación, who would later wed Jesús María Ortiz, son of Tomás and Josefa Clementa Elías. Captain Comadurán's wife assisted with the baptism of another infant who was closely related to her—a male child born to Antonio Ramírez, apparently her nephew, and his wife Josefa Orozco. The godfather was Leonardo Orozco, who had been the second justice of the peace at Tubac only a year and half before.

From Tucson, García Rojas moved south to San Xavier on May 13th, pausing long enough to baptize eight children. Since the Pimas and Papagos, all of whom had Spanish names, no longer were listed as Indians in the baptismal registers, it is difficult to separate Mexican and Indian families. However, the number of Mexican residents at the mission was increasing and soon would grow even more.

In spite of the migration of several prominent Tubac families to Tucson by the late spring of 1846, the older post was by no means deserted when García Rojas reached it on May 15th. There were some changes though. First, he recorded in his register that seven of the ten Mexican infants he baptized were "natural children," or *hijos naturales*. The names of their unwed mothers are ones long represented in the community, some even of the elite.[13]

Among the legitimate children baptized by García Rojas was another daughter of Lieutenant Colonel José María Martínez, who was probably still waiting to be called into service against the Apaches. The child was given the name María Policarpia.

War!

By the time President Polk announced that a state of war prevailed between the United States and Mexico, the political situation
in Mexico City had deteriorated even more. General Paredes proved
a more arbitrary tyrant than Santa Anna, and both soldiers and
civilians in the capital quickly tired of his rule.[14] In September,
1846, he was overthrown, leading to the restoration of federalism
and soon after, the return of Santa Anna. Meanwhile in Sonora,
Colonel Cuesta was making the most of his new power base. After
deposing Gaxiola, he took it upon himself to appoint a new departmental assembly. Perhaps in order to deal a further blow to Urrea
partisans, he filled it with persons whose sympathies clearly lay
with Gándara. Its head—*primer vocal*—was Gándara's brother
Juan.[15] The way was now paved for Manuel María and his adherents
to regain control of Sonora, and the governmental changes in Mexico City would make it easier for them to do so.

Once the war was officially underway, the United States devised
a three-pronged strategy for the invasion of Mexico. Texas was to
be the take-off point for one of these. Another called for a seaborne
attack on the Veracruz coast. The third involved a march westward
into California that would place in American hands the territory
Polk tried to purchase earlier. The Hispanic population of southern
Arizona would be directly affected only by the last, although men
like General Urrea would take part in campaigns elsewhere.

The United States Army of the West, under General Stephen
Watts Kearny, was assigned responsibility for conquering the Mexican northwest. In June, 1846, just a month after the war began,
Kearny left Fort Leavenworth headed for Santa Fe. The conquest
of New Mexico proved easier than he had imagined and by August
he was in full control. In October and November he led part of his
army down the Gila River into California.[16] Kearny did not pass
through any of the Mexican settlements in the Pimería Alta, all of
which lay to the south of his route.

At the time he left Santa Fe, Kearny had been expecting a battalion of Mormon soldiers led by Lieutenant A. J. Smith of the
First United States Dragoons. He left instructions that when Smith
and his men reached New Mexico, they were to follow him to
California over a southerly route that would take them close to the

frontier towns of Sonora. Organized in Nauvoo, Illinois, the Mormon force consisted primarily of men whose motivation for enlisting was as much religious as patriotic. They hoped that their willingness to serve might help relieve some of the discrimination they had experienced at the hands of their midwestern neighbors. Like Kearny before them, they began their march westward at Fort Leavenworth and reached Santa Fe on October 12th. In accordance with Kearny's instructions, they were to be led from this point by Lieutenant Colonel Philip St. George Cooke, a graduate of West Point.[17]

After dismissing those soldiers considered too old or otherwise unfit for combat, Cooke led the battalion out of Santa Fe on October 19th. On November 9th, he decided to send back more than fifty other recruits[18] who either were ill or had demonstrated little capacity for soldiering. With what was left of the original group, including some women, he resumed the march.

Among the scouts accompanying the Mormon Battalion were mountain men Antoine Leroux and Pauline Weaver, who had been with the David Jackson party that passed through Tucson fifteen years earlier. The farther south the battalion went, however, the less Leroux and Weaver knew about the region. On November 20th, they did report water at a location they thought was close to the abandoned San Bernardino Ranch, a grant belonging to the Pérez family. Cooke decided to head for the ranch. He had heard about it, but did not know its exact location. It turned out to be farther than Leroux and Weaver had calculated but with the aid of Mexicans encountered along the way, the battalion reached the site on December 2nd.[19]

Judging from the available accounts of the Cooke expedition, San Bernardino made a favorable impression on the members of the battalion, not only because of its beauty but because of the free access to fresh meat that it provided. Large herds of cattle—mostly bulls according to Cooke—roamed the area and could be hunted like buffalo. Henry Standage, one of Cooke's soldiers, wrote in his diary that the meat of these animals was "really sweet." Another trooper named Bliss described it as "fat and tender, the best meat I ever eat." Henry W. Bigler noted similar comments in his journal, but observed also that Captain Jesse D. Hunter of B Company told his wife the animals were heifers so that she "might relish the beef with a better appetite." According to Bigler, during the soldiers'

Lt. Colonel Philip St.
George Cooke (U.S.
National Archives)

twelve-mile march on December 4th they saw four or five thousand head of wild cattle.[20]

Several times on their journey to the San Bernardino, members of the battalion encountered Apaches who told them of their great enmity with the Mexicans but did not threaten the Americans. They did, however, rob one trooper who became separated from the group, stripping him of his clothing and weapons.[21] Cooke did not care much for the appearance of the Apaches, but observed that "they ride fine horses and are armed with formidable lances, guns, and bows."[22]

From San Bernardino, the *Yanquis* marched southward to a point about fourteen miles north of the old presidio of Fronteras, then turned westward in search of the San Pedro River, which they reached on December 9th. Along the route they encountered more wild cattle and horses, as well as antelope. The size of the cattle herds increased as they proceeded north along the river, passing through the ranches of San Pedro and San Rafael del Valle, both of which were grants belonging to Rafael Elías González, brother of José María. On December 10th, at the southern end of the San Juan de las Boquillas grant, they encountered a herd of wild bulls. Sixteen-year old Robert Whitworth, an Englishman, described the incident:

> *December 10.* Followed the river for 15 miles. We had a very serious fight with wild cattle today. They would charge our ranks, Waggons, or Mules without any fear. One man was gored in the thigh, and Leut Stoneman had his thumb hurt by the bursting of two loads at once in his sixteen shooter. We had four mules Slain, and I counted 19 dead Bulls close along the road.[23]

In another account of the event, Henry Bigler stated: "One lead mule in a team was thrown by a bull over his mate and so gored that his entrails hung down a foot or more."[24] Cooke himself reported that a coal-black bull charged him and a Corporal Frost who held his fire until the animal was close to them; then dropped it with one shot.[25]

On December 12th, Leroux and other guides informed the battalion commander that the Tucson presidio lay some fifty or sixty miles distant along a trail that left the river and did not offer any water for a stretch of about twenty miles. In addition, they mentioned that in their explorations they had come upon a party of Apaches and Mexicans who were distilling mescal. Several Mexican soldiers accompanying the party told them that the Tucson garrison included 200 men. Dr. Stephen C. Foster, interpreter for the battalion, was skeptical about this piece of intelligence and set off by himself to have a look at the situation.[26]

The battalion left the San Pedro River on December 14th,[27] reaching the mescal camp during the day. According to Bigler, "We passed a Mexican distillery where they were making whisky out of roots they call 'mescal'; the tubs or vessels were made of rawhides with the hair on. Some of the men tasted the whisky and say it is poor stuff."[28]

In his journal, Cooke reported that there were four or five Mexican soldiers at the place where the battalion camped for the night. He noted that they appeared to be quite unconcerned about the fact that the Americans were nearby, and described their behavior as "strange simplicity . . . indicating a conviction that the savages were their natural and only enemies."[29]

A Mexican sergeant among the soldiers at the distillery told Cooke that the people of the presidio were greatly disturbed by the reports of the battalion and many were ready to flee. He stated further that his commanding officer had sent him to request that Cooke and his troops not come into town—which the garrison had been ordered to defend—but to pass on either side of it. Cooke informed the sergeant that it was not his intention to molest the garrison and that he should tell the people of the fort that the Americans were their friends.

On the morning of December 15th, as the battalion continued its march toward Tucson, the Americans encountered four soldiers from the presidio headed in their direction. One of the quartet was a corporal who, Cooke learned, was a son of Captain Comadurán.[30] The Mexicans informed the battalion commander that Dr. Foster was in Tucson under guard but that they had begged him to come with them and he had refused. Thereupon, Cooke took the Mexicans into custody and told them they would be kept as hostages pending Foster's release. He dispatched a messenger to inform the presidial commander that he should free the doctor without delay.

In the early morning hours of December 16th, two Tucson officers brought Foster to Cooke's camp. One represented himself as a "commissioner" who was authorized to make a special armistice. Following a lengthy discussion,[31] Cooke told the visitors they would have to deliver a few arms to him "as tokens of surrender" and agree not to serve against the United States "during the present war. . . ."[32] The Mexicans departed, telling Cooke they did not consider his terms acceptable.

At eight on the morning of December 17th, 1846, the Americans were again on the march.[33] A few miles outside Tucson, they were met by a "fine looking cavalryman well armed" who delivered a communication from Comadurán refusing the surrender terms offered earlier that day. Cooke immediately prepared his men for combat and resumed the march. They had gone only a short distance when they were intercepted by two Mexican civilians who informed them that the Mexican troops had left the fort. The American soldiers then proceeded and on their approach to Tucson were met by a dozen "well mounted" men who escorted them to the edge of the town. Although all the Mexicans were in civilian garb, Cooke observed in his journal that some were "reported to be soldiers."[34]

Cooke and his men were not aware as they neared Tucson that the governor and military commander of Sonora, Colonel Fernando Cuesta, was scarcely fifty miles away. The Sonoran chief executive with a small escort of men was approaching Tubac from the south when a messenger apparently sent by Comadurán early on the morning of December 17th arrived with the news that an American force of 500 soldiers had reached the fort. Cuesta must have turned back immediately, for only a little over a week later from the Sonoran capital, he informed the people of the occupation of Tucson. He also announced that he was making plans to defend the state.[35]

It was just after midday when the Mormon Battalion marched through the streets of Tucson on their way to a site outside the fort where Cooke ordered the Americans to make camp.[36] About a hundred of the "perhaps five hundred" Mexican inhabitants remained in the town. Most apparently were elderly persons and children, and as the Americans rode or walked by, they offered them water—perhaps the most hospitable gesture a desert people could make. Before the day was out, Cooke had also obtained wheat and some badly needed salt.[37]

For most of the members of the Mormon Battalion, Tucson was completely unknown, even as a place name. In his diary, Robert Whitworth referred to the "Town of Teusone." Standage spelled it "Touson" and Bliss recorded it in his journal as "Tubson."[38]

In general, the American soldiers found the Tucsonenses pleasant and kind people. Bigler commented that the few persons left were "old men and infirm, with a few children, who were at our mercy and were badly frightened on our approach, but as we showed no sign of fight, they became friendly and sociable, though close in their dealings."[39] Standage noted that the Mormons "were kindly treated by the people . . . who brought Flour, Meal, Tobacco, Quinces to the camp for sale and many of them giving such things to the soldiers."[40] Bliss observed that "the people here are the most friendly and intelligent I have seen of all the Spaniards. . . ."[41] His comments were seconded by Samuel Hollister Rogers who described Tucson's Mexicans as "more intelligent than [those] at Santa Fe."[42] Rogers also mentioned the presence of "some fine farms," and Nathaniel Jones wrote that he traded clothing to the Tucsonenses in exchange for beans and flour.[43]

For at least some of the soldiers, Tucson was a welcome sight after many days marching through deserted countryside. "It looked good to see young green wheat patches and fruit trees," according to Bigler, "and to see hogs and fowls running about, and it was music to our ears to hear the crowing of the cocks. Here are the finest quinces I ever saw." Bigler also noted the presence of two "little mills for grinding grain . . . run by jackass power; the upper millstone moved around as fast as Mr. Donkey pleased to walk."[44]

The earliest rumors that had reached Cooke concerning the size of the military force at Tucson suggested the presence of more than 200 troops in the area, including reinforcements from the garrisons at Tubac, Santa Cruz and Fronteras. However, Dr. Foster, following his captivity, estimated the number at 130.[45]

When they hastily evacuated the presidio, the Mexicans troopers went to San Xavier. Late in the afternoon of December 17th, Cooke sought fifty volunteers to accompany him on an expedition to the old mission to confiscate arms and supplies from the Mexican force. As soon as he had the men he needed, Cooke led them south along the river. They had travelled only a mile or two, however, when they encountered a mesquite thicket so dense the battalion commander feared it might provide the enemy cover for an ambush. He ordered the volunteers back to the presidio and posted a heavy guard. Later, he learned that Comadurán had not contemplated an ambush and on hearing that Cooke and his men were heading toward the mission, the Mexican commander had withdrawn his force even farther. By this time, also, the Mexican troops from other forts had started to march back to their posts.[46]

To keep his men alert, Cooke may have deliberately kept the revised estimate of the size of the Tucson garrison from them. Standage was apparently under the impression that the Mexican forces vastly outnumbered them and enjoyed other strategic advantages. Remarking on the decision of the Mexicans not to resist, he wrote in his diary, "I am led to exclaim that the Lord God of Israel will save his people in as much as He knoweth the cause of our being here in the United States Service."[47] The Mormon soldiers appear to have been no more eager for battle than the Mexicans. In his diary entry of December 16th, Whitworth states that the soldiers of the Battalion marched twenty-two miles "almost on the trot" to the fort, "expecting to have a fight, but the soldiers (about three hundred) cleared out in good time to save their Bacon and ours too. . . ."[48]

At midnight, following the return of the volunteers to their Tucson camp, some of the civilian settlers began coming back from San Xavier. One of the guards awakened Cooke to inform him that "a large Mexican army was coming. . . ." The American commander was not inclined to take the report seriously until he heard from the officer of the day that a picket had fired upon a body of men approaching Tucson from the south. He then ordered the trumpets sounded and when the troops were assembled, sent a company into the presidio. He also dispatched Lieutenant Stoneman with a small reconnaissance party to search the surrounding area. Cooke recorded in his diary that "nothing was discovered."[49]

On the morning of the 18th, Cooke led the battalion out of the Tucson area headed for the Pima villages on the Gila River. They expected to find abundant water at Picacho Peak which Bigler described as "resembling a cow's horn."[50] It was apparently an unusually hot December day, and when they reached their destination the Mormons were exhausted and extremely thirsty. The only water they found was in small puddles. They lay face down to drink, and Bigler commented that it brought to his mind "Gideon's army lapping water like dogs, Judges 7, Verse 51."[51]

On their march from Picacho to the junction of the Gila and Colorado rivers, which they reached on January 8th, 1847, the soldiers met only one other party of Mexicans. Bigler says the group included several families who camped near the battalion on the night of December 31st. He states in his journal that they were on their way to Chihuahua and had met General Kearny eighteen days before.[52] Cooke, on the other hand, refers to encountering two travellers—a Chilean and a "California refugee" who "gave very confused information of a renewed state of war in California, and of bodies of armed men . . . coming to Sonora."[53]

From the Gila River Pimas, Cooke obtained some mules and merchandise that Kearny had left with the Indians for safekeeping. The chief, perhaps Culo Azul, informed Cooke that a party of Mexicans from Tucson had a few days before attempted to obtain the goods by representing themselves as part of the American army. According to the Indian, they had demanded the supplies, saying

Colonel Cooke had sent them. Unconvinced, the Pimas refused to part with the things placed in their keeping.[54]

Before leaving Tucson on the morning of December 18th, Lieutenant Colonel Cooke had prepared a note for Captain Comadurán and enclosed with it a letter addressed to "his Excellency, Señor Don Manuel Gándara, Governor of Sonora," noting in his journal that Gándara was said to be "very well disposed toward the United States." Because several years had passed since Gándara had been governor, and another six months would go by before he would again occupy that office, it is unknown why Cooke thought Gándara was Sonora's chief executive. On the other hand, Sonora had gone through so many political changes during the preceding ten years that even the people of the area may not have understood clearly who headed the department.

The communication intended for the governor placed deliberate emphasis on the differences between Sonora and the central government in Mexico City. Cooke stressed that Mexico's government had been of no service to Sonora in fighting the Apaches and he hinted that this could only be accomplished by a union of Sonora and her northern neighbors. Cooke stated with pride that he had made a wagon road "from the streams of the Atlantic to the Pacific Ocean, through the valuable plains, and mountains rich with minerals, of Sonora."[55]

The departure of the Mormon Battalion from Tucson after a stay of less than twenty-four hours may have prevented a battle between the American and Mexican forces, although when he left the presidio Cooke was not aware that any such possibility existed. Governor Cuesta, on his way south from Tubac, had sent a messenger ahead to instruct Colonel José María Elías González to ride to Tucson with a detachment of troops as rapidly as possible. It apparently took Elías a few days to assemble and equip such a force and it was almost the end of December before he and seventy infantrymen reached the fort. By that time the Americans were halfway to California.[56]

The presence of Colonel Elías and his men at Tucson apparently gave Father García Rojas a greater feeling of security, and he chose the months of January and February for visits to Santa Cruz, Tumacácori and San Xavier. His sacramental registers do not show that he entered the presidios of Tucson and Tubac, but he almost certainly performed baptisms for families from those communities when he was at San Xavier on February 12th and Tumacácori on February 14th. While visiting San Xavier, he baptized fourteen children, a greater number than on the previous occasion; at Tumacácori, he baptized six, compared to none the preceding May.[57]

The overthrow of General Paredes y Arrillaga in September of 1846 led to important changes in the governing structure of Mexico, including the partial reestablishment of the federalist system. One result of this restructuring was the convening of elections to choose new representatives to congress and to the state legislatures. In December, after returning from his trip to the north, Colonel Cuesta scheduled such elections for Sonora. He and other state officials met at Ures in January to work out the details, and one of their first acts was to name an interim governor. They picked don Luis Redondo, member of a family that had long been prominent in the Altar Valley. Through his mother, Redondo was related to the Gándaras, and followers of Manuel María may have influenced the selection. On January 6th, 1847, Colonel Cuesta turned the chief executive's office over to Redondo in whose hands the new legislature would soon place special powers for dealing with the possibility of an American invasion.[58]

II

The War Years, 1847-1848

The brief occupation of Tucson by the Mormon Battalion heightened the Sonorans' fear that their state, like New Mexico and California, would be the target of American attack. The invasion of Chihuahua in February, 1847, removed any lingering doubts about the intentions of the United States to seize all of northern Mexico.[1] On February 18th, the Sonoran legislature conferred extraordinary powers on Governor Redondo, allowing him to take whatever actions he might deem necessary to defend the state.[2] One of Redondo's first moves was to place Colonel José María Elías González in charge of the Sonoran defense effort. He was authorized to organize a force of regulars and auxiliaries and prepare to meet an invasion, regardless of the direction from which it came.

Early in April, word reached Ures that Americans were joining with Apaches for an attack on Fronteras. On April 23rd, Mariano Morales, the municipal president of Arizpe, informed state authorities that a large force of Americans and Apaches had reached Las Boquillas on the outskirts of Fronteras. Colonel Elías then notified Governor Redondo that he would go immediately to the area to try to stop the invaders. He noted that the presidial forces were lacking arms, ammunition and horses, and commented that all they had to fall back on was their courage and patriotism.[3]

Within a week after leaving Ures, Elías and the 300 men under his command were established in Fronteras. On April 30th, the colonel reported there were Apaches in the area but few if any Americans. He noted that Arizpe's municipal president had obtained his information from a pair of mule drivers who had passed through the Fronteras region. Elías said he, too, interviewed the *arrieros* but got a different story from them—one that included no mention of Americans.[4]

When the war between the United States and Mexico started, there were a number of Americans making their homes in Sonora. Some had become Mexican citizens; others had not. The largest concentration of *Yanquis* was in Hermosillo which, by 1847, was the largest Sonoran town. At least a few of the Americans were confident that armies from their country would soon control Sonora and they made no attempt to hide their contempt for the Mexican army and selected aspects of Mexican culture. Late in June, 1847, the official newspaper in Ures reported that Americans residing in Hermosillo, in spite of being protected and shown great courtesy by the Sonoran government, were constantly abusing the Mexicans, speaking with contempt about their authorized armies, and praising the fighting prowess of their own nation. Furthermore, they tried to make the people believe that the American government was waging war in Mexico solely to free the Mexicans from the oppression they had suffered.[5] The author of the article commented that he felt his own government was remiss in not putting a stop to this outrageous talk and conduct.

Gándara Becomes Sonora's Constitutional Governor

Early in May, 1847, Luis Redondo stepped down as Sonora's governor and turned the office over to Manuel María Gándara, who had been elected to that office a short time before. Patience and persistence had paid off for him, and Gándara or men associated with him would rule the state for most of the next decade.[6]

In addition to the threat of an American invasion and continuing raids by the Apaches, the new governor found himself confronting a major problem of banditry in the countryside. Particularly troublesome were a highwayman named Pedro Espinosa, who was popularly known as *El Chivero* ("the mountain lion"), and a trio of Yaqui Indians. Early in August of 1847, Gándara issued a circular calling for the arrest of the leaders and members of their gangs.

Less than a month later a Mexican from Bacanora with three Indians allies apprehended Espinosa who had a young boy with him. The robber was turned over to authorities and a short time later was shot to death by a prison guard.[7]

While the Mexicans hunted bandits to the south, Father García Rojas made another round of the Santa Cruz Valley settlements. He visited Tumacácori first, baptizing one infant there on August 26th. Two days later he was in Tucson. Between August 28th and September 1st, he baptized twenty-six children at Tucson and San Xavier. More graphic evidence of the population concentration can hardly be provided.

Shortly after Father García Rojas' visit to Tucson, Captain Comadurán led another expedition into the field against Apaches. For some months, the principal chief of the Pinaleños had been sending messages to Comadurán that he was eager to make peace with the Mexicans. At the same time he made the overtures, however, he and his warriors continued to attack Tubac and San Xavier at regular intervals. Finally, the *comandante* sent word to the Indian leader that if he and all the families under his control did not surrender, the troops of the garrison would punish them. When he received no response, Comadurán chose to act.

On September 10th, 1847, Tucson's commanding officer rode out of the fort in charge of 210 men. Included in the party were fifteen soldiers from Santa Cruz, seventeen from Tubac, and forty-five from Comadurán's own garrison, plus Mexican auxiliaries from Tucson, along with Pimas and peaceful Apaches. The captain's ability to put together such a formidable force may reflect the fact that some of the soldiers who came to the presidio with Colonel Elías nine months earlier had remained to strengthen Tucson's defenses.

After a four-day march, Comadurán and his men reached Arivaipa Canyon on September 14th, where they engaged the heavily outnumbered Pinaleños. This time, the Mexicans and their Indian allies came out considerably better than in previous encounters. The captain reported a total of sixteen warriors, seven women and four boys killed, and fourteen persons of both sexes captured. Thirty horses and eight cattle taken by the Indians in earlier raids were recovered.

Comadurán's forces, in spite of superior firepower, did not escape without losses. One of the soldiers from Santa Cruz died in battle, along with a Tucson civilian named Pedro Ruelas.[8] Four Tucson soldiers were wounded. After the Apaches fled the battlefield, they continued to send peace messages to Comadurán but when he invited them to the camp to discuss terms, they would not come.[9]

The first and only American occupation of Sonora during the war began the month after Comadurán's expedition against the Pinaleños. On October 16th, 1847, three American vessels anchored off Guaymas between the islands of Pájaros and Almagre Grande. E. A. T. Lavallete, the commander of the small fleet, sent a note to his Mexican counterpart demanding unconditional surrender of the port. The demand was refused and the Americans opened fire. Believing they could not hold out against the superior firepower of the invaders, the Mexican soldiers abandoned the plaza and retreated some distance from the town. Shortly thereafter, American sailors entered Guaymas and the ships offshore established a tight blockade of the port that lasted until June, 1848.[10]

Most standard histories of Arizona make no mention of any American penetration of the upper Pimería Alta during the war years other than those of Kearny and Cooke. However, a curious article published in the *Arizona Weekly Citizen* on June 15th, 1889, suggests there may have been one.[11] The article is concerned with the visit to the city of a Californian, called Judge F. Adams, who told a reporter that he had been in the Tucson area in November, 1847, with a company of soldiers carrying dispatches to General Kearny in California. According to Adams, the Americans tried to seize the presidio but were unable to do so. They contented themselves with surrounding it and holding captive those who were inside. Shortly after their arrival, they were joined by five American soldiers from El Paso who carried orders for them to return to Fort Bliss. The next day, they abandoned their siege. Adams reported that soldiers from the presidio followed them as they retreated southward, but would "scamper back in the direction of the town at a great rate" whenever the Americans turned to face them.[12]

In the story, Adams mentioned that the men in his party killed several Apaches near Tucson and San Xavier and another in the vicinity of a place called La Canoa. These were without doubt peaceful Indians from the long-established camps at the Arizona presidios. Had the Americans continued south as far as Tubac, they might have been tempted to attack that place, mistaking it for a

Battle in the streets of Guaymas between American sailors and Mexican soldiers
(Villa, *Historia del Estado de Sonora*)

hostile Apache community. Certainly, by late 1847, there were
more Indians than Mexicans in the town. The Apaches, in fact,
may have constituted as much as two-thirds of the total population.[13]

Early in February, 1848, the United States and Mexican negotiators agreed on terms to end the fighting. Although several more
months would pass before the Treaty of Guadalupe Hidalgo was
ratified by the national legislatures of the two countries, the war was
over.[14]

Massacre in the Sierra de las Mesteñas

It is not recorded when Sonorans learned of the peace treaty, but
they must have anguished over the news that Upper California,
New Mexico, and all the region north of the Gila River would soon
become part of the United States. For several years, Americans had
been turning over arms and ammunition to the Apaches in exchange for horses and mules stolen from the Mexicans. The situation would surely worsen.

Beginning in February, 1848, the month in which the terms of
the treaty were agreed to, the Sonoran General Command suspended the bimonthly wheat ration previously provided presidial
soldiers. The blockade of Guaymas had deprived the departmental

government of income from taxes on exports and imports. Bankruptcy threatened.

By mid-spring, many residents of Tucson faced starvation. Short of weapons, mounts and food, the Tucson troopers rebelled against further military duty. Captain Comadurán departed hastily for Ures to carry the bad news to his superiors and to seek their help. While he was away, Tucsonans organized an expedition to round up wild cattle at the abandoned Babocómari ranch. The acting *comandante* provided a small military escort. On May 10th, the party, at least fifteen strong, rode into an ambush at a watering place in the Whetstone Mountains (La Sierra de Las Mesteñas) called La Agua de las Mesteñas. All perished.

It was sometime after the massacre before Comadurán returned from Ures and the Tucson residents were too frightened initially to send an expedition to recover the bodies.[15] When finally they did mount the effort, they found the dead too badly decomposed to carry. In July, troopers from Santa Cruz put the bodies in sacks and transported them to that post for burial.[16]

As the victims were being removed, Comadurán forwarded to Manuel María Gándara a letter from nine Tucson widows whose husbands had fallen at the waterhole. The letter reveals the names of the dead. Corporals Zeferino Luque and Juan Rodríguez headed the expedition, accompanied by drummer Ignacio Camacho and soldiers Pedro Urías, Tomás Ocoboa, Juan Martínez, Rafael Ramírez, Manuel Rodríguez and Manuel Castillo. In the letter he wrote to accompany the widows' plea, Comadurán declared all of them worthy of assistance, and seconded their request to Gándara for help from the military fund for widows and orphans.[17]

In September, following the devastating ambush, a large Apache war party laid siege to Santa Cruz. They did not kill any of the settlers, but escaped with 60 cattle, 10 horses, and three mules. Alférez Manuel Romero and a small force of soldiers pursued them and succeeded in recovering some of the booty, but could not defeat the Indians in battle. The Santa Cruz *comandante*, Captain Francisco Villaescusa, reported that the Apaches were impoverishing the Hispanic settlers and that many soldiers were deserting.[18]

In October, 1848, a caravan of Sonorans left Hermosillo headed for California to search for gold. In no time, the migration would become a floodtide, and over the next five months alone more than

5,000 people would head for the northwest.[19] The exodus of able-bodied males from some of the frontier areas would leave those remaining behind even more vulnerable to Apache attack.

Graham's Trek Through Pimería Alta

The first descriptions in English of Santa Cruz Valley settlements south of Tucson come from the pens of soldiers accompanying Major Lawrence P. Graham from Monterrey, Nuevo León, to Los Angeles in 1848. In October, the company passed through what later became southern Arizona. The most complete account is by Lieutenant Cave Johnson Couts. Major Graham seems to have been inebriated much of the time, and, understandably, has provided no information about it at all.

From abandoned San Bernardino, which they reached on October 5th, the Graham party moved westward to the San Pedro River, passing through a location called Agua Prieta near the modern town of that name. Rather than follow the river northward as Cooke had done, Graham.chose to head across country in the direction of the Huachuca Mountains. Finding them too formidable a barrier, he turned south around the range, and on October 14th he and his men arrived at Santa Cruz, which had been under persistent attack from the Apaches most of the preceding month.

In his diary, Couts reported that the presidial garrison included "seventy or eighty" soldiers, none of whom impressed him much. The women of the town came freely into the visitors' camp to trade for soap and sugar. The Americans were also able to obtain pork, chicken and corn from their hosts.[20]

The Graham contingent left Santa Cruz on October 20th, heading downriver toward Tucson. The next evening, they camped near the old mission site of Guevavi. Along the way, they had passed deserted ranches and haciendas whose owners and inhabitants had long since been driven out by hostile Apaches. Near Guevavi, the Americans found a group of about twenty Mexicans mining for gold. As the Americans approached, the miners, taking the intruders for Apaches, scattered in all directions. Later, Lieutenant Couts learned that because of the Indian menace, mining was not a continuous process; rather, it took place at intervals of never more than two weeks in length. The owner—or at least the proprietor—of the mine implied that it was not particularly productive, although he was in possession of a nugget weighing two-and-a-half ounces.[21]

While en route to Tubac on October 22nd, the Americans passed through what Couts described as "a nice Indian village" just south of the presidio. It was Tumacácori and, according to Couts, "the Church looked very well." As for Tubac, the American officer wrote that it might as well be considered an Indian village "for there are two or more Apaches to every one Mexican." A man he described as "the General in Chief" of all the Apaches was in Tubac that day and he delivered a speech to his fellow Indians, cautioning against stealing from the visitors or interfering in any way with them. Couts was impressed that all, or nearly all, of the Apaches "talk Mexican."

The American lieutenant noted in his journal that the unit marched only nine miles on the 23rd, an observation that suggests they probably spent the night at the site of the Canoa ranch where water would have been available. No members of the Ortiz family lived there at the time. The following day, the Americans marched the distance to San Xavier.[22]

Both Couts and soldier Samuel Chamberlain were impressed with the remarkable state of preservation in which they found the old mission structure of San Xavier del Bac.[23] The lieutenant noted that the church was said to be "the *finest* in Sonora." He commented that its domes and spires which projected above the mesquite suggested "a City with *many* churches and other large and fine buildings." He also observed that it was constructed of burnt brick, "the first any of us had seen in Mex.," and that its wax figures and paintings "were particularly fine." The exterior, Couts wrote in his journal, "shows no age: on the contrary looks rather new: but there is an appearance of age about the interior which rather adds to than detracts from the sublimity of the picture. It is kept by these Pimas with incredible care and neatness."

Chamberlain was so taken with the church that he set out to make a sketch of it. While engaged at this task, he was interrupted by his commanding officer, perhaps intoxicated as seemed often to be the case, who demanded to know what he was doing. When the soldier replied, Major Graham ridiculed his drawing ability, snatched the pad from his hands, glanced at it; then threw it in Chamberlain's face. Next, he had the soldier handcuffed and left standing for two hours in the sun. A similar incident the following day in Tucson persuaded Chamberlain that further military service under Graham was not for him. He decided he would rather face the penalty for desertion and gave up soldiering shortly afterward.

The men of Graham's detachment were disappointed that Tucson was not the large, thriving city they expected it to be. Couts introduced his observations about the town with the comment that "the big place, the 2nd Chihuahua, is no *great deal* after all." However, he went on to record that, counting the Indians and Mexicans together, it was probably the largest settlement they had seen since their departure from Chihuahua. The people, he wrote, "are much in advance of some that we have passed, think Americans are *every thing*."

The courteous treatment that Graham's soldiers received from the Tucsonenses was similar to that noted by Cooke and his men two years before. The presidial commander, almost certainly Captain Comadurán, went to call on Major Graham the morning after their arrival, but the latter had "already got drunk and come on into town." The Mexican officer remained at the camp of the Americans all day waiting for Graham to appear and, Couts wrote, because it was cold and rainy, he was "nearly frozen" when Captain Kane "had the old fellow put into a wagon and brought home."[24]

Regrettably, Couts and Chamberlain have left much less information about Tucson and its inhabitants than is provided in the combined accounts of the various members of the Mormon Battalion. Major Graham and his troopers spent only one day at the presidio. According to Couts it rained the entire time. Chamberlain offers a substantially different account of the weather. Undaunted by his experience at San Xavier, he set out to sketch the walled town. Again, Major Graham caught him in the act and prescribed punishment. He was handcuffed and left to face the elements. "This Tucson is a very hot place," Chamberlain wrote in his autobiography, "and being tied up in the sun I was in a fair way of becoming *tasajo* [beef jerky].[25] I could feel my brains sizzling and my skin was commencing to crack. . . . " The soldier then relates how he was released from his misery by a "strange white man . . . dressed in a half Indian, half Mexican costume and armed with a heavy Kentuck rifle, revolver, and a huge Bowie Knife." The stranger's name, he later learned, was Tom Hitchcock and he belonged to John Glanton's band of scalp hunters "employed by Don Jose Urrea, Governor of Sonora."[26]

Sketch said to be the Tucson presidio in 1848 (Chamberlain, *My Confession*)

Couts gives the impression in his journal that the Pima Indian village at the foot of Sentinel Peak (modern A Mountain), long known to the Mexicans as El Pueblito, was abandoned at the time of his visit. The lieutenant thought that it had been a Spanish settlement and wrote that nothing remained but the residue of an "old Crockery furnace." The ground was "a complete dog town covered with old broken earthenware." Couts observed that it was at about this location "where the branch [of the Santa Cruz River] disappears into the sandy desert."

Like the troopers who preceded him with Cooke's expedition, Couts was fascinated with the burro-powered grist mills that he found in Tucson. Whereas one of his predecessors had mentioned only two in the community, Graham's lieutenant stated that "Every house in Tucion [sic] furnished with a Buro [sic] *flour mill*, and are kept going incessantly, probably grind a half bushel of wheat in 24 hours."[27]

On the morning of October 27th, 1848, the California-bound column left Tucson and marched northwestward toward the Gila River. Couts stated that the troopers obtained water from a place called the Charco de las Yumas, twenty-two miles south of Picacho.[28] The soldiers also passed by the famous old ruins of Casa Grande. They were well received by the Pima and Maricopa Indians of the Gila River villages, some of whom had just returned from a major battle with the Yumas who had killed thirty of their warriors and their "king." From the Pima towns, Graham's contingent followed the route previously covered by Kearny and Cooke.

Major Graham's trek through southern Arizona came just five

months after the Mexican congress ratified the Treaty of Guadalupe Hidalgo, officially bringing an end to the war between the two countries.[29] Had they travelled north of the Gila River, they would have been in the territory of the United States all the way. As it was they were trespassers on foreign soil; many others would soon follow them.

The Sonoran Census of 1848

Couts' account of his visit to the Hispanic settlements of the Pimería Alta is filled with references to the desolation caused by the hostile Apaches. While at Santa Cruz, he noted that three weeks earlier the fort had suffered the loss of its entire horse herd. He remarked on the number of abandoned ranches encountered between Santa Cruz and Tubac, including such long-established haciendas as that of Santa Bárbara. At Guevavi, he observed the extent to which gold-mining operations were subject to the whim of the Indian raiders. He wrote that Tumacácori had no Hispanic residents; he commented that Tubac might also be referred to as an "Indian village" since the native inhabitants greatly outnumbered the Hispanics.

The devastation that the Americans observed in the Santa Cruz Valley was common elsewhere along the frontier as well. According to an official government report issued earlier in the year, Apache raids had caused the depopulation of twenty-six mining camps, thirty haciendas and ninety ranches. This count did not include any locations in Sahuaripa and several other districts for which local officials had not provided data. Nor did it include the towns of Chinapa and Cuquiárachi, sacked and burned a few months before.[30]

At the time of Couts' visit to Tubac, the number of resident Mexican families was probably fewer than a dozen. A month before the Americans arrived, Gándara circulated a notice of the forthcoming municipal elections, including information from a recently completed census of the state. The count had been taken at least six months before, and it showed Tubac with a population of 249, about two hundred of whom must have been *Apaches Mansos*. Tucson was larger but it boasted only 760 inhabitants. The statistics provide clear evidence that the European-derived population of the

Sonoran frontier at the end of the war between the United States and Mexico did not exceed a thousand persons.

One of the most dramatic disclosures of the 1848 Sonoran census concerns Arizpe. The census takers counted only 1,491 persons there, a figure that was down from 7,000 about a dozen years before. The transfer of the capital to Ures had, of course, contributed to the population decline, but Apache raids had taken their toll as well. For several years, the Sonora River Valley, with its rich haciendas and ranches, had been a favorite target of the raiders.

Hermosillo, with a population of 11,635, was clearly the major Sonoran city in 1848. Alamos with its surrounding ranches and mining settlements was smaller by about five hundred. Guaymas was not included because of the American blockade and the only other community with more than 5,000 inhabitants was the mining town of Baroyeca. Its population stood at 7,484. The mines were playing out, however, and within a few years no one would be left there.

Ures, which would be Sonora's capital until 1879, was a town of just under 4,000 inhabitants at the time of the census. The municipalities of Cucurpe, in the San Miguel River Valley, and Baviácora, in the Sonora River Valley, were both about the same size as Arizpe, and Santa Ana and Altar were slightly smaller. San Ignacio, Magdalena and Tubutama had 100 or so more inhabitants than Tucson and Pitiquito was about the same size.[31]

Shortly before issuing the election notice that included the census report, Gándara had put out another circular lamenting the tragic circumstances in which the state found itself as a result of the Apache attacks. "All is misery," he wrote, "and the government finds itself lacking even the capacity to make use of the few available resources to ward off the most serious ills."[32] He noted that in February the government had made an effort to provide 7,500 pesos per month to meet the expense of fighting Apaches. Some of the municipalities that were expected to contribute these funds complained, however, that they could not meet their quotas. Gándara then sought a "forced loan" from certain of the wealthy citizens of the state, "but even that failed."

In December, 1848, the Sonorans chose José de Aguilar, who had previously been chief justice of the state supreme court, as their new governor. A member of one of the wealthiest families of the San Miguel River Valley, Aguilar was born in 1804 at San Miguel de Horcasitas. He was widely known throughout Sonora and before his death in 1881 would make many contributions to the development of his native state.[33]

Teodoro Ramírez, First Citizen of Tucson

As the Mexican period of control in northern Pimería Alta entered its closing years, the individual who seems to have been most called upon to serve his neighbors was don Teodoro Ramírez, a man who enjoyed the respect of all the residents of the Santa Cruz Valley—both Indian and Hispanic. Some of the ways in which he served have already been mentioned. On at least two occasions, he was personally responsible for seeing to it that the soldiers and their families did not go without food. When a reliable translator was needed for negotiations with Pimas and Papagos, don Teodoro was invariably the person to whom both the Indians and the Mexicans turned. If a document of some special kind had to be drafted, again it was Ramírez who served as scribe, and probably author as well. Thanks to his godfather, Pedro de Arriquibar, he was better educated than most of his associates.[34]

In spite of enjoying the respect of his neighbors and greater wealth than most, by late 1848 Teodoro Ramírez was a man who had suffered more than his share of grief. Over a two-year span, he had experienced the loss of four adult relatives and an infant daughter. First to go was his beloved older brother, Loreto, who died on October 8th, 1846. His sister Petra died in March of the following year. In August, 1847, he and María de los Angeles lost a day-old infant daughter. Apaches killed his nephew, Rafael, in May, 1848 and two months later, Teodoro mourned the death of his brother Antonio.

Along the way, there were a few blessings to count. The year before Loreto's death, the Ramírez couple became the parents of a girl they named María Manuela Martina. In April, 1846, they took her to San Ignacio for baptism on Easter Sunday.[35]

The Tribulations of Captain Comadurán

Although Tucson's *comandante* welcomed Major Graham's forces to Tucson in October, 1848, his heart was troubled at the time. A

few days before the Americans arrived, the presidial soldiers protested their lot with the second strike that year and went so far as to
send a delegation to Ures to meet with Gándara, who was both
governor and military commander of the state. At the capital, the
troopers learned that the departmental government could do nothing to improve their situation. Gándara told them he would order
Comadurán to relieve them of military duties so they might earn a
living at other pursuits.

Soon after their representatives returned from Ures, the soldiers
confronted Captain Comadurán, insisting that he carry out Gándara's orders. He told them he had received no orders and could not
meet their demands. Following a long discussion, the *comandante*
agreed to a compromise. In return for their promises not to abandon the fort, he would ask them to perform only guard duty. Field
service, for the time being, would not be required.

At eight o'clock on the evening of December 9th, 1848, a messenger from Tubac arrived at Comadurán's quarters with the news
that Tucson's sister fort was under attack. The Apaches had already
killed several soldiers and civilians. Knowing it would be useless to
try to assemble a force of troopers to send to the rescue, the *comandante* sought help from the town's justice of the peace, who rounded
up twelve civilian volunteers, himself among them. Comadurán
assigned Corporal José Romero to lead the rescue mission. When
they arrived at San Xavier, they learned that villager Ygnacio Saenz
had already departed for Tubac with a force of twenty Papagos.

Corporal Romero and his party caught up with Saenz at La
Canoa, where they were joined by a Tubac *vecino* and several tame
Apaches who told them the raiders had departed. The residents had
also abandoned the site. Romero and eight Tucsonans went on to
investigate the destruction while the others turned back.[36]

Late in January, the Sonoran general command ordered Comadurán to send twenty men to reoccupy the now-empty Tubac
presidio. The captain replied that he had earlier attempted to do so,
but the twelve-man force he had assembled under Corporal Solano
León got only as far as San Xavier, where the soldiers rebelled,
saying they had no shoes and were freezing.

Comadurán also informed his superiors that the Tubac *comandante* and his small force of men were in Tucson, where they lived
on what limited rations his post could provide. Some of Tubac's
vecinos were also in Tucson; others had gone to San Xavier and the

mining community of Soñi; still others had joined a few Tucsonans headed for California. The captain observed that the soldiers under his command were also rumored to be planning a trek to the gold-fields. The only persons left to die of hunger or to fall victim to the Apaches, he observed, would be those with large families who could not undertake the journey.[37]

12

The Yanqui Forty-Niners

In January, 1849, Tucson officially ceased being a presidio—a status it had enjoyed for almost three-quarters of a century—and took on the new designation "military colony."[1] The shift, decreed six months early by President José Joaquín de Herrera and his advisors, was intended to bring tranquility to the region and to promote settlement. Herrera feared new *Yanqui* moves to acquire Mexican territory and viewed the largely vacant borderlands as particularly vulnerable. At first the change would hardly be noticed. Within a few years, however, the old-time residents of Tucson would come to view it as an abomination.

The handful of persons still living in the remote northern villages of Sonora probably received the news of the establishment of military colonies with mixed emotions. On the positive side, they saw it as a move that could increase their capacity to withstand the Apache attacks that were now more frequent and more deadly than at any earlier period. Through long experience, however, they had grown dubious about the ability of the politicians in Mexico City to sustain an interest in the frontier long enough to accomplish anything.[2] There were questions, too, about the capacity of the bankrupt central government to support a program of sufficient magnitude to accomplish its objectives. In that regard, Article I of the decree was not particularly encouraging. It provided that "the budgets for these [military colonies] shall not exceed that prescribed for the presidial companies created by the law of March 20, 1826."[3]

Among those in Tucson at the time of the change in status was Father Lorenzo Vázquez from Altar, who was completing one of the most exhausting religious expeditions since the days of Garcés. He had travelled nearly 200 miles before he reached the town in late December.[4] Facing him at Tucson and San Xavier was a large accumulation of sacramental responsibilities. While in the area, he baptized forty-three persons, confirmed 118, confessed 120 and married four couples.[5] Sometime before the middle of January, he was back at his home base.

Gándara and Elías Disagree

Tubac and Tumacácori did not suffer alone in the closing days of 1848 and the first two months of 1849. On the contrary, much of northern Sonora sustained at this time the most devastating series of Apache raids ever experienced in the region. Acting Governor Juan B. Gándara on February 3rd sent a communication to Military Commander José María Elías González outlining the damage done in a two-week period between January 10th and January 23rd. He also predicted that if Elías could not put a force of 600 to 700 men in the field, many of the towns in the Arizpe, Moctezuma, San Ignacio and Altar districts would soon be abandoned. He noted that eighty-six persons had been killed by the Apaches during the period under review, in addition to the nine who had lost their lives at Tubac. Gándara urged the old soldier to get into action immediately.

Apparently stung by the implied criticism of his previous efforts against the Apaches, Elías wrote the acting governor on February 4th that Gándara's brother, Manuel María, had repeatedly placed obstacles in the way of his mounting a proper offensive against the Indians. Furthermore, Elías complained, only a month before, Juan himself had ordered two companies of soldiers into the field without so much as consulting him. To make matters worse, the acting governor had placed the troops under the command of men who were "notoriously incompetent."

From this point, Sonora's most experienced Indian fighter went on to blame the Gándaras for neglect of the presidios that had resulted in shutting down those at Fronteras and Bavispe. "If your

predecessor [and brother] with all his prestige, power, and resources could not remedy these evils," he asked, "how do you
expect me to do it in two months with no means whatsoever?" A
decade of frustration poured from Elías' pen as he defended his
honor, and he concluded with a challenge to Gándara to provide
him some resources so he could chastise the Apaches in their own
villages.[6]

Although he placed the emphasis on a lack of resources, Colonel
Elías certainly knew as well as Acting Governor Gándara that one of
the most important reasons for their inability to control the Indians
was the rapid depopulation of the frontier communities, whose
residents were heading for the California gold fields in ever increasing numbers. The problem grew in the early months of 1849 as
some of the first migrants returned with reports of great wealth to
be had for little effort.[7] In March, Father Vázquez wrote the bishop
that the outbound expeditions to California from Tucson and the
Altar Valley were leaving the remnant population of his parish open
to Apache attacks which were now coming with ever greater in-
tensity.[8]

Tucson's Isolation Breaks Down

While Sonoran political and military leaders were preoccupied
with the collapse of the frontier towns as a consequence of both
migration and Indian attacks, thousands of adventurers from the
United States and other countries were busy organizing expeditions
to California and before the end of 1848 some parties were already
on the move. The first news of the gold discovery had reached the
east coast in August, but many persons remained doubtful about
the matter until President James K. Polk delivered his annual message to Congress on December 5th. In that address, he stated that
the California mines were probably more valuable than had been
anticipated, and that an abundance of the ore that "would scarcely
command belief" had been corroborated by reports from military
officials.[9]

The first known civilian group bound for California to pass
through Arizona was a party of twenty-five headed by John C.
Fremont. They reached the area during March. Regrettably, the
man who later would be Arizona's territorial governor and a short-

term resident of Tucson recorded only a few cryptic notes about the experience. Fremont reported seeing peach trees in bloom somewhere in the Santa Cruz Valley (probably at either Tubac or Tumacácori) and that he encountered a party of Mexicans also headed for California who told him of the gold strike.[10]

Behind Fremont was the Kit Carson Association of New York, often said to have been the first real "Forty-Niner" party to follow the Gila trail to the goldfields. Harvey Wood of that company provided a few details of the journey, but included nothing concerning the residents of the Sonoran frontier. His notes do offer some insights into Mexican and Apache relations, however, especially in the portion concerned with the old Chihuahua fort of Janos which, by early 1849, had a dwindling population of about three hundred. He reported that the town was "in the possession" of six Apaches who were riding from store to store and making the proprietors furnish them with liquor "or anything else they demanded." These Indians purported to be part of a much larger group lurking on the outskirts of the community. They were well mounted, he observed, and "professed to be friendly to Americans."[11]

Writing about the journey from Janos to Tucson, Wood commented only that the party passed by several villages completely deserted, "caused by Apaches making a raid on the place, killing a few of the inhabitants and helping themselves to stock or anything else they fancied."[12] From the tenor of his comments, it is apparent that Wood had a low opinion of the Sonorans' courage to face up to the Apaches, an opinion others would also later voice.[13]

In his account of dealing with the Pima and Maricopa Indians, Wood makes clear that in spite of what was taking place in California, northern Sonora was not yet on the gold standard. Members of the Kit Carson Association offered the Indians $10 gold pieces, but found them reluctant to take these coins, whereas they readily accepted silver half dollars.[14] A few months earlier, Lieutenant Cave Johnson Couts and his fellow soldiers had found that the Mexicans also preferred silver to gold.[15]

Wood was generous in his praise of the Gila River Indians, especially of their chief who seemed to have great control over the rank and file. When one of the Carson party had a buffalo robe stolen, the Indian leader called together a group of warriors, talked to them about the matter and secured the return of the garment.[16]

The Kit Carson party reached the Colorado River shortly before mid-June, and crossed the stream on the 15th of that month. Wood does not provide any dates for visits to Santa Cruz and Tucson, but given the pace of later emigrant parties, it seems likely they passed through these communities around the middle of May. Within another two months, the dust of the Forty-Niners would fill the air over southern Arizona, and before the end of the year many thousands of travellers would reach California over the Gila route.

Between the visits of the Fremont and Kit Carson parties, the residents of the frontier communities of northern Sonora pondered their fate. Many undoubtedly felt that if the central government did not immediately supply arms and experienced soldiers, they would have no choice but to migrate, either farther south into Mexico, or to California. Before the December attack on Tubac, the settlers there, as well as those in Tucson and Santa Cruz, had petitioned the governor of Sonora for help, but spring had now come and no aid was in sight.

At Tucson, Captain Antonio Comadurán undoubtedly knew about the heated exchange that had taken place between Elías and Acting Governor Juan Gándara a short time before. Because of his close personal relationship with the general commander, he may also have been aware that following this exchange Elías had written the secretary of war in Mexico City insisting on immediate financial assistance. On March 26th, the secretary responded by sending a draft for 11,000 pesos, made out to the general commissary of the state of Sonora. An accompanying letter promised additional amounts. Elías was directed to use the money to make certain that the Sonora and Sinaloa garrisons were provided their full complement of soldiers, and that the troops had the required number of horses.[17]

By the time the federal draft reached Sonora, Juan B. Gándara had departed, and the Constitutional Governor José de Aguilar occupied the chair of chief executive. On April 30th, he sent a communication to the commanding officer at Santa Cruz advising him that fifty muskets were ready for delivery to the inhabitants of his community, as well as those of Tucson and Tubac. (He apparently overlooked the fact that no one had been living at Tubac since the Apache attack.) Aguilar stated that the local authorities of all three places were being asked to provide an escort to deliver the arms and munitions.[18] Shortly after Aguilar wrote to the Santa Cruz *comandante*, the community was visited by a large party of Ameri-

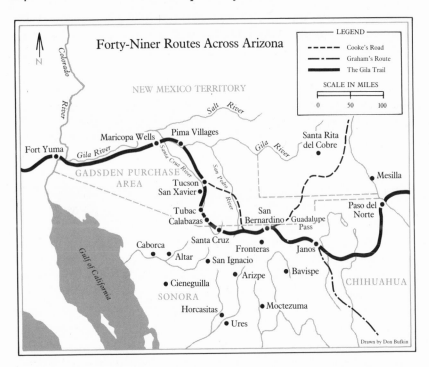

Forty-Niner Routes Across Arizona

LEGEND
- - - - - Cooke's Road
- · - · - Graham's Route
▬▬▬ The Gila Trail

SCALE IN MILES
0   50   100

can gold seekers who had left New Orleans on March 4th. The *Yanquis* were accompanied by John E. Durivage, correspondent for the *Daily Picayune*, who, fortunately, kept a diary of his adventures and reported them back to the paper.

The New Orleans travellers entered Arizona about May 15th, having journeyed overland from Brownsville, Texas. Like the soldiers who passed through before them, they encountered large herds of wild cattle not far from the old San Bernardino ranch, and sustained themselves for several days on meat from the animals. On May 23rd, they approached Santa Cruz where they came upon six horsemen whom they took to be Apaches. On closer inspection, however, the riders turned out to be Mexican soldiers from the old fort. The presidials, thinking the Americans were Apaches, had ridden out to challenge them. Durivage and his companions were apparently quite disappointed with what they found when they accompanied the soldiers to the town. The reporter described it as "old, dilapidated, and the poorest of the poor." He observed further that "there was no such thing as a store in the whole rancho." Durivage's account indicates that the New Orleans party was not the first to visit Santa Cruz after the Kit Carson Association passed through. Only a few days before their arrival, a company headed by a "Captain Fair" was there and, according to Durivage, had "skinned the place of flour, sugar, and bread. . . ." Wood's earlier observations about the reluctance of the Pima and Maricopa Indians to accept gold in preference to silver was confirmed by Durivage for the residents of Santa Cruz. Although he described the people as "poor as churchmice," he noted that "you cannot procure anything for gold . . . silver is the circulating medium."

The New Orleans newspaperman noted as another sign of the town's poverty the fact that it had no resident padre. Services were performed, he said, by a *maestro* or lay priest. Since Tucson was in a similar situation at the time, it is probable that a *maestro* also provided for the spiritual needs of the Tucsonenses on an interim basis.

In spite of great difficulties in securing food from the residents of Santa Cruz, Durivage had words of high praise for the *comandante* of the new military colony. The commander invited some of the American emigrants to dine at his home, where he provided them the best of what little was available, accompanying the serving of each new dish with an apology for its "inferior quality." When asked what the visitors should pay for the meal they had enjoyed, he responded "with the air of a Spanish nobleman: *Es* [sic] *no vale nada, señor.*" Durivage concluded that "It is like finding an oasis in a desert to light on a liberal Mexican gentleman."

Passing downstream from Santa Cruz, the Durivage party camped at the site of the deserted Santa Bárbara Ranch, one of the oldest and for many years one of the most important haciendas in Sonora. The reporter commented on the beauty of the valley and the vast quantities of gold-colored mica in the streambed. Some of his fellow travellers panned the sand, hoping they might encounter some of the genuine article but none was successful. Durivage apparently confused the settlements of Tubac (which he called La Vaca) and Tumacácori, but did note that both were abandoned. They camped eight miles north of Tumacácori just above the point where the river disappeared into the sand.[19]

The following day, Durivage and a doctor accompanying the New Orleans party pushed on ahead to San Xavier which the reporter described as inhabited "by Pima Indians and a few Apache touters." Both the visitors were impressed with "the old cathedral, a splendid edifice erected at an enormous cost, in a very fair state of preservation externally and internally." In contrast, Durivage described the houses of the Indians as "mud hovels, scarcely big enough for a sow and her litter, and little better than a sty or a dog kennel." On the other hand, he called the Indians "bright and intelligent people."

At sundown on May 28th, Durivage and his companion reached Tucson, "a miserable old place garrisoned by about one hundred men." Provisions were scarce here, as they had been in Santa Cruz, but the men were able to acquire flour and a small quantity of corn. The reporter noted that near the town were the remains of an old mission whose gardens were well stocked with fruit. Durivage was impressed with the number of saguaro cactus growing on a "large, pyramid-shaped mountain" near the ruined mission.

On May 29th, the remainder of the New Orleans caravan arrived at Tucson and stopped a mile below the presidio. Throughout the remainder of the day "Mexican women and Indians" visited the camp, eager to trade. Needles and thread were among the items most sought after. In his journal, Durivage noted that "a few good purchases in mule flesh were made" by the Americans. In wandering about the community, he discovered the presence of the camp of tame Apaches who, in his eyes, were cowardly and imbecilic. He could not find in them a "single captivating trait of character," and he described them as "unequivocally a miserable, degraded set." He observed, however, that they were treated with great consideration by the Mexicans "and are wholly supported by them."

At 4 a.m., June 1st, the New Orleans party began the journey to the Gila River which Durivage considered the most difficult part of the entire trip. (This observation would later be shared by the members of many other parties.) They travelled until 2 a.m. the following morning and after a rest of a couple of hours pushed on. Durivage, more dead than alive, reached the river about 2 p.m., June 2nd. Others had arrived earlier. Their horses were so famished for water that they dashed for the stream, leaving riders on the ground, hanging in trees and thrashing about in the river.

For the next several days, the caravan visited various Pima villages, purchasing and trading for food. On June 6th, Pima leader Antonio Culo Azul invited the emigrants to attend a scalp dance which the Pimas and Maricopas were holding in celebration of a victory over the Apaches. They had in their possession six scalps and twenty-five women and children prisoners. The Americans declined, but others coming along later would observe such ceremonies.

After passing the painted rocks area, on June 11th Durivage and his comrades encountered a party of Mexicans who had travelled overland from San Blas in Nayarit. They were accompanied by "Captain Lewis of New York and five companions who had come by the way of Veracruz and Mazatlán." The Americans had hoped to obtain passage by sea from Mazatlán, but had been unsuccessful in that effort.

On June 19th, the New Orleans party reached the Colorado River, where they learned that a few days before Captain Allen of St. Louis and two members of his group had been drowned attempting to cross. After spending some time scouting the area and deciding on the best way to get over to the California side, the Americans made their crossing on June 22nd.[20]

Only a few days behind the New Orleans caravan was a party of New Yorkers who, after landing at Brazos Santiago on the Texas coast, had followed the same overland route as Durivage and his associates. This group called itself the Hampden Mining Company, and their chronicler was Asa Bement Clarke. He described the ruins of the Rancho San Bernardino as "situated on a rise of ground with a beautiful, grassy flat on each side, with a small stream running through a bluff from ten to thirty feet high. . . ." Not far away, the Hampden company came upon the first herds of wild cattle.

When the party reached Santa Cruz on May 25th, they experienced less difficulty than the New Orleans emigrants in obtaining food. Clarke mentioned the presence of a flour mill that "was erected by a Yankee who afterward went to California." He stated that *pinole* was plentiful, and proceeded to explain the process by which it was made. According to his description, "The wheat is soaked in hot water, then put into frames to drain, from which it is taken and spread on hides to dry in the sun; it is then put into a large oven and parched or baked, when it is ready to grind. . . . Penole [sic] makes an excellent food for the journey, made into a pudding, or porridge; sweetened and stirred in water, it makes a very refreshing drink." According to Clarke, the members of his party visited many houses in Santa Cruz, "entering without ceremony." He spent several hours watching a family bake bread, but commented unfavorably on the sanitary habits of his hosts after he observed a woman wash her hands in a gourd atop a water jar from which other persons were drinking.

Clarke contributes several items to the negative stereotype of the Mexicans as Indian fighters. Observing villagers carrying arms along with them to the fields, he asked one of the company's mule drivers (whom he identified as "a Santa Fe man") what they intended to do with their guns and lances. He was told "When they see the Indians coming, they throw them down and run like h___l." In his diary, Clarke also recorded another anecdote concerning Apache intimidation of the Mexicans: during the planting season while the men were working in the fields, a group of Apaches rode by and demanded they be given the best horse in town; the owner handed it over without hesitation.

Like some of the other diarists who would follow, Clarke confused the Santa Cruz and San Pedro rivers, giving the latter name to the stream the argonauts followed after leaving the town of Santa Cruz. At Tumacácori, the Hampden party found peaches, pears and quinces in the mission orchard, and at Tubac they noted that the residents had departed in such haste that they had left many of their possessions behind. Commenting on the beauty of the river valley, Clarke's obvious disdain for the Mexicans got the better of him. "It must be a miserable race," he wrote, "that could deliver up such a valley with its delightful climate."

On May 30th, members of the Hampden Mining Company reached San Xavier which Clarke identified as San Gabriel. As with other visitors, he was taken by the beauty of the church, recording that it must have cost as much as all the other buildings in town. While passing through Tucson later in the day, the emigrants were able to buy meat, bread and flour, as well as milk—the last delivered to them in baskets "woven so closely, that they are used for containing liquids."

In describing the Tucson garrison, Clarke again allowed his prejudices to surface. "There is a band of organized troops stationed here," he wrote. "The soldiers make a contemptible appearance, lounging about their quarters. Their pay is the promise of three bushels of wheat, and a small sum of money per month. The wheat they get, the money they do not. They, however, receive more than their services are worth."

Clarke was one of the first of the Forty-Niners to see the Tucson meteorite, or at least to write about it. He had gone to a blacksmith shop, presumably that of Ramón Pacheco, to obtain mule shoes and saw what he described as "a piece of native iron from a neighboring mountain, used for an anvil." It was between three and four feet long, with two large legs. The Americans judged its weight at about 2,000 pounds. In the part of his diary where he described the meteorite, Clarke expressed his surprise that the smith using it claimed that he did not know how to shoe mules.

For part of the distance between Tucson and the Gila River, members of the Hampden Mining Company apparently shared the trail with Durivage and his group. Clarke mentions that several of the emigrants had "fainted" before getting to the stream, including a "gentleman from New Orleans, formerly connected with the *Picayune* who gave out a few miles back. . . ." The reference is unquestionably to Durivage who came close to experiencing sun stroke.

Quite evidently by early summer of 1849, traffic along the Gila trail had become intense. Clarke's description of the journey from the Pima villages to the Colorado River makes reference to several other parties just ahead of his or just behind. Included were a company of Mississippians (possibly the Durivage party) and the North Adams Company from Massachusetts. He also mentions parties of Mexicans. On June 24th and 25th, the members of the Hampden Mining Company crossed the Colorado.[21]

Yankee Arrogance Causes Problems

The negative appraisals of Mexican villagers and their way of life that are reflected in the writings of men such as Asa Bement Clarke are probably typical of most Forty-Niners' point of view. The United States had just concluded a successful war against the Mexicans and the spoils of the conflict had greatly increased the size of the nation. Winning had been almost unbelievably easy and many Americans felt nothing but contempt for the defeated enemy. In his book *Mexico and the Hispanic Southwest in American Literature*, Cecil Robinson notes that

> more or less ragged fringes of Mexican society were not such as would favorably impress American frontiersmen, who by and large held the plains Indians in higher regard than they

did the Mexicans. Such nomadic warriors as the Apaches and Navajos had certain stoic virtues that could be readily understood and appreciated by the rather simple frontiersman, yet even the most forlorn Mexican represented to a degree a complex culture that these Americans either could not or would not understand.[22]

The first serious incident resulting from this arrogance occurred early in June at the old gold mining town of Cieneguilla south of Altar. A party of more than 30 Americans sacked the town with no regard for the fact that the local people had welcomed them and treated them kindly. The raiders began their mischief by placing a rope around the neck of the village priest—Father Francisco Javier Vázquez—hanging him several times for short intervals, then dragging him about. The elderly priest almost perished of fright and outrage. The Americans then mistreated his sister in similar fashion and carried her off to the house in which they had been living. Before abandoning the town later in the day, they rounded up other citizens, stripped them of their belongings and locked them in their houses.[23]

After departing Cieneguilla, the Yankees headed for Caborca, passing through there about 3 p.m. on June 3rd. Although the horses ridden by the Forty-Niners were tired and the riders low on water, the Americans apparently hurried through town without attempting to get new mounts or assuage their thirst. José María Bustamante, president of the Caborca council, wrote the governor that he did not pursue the invaders because most of the able-bodied men of the district were away in California.[24]

A month after the assault on Cieneguilla, a party of Texans subjected Santa Cruz to a similar demonstration of *Yanqui* disregard for local authority, law and custom. They reached the old fort on July 3rd and were treated to a *fandango* by the local residents. The following morning, the Mexicans urged them to camp within the town limits because of the Apache danger, but the travellers, apparently confident they could stand up to the Apaches, declined.

The Americans' disregard for this danger may have stemmed from the fact that a few days before, they had made an attack on an Apache camp and forced the inhabitants to flee to the nearby hills. In their haste to escape the unexpected onslaught, the Indians left

Valley leading to Santa Cruz, Sonora (Bartlett, *Personal Narrative*, volume 1)

Sketch of Santa Cruz in the 1860s (Browne, *Adventures in the Apache Country*)

behind a mare and thirty-nine cows with Mexican brands. Two days after arriving in Santa Cruz, the Yanquis learned that Mexican law required them to put the stock in the public corral so the animals might be claimed by their owners, who were to pay a sum equal to about fifty cents per head to those who had made the recovery. According to Benjamin Butler Harris, a member of the Texas party, the Americans refused to surrender the animals under these terms, whereupon the Santa Cruz *alcalde* forbade the Mexicans of the town to receive any beef from the visitors or to stage any more dances for them. The captain of the American party then prepared a defiant message for the *alcalde* and had it translated into Spanish. He delivered the communication personally and threatened the Mexican official with a long-bladed Bowie knife.

That night the rampaging *Yanquis* broke into a private home where a number of the village young ladies had been locked up for their protection. They persuaded the twenty-five girls in the house to join them for a dance. Some of the officers of the garrison rushed in to confront the intruders, but backed down when they found themselves outnumbered by angry Texans with drawn pistols.

In his diary, Harris recorded that the Forty-Niners found sympathy the following day from some of the local Mexicans. They butchered a beef for these people. After distributing meat, the Texans threw the entrails into the house of the *alcalde*. When they finally left Santa Cruz on July 7th, they gave the townspeople the remaining stock.

The Mexican account of the Santa Cruz outrage reads somewhat differently from Harris'. On August 3rd, *El Sonorense* published part of a letter from Colonel Elías González to Governor Aguilar dated July 24. In the letter, Elías quoted the commanding officer of the Santa Cruz military colony, Captain José María Villaescusa, concerning the events that took place earlier in the month. According to Villaescusa, there were more than eighty Americans in the Texas party and they demanded payment of three pesos per animal to comply with the Sonoran law. When the Mexicans refused because they could not afford such a high payment, the Americans began butchering the cows and selling beef. Villaescusa described the visitors as the most audacious and disorderly people he had ever seen.

After leaving Santa Cruz, the Texans proceeded to San Xavier where they administered thirty-nine lashes to an Indian who had pilfered some items from their goods. The Papago headman himself had the culprit arrested and turned over to the Americans.

News of their reputation apparently did not precede the Texans to Tucson, where members of the party attended many *fandangos*. Harris reported that "immigrants to the number of four to five hundred filled the little frontier town. . . ."[25]

A third example of American rowdiness occurred in August and, although milder than the previous events, it also contributed to the unfavorable stereotype of the argonauts. In this case, the party was headed by naturalist John Woodhouse Audubon. After losing their way, the company struggled south along the slopes of the Sierra Madre to the vicinity of Yécora, Sonora, where they turned west. On August 22nd, more dead than alive, they reached Ures and decided to spend a week recuperating. The therapy some of the men chose for themselves involved the ingestion of large quantities of the local mescal, perhaps the variety known as *bacanora* for which Sonora was famous even then. Several became so boisterous and obnoxious that they were incarcerated and Audubon found himself obliged to pay to secure their release. Shortly thereafter, the group resumed its March and reached Altar on September 12th. Here, they met Mexicans returning from California who lifted their spirits with tales of abundant gold. The Americans hastened to hire a Papago to guide them along a trail where water could be found. The Indian accepted payment in advance consisting of a pair of shirts, a sheath knife and $5. He disappeared a few days later.

The argonauts eventually made it to the Colorado River on October 15th. By that time, they were in such dire straits that they had to obtain food from the contingent of U.S. Dragoons stationed at the crossing. These soldiers were commanded by Lieutenant Cave Johnson Couts, who had made the trip through Sonora the preceding year with Major Lawrence P. Graham. From the soldiers, Audubon party members learned of the recent drownings of four men—an army officer, one of his men and two Mexicans.[26]

Apache Attacks Continue

Through much of 1849 the Apaches refrained from preying on the Forty-Niner caravans, although as early as June, the Texas party that later caused problems at Santa Cruz encountered an ambush laid by Mangas Coloradas and his warriors between Janos and Guadalupe Pass. Following a short skirmish, the Indian leader called for a parley. When it was granted, he told the Americans that he loved them and that he hoped they would join him in driving the Mexicans (*cristianos malditos* he called them) from the area.[27]

Although the first accounts by the Forty-Niners of their travels through northern Sonora do not mention trading arms to the Indians, the practice had been engaged in for some time by Americans residing in New Mexico and had certainly contributed to the increased tempo of Apache depredations on frontier settlements. In spite of the summer heat, hostile Apaches raided widely across northern Sonora during July and August. The Texas argonauts encountered an Apache party between Agua Prieta and Santa Cruz early in July, and on the 30th of that month, the Indians assaulted Santa Cruz with a force of more than fifty warriors. They plundered livestock, killed a visitor from Altar and kidnapped three residents.

Farther south, the Mexicans struck back early in August but the results were tragic. Captain Teodoro Aros led a small group of soldiers in pursuit of Apaches raiding in the area of Arizpe and succeeded in killing four and wounding several others. After the battle, the Mexicans recovered ninety head of cattle, four mules, three horses and a donkey. Aros detailed Sergeant Serapio Olguín to escort the animals to Arizpe. Along the way, Olguín and his party, including twenty civilians, were ambushed by Apaches at a site known as Los Berrendos. The sergeant and four civilians were killed outright, two soldiers were wounded but escaped, and thirty-two persons, among them six soldiers, were taken prisoner by the Indians.

A few days later, on August 12th, a force of more than sixty Apache warriors assaulted ranches in the lower San Miguel Valley not far from Horcasitas. Rumors reached Ures that they planned to attack the large hacienda of Alamito and then go on to Hermosillo.[28]

Two weeks after the attack on Santa Cruz, an American party calling itself the Defiance [Ohio] Gold Hunters reached that town. George W. B. Evans, a member of the group, kept a diary of his experiences, but included next to nothing about either Santa Cruz or Tucson.[29] Of the former, he wrote only that it was "poor and almost deserted." He also noted that the company left its wagons there and formed a pack train to continue the journey. Evans and his associates were apparently pleased with their reception from the

Pimas at San Xavier who gave them beef. The diarist noted that
these Indians were "civil and polite and extremely grateful for the
least favor granted." Of Tucson, he said only that it was "little
better than the Indian town."[30]

Not far behind the Ohio party was the Little Rock Company of
Arkansas, one of whose members found Santa Cruz a good place to
trade jewelry. For an item that had cost him seventy-five cents he
secured two and a half bushels of flour, several pounds of sugar,
and a number of "other little articles." To attract the women, he
borrowed a fiddle and played it. After shutting down his business
for the day, he joined some of his companions and a group of local
ladies for a *fandango*. The chronicler for the Little Rock Company
commented at some length on the beauty of the abandoned Santa
Cruz Valley, observing that "The whole country abounds in rich
gold and silver mines. But as soon as a town or rancho is built, the
Apaches tear it down and kill all the males and carry off all the
females." Like others before him, and some who came later, he had
nothing good to say about the Mexican troops. Writing of those in
Tucson he stated that "as soon as they go outside the town, the
Apaches drive them in again. They are like all Mexican soldiery."[31]

Close on the heels of the Arkansas company was another Texas
group, this one headed by Lewis Birdsall Harris. Although ostensi-
bly one of the best organized and directed of all Forty-Niner caravans, it was plagued with innumerable problems. Cornelius C. Cox,
who travelled with the group, noted that they were delayed for
more than a week near the San Pedro River between Agua Prieta
and Santa Cruz because of the illness of a woman in the party. They
finally made progess on September 1st, but three days later the
woman's condition worsened and she and her husband left the
group.[32]

Cox's description of Santa Cruz is brief but informative:

This place has a population of about fifteen hundred—com-
posed chiefly of the lower order called Peons. There is an
Arsenal, a Church, and several grist mills in the place. The
chief productions of the valley are Corn, Wheat, and Beans.
The corn is in roasting ears and proves the excellent quality of
the land. Wheat is worth $3 per Fanagar [*fanega*], Flour Six.
Mrs. Harris laid in a good supply of vegitables [sic], Eggs, and
Chickens which we are enjoying with an Epicurians taste."[33]

Cox followed other observers in extolling the beauty of the Santa Cruz Valley and commenting on the abundance of fruits in the orchards of abandoned villages. His diary entry on San Xavier (again mislabeled San Gabriel) exhibits some newly acquired Spanish. He noted that the "*Elacia*" (*iglesia* or church) was "really a splendid looking building, the interior of which presented a solemn and imposing scene." At Tucson, the Texans replenished their supplies, attended a *fandago*—apparently by now a standard event— and talked with some Mexicans returning from California, one of whom was carrying a quantity of gold dust estimated to be worth $20,000.

Tucson was evidently enjoying a new measure of prosperity by early September, 1849. With greater frequency, the Forty-Niner diarists described finding substantial quantities of food available for sale or trade. Cox mentioned that the Harris party purchased cattle from residents of the military colony at a price of $12 per head. The Mexican women were eager to acquire items of jewelry that the Americans brought with them, and Cox reported that some of the Texas company "made handsome profits upon their little stocks of finery trinckets etc."

Just before reaching the Colorado River, the Harris party encountered members of the Audubon company. "Here was the first instance of distress that I had seen on the road," Cox wrote. "Many of these men had not a day's provisions on hand, and some were entirely destitute." Cox described in some detail the drowning of the American officer, Captain Herman Thorne, and his three companions, an event that was also recorded by members of the Audubon party.[34]

As traffic along the Gila Trail continued to increase during the month of September, Colonel José María Elías González put the finishing touches on a plan to confront the Apaches in their mountain havens. Available to help cover the expenses of such an expedition were central government funds destined for the support of the military colonies, as well as local contributions of money and equipment. On September 22nd, near the abandoned San Pedro Ranch, Missouri parties headed by Captains Samuel Berry and John Robards encountered a Mexican officer leading troops to a rendezvous with the Elías expedition. The Americans were impressed with the officer's English and were surprised to find that he had been educated in England. He reported that there were more than eight hundred soldiers and militiamen in the Mexican force which was headed for the Dry Lake area (modern Willcox Playa) where a large body of Apaches had been sighted.[35]

Several other American parties were in the San Pedro region at the time the Mexican troops went north on their Apache campaign. One was the Peoria Company and it included a Quaker named Charles Pancoast. Like much else that he encountered while passing through this part of Sonora, the Mexican troops provided Pancoast with subject matter for his sarcasm. "Soon after we camped," he wrote,

> there came over the Mountain a Company of Mexican Cavalry, armed with long Swords, wearing sugar-loaf caps of leather adorned with Crow or Rooster feathers or old Revolutionary cockades, blue coats with brass buttons (many of which were missing) and Pants too short for them, and riding miserable Broncho Horses: altogether bearing too much resemblance to Don Quixote's Company. Not knowing that we were in the Mexican states, we at first took them to be a band of cut-throat Guerillas. They did not condescend to speak to us, but figured around for a time, and then galloped off down the mountainside.

Pancoast's strong distaste for the local population was again manifest in a diary entry recorded two days later. This time he noted, "We camped near the beautifully located but scrawny Town of Santa Cruz, inhabited by about three hundred miserable-looking Mexicans commonly termed 'Greasers.' All of them appeared to be constitutionally tired, and to have an abundance of time to rest."[36]

Colonel Elías' forces did not remain long in the San Pedro-Santa Cruz area. When the Illinois Company passed through a few days after Pancoast and his companions, the Mexican soldiers had already moved north into the heart of the Apache country. H. M. T. Powell, who provided an extensive account of the experiences of the Illinois party, did not single out Mexican soldiers for unflattering comments, but extended them to all and sundry. "There is everything here to make country life delightful," he recorded, "and yet the imbecile Mexicans permit a few Apaches to drive them out of as beautiful a country as heaven ever smiled on."

On Santa Cruz and its inhabitants, he commented that the place looked very old and dilapidated with "grama grass growing on the tops of the houses." He observed two churches. One provided quarters for soldiers, half of whom were in town and the other half "out on country parties after the Apaches who stripped them last spring of everything except a few sheep and goats." Many people of the town, remarked Powell, were attending a grand festival in Arizpe in spite of the Apache danger. "They are certainly a very imbecile, trifling people," he commented, then followed his insult with a left-handed compliment, noting that the Santa Cruz residents looked "better than those I saw in New Mexico. They have a brighter and more intelligent look." Many, he noted, were suffering from "fever and ague."

Powell and his companions paid $6 a *fanega* (two-and-a-half bushels) for unbolted flour, and twelve and a half cents each for cakes of sugar. One member of the party also sold a cart in Santa Cruz for $10. Taken together, these transactions reveal that by early October, 1849, U.S. currency had become the principal means of exchange in Mexican towns along the Gila trail.[37]

While most of the troops from the frontier military colonies were chasing Apaches with Colonel Elías, a veteran soldier from the Tucson garrison, now a national guard captain, was doing some campaigning of his own with the aid of 130 Papagos from San Xavier. During the first week of October, Guadalupe Luque, a descendant of one of Arizona's oldest Hispanic families,[38] rode at the head of the Papago force to Arivaipa Canyon where they attacked several camps of Apaches whom they considered responsible for recent raids on Tucson. The Papagos killed six warriors and five adult women, and took twelve children as captives. Captain Luque permitted them to keep as booty the ten horses and fifteen cattle recovered from the Arivaipa Indians.[39]

The two Missouri companies and the Peoria party, the same three Forty-Niner groups that had encountered Mexican soldiers while in the San Pedro area, arrived at San Xavier as the Papagos were preparing a scalp dance to celebrate their destruction of the Apache camp. Although such affairs must certainly have been familiar to the Hispanic population of the area and accepted as normal Indian behavior, the Americans were horrified by the proceedings.

On the night of October 3rd, members of Captain Berry's Missouri party, who were camped on the outskirts of San Xavier, noted that the Papagos were in a very excited state because of the victory they had gained over their enemies. The Indians told them they had slain ten Apaches and taken ten children as prisoners. They had two scalps which an old man, with much ceremony, arranged on a spear. Then the Papagos began to dance. The "yells and frantic gestures of the performers," diarist William H. Hunter wrote, "were truly disgusting and fearful. . . ." The following morning, the Missourian noted that the "screams of the savages as they carried on their diabolic orgies, resounded through our camp and prevented many of us from sleeping."

The Indian ceremonies continued into the evening of October 4th when, according to Hunter, "they paraded their prisoners, amongst them a clean limbed active little fellow about 10 years old who had been shot in the back of the neck. In the wound maggots were already rankling eliciting neither sympathy nor compassion." This young Apache then became the object of "torment and vengeance" especially by an elderly woman whom Hunter described as "an old fiend-like looking squaw." He concluded with this description:

> The little prisoners grouped in a circle around the scalp spear, at first evinced some agitation on seeing their persecutors brandishing their knives, tomahawks, etc., but after the dance had commenced . . . it was surprising to watch their stoical apathy. The squaws would every now and then brandish their knives about their throats, and then rushing furiously upon them, seize them by the hair, and with a stroke which nothing but practice could have rendered so apt, sever a lock of hair from their heads, as near the skin as possible. The old squaw aforementioned would then seize the scalps and shaking them wildly in the air, with apparent imprecations, thrust them into the faces of the little unfortunates. The boy, however, above alluded to, quailed not. His gaze never once encountered the mementoes of the dead, but was steadily and unblanchingly fixed on that of his human tormentor. And never did the lion in all his pride and power, cast a more disdainful, withering look of scorn and contempt on his most pusillanimous assailant, than that which decked the brow of this stripling of the desert toward his persecutors.[40]

Camped in the vicinity of San Xavier at this time was the Peoria Company to which Forty-Niner Charles Pancoast belonged. These

Americans were also attracted by the tumult, and seeing painted Indians waving weapons through the air, thought for a time they might have to fight. When they finally determined what the excitement was all about, they retired to camp to consume their evening meals. Later some went back to view proceedings in the Indian village. Pancoast's description of these events resembles that of Hunter except in one important particular.

> The first thing that attracted our attention was a number of bloody scalps set up on Spears that had been driven into the ground. But what we found still more interesting was a captive Indian girl, twelve or thirteen years of age, sitting on the ground in the Arbor. Notwithstanding her awful position with all those horrid painted Savages dancing, yelling and posturing about her. . . . she sat apparently unmoved, with no look or utterance expressive of the terrible emotions that must have prevailed within her. One of the Indians could speak a little Spanish, and our Interpreter asked if they intended to scalp or kill the little Girl, and he answered in the negative, but said they would make her work for them.[41]

The San Xavier Papagos were apparently sharing their village with both Apaches and Mexicans in October, 1849. The anonymous chronicler of the Robards' party observed that Apaches were living to the north of the church, and a comment in Hunter's diary suggests that some of the Tubac refugees may have been occupying temporary quarters inside the mission. "Around the wall," he wrote, "on the interior, was rooms or cells for the residence of the servants of the Church, now occupied by Mexican families who are suffering, and perhaps helping, the Edifice to pass quickly into ruin and decay."[42]

Pancoast, Hunter, and the unidentified writer mention Tucson, but Pancoast notes only that he obtained a horse from one local resident in exchange for six brass buttons, a box of paints, and two small mirrors.[43] He and his companions visited the military colony on October 7th, two days after the Robards' party, and a day after the Berry company. Hunter reported the town's population to be about "eight hundred to a thousand"; the Robards' diarist guessed "five hundred."

Hunter is unique among Forty-Niners in commenting favorably on the appearance of Tucson. He described it as "better laid out" than any town they had seen since leaving Santa Fe. The Missourians had heard that Tucson was crowded with emigrants who were unable to proceed further. However, they did not find this to be true. The Tucsonenses told them that the biggest group of stranded Forty-Niners, as many as 800, was at the Pima villages on the Gila River.

Hunter reported in his journal that he visited the Tucson *alcalde* (actually the *juez de paz*) who communicated to him wondrous tales of the riches in California that "were altogether beyond the reach of credibility." He also noted that there were three or four other caravans camped near the old presidio and that the members of these companies were busily engaged in trading with the natives for cattle and provisions, "for which they seemed to be paying tolerably high." His concluding comment about Tucson was that the town looked "as though it may have seen better days."[44]

About four days behind the Missourians and on the heels of the party from Peoria was the Illinois Company, whose chronicler, H. M. T. Powell, provided history with some of its best descriptions of travel along the Gila Trail. Powell and his companions rode into San Xavier on October 9th, having encountered a small party of Mexicans travelling from Tucson to Santa Cruz the previous day. Two members of the group were soldiers and Powell wrote of them: "Any one of Falstaff's ragged regiment was well dressed in comparison."

Powell was less taken with the San Xavier church than some of his predecessors, but still considered it important enough to merit a sketch. He commented that the interior was very elaborately carved and gilded "with a number of large oil paintings, but none of any worth that I could see." He also noted that the roof leaked and the water was running down inside "over paintings and all" and accused the Papagos of being too lazy to mend it. Before leaving San Xavier for Tucson, members of the Illinois party heard that a local Mexican had recently returned from California with $60,000 worth of gold.

Powell was the first of the Forty-Niners to identify any Tucsonans by name, reporting that he sold his wagon to Ygnacio Saenz for a mule and a pony. He apparently struck up something of an acquaintanceship with the Mexican as well, and learned from him that the Papagos were Christians, in spite of their "brutish" appearance; that they were very brave, and that they were helpful in

H.M.T. Powell's 1849 sketch of the mission church at San Xavier del Bac (*The Santa Fe Trail to California 1849–1852*)

keeping the valley cleared of Apaches. Nevertheless, Powell described the Indians as "ugly as sin and black as the devil."

Although Powell was critical of many things he encountered along the way, including the appearance and behavior of the natives of the region, he included in his remarks about Tucson some very flattering statements about the local residents. "As our Train passed through the town," he wrote, "there was quite a crowd in the street to look at us—they were the best looking and best dressed Mexicans I have seen. Many of the men were quite good looking, more intelligence was marked on their faces than I have seen in any other town I have passed through."

Another piece of information he obtained from Ygnacio Saenz related to El Pueblito, the abandoned Pima community at the foot of Sentinel Peak. Saenz told him it contained the second oldest building erected in the valley, referring undoubtedly to the two story structure later known to Tucson residents as "the convent." Powell noted in his journal that he regretted the fact that he was not able to pay a visit to the site. In conclusion, the Illinois diarist observed that the Tucsonenses were benefiting from the willingness of the Forty-Niners to trade weapons for other goods. One villager showed him a pair of revolvers he had purchased for $2 apiece, as well as a good rifle obtained for $4. At the home of the *alcalde*, he had seen an artillery sword (worth $20 on the St. Louis market) that had been acquired by the mayor for only $3.[45] Powell also saw seven or eight wagons that Tucson residents had obtained from Forty-Niners in exchange for horses and mules.[46]

Although often lauded for their honesty by the earliest of the argonauts, by the fall of 1849 the Pima Indians of the Gila River had acquired light-fingered tendencies that the gold seekers negatively contrasted with other more admirable characteristics. Powell stated that members of his party were "perfectly astounded" at the amount of goods they "lost" while passing through the Pima villages. On the other hand, they were impressed with the ability of the Pimas to chastise the Apaches.

Like others before it, the Illinois party with which Powell was associated met many Mexicans returning from the goldfields. Not far from the Pima towns, they encountered a group of seven from whom they acquired "a good deal of useful information" about the route ahead. Powell wrote that they were taking home a large amount of gold, "how much I do not know, but our Captain and some of the others of our Train saw a double handful of it."[47]

By the middle of October, 1849, Colonel José María Elías González and his miscellaneous assortment of presidial soldiers, national guardsmen, and members of the Sonora militia had carried their campaign against the Apaches into the area of New Mexico just south of the Santa Rita mines. They skirmished with the Indians on the morning of October 15th, losing three men while killing seven of the enemy and wounding an undetermined number. After the battle, they encountered a group of Americans belonging to a party calling itself the Fremont Association. The Mexicans and Americans exchanged goods and Colonel Elías left two of his men with the Forty-Niners to serve as guides. He also turned over to them a ten-year-old Apache boy whom the Mexicans had captured.[48]

Unlike many of the caravans that had preceded them, the Fremont Association decided not to turn southerly and follow Major Graham's route; rather they continued due west from the vicinity of present-day Lordsburg toward Tucson, becoming the first Forty-Niner party of record to travel this way. On October 24th, they entered Apache Pass and completed their journey through it the following day.[49] During the next week they traversed the upper reaches of the Sulphur Springs Valley, finally striking Cooke's 1846 route at the San Pedro River near modern Benson on November 1st.

The Fremont Association proceeded leisurely along Cooke's road to Tucson, where they camped on the evening of November 6th. The following day, Robert Eccleston, chronicler for the group, rode out to see the town which he referred to wryly in his diary as "the famous city." He found it a "tolerable respectable" place "composed of Mexican adobes and a few Indian huts." He noted that the church was much dilapidated. He also observed that the townspeople had become shrewd traders. He bought a few items, nevertheless, including tortillas and milk which he found quite satisfying. Sugar and molasses were not available, but corn and wheat were abundant. The only fruit was quince; pumpkin and peppers were the only vegetables. Sheep, goats and burros were plentiful. On the night before the Americans' departure the local Mexicans staged a dance for them.[50]

For some Tucsonans, 1849 brought a limited amount of prosperity not previously known. For others, all the excitement about gold created a restlessness that inspired them to join Americans on the trail west. But the year had its ill omens too. From the east and south an epidemic of cholera was eating its way toward Sonora. Many of the Forty-Niners had encountered it along the way and some companies had disbanded or turned back because of it. In August, the illness caught up with General José Urrea at his home in Durango and killed the famous Tucsonan.[51]

To the disappointment of the frontiersmen, the arrival of the Americans had brought no relief from Apache attacks and the new year would get underway with hostile Indians again at the doorstep.

13

California Sours for Sonorans

The lure of the goldfields remained strong for Sonoran frontiersmen as 1850 got underway. At least 5,000 had made the trek west the year before and many more would follow them.[1] A favorite destination for the Sonoran argonauts was the San Joaquín River and its tributaries and by 1849 part of that region was being referred to as "Sonora." Some of the earliest miners unquestionably prospered. One contemporary observer reported that about 250 returnees checking through customs at Guaymas in November and December, 1849, declared the impressive sum of 426,000 pesos.[2] Several were experienced miners who had been grubstaked by wealthy Sonorans to locate the deposits and extract the precious metal in return for a percentage of the proceeds. Even those who lacked this kind of backing, however, knew more about what they doing than did the average adventurer; they brought to the California goldfields the mining techniques of their Spanish forebears.[3]

The possibility of becoming wealthy was one factor that drew Sonorans to California, but escaping the continued Apache menace was an equally powerful incentive to leave the frontier. Stories of Indian raids continued to fill the pages of state newspapers through the early months of 1850. On February 1st, a special column in *El Sonorense* devoted to Apache matters reported Indian attacks as far south as Batuc in the lower Moctezuma River Valley. It also described raids on Santa Cruz and Tucson that had taken place in late

December and early January. The civilians and soldiers at Santa Cruz had successfully resisted with very slight losses of livestock. Tucsonans had not been so lucky. On January 6th, a large body of Indians, all well mounted, rode through the outskirts of the town and drove off a herd of cattle tended by a lone *vaquero*. Short of horses, the soldiers were unable to give chase.[4]

A month after the raid, Tucsonans voiced their opinions about another shortage that was troubling them. More than a year had passed since any priest had visited the community. Many children had not been baptized and couples were sinfully living together because there was no one to perform the marriage ceremony. Tucson's Justice of the Peace Antonio Sotelo prepared a petition calling for the assignment of a priest to the military colony. Recognizing that incorporating the Papagos into the petition might give it added strength, he cited the needs of the residents of San Xavier. "The children of fifty Indian families are growing up as heathens," he wrote. In addition to Sotelo, nine others signed the petition, among them Antonio Comadurán and Francisco Solano León.[5]

On April 24th, 1850, the Sonoran government issued an official announcement on the migration to California that had occurred over the preceding year and a half. The smallest number of emigrants, only 130, had left the San Ignacio district (which included Tucson). By contrast, 2,000 had made the trek from Hermosillo, among them eighty women and children.[6]

The Foreign Miners' Act

Well before the end of 1849, Anglo-Americans in California had developed strong biases against many groups of incoming foreigners. Feelings against Hispanics were particularly strong and even the native Californians became victims of this xenophobia. The tension reached a peak in May, 1850, when the California legislature enacted what became known as the Foreign Miners' Tax Law. Attempts to enforce the $20-per-month payment led to bloodshed in several places.[7]

By late summer of 1850, Sonoran newspapers commented on this negative turn of events. *El Sonorense* reported on August 16th that those returning from the goldfields did not have the same cheerful dispositions as others who had come back the year before. Not only were the gold deposits dwindling, but Sonorans were suffering from the new tax. In addition, the selling price for Mexican mules (which frontiersmen took with them to barter) had declined drastically and the market for these animals was now better in Mexico than in California.

The author of the *El Sonorense* article was particularly bitter about the miners' tax. "This law," he wrote, "has been conceived with the aim of depriving foreigners of the discoveries they have made, so that those in power can take advantage of the situation." He went on to point out that even when foreign miners paid their tax and received the necessary work permits, American outsiders would invade their claims, tear up their permits and throw them out. "Such is the behavior of illustrious free men in civilized Northamerica," he observed. The *El Sonorense* writer pointed out that there were Anglo Californians who opposed the miners' tax, but that their opposition would have no immediate effect since the legislature was in recess and had no plans to resume deliberations.

A month later, Sonora's official newspaper published without comment a set of resolutions adopted July 21st by a group of Californians in the town of Sonora. The first identified as personae non grata all foreigners in Tuolumne County, except those with respectable, permanent businesses. Anyone not in that category was to leave the county within fifteen days unless local authorities granted them special permission to remain. Among the other resolutions was one calling upon all foreigners to surrender their arms immediately. It also authorized "good citizens" to disarm the outsiders.[8]

The Colorado Crossing

For Mexicans, as well as Anglos, the overland route to California crossed the Colorado River near its junction with the Gila. During most of 1849, travellers relied on makeshift arrangements to get themselves and their equipment over the river. The Quechan, or Yuma, Indians operated a small ferry some of this time, but the service was not always dependable. At the end of September Lieutenant Cave Johnson Couts, who commanded an escort for the United States-Mexico Boundary Commission, established Camp Calhoun on the California side of the river. During the next two months, he and his men would help travellers cross the stream safely. They would also collect duty from Sonorans returning to their homes with gold from California mines.[9]

Mexican representatives to the boundary commission replaced Couts and operated the ferry during December, 1849. The group included a son of Agustín de Iturbide, Mexico's short-lived emperor, and José María Carrasco, who would later serve as Sonora's military commander.[10]

Sometime early in 1850, Able B. Lincoln began operating the ferry and grossed over $60,000 in three months. Against his will he acquired an unsavory partner, former scalp hunter Joel Glanton, who ruthlessly eliminated a competing Indian ferry operator. Glanton charged exorbitant fares for all passengers but apparently gouged Sonorans more than any others. A day of reckoning for the partners was not long in coming. On April 21st, 1850, the Quechans sought their revenge. Surprising the Americans in their camp, the Indians murdered Glanton, Lincoln and several of their associates.[11] The Indians went back into the ferry business after the attack, but new competition was not long in coming. By late June or early July, a party of Americans from California under the leadership of George Alonzo Johnson was collecting fees from travellers for taking them across the stream. The Quechans were understandably hostile to the newcomers and harassed them constantly.

Sonorans returning from the goldfields suffered abuse at the hands of American ferry operators beginning with Lieutenant Couts, who collected duty on the instructions of "Colonel" James Collier, California's first customs director. Colonel Collier went so far as to suggest that Couts pocket the proceeds. Charles Pancoast, the Quaker Forty-Niner, was shocked at the tactics used by the Americans. Among other abuses, American soldiers crossed on to Mexican soil to collect duty from returning Sonorans.[12]

By the fall of 1850, reports of ill treatment were common in Sonoran newspapers. In November, Altar Prefect Antonio de Urrea sent Governor Aguilar two letters about the matter. In the first he noted that since October, 1849, when American troops began manning the ferry to protect Forty-Niners against the Indians, Mexican citizens had been the victims of harassment. Urrea had received reports that Mexicans were deprived of arms and other valuables in clear violations of the treaties. Perhaps, he suggested, force should be answered with force. His second letter was more specific. Urrea wrote that on November 7th a party from Ures had arrived in that community with a complaint against some Americans who had attempted to assault and disarm them after they had crossed the river into Mexican territory. In self-defense the Mexicans fired at the attackers, who fled. One of the Mexicans was slightly injured in the encounter.[13]

On November 16th, Governor Aguilar sent a directive to justices of the peace in various frontier towns requesting depositions from local citizens concerning abuses they had suffered at the hands of American troops stationed near Yuma crossing. A few days later he wrote the minister of foreign relations in Mexico City to describe some of the violations he had heard about and to request that the national government make an official diplomatic protest. The minister responded a month later saying that the president of Mexico had agreed to submit a protest once Governor Aguilar had completed his investigation and submitted all the depositions he had collected. He was encouraged to include full details.[14]

Tucson Under Attack

Early on the morning of December 16th, 1850, as Tucsonenses tended their fields and animals, "enemy Indians" in considerable numbers descended on the town. The drama is best related in the words of Captain Antonio Comadurán who described it the following day in a report to his kinsman and superior officer, Colonel José María Elías González.

Yesterday, the 16th of the month at about nine in the morning, a large group of enemy Indians, mounted and on foot, approached this plaza as the populace was moving about, scattered to the four winds. Some hastily set about gathering their livestock, while others skirmished with the Indians who were trying to force their way into the fort and, thus, cut off the passage to San Xavier.

Approximately forty men of the town were at the dam and, lacking weapons, they sought refuge in the convent of the mission. Another ten, with their livestock, headed for San Xavier. The remaining civilians and the small force of soldiers, most of them without arms, stood with their backs to the wall resisting the intrepid enemies who had come up to the row of houses just outside the fort.

The Indians killed three civilians on the south side and carried off a boy woodcutter, four peaceful Apache women, and a boy carrying firewood. They killed another civilian on the north side and gravely wounded a second, while driving off the livestock: cattle, horses, mules and oxen. They burned a sack of wheat and plundered a nearby ranch house. Since the enemy had the town completely surrounded, we could not hinder them from rounding up all the animals wandering loose through the area.

After collecting all the livestock, Comadurán continued, the Indians gathered outside the north wall of town stating that they wanted to live at peace with the Mexicans. Corporal Tomás Gastelo, with nine men who had valiantly defended the gateway of the fort, went out to meet them. The enemy parties embraced and exchanged small gifts as a sign of good faith. The Apaches indicated they were willing to return the animals they had rounded up, as well as the captives, and would return other prisoners from Santa Cruz whom they were holding at a nearby location. Furthermore, they would send José Antonio Acuña, a Mexican who had been captured as a small child, to serve as their agent in negotiating the peace.

As Gastelo and his companions escorted Acuña into the village, a rescue force of Papagos swept in from San Xavier. There was no time to tell them of the peace proposal and they immediately fell on the enemy, killing three warriors and wounding many others. The Apaches fled in disorder with the Papagos close behind. Sometime later, the Papagos returned to Tucson saying that they had decided to give up the chase after determining the size of the enemy force. Fearing for their families at the mission, they declined to join the soldiers and others from Tucson in further pursuit of the Apaches.

Captain Comadurán later learned from Acuña that the Apache leaders were sincere in their desire for peace. What they longed for, he reported, was to be able to come and go as they pleased, to deal with the Mexicans as friends and to eat their tortillas. If their peace offer was rejected, however, they would continue the war, day by day, until the Mexicans were exterminated or driven out. Acuña also told Comadurán that the Apache force numbered 361 warriors, all well-armed with rifles obtained from the Americans in exchange for mules. He said that on the road to Tucson several of the Apache bands had quarreled over strategy. The Pinals did not want to attack the town and it was they who had brought their female captives from Santa Cruz to demonstrate their sincerity. When others insisted on the raid, the Pinals withdrew and waited with the Santa Cruz prisoners at a point "north of the Cañada del Oro." The Cerro Colorado and Tonto bands were opposed to any offer of peace and intended to carry away any livestock they captured.

Comadurán appealed to his commanding officer to supply Tucson with the men, horses and arms needed to defend the colony. He pointed out that the Apaches were well aware how defenseless the Mexicans and peaceful Indians were. Without doubt they would soon be back to make another assault on Tucson and San Xavier. He closed with the reminder that if Tucson were abandoned by its residents, the Indians would have an opening into the interior of Sonora.[15]

Cholera Provides a New Threat

In the same month that the Apaches struck Tucson, Hermosillo was hit with a cholera epidemic that took many lives and sent Sonorans fleeing to other parts of the state. According to an article in *El Sonorense*, the first outbreak of the disease had occurred shortly before in Guaymas. The carriers were miners returning from California by ship. They transmitted the cholera to residents of the port where the general effect was moderate. Early in December, however, a few Indians in Hermosillo began showing signs of affliction and in less than two weeks the disease spread throughout the community. People abandoning Hermosillo apparently carried illness to Buenavista, San Miguel de Horcasitas and Ures, the most recent towns to suffer outbreaks. *El Sonorense* reported that families were emigrating northward from Ures to escape the scourge.[16]

In January, 1851, as the epidemic spread slowly north, a man who later would become the most powerful figure in Sonora suffered a devastating defeat at Indian hands. Captain Ignacio Pesqueira, in command of a small force of national guardsmen from Arizpe and Bacoachi, engaged the Apaches at a place known to the Mexicans as *Ojo Hediondo*, or "Stinking Spring," not far from Cumpas in the Moctezuma River Valley. When the fighting was over, the Mexican dead included Captain Manuel Martínez and twenty-five guardsmen. Forty-three men were wounded, among them Captain Pesqueira and Rafael Angel Corella, commanding officer of the cavalry unit from Arizpe.[17] Flushed with victory, the Indians attacked Bacoachi, most of whose able-bodied men lay on the battlefield at *Ojo Hediondo*. The Apaches finally rode off with over a thousand head of livestock. They left behind six dead residents of Bacoachi, including Justice of the Peace Teodoro Bustamante.[18]

News of Pesqueira's defeat and the sacking of Bacoachi must have sent tremors of fear through Tucsonans, who had so recently undergone an ordeal of their own. In February, Captain Comadurán and the other residents did what they could to prepare for the inevitable and imminent onslaught.

At sunrise on March 3rd, a peaceful Apache woman from the Tucson camp called at Comadurán's quarters to deliver him a message. She had been one of those captured in the December assault but had managed to escape five days earlier. She reported that all the Apaches from the White Mountains to the Colorado River were planning a joint attack to destroy Tucson as they had destroyed other Sonoran communities. The woman stated that the Indians were drunk and had been filling themselves with mescal since the day of her capture. They were also dancing, eating the beef they had stolen and discussing strategies for the raid. The Indians planned to attack during the month's full moon and there would be enough Apaches to drive all the Mexicans from the area. The former captive also commented that the Indians would be accompanied by Americans who were their principal suppliers of arms and munitions.

The *comandante* wasted no time in relaying the information to his new superior officer, Colonel José María Carrasco. In his letter to the commanding inspector general, Comadurán repeated his plea for enlargement of the military colonies which had received almost no help in spite of the great plans by Mexico's central government.[19]

Cynical as he may have been, Comadurán probably expected some action from Carrasco, a respected veteran of the war between Mexico and the United States who had later served briefly at the Colorado River crossing. The new commander had reached Ures in January of 1851 and immediately issued a proclamation promising severe penalties for Sonorans trading with the Apaches or offering excessive ransom for prisoners. He had followed that initiative with an attack on the *Apaches mansos* of Janos, believing them responsible for Pesqueira's defeat.[20]

In spite of Comadurán's expectations, Carrasco's reply from Ures on March 28th was a disappointment. He sympathized with the Tucson *comandante*, but did not promise any immediate help.[21] On the same date as his response, however, Carrasco took an action that pleased the presidial commanders. He issued a circular setting forth the amount of pay military personnel would receive and the conditions under which the money would be distributed. Ordinary line soldiers and those of the military colonies would get three *reales* per day. Corporals were to receive the same amount plus perquisites. In addition, corporals and privates would be entitled to two *reales* monthly for ordinary expenses and infantrymen six *reales* for *taguas* (sandals). Cavalrymen were to be provided a pair of shoes per month whatever the cost might be. The soldiers could draw clothing and equipment as needed but rations of fodder would not be provided after the troopers' August harvest of forage. Carrasco stated in his circular that he hoped these changes would ease recruiting, prevent desertion and simplify accounting procedures.[22]

In June, Carrasco issued additional orders that must have left no doubt about his intention to activate the military colonies. The first indicated that beginning June 17th, the colonies would receive their grain from private parties under contract. The soldiers would be permitted to continue growing crops of their own but the government would contract for enough grain to supply 150 men for a full year. The second order clarified the roles of civil and military officials in the military colonies. In Santa Cruz, Tucson, Bavispe and Altar—where civil governments had long been present—the *comandantes* would have no jurisdiction over civilians except in time of crisis when the Apaches threatened the villages. At Fronteras, which had been abandoned and then founded anew as a military colony, the *comandante* would have both civil and military responsibilities.[23]

During 1850 and 1851, Tucson Justice of the Peace Ygnacio Saenz busied himself locating vacant land for the Tubac refugees and accommodating the demands of the new colonists. Doing so required negotiating with San Xavier Indians who had dominion over certain irrigable plots that lay fallow. Early in 1851, José María Martínez, who had abandoned his Tubac grant a year earlier, sought property near San Xavier mission. The Papago governor at that time was José Golosa, adopted son of the former governor Ignacio Zapata. It was with Golosa that the Mexicans had to negotiate. Teodoro Ramírez played a key role, serving as a witness for the Papagos and drafting the grant documents, which were signed by Saenz on February 24th.[24]

Americans, dissapointed at not finding gold in California, added to Tucson's military and civil problems in 1851. After leaving the Pacific Coast, they began to drift back into Sonora where the mining potential had been romanticized by the legend of the Arizonac discovery.[25] While returning to his post on July 6th, the *comandante* of the Santa Cruz colony encountered a party of nearly fifty *Yanquis* camped about a league south of San Xavier, apparently with intentions of remaining. José María Flores, Sonora's assistant inspector general, reported his sighting to the governor on July 9th, adding that four of the San Xavier group had been in Ures to request permission to mine in Sonora. He noted that they had no passports or official papers of any kind.

In his letter to the governor, Flores also mentioned that the military colony of Tucson was in no position to defend itself against armed Americans because there were only twenty-odd able-bodied men available. Nine soldiers had recently died of cholera which was raging in the community and others had been stricken by the disease but were convalescing.[26]

Although Flores did not identify any of the Tucson cholera victims, one of them may have been Captain Antonio Comadurán. The March communication of the *comandante* concerning the expected Apache attack is the last document signed by him that has been found in the Sonoran archives. Six weeks after Tucson's *comandante* prepared his report of Apache plans, a party of these Indians attacked a supply train headed for Tucson from Altar. An officer named Mariano Surita (rank undetermined) described the engagement to the Sonoran general command. Apparently Surita was in charge at Tucson on the date of the incident—April 19th. He makes no mention of Comadurán, who may have been bedridden or already deceased by that time.[27]

Tucson was not the only community in northern Sonora besieged by cholera in July, 1851. In his letter to the governor, Flores stated that Santa Cruz also suffered from the illness. Furthermore, towns of the Altar Valley were hit harder than either of the frontier military colonies. A tally prepared on July 27th by Father Lorenzo

Vásquez shows that 1,116 people in his Altar Valley parish had died from the disease.[28]

Another July tragedy that affected the residents of the military colonies was the death of Commanding Inspector General Carrasco. Cholera took his life near Guaymas on the 21st of the month. He was only thirty-eight.[29] Had Carrasco lived, the military colonies might have achieved the goals set for them; unfortunately, his successors lacked both his ability and his charisma.

On the last day of July, a group of peaceful Apaches from Tucson were attacked by a party of their wilder brethren at a location near Calabazas. Fifty-one of them were either killed or captured. Two Tucson citizens who had gone to the Apache camp to get acorns also lost their lives in the conflict.[30] The incident was reported to higher authorities by the Tucson justice of the peace, rather than the *comandante*—further evidence of Comadurán's absence.

Tubac Becomes a Military Colony

Sometime in the late summer or early fall of 1851 Tubac was reoccupied with the new status of military colony. Whether this represented a decision made by Carrasco before his death or a decision by someone else is not clear. Nor is it certain just when the resettlement took place. A scouting party for the United States-Mexico Boundary Commission was in the area between the 13th and 17th of September and found no residents.[31] The San Ignacio prefect, however, reported to Sonora's governor that twelve soldiers from the Tubac military colony were attacked by an Apache war party a few leagues north of Imuris on August 27th.[32] Whatever the exact date of its reoccupation, Tubac had gained a new lease on life by the fall of 1851 and among its initial settlers were members of a Mormon party headed for California. Passing through the Santa Cruz Valley in one of the nicest seasons of the year, the Mormons were persuaded to remain in exchange for concessions of land.[33] (They did not, however, stay for long.)

As Tubac began another chapter in its history, Lieutenant Colonel José María Flores replaced Colonel Carrasco as commanding inspector general of the northern frontier. Sometime late in the fall of 1851, he led a large party of professional soldiers, national guardsmen and men from the military colonies on an Apache chase that took him as far as the Gila River. In addition to harassing the Indians, Flores' mission was intended to intimidate American free-booters roaming the area.[34]

The new inspector general lacked the tact of his predecessor and before his campaign ended he managed to alienate many of the residents of the military colonies. On December 27th, the Santa Cruz justice of the peace wrote the Altar prefect to complain that Flores was billeting his troops in the town church. Four days later, Tucson Justice of the Peace Miguel Pacheco wrote a similar letter, commenting that the old presidial chapel was in very bad shape but it was still "the house of god."[35] The volleys from Santa Cruz and Tucson were just the first rounds in what would become a pro-longed attack against high-handed civil and military officials. The long-time residents of the former Spanish presidios voiced legiti-mate complaints about how the bureaucrats dealt with them and their property.

When Captain Comadurán passed from the scene in 1851, no officer of comparable rank replaced him. Surita apparently com-manded for a brief interval but the responsibilities soon fell on First Ensign Manuel Romero, who must have been in charge during the closing months of 1851 and early 1852. For most of the next two years, the command at Tucson would be unstable and the effective-ness of the garrison diminished.

Determining the Boundary

In the first three years after the war between the United States and Mexico ended, little was accomplished to determine the precise location of the boundary between the two countries. John B. Weller, the first United States boundary commissioner, was removed from office early in 1850 and replaced by John C. Fremont. Within a matter of weeks, Fremont was elected to represent California in the Senate and resigned his appointive post. Next to be named was John Russell Bartlett, who reached El Paso in mid-November and shortly after began the first of his field labors with the commission.

Bartlett and his party did not set out for Sonora until May, 1851, when they travelled from the mines at Santa Rita del Cobre to the old presidial town of Fronteras. Part of the journey was along the route followed by many of the Forty-Niners and in his description of the trip Bartlett wrote of such places as San Bernardino and Agua Prieta, names then familiar to many American travellers. When they reached Fronteras, they met Colonel Carrasco (whom Bartlett referred to as "general"), who was about to lead an expedition against the Apaches. He had just returned from the campaign against the "peaceful" Indians at Janos.

Bartlett's description of the provisions carried by Carrasco's troops provides a more detailed account of this aspect of Mexican soldiering than any other available. In addition to a musket, forty rounds of ammunition and a blanket, each soldier carried six-days' rations: twelve pounds of *pinole*, three pounds of dried beef and three pounds of *panocha* (brown sugar). Carrasco's force was also accompanied by a pack train of sixty mules with tents and other camp equipment, as well as additional ammunition and provisions. Bartlett considered it a meager outfit for an army of 400 men.[36]

From Fronteras, Bartlett and his aides travelled to Arizpe which they reached on May 30th. They remained in the old Sonoran capital until June 3rd, when they returned to the copper mines. Their route again took them through Fronteras where they lingered a few days to enjoy a gift of beef offered by Captain Bernabé Gómez. The meat was from one of the many wild bulls still roaming the area. On June 23rd, they concluded their first Sonoran venture.[37]

Shortly after returning to Santa Rita, the surveyors had an experience which, according to Bartlett, would long be remembered—one which exposed them to a new aspect of the reality of life on the Sonoran frontier. On the evening of June 27th, a party of New Mexicans rode into the village seeking provisions. With them they had a young Mexican girl purchased from the Apaches, whom they planned to sell or otherwise dispose of at the highest possible price. The Americans were shocked at what they saw and Bartlett immediately called on Lieutenant Colonel Craig, leader of his military escort, to have the girl released. He cited as his authority provisions in the Treaty of Guadalupe Hidalgo prohibiting the purchase of any Apache captives. Once the girl was freed, Bartlett interviewed the New Mexicans and learned that she had been held by the Pinal Apaches.

Later, the girl told Bartlett that her name was Inez González and that she was from Santa Cruz. She had been captured near Magdalena in September while on her way to the annual festival of San

Sketch of Arizpe, Sonora in 1851 (Bartlett, *Personal Narrative*, volume 1)

Francisco. At the time the Indians took two other women prisoners and a boy named Francisco Pacheco. Without doubt she and her companions were among the Mexicans the Pinal Apaches had brought to Tucson in December.[38] Had the Papagos from San Xavier not intervened when they did, she might have gained her freedom then.

Not long after the incident Bartlett was again confronted with a captive problem. Two Mexican boys escaped from a group of Apaches while the Indians visited the commissioner's camp. Mangas Coloradas (referred to by Bartlett as Mangus Colorado) and another important Apache chief named Delgadito conferred with Bartlett, suggesting he purchase the escapees. The commissioner refused to do so saying that his responsibility was to free captives not buy them. A tense situation developed and continued for several days. Finally, Bartlett proposed that one of the Mexicans with the survey pay the Apaches for the boys, thus making the purchase

Sketch of doña Inez (Browne, *Adventures in the Apache Country*)

personal not official. After considerable negotiation, a bargain was struck and the Indians received goods worth about $250. By the time the issue was settled, the former captives were safely in the hands of Mexican authorities in Janos.[39]

On August 28th, the survey party left Santa Rita for a rendezvous with General Pedro García Conde, the Mexican commissioner, and his staff. The two groups met at a point not far from the Chiricahua Mountains and a day's journey east of the San Pedro River. After reaching an understanding on how the survey work would be done, both commissioners decided they would go to Santa Cruz for provisions. They established a camp on the San Pedro and General García set out first. Bartlett followed shortly after but got lost and spent several days wandering about the countryside.

Mexican Boundary Commissioner   U.S. Boundary Commissioner John
Pedro García Conde (Villa, *Galería*)   Russell Bartlett (Arizona Historical
                                        Society)

Fortunately for Bartlett and his companions, two members of
their company stumbled upon a group of Mexicans from Santa
Cruz hunting wild cattle on the San Pedro. When the *vaqueros*
heard that the party had Inez González with them, they readily
agreed to help the Americans find their way. Among the Mexicans
were the stepfather and other relatives of Inez. They were reunited
with the lost girl at Bartlett's camp on September 20.[40] Three days
later there was another more emotional reunion when they reached
Santa Cruz and Inez rejoined her mother and younger brothers.[41]

In his diary Bartlett commented on the destitute condition of the
Santa Cruz citizens and stated that the town had been completely
abandoned for a short time the previous fall. The representatives of
the commission were the victims of considerable pilfering by some
of the local residents and Bartlett appealed to Father Bernardino
Pacheco for assistance in controlling the larcenous tendencies of his
parishoners. The priest told the commissioner there was little he
could do, so Bartlett closed his camp to further entry by local
inhabitants.[42]

Father Pacheco was also a new arrival in Santa Cruz and may not
have felt confident in his ability to turn the situation around. He
had been appointed to the post in May and given responsibility for

the inhabitants of Santa Cruz, Cocóspera, Tumacácori, Tubac, San Xavier and Tucson. Shortly before Bartlett's arrival, Pacheco had toured the circuit. On August 29th, he was in Tucson where he baptized Juan Manuel Ramírez, a son of Teodoro and María de los Angeles Salazar. The baby was almost eight months old.[43]

Because he could not obtain needed supplies in Santa Cruz, Bartlett decided to push on to Magdalena and hired Jesús Ortiz, stepfather of Inez González, to lead him there. The commissioner's party was briefly detained while en route by a representative of the prefect of San Ignacio who was under orders to determine the legitimacy of the Americans' business before allowing them to pass on. Bartlett, with many letters from both American and Mexican officials, had no difficulty in satisfying the official but the incident prompted him to record in his diary the misdeeds of Americans passing through Sonora. "These reckless adventurers," he wrote,

often set at defiance all law and propriety, and we had many accounts of their shameful and brutal conduct. The fields in this country are seldom fenced, and it is no uncommon thing for a party of these men to encamp and turn their animals into a field of corn, on which the helpless ranchero and his family are probably depending for their chief support. They will enter a house, pistol in hand, demanding whatever it affords; frequently they help themselves, without the ceremony of paying for what they take; and commit other outrages which make one who has any national pride blush to hear recited.[44]

Bartlett was unable to locate supplies in Magdalena either, so he decided to go to the capital city of Ures. He fell ill along the way, however, and was detained at Ures until late December. On the day before Christmas, he learned that General Pedro García Conde, his Mexican counterpart, had died five days earlier at the family home in Arizpe.[45] Bartlett decided to sail from Guaymas for San Diego, where he could rejoin the other members of the survey team who had been moving down the Gila. He boarded a ship early in January, 1852.[46]

14

The End of Mexican Rule

Late in 1851, The American ferrymen withdrew from Yuma Crossing. Plagued by supply problems, the U. S. Army also abandoned the site. The Gila route, however, was important for bringing livestock into California and the ferry had to be maintained.[1] Soldiers in greater numbers returned early in 1852. Assured of better protection against the Indians, Louis J. F. Jaeger reopened the ferry[2] and the American invasion continued. The incoming *Yanquis*, however, were not the most serious threat that the Mexicans faced. The Apaches continued their attacks and the ongoing squabbles between civil and military authorities provided little relief—in fact the bickering between soldier and statesman created new problems.

In establishing the military colonies, the Mexican government had intended that the soldiers raise crops to support themselves and their families. Knowing that land and water resources on the Sonoran frontier were limited, Colonel Carrasco had not pressed this issue; instead he had made arrangements for buying grain from private contractors.[3] José María Flores, his successor, took a different tack. Late in 1851, he pressured civil officials of the colonies to turn over land to the *comandantes*. Tucson Justice of the Peace Miguel Pacheco, whose duties involved matters related to local land and water, was caught in the middle. During the winter of 1851, Pacheco found himself in the unenviable position of ordering retired soldier Francisco Herrán and others off their fields near the old San Agustín mission. They would have to turn the property over to the military. Herrán, son of a former Tubac presidial commander, immediately protested.

In his complaint, Herrán reported that he had served as a distinguished soldier in the Tucson company for twenty-four years before his retirement in 1829. Shortly after leaving the army, he had paid 68 pesos to one of the Indians at El Pueblito to obtain a plot of land for cultivation. Finding this acreage insufficient for his family to subsist on,[4] he sought a small grant of nearby land and had it confirmed by the justice of the peace. Herrán stated that he had been cultivating both plots for the past twenty-three years; without them he would be totally insolvent. Francisco González, the prefect to whom Herrán directed his protest, forwarded it to Governor José Aguilar. In an accompanying letter, he described attempts to apply the military colony regulations to Tucson as obvious injustices. The rules were appropriate only for more remote frontier areas with vacant lands.[5]

A little over a week after Herrán sent his complaint, several Tucson citizens acted to bring the whole problem of land assignments to the attention of Governor Aguilar. Ygnacio Saenz, who had replaced Pacheco as first justice of the peace, signed a lengthy letter to the governor which also bore the names of Dolores Gallardo, second justice of the peace, Jesús Castro, attorney-treasurer (*síndico*), and José Golosa, governor at San Xavier. The officials wrote that Acting Inspector General Flores had threatened to move Tucson soldiers to Tubac if Tucsonenses did not contribute land for the military colony. Fearing he might carry out his threat, they agreed to stop farming half the acreage at the San Agustín site, even though it would create a great hardship for certain families—like Francisco Herrán's.

The correspondents noted that they had used these fields for many years[6] and if the land was declared vacant and given to the military colony the town would face ruin. They protested that the soldiers were employed as farmers when they should be keeping the Apaches at bay. Shortly before, the raiders had driven off most of the San Xavier livestock and the soldiers from the colony could not even find their trail. Soon, the Apaches would be stealing the very oxen upon which the citizens depended![7]

Four days after Ygnacio Saenz and his associates wrote Aguilar, Ensign Manuel Romero, Tucson's acting *comandante*, signed a certificate to accompany another message for the governor. This correspondence could only have provided further embarrassment for the soldier-farmers of the colony. During the last days of April and the first week of May, National Guard Captain Guadalupe Luque had again been in the field with his San Xavier warriors, a few Gila River Pimas and some peaceful Apaches from Tucson. Somewhere along the Black River, they encountered a large Apache camp, and on May 4th at three in the morning, they launched their attack. Fourteen enemy were killed and two Papago captives recovered.[8]

The Apaches retaliated quickly. About mid-morning on June 17th, more than 300 warriors burst out of the heavy mesquite thicket surrounding Tucson. In minutes they stole a herd of oxen whose caretakers fled for the protection of the walled fort. Soon the Indians also held many mules and horses, over 300 cattle and more than 1,000 sheep.

Captain Agustín Romanos, Tucson's new *comandante* who had been at the colony for less than a month, gained his baptism of fire in the assault. When he learned of the attack, he assembled his men and ordered Ensigns Manuel Romero and Miguel Romanos to lead a twenty-five-man detachment against Apaches approaching from the north. Justice of the Peace Ygnacio Saenz and several other civilians, along with fourteen Papagos, sallied forth to confront those coming from other directions. Sergeant Joaquín Morales led ten infantrymen and a few civilians against Indians who were trying to hold onto the stolen livestock.

The battle continued for the rest of the morning and into the early afternoon. Finally, the Indians abandoned most of the animals they had taken and rode off to the north. Romanos, thinking that the colony had fresher horses and men than the Apaches, decided to give chase. It was late afternoon, however, before he could put together the necessary force. Shortly after four p.m., Ensigns Romero and Romanos rode out of town at the head of more than 100 soldiers, civilians, peaceful Apaches and Papagos. In the group were twelve Frenchmen, colonists who had arrived in the Tucson area shortly before.[9]

As had so often been the case, the pursuit proved fruitless. The raiders had retreated all the way to the Cañada del Oro without stopping. When the Tucsonans reached that point they decided they were too far behind to continue the chase. They returned the next day and reported to Captain Romanos that they did not see any

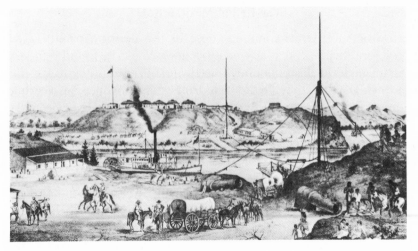

Fort Yuma (Arizona Historical Society)

Ferry operator Louis
Jaeger and Yuma Indian
manservant (Arizona
Historical Society)

cattle or sheep tracks among those of the fleeing Apaches and, therefore, believed that any missing stock would be found wandering through the desert not far from the fort. They also informed the *comandante* that they found footprints made by people wearing American shoes, suggesting that the Apaches might have been assisted by United States citizens.

Romanos reported to General Miguel Blanco, Sonora's new military commander, that the only Tucson casualty was a citizen named José Antonio Martínez, who had been gravely wounded by an Apache bullet. Corporal Ramón Comadurán, son of the former Tucson *comandante*, barely escaped with his life after being surprised outside the fort by the Indians. Having removed the saddle from his horse, he rode off bareback. To make matters worse, the barrel of his musket exploded as he fired at his foes. Somehow, he escaped without injury.[10] Romanos was generous in his praise of all the defenders. He singled out for special mention Justice of the Peace Saenz, M. Lepine de Ligendes of the French colony, and the Tucson Papagos. He also reported that the Papagos of San Xavier, when notified of the Apache attack, assembled a large force to come to the rescue but they arrived after the enemy had fled.[11]

The Boundary Commission Visits Tucson

John Russell Bartlett and others of the boundary survey party reached the Colorado River from San Diego on June 9th, 1852. Their task was to proceed east, surveying the Gila River, the dividing line between the United States and Mexico. The atmosphere in their camp was notably subdued. Three days earlier, Lieutenant Colonel L. S. Craig, head of the commission's military escort, had been murdered by a pair of army deserters whom he had tried to persuade to return to duty.

On June 11th, Lieutenant Amiel Weeks Whipple, the astronomer in command of the survey party, crossed the Colorado and began his work. Bartlett did not follow until June 18th when, as usual, he was more preoccupied with exploring the countryside than with the basic duties of his office. Proceeding leisurely up the Gila, he visited with the Pimas and Maricopas in their villages. On July 10th, Bartlett and his companions encountered a small party of

Sketch of San Agustín del Pueblito in 1852 (Bartlett, *Personal Narrative*, volume 2)

Tucson citizens who had come to the Gila to trade with the Indians. The Mexicans told the commissioner that in the ninety miles between Tucson and the first Pima village no water was available. Fortunately, however, it rained heavily the following day and from Picacho to Tucson Bartlett and his men had problems keeping dry.[12]

The commissioner reached Tucson early the 16th and found the town full of soldiers. General Miguel Blanco, Sonora's newly appointed military commander, was in the area campaigning against the Apaches who had attacked the colony a short time before. Blanco told Bartlett that in following the trail of the Apaches, he and his men had again found prints left by American-made shoes. He reported that these were distinguishable because of their large size and the nature of the heel marks.[13]

The surveyors camped on the banks of the Santa Cruz River near Tucson, close to an American party led by a man named Coons who was on his way to San Francisco with a flock of 14,000 sheep. A force of forty-five Americans and fifteen Mexicans watched over the animals.

From the slopes of Sentinel Peak, Bartlett sketched the buildings of San Agustín del Pueblito with Tucson in the background.[14] The large two-storied structure popularly known as the convent was still roofed at the time and the adjacent chapel appears in restorable condition. The drawing shows an idyllic setting with cultivated fields and livestock grazing in small pastures. Bartlett reported that only a small portion of the lands along the river were in production. He commented that these fields yielded bountiful harvests of maize, peas, beans and lentils. The Mexican also grew onions and pumpkins and the orchards provided apples, pears, peaches and grapes.

Bartlett was not much impressed with Tucson proper. "The houses . . . are all of adobe, and the majority are in a state of ruin," he reported. He went on to remark that no attention was given to repair and that as soon as a dwelling ceased to be habitable, the "miserable tenants" moved into "some other hovel where they may eke out their existence." In one passage he reported the total number of inhabitants to be about a third of the town's one-time population of "a thousand souls"; in another, he wrote that there were "three hundred soldiers in the place, although the average number for some years past has not exceeded twenty." Without doubt, most of the military personnel in the community at the time of Bartlett's visit were part of Blanco's army and not residents of the colony.[15]

On July 19th, the Americans moved on to San Xavier. The commissioner described the church as the largest and most beautiful in Sonora. He wrote unflatteringly, however, of the Hispanic mode of colonization compared with the Anglo. (In spite of his superior education, Bartlett could match the humblest of the Forty-Niners when it came to ethnocentrism.)

When the surveyors reached Tubac, Bartlett learned that Inez González, the captive girl he had rescued from the Apaches, was there in the household of Captain Bernabé Gómez, commanding officer of the new military colony. Gómez had been a friendly host to Bartlett at Fronteras the year before and they had struck up a cordial relationship. This time, however, Bartlett was morally offended by the way the captain treated Inez. For the next few days he would do all he could to free her from what he considered to be the lecherous grasp of the Mexican officer. He even appealed to Father Pacheco at Santa Cruz; when that failed, he protested to Sonora's governor.[16]

It is highly unlikely that Inez shared Bartlett's concern. Gómez was a respected young officer with a bright future—an excellent catch by frontier standards with or without benefit of clergy. Furthermore, only a year earlier, the young Mexican woman had almost certainly been the wife of an Apache—an uncomfortable status at best; a deadly one at worst.[17]

Twice while travelling from Tubac to Janos in late July and early August, 1852, Bartlett and his companions encountered soldiers from Tucson's military colony. The first meeting took place south of Tumacácori on July 22nd. Shortly after making camp that day, the surveyors were overtaken by a small party of men bearing a litter on which, according to Bartlett, "their colonel" lay. The soldiers were on their way to Arizpe to seek medical attention for the ailing officer, perhaps Agustín Romanos. Not far behind the litter-bearers was a second group of soldiers who camped near the Americans. The commission next ran into Mexican troops on August 2nd not far from the deserted Rancho San Bernardino. This time it was a much larger group—200, according to Bartlett. They were commanded by Hilarión García, a veteran officer whom the commissioner had met at Santa Cruz the year before.[18]

Bartlett's description of the Mexican soldiers closely resembles that of some of the Forty-Niners who seemed to enjoy addressing the subject in their journals. "A more miserable set of men I never met," he wrote, "certainly none calling themselves soldiers. Some . . . were destitute of shirts, others of pantaloons, and some had neither coats nor hats. Some wore overcoats, without a rag of clothing beneath."

Along the route between Tucson and Janos, the boundary party crossed paths with several companies of Americans headed for California. Although the search for gold was no longer rewarding for most of the prospectors, the romance continued to attract the venturesome.

For Sonorans, California had ceased to be viewed as the promised land by 1852, at least for making a fortune with a prospector's pan or at the end of a pick. Those who continued on the westward trek were more likely to be entrepreneurs interested in selling livestock or other goods to the Americans. Mexican drovers were treated better by the American soldiers than the miners had been, and following the establishment of Fort Yuma in 1852, the size of their flocks and herds crossing the river increased impressively. On August 28th, Lieutenant Sweeny reported that a Mexican party driving 28,000 sheep and eighty mules crossed the Colorado near its confluence with the Gila.[19]

The French Threaten

When General Blanco visited with Commissioner Bartlett in Tucson on July 16th, 1852, he told the American that he was planning a major campaign against the Apaches in October when the weather would be cooler and the rainy season over. The Mexican troops would begin their assault on Apache encampments along the Gila, then move eastward to the Mogollon Mountains of New Mexico.[20] Any pioneer Tucsonan within earshot of the general would likely have sneered at the probability of any such campaign. Over the past twenty-five years, they had heard many times of such ambitious plans—from Gándara, Urrea, Elías and others. Inevitably, events farther south had intervened to postpone or significantly reduce the number of soldiers available to fight hostile Indians.

By late September, 1852, it was obvious to the residents of the Pimería Alta that a new Sonoran crisis was about to change any ideas Blanco may have had for eliminating the Apache threat. A French count named Gastón de Raousset Boulbón had arrived in Sonora the previous June from San Francisco, and he and his followers were in open rebellion against the local government. The filibusterers had also been joined by some of the French colonists previously settled at Tucson and Cocóspera. On the 1st of October, the invaders captured Magdalena, and by the 13th they were camped on the outskirts of Hermosillo. The Apaches would have to wait. For now, General Blanco's primary concern was to prevent the foreigners from taking over the Sonoran government. Although the French did capture Hermosillo they failed to find adherents among the Mexican population and decided to withdraw. Raousset, seriously ill, sailed from Guaymas at the end of 1852.[21]

The French interlude, which in little more than a year would be repeated on a somewhat less serious scale, tied up much of the Sonoran army through the winter and left the frontier relatively defenseless. Late in January, 1853, Francisco González, prefect at San Ignacio, wrote Sonora's governor that Apaches "in considerable numbers" had attacked the old settlement of Cocóspera on the 25th, killed a French priest still living in the area, and escaped with many head of livestock. The Indians also raided the San Miguel Valley near Cucurpe, and rumors were circulating that they planned to organize a great offensive against Santa Cruz and Tucson to destroy both colonies.[22]

In spite of the bad news from the northern frontier, Manuel María Gándara, between governorships, decided to risk some of his capital in setting up a sheep ranch on the Calabazas grant, the title to which was held by his brother-in-law Francisco Aguilar.[23] Gándara was aware of the California market for mutton and intended to take full advantage of the situation. In December, 1852, at the Hacienda de Topahue between Hermosillo and Ures, Sonora's most persistent politician signed a contract with several German immigrants to establish and operate the Calabazas ranch for him. He agreed to stock it with 5,000 sheep, 1,000 goats, a small herd of cattle, and any draft animals needed for plowing and hauling. The livestock were to be delivered in March and April, 1853.[24]

Although the exact date of the reoccupation of Calabazas is unknown, it is not likely that Gándara was able to deliver the animals on schedule. On February 1st, 1853, following reestablishment of the Santa Anna dictatorship in Mexico City, Manuel María moved back into the familiar surroundings of the governor's office. By the end of June, he held the additional post of military commander.[25] Gándara's assumption of control over the state's military forces coincided with a change in command at Tubac. Late in June, Captain Andrés Zenteno, a man close to the governor, took charge of the small garrison. His appointment may well have represented an effort on Gándara's part to protect the investment he had made at nearby Calabazas.

Shortly before Tubac's new *comandante* arrived, the residents of the colony found themselves exposed once more to the hazards of frontier life. On June 11th, a servant of José María Martínez appeared in town to report that the Apaches had attacked them at La Canoa and carried off his master. Corporal Dolores Rodríguez led eight men to the rescue. Not far from Tubac, they found a large band of Apaches who had just murdered two postriders from Tubutama. They turned back to warn the Tubac residents, but the Apaches beat them to the presidio, taking one captive and killing four yoke of oxen. The Indians next rode north to attack a small

Sketch of Gándara hacienda at Calabazas in 1854 (Gray, *Report*)

party of postriders from Tubac, killing José María Galindo who was riding with them.

A larger group of Tubac troopers then gave chase and caught up with the raiders in the Santa Rita Mountains. Remarkably, they were able to liberate Martínez. Carlos Cota, who reported the events to Gándara, commended First Sergeant José Paredes, corporals Rodríguez and Cirilio Tánori and citizen José Ortega. He also beseeched his superior to provide ammunition for the colony's small cannon, as well as muskets and flints which were in short supply.[26]

One of Zenteno's first tasks was to resettle at Tubac a group of tame Apaches who had been living at Tucson. A contingent of the Indians arrived about the middle of July, and shortly afterward the *comandante* wrote Gándara for help in supplying them with the basic necessities. The response he received was that he should provide the Apaches with lands to cultivate since the government had no other means to help them. He was also to give the Indians weapons, but only after the captain was sure of their allegiances. The arms were to be used only in defense of the colony.[27]

Eager to display his military skills, Zenteno, in late July, began planning an offensive against the Apaches. Since he had only twenty-five soldiers, he sought help from the Tucsonenses. Lieutenant Manuel Romero and Justice of the Peace Jesús María Ortiz turned him down. Angered by the lack of cooperation, Zenteno wrote

Gándara asking him to order the frontier commanders to furnish each other help when requested. While the Tubac commander seethed over the responses from Romero and Ortiz, a small party of Apaches rode close to the wall of the Tubac fort and murdered don Ignacio Iberri, a prominent Sonora citizen travelling down the river from Santa Cruz. Zenteno wasted no time in letting Gándara know of this latest incident.[28]

By August, the *comandante* was beginning to have his fill of the peaceful Apaches. A delegation of them visited him early in the month seeking permission to travel to Ures to present a grievance personally to Gándara about the way they were being treated. Later, Sonora's chief executive would agree to provide them a weekly wheat ration.[29]

More Squabbles Over Land

The dissatisfaction of the old settlers in the military colonies increased throughout 1852;[30] by the summer of the next year their frustration had peaked. In September, 1853, Tucson Justice of the Peace Jesús María Ortiz[31] filed a new set of complaints with Prefect González. The high-handedness of the *comandante* deprived people of land and water, he wrote; as a result, many were leaving for California.

González wasted no time in forwarding Ortiz' report to Governor Gándara. His letter of transmittal is a masterpiece of indignant prose:

> The soldiers have been transformed into laborers and servants of the commanding officers . . . working only for the utility and advantage of the latter, and not for their own benefit, that of the treasury, or the fatherland. They are chained to the plow and the spade when they should be instructed in the use of arms and employed against the barbarians who every day invade, assault, and destroy the state.

He blamed General Commanders Flores and Blanco for all the problems of the colonies, stating that they had followed rigid policies that resulted in unjust seizures of farmlands.[32]

González concluded his letter by observing that if all the money wasted on the military colonies had been spent in providing aid to the communities, the enemy would long since have been contained and taught a lesson. He predicted that unless Gándara intervened to restore land and water to the original settlers, all would soon migrate.[33]

About the time González prepared his fiery message, Sonora's governor responded to the series of letters he had received from Zenteno in Tubac. On September 13th, he sent a circular to the commanding officers of the military colonies. Henceforth, he told them, they would be expected to help each other whenever called upon.[34] Two weeks later, he stepped in to settle the problems at Tucson and Santa Cruz. Citing the presidial regulations of 1772, Gándara ordered the *comandantes* to return all farmlands taken from residents of those communities immediately. "Theirs is the right to harvest these lands," he wrote. Remarkably, his order seems to have been ignored in Tucson, at least in the case of outlying fields that had been taken from the settlers.[35]

By the fall of 1853, Tucson had apparently gone more than a year without a high-ranking officer.[36] Part of the time, command responsibilities rested with Manuel Romero, aided by Joaquín Comadurán, son of the old commander. On November 9th, Gándara placed Captain Andrés Zenteno in charge of Santa Cruz and Tucson, as well as the military colony at Tubac. The Governor's instructions were quite specific. Zenteno was to assess the strength of his command and make sure the men were ready to turn back "any group of adventurers that might appear on the scene." Also, he was to thank the Gila River Pimas and the Papagos for their past help and assure them they could keep livestock captured from the Apaches. In return, however, the Indians must promise to supply mounted men to reinforce and aid the Mexicans if necessary. Tubac—with its contingent of soldiers—was to be his headquarters but Zenteno was to keep sufficient troops at each of the other posts to protect the settlers.

In his instructions to the new commander of the Tucson sector, Gándara did not forget his own economic interests. To protect the Calabazas sheep ranch—apparently operational by then—Zenteno was to station a detachment of six men there in case of emergency. The troopers could help with rounding up the animals and keeping them out of danger.[37]

The change in the Tubac captain's status did little to relieve his frustrations and in fact may have increased them. Gándara's directives were not accompanied by any supplies and Zenteno was obliged to continue calling on his neighbors for whatever charity they could provide. In January, 1854, with troop rations completely exhausted, the *comandante* borrowed mules and gunny sacks from the German overseers at Calabazas and put together a small supply train to go to Santa Cruz for food. Corporal Dolores Rodríguez and six Tubac soldiers were in charge. A mile from the old ranch of San Lázaro the Apaches attacked, cut loose the oxen and drove off all the mules. Troopers Martín Santos and Ramón Grijalva were killed; Petronilo Miranda disappeared. Rodríguez and the other three soldiers carried the bad news back to Tubac. When he reported to higher headquarters, Zenteno wrote that if he did not get help from the Sonoran government soon, he would move to Santa Cruz, even if he had to face a court martial.[38]

The Gadsden Purchase Treaty

Two weeks before Zenteno informed his superiors of the dismal experience of the Santa Cruz supply train, James Gadsden, United States minister to Mexico, negotiated a treaty which moved the boundary between the countries south to include the only portion of Arizona with an established European-derived population.[39] The diplomats signed the agreement on December 30th, 1853. Mexican and American legislators would ratify the agreement within six months of that date.[40]

For Sonorans, the significant aspects of the treaty were the loss of the northern part of the state and a concession by the Mexicans relieving the United States of responsibility for preventing invasion of Mexican territory by members of "savage tribes" residing on the American side of the boundary.[41]

One goal of the U.S. negotiators was to obtain land south of the Gila River for a railroad right-of-way and even before the agreement was final, the U.S. Army Corps of Engineers made plans to survey a route along the 32nd parallel. With President Santa Anna's permission, Lieutenant John G. Parke started the survey in January of 1854. When he and his crew passed through Tucson in February, they camped beside the Santa Cruz River, at the time a running stream about a foot deep. Parke judged the town's population at six hundred.[42] A private surveying party sponsored by the 32nd Parallel Railroad Company worked in the opposite direction from Parke and reached Sonora two months later. Colonel Andrew B. Gray was in charge. One member of the team was a young Naval Academy graduate named Peter Rainsford Brady, who would later become an important figure in territorial Arizona. The Gray expedition reached the Tubac area in April.[43] As they approached the site of the Calabazas Ranch, they encountered a large group of Apaches bent on the destruction of the Gándara hacienda. Two Mexican captives, who were leading the Indian war party, talked freely to Brady of their intentions. The American was impressed by the ugly countenance and ferociousness of one of these individuals—a man who called himself Romero.

After the meeting, the members of the survey crew came upon a large force of peaceful Apaches and Mexican soldiers under Captain Hilarión García, who had apparently taken charge of the Tucson garrison. García told the Americans that they were lying in wait for an Apache attack which had been expected for several days.

Gray and his party camped a few hundred yards from the old church at Calabazas which German Friedrich Hulsemann and his men had converted into a ranch house. As the Americans ate lunch, Mexican herders hurriedly began crowding the stock into corrals, while women and children ran for the adobe structure. At the sound of a bugle, García's troopers attacked the approaching Apaches and the hostiles were completely routed. Later, the victors displayed the severed head of Romero, and a string of Apache ears two-and-a-half to three feet long.[44]

The Calabazas battle was one of the most important victories over the Apaches during the 1850s and Brady's recollections of the event differ only in minor details from Captain Zenteno's April 25th official report. Writing to Assistant Inspector General Gómez, the Tubac commander stated that the Indians had been impressively beaten two days before. He sent fourteen pairs of Apache ears as evidence of the number of enemy killed and made a point of informing Gómez that the dead included the Mexican captives Marcial Gallegos and Romero, leaders of the force of two-hundred Pinal and Sierra Ancha warriors.[45] While commending all his men for bravery, Zenteno particularly lauded Sergeant Santos Michelena and Captain Guadalupe Luque, who was probably the most effective commander on the Sonoran frontier at the time. The Tubac officer said nothing about Hilarión García, who provided his own report.[46]

Not long after the Calabazas battle, Captain García replaced Zenteno as overall commander of the Tucson sector. García was also promoted to chief inspector for all military colonies in the region.

Preparing for the Change of Command

With the ratification of the Gadsden Purchase in June, 1854, Sonorans found themselves confronted by a new threat from Count Raousset Boulbón and his French filibusterers. This one, however, was short-lived. On July 13th, the invaders were soundly trounced by General José María Yañez, who had replaced Gándara as governor and military commander of the state. The French leader was captured and a month later he was executed.[47] In spite of the filibusterers and the changes caused by the Gadsden Treaty (when much of the area long known as the Pimería Alta became a part of the United States) life for the Hispanic frontiersmen went on as usual. The Apaches continued their raiding, accompanied by an occasional peace offer, and the Mexican soldiers, civilians and Indian allies continued to pursue them through the countryside, usually with negligible results.

Captain García followed his Calabazas victory with an expedition against the Arivaipa Apaches and recovered a small herd of cattle stolen from Imuris. The *comandante* did not immediately return these animals to their Mexican owners, though, and became the subject of a petition to General Yañez. The general quickly ordered García to deliver the cows to the rightful owners in Imuris.

In mid-July of 1854, perhaps because of the effects of the Calabazas and Arivaipa campaigns, some of the Apache leaders sent women emissaries to Tucson to seek peace with the Mexicans. García reported the incident to Manuel María Gándara and asked for instructions. Gándara responded that the Mexicans could not enter into treaties with the Pinal, Sierra Ancha and Sierra Blanca bands because they resided north of the Gila River. Surprisingly, he endorsed the idea of a treaty with the Arivaipa Apaches, even though their territory had come under the jurisdiction of the United States as a result of the Gadsden Purchase. Gándara was quite specific in stating that any Apache treaty should include provisions requiring that the Indians give up their Mexican prisoners and settle in the vicinity of Tucson or Santa Cruz where they would receive rations of wheat and corn. They should also be promised the sum of one *real* per day for military service against hostile brethren.[48]

In September, 1854, the Mexicans collaborated with a party of Texans in a successful battle against the Apaches. The Americans were after cattle stolen from them and revenge for the death of one of their number. A man named Callahan invited the acting commander at Santa Cruz, non-commissioned officer Angel Elías, to help recover the animals. The only soldier available was the armorer but Elías persuaded twenty-five civilians to take part in the chase. They encountered Apaches, killed twenty-one, and recovered fifty-seven cattle—all with Mexican brands. They also freed Tucsonan Antonio Munguía, who had been captured by the Indians four years earlier. Miguel Miera lost his life in the battle after slaying two Indians with a machete. Although the cows belonged to Mexican owners, Callahan took it upon himself to decide what would be done with them. He chose to distribute the animals among all who had participated, setting aside a share for Miera's widow as well. Familiar with Mexican law regarding livestock recovered from the Indians, Elías opposed Callahan but the Texan assured him he would discuss the matter with Captain García, Elías' commanding officer, when he reached Tucson. The young soldier acquiesced. Two weeks later, however, García had still heard nothing from the American.[49]

As the governments of the United States and Mexico arranged for another boundary survey, Americans—intent on staying—began moving into the newly acquired territory. Some were attracted by tales about such great mineral discoveries as the *planchas de plata*. Others, disappointed with their luck in California, wanted to investigate reports of gold deposits along the Gila River. One group of *Yanquis* passing through the newly acquired region in July, 1854, paused long enough to survey a townsite on the east bank of the Colorado River near its junction with the Gila. The party, which included Charles D. Poston, had been exploring the area since March. They had left California in late February under the false impression that all of Sonora was to become American territory. By the time they reached Fort Yuma, however, they were aware that most of the country they had passed through would remain part of Mexico.

Satisfied that a railroad linking Texas and southern California would cross the Colorado River near its junction with the Gila, the Poston party decided to lay out a townsite on the east bank of the stream. Sometime after July 14th, they carried out their survey. Title to the townsite was filed in the names of Poston, John C. McLemore and Herman Ehrenberg. They called the place Colorado City.[50]

Several months after Poston and his companions left, another group of fortune hunters moved in from California. Included were Peter Brady, who had been with the Gray survey crew earlier in the year, and Frederick A. Ronstadt, a German-Mexican who was managing Manuel María Gándara's Topahue hacienda when Bartlett visited in 1851.[51] Organized as the Arizona Mining and Trading Company, members of the group discovered the extensive copper deposits at Ajo. Several remained at Ajo, while others went on in search of the silver lode at Arizonac.

A party of Sonorans from Altar, including the district prefect, attempted unsuccessfully to drive away those who stayed at Ajo. The other members of the group reached Arizonac, meanwhile, where they found a large piece of raw silver. The Mexican authorities learned of their presence and challenged them also. At this point, the Americans decided to return to California to report what they had found and to seek the financing they needed to return.[52]

Cattlemen joined the invasion as well as prospectors. A cattle train from Texas passed through Tubac in September, 1854 and found a few soldiers still stationed there.[53] The troopers must have departed shortly afterward, however, for subsequent accounts do not mention them. Some Hispanic settlers and peaceful Apaches may have lingered briefly after the soldiers exited but they, too, soon went elsewhere.[54]

For a few months following the Calabazas defeat, hostile Apaches did not disturb the sheep ranch,[55] but they were raiding again by late summer. In September, Gándara, back in office for a brief period, expressed hope that the Americans would send troops to the area to help protect his investment. Shortly before, the Indians had swept in, killing fifty sheep and driving off other livestock.[56]

The Mexican and American members of the new boundary com-

Frederick A. Ronstadt (courtesy of   Peter R. Brady (Arizona Historical
Ed Ronstadt)   Society)

mission met in December, 1854, and quickly agreed on how the
survey would proceed. On January 31st, 1855, the first monument
was set in place at El Paso. One group of surveyors, under William
H. Emory, the American commissioner, moved westward from the
initial monument as far as a site known as Los Nogales de Elías.[57]
They passed through the Santa Cruz Valley in May and observed
that the Gándara sheep ranch was still occupied by its German
proprietors.[58]

   While Emory was busy in the east, Lieutenant Nathaniel Michler and his Mexican counterpart, Francisco Jiménez, began the
survey at the western end. They were accompanied by Captain
Hilarión García, Lieutenant Romero and a contingent of troops
from Tucson. First Ensign Joaquín Comadurán remained behind to
command the soldiers protecting residents of the military colony.

   Because of a shortage of water, Michler and Jiménez abandoned
their work in May and traveled to Tucson via the Gila River. As
they came through the Indian villages, Pima and Maricopa leaders
expressed anxiety about their future under American rule. The
following month these leaders, along with two from San Xavier,

met with Emory at Nogales and received assurances that any land rights they enjoyed under the Mexicans would be respected.[59]

Anticipating the withdrawal of official representatives of the Mexican government, Ensign Comadurán, in May, 1855, inventoried all the furnishings at the Tucson, San Xavier and Tumacácori churches and forwarded a copy to the assistant inspector general. He then locked the buildings. José María Martínez was given the keys to the San Xavier and Tumacácori churches. His orders were to open them only when priests visited and to put everything back in its proper place when they left.[60]

Late in the summer of 1855, Ensign Comadurán was given another assignment. He was to compile a roster of military personnel assigned to the Tucson post, showing the duty status of each. The register was completed and signed on September 1st. Nearly half of the soldiers were not at their post. Rather, they were busy escorting the boundary surveyors and carrying out special assignments in Ures. One man who had deserted the survey party was in jail.[61]

Many of the names on the 1855 roster had been well-known in Pimería Alta for more than a century: Romero, Ramírez, Granillo, Grijalva, Gallegos, Ortega, León, Bojórquez, Barragán and Azedo. On the list, too, were both of Ensign Comadurán's brothers. Antonio, the youngest, was the armorer for the company. Ramón, a cavalry sergeant, was riding with the surveyors. Within a few months, these men would face the decision of changing their citizenship or abandoning the home their ancestors had fought and died for.

The old Mexican families were not the only ones represented in Tucson when Comadurán prepared his roster. There were also newcomers with non-Hispanic names. Two in particular—John M. Pinkston and German-born Friedrich Goerlitz—were already involved in the community's affairs. By early September, 1855, they and their Mexican neighbors knew that the soldiers of the Tucson garrison would soon be on their way south of the new boundary, leaving Tucson without protection against the Apaches. Goerlitz helped draft a petition for Brevet Brigadier General John Garland, commanding officer for the Department of New Mexico, in which the Tucsonans requested that American troops be assigned immediately to the area to replace the departing Mexicans. In the petition (written in Spanish), they noted that Tucson had lost a substantial part of its population to the cholera epidemic and the exodus to California. They also reminded the general that the presence of troops would help make possible the development of abundant mineral resources.

In addition to signing the petition for himself and for fifty-four Mexican residents, Goerlitz attached a letter identifing himself as one of eight American citizens who had been in the area for more than a year waiting for the United States to take possession. He did not name any of the others but one was Pinkston, who wrote the transmittal letter for the petition as well as a separate personal message.[62] The others must have included John Warner Davis, Henry Alfing and John C. Clarke who had been working at Gándara's ranch for at least a year; Peter Kitchen was in temporary quarters at Canoa; and Colonel James W. Douglass and C. C. Dodson had settled at Sópori. Mark Aldrich and the Contzen brothers may have been on the scene by the fall of 1855 also, along with H. H. (Paddy) Burke and Edward Miles. Five other Americans—including William H. Kirkland, Nelson Van Alstine, and V. S. Shelby—reached Tucson in January, four months later.[63]

Toward the end of 1855 or early in 1856, some of those who had visited the Ajo region a year earlier returned with equipment to begin mining. Peter Brady was not in the group; he had chosen instead to join Major Emory's boundary survey crew, this time as an interpreter. After his assignment, illness kept Brady in California and he did not return to Arizona until 1857, when he was appointed Indian agent at Fort Yuma.[64]

Captain García and his fellow soldiers completed their duties with the boundary commission in the fall of 1855 and returned to Tucson. By now, however, it was clear that the old fort lay in United States territory and the days of the Mexican garrison were numbered. García, a veteran soldier with ties to other parts of Sonora, knew that his future lay to the south. For many in the Tucson company and for most of the civilian population, the Santa Cruz Valley was all they had ever known and now they must decide whether to leave it.

Departure of the Mexican Troops

About January 1st, 1856, Adjutant Inspector Ignacio Pesqueira, who was on the threshold of becoming the most powerful political figure in Sonora, directed the transfer of all but a handful of Tucson's soldiers and their families to a new bivouac in Imuris, a hundred miles to the south.[65] Ensign Joaquín Comadurán, Sergeant Joaquín Morales and a small force of enlisted men were left behind to guard equipment and supplies. In the absence of an elected justice of the peace and other civil officials, these men would govern for the last days of Mexican rule.[66]

Early in March, 1856, Captain García and some of the soldiers who had left with him in January returned to supervise the final transfer of men and goods. About this time, too, Angel Elías came north from Santa Cruz to escort departing civilian families to his post. The transition promised to be painful at best for everyone involved but it was made more so by the insensitivity of some of the Americans living in Tucson and by the inclement weather.

As the forlorn group of Mexican soldiers marched from town, several Anglo newcomers raised an American flag over an adobe store recently established by Edward Miles. The act was in violation of an agreement between the boundary commissioners that the stars and stripes would not be displayed until the last of the Mexicans had departed. When Captain García heard what was happening, he approached the men and asked them to desist. They not only refused but drew their arms and made it clear that they would fight to keep the flag in the air. García chose to carry the matter no further.

As the soldiers and civilians headed south, they encountered an unusually heavy March storm. Both groups were delayed but those in Elías' party may have suffered the most. Recalling the event many years later, Elías said they left on foot, travelling as far as Tubac before resting. The children cried of hunger and some of the older people were close to death. Still, they reached Santa Cruz and settled there with the remnants of the Tubac garrison that had been transferred some time before.[67]

15

Epilogue

Acting Comandante Joaquín Comadurán occupied himself with more than military matters in the final days before the departure of Mexican troops from Tucson. His duties included certifying land titles, sales and exchanges for both Anglo and Mexican residents and the documents he prepared attest some of Arizona's oldest recorded property claims.

During both the Spanish and Mexican periods, the approach to land ownership, occupation and use throughout the Pimería Alta had been casual at best. In towns exclusively controlled by civil authorities, *alcaldes* and *jueces de paz* probably insisted on more formal procedures than were followed in presidios and missions; in all the areas, however, traditional understandings, rather than legal documents, provided the foundation for land tenancy. Even when officials followed formal granting or confirmation procedures, papers had a way of getting lost, eaten by rodents or insects, and burned or carried off by Apaches.

During his Tucson visit in the early 1850s, Bartlett noted that when residents of the town were obliged to leave a dwelling because of its deteriorated condition, they simply packed their belongings and moved into a more habitable abode nearby.[1] If questions of previous ownership arose, they did not come to the commissioner's attention. The panic that began to affect the community shortly before Bartlett's visit certainly was related to the fact that persons cultivating fields near the old Indian village of El Pueblito lacked documentary proof of any legal right to be there.

The Gadsden Purchase Treaty incorporated Articles VIII and IX of the earlier pact of Guadalupe Hidalgo assuring persons who remained in the ceded area "enjoyment of their liberty and property" and guaranteeing that Mexicans who moved out would have their property rights "inviolably respected . . . as if the same belonged to citizens of the United States." With respect to land grants, however, Article VI stipulated that only those "located and duly recorded in the archives of Mexico" would be "respected." Perhaps because of uncertainty about how the term "grant," or *merced*, would be interpreted by the American government, some of Tucson's more sophisticated residents made last minute efforts to create a written record of their landholdings. First in line was don Teodoro Ramírez, who approached his nephew, Ensign Comadurán, in March, 1855, shortly after the young officer became acting commander. He was concerned primarily with getting a copy of the official account of his land purchase from the tame Apaches in 1828. Joaquín found it in the post record book, placed there by his father Antonio.

After preparing a copy and presenting it to his uncle, Comadurán gave his blessing to Teodoro's purchase of two adjacent pieces of land. One was a field that had belonged to Alejandro Granillo since 1833. Granillo's widow, María Petra Parado, was willing to sell it for 60 pesos. The other had long been in the Martínez family and María Gertrudis Acuña, widow of Pedro Martínez, was willing to part with it for the same price. Sergeant Solano León, on leave from his duties with the boundary commission, represented the widow Martínez in the transaction. When he left his nephew's quarters that day, Teodoro had three new pieces of paper proving his ownership of fields to the north of the walled town.

Ramírez was back to see his nephew again in May, this time to register a fourth piece of land that he had owned since 1828. It was, in fact, the first property he had bought near the tame Apache village. He showed Comadurán a document dated January 15th, 1828, that recorded his purchase of land from Francisco Granillo, María Castro, Juan Acuña and José Solares.[2]

Comadurán's next involvement with real estate concerned a house and lot, or *solar*, claimed by Eustaquio Ramírez, brother of Teodoro. On September 15th, the old man came to see whether his

young kinsman could supply him with a *documento de la casa*, or
"house document," confirming his right to the property. He testified that he had bought it from don Clemente Telles on an unspecified date in the past. Comadurán summoned Telles, placed him
under oath, and inquired whether he could recall the transaction.
Telles assured him that he could, testifying that Ramírez was in
legal possession of the premises. Two other elders—José Herreras
and Ygnacio Saenz—appeared before the *comandante* and corroborated the testimony given by Ramírez and Telles. They informed
Comadurán that Telles had inherited the property from his father
who had constructed the house on it more than forty years earlier.
Although none of the witnesses produced evidence of an original
deed in the name of Telles' father, Ensign Comadurán prepared an
ownership document for his uncle.[3]

In January, 1856, shortly after Adjutant Inspector Pesqueira directed the transfer of the Tucson garrison to Imuris, Comadurán
recorded the first American purchase of land from Mexican residents of Tucson.[4] George Leach, who had probably been in town
only a few days, bought two pieces of property, one a field (*tierra de
pan llevar*) belonging to a widow named Juana Rosario, who had
purchased it many years before from an Indian resident of El
Pueblito. Doña Juana had been able to keep the property in spite of
challenges from officials of the military colony and from Juan Manuel Burruel, a fellow Tucsonense. On January 20th, 1856, after
receiving a deed from Ensign Comadurán, she promptly sold the
land to Leach for 20 pesos.[5]

Later the same day, Leach cooled his heels outside Comadurán's
quarters while the *comandante* considered a request from soldier
Fernando Galas for a house document that would also permit him
to make a sale to the American. After listening to Galas' plea and
summoning witnesses, Comadurán awarded the requested document. Two days later, Galas surrendered his property and his new
"piece of paper" to Leach in exchange for 10 pesos.[6]

The chain of title for the Galas property during the next three
years clearly demonstrates the transient character of Tucson's Anglo population just after the Mexican troops left. On April 9th,
1856, Leach passed the property on to Frederick A. Ronstadt, who
was in the village briefly before going to Ajo to begin mining operations there. Ronstadt paid him $75, certainly a tidy return on his

original investment of 10 pesos. In October, Ronstadt sold the property to Albert Bowman, who handed it on to R. M. Doss three months later. The Miles brothers purchased it from Doss in November, 1857, and they kept it briefly before turning it over to James McCoy. Solomon Warner acquired it in March, 1859, and William S. Oury recorded it in Warner's name in his 1862 property record.[7]

On the same January day that Joaquín Comadurán busily approved transactions involving American George Leach, he found the time to prepare a title document for elderly widow Ursula Solares, one of Tucson's principal property holders. She claimed ownership of a plot across the arroyo just south of the walls of the old fort. She told Comadurán it had been in her family a long time. In fact, the original grantor had been Pedro de Allande y Saabedra. Comadurán recorded her testimony, then gave her the deed.[8]

Another January visitor to Comadurán's quarters was relative Pedro Ramírez who came to see the *comandante* about money rather than land. For some time he had been the voice of law and order in the community, serving in the combined position of civil and military constable. His salary was not much but as he contemplated the withdrawal of Mexican troops, Pedro realized that he had better collect the small amount that was owed him now or he would never see it. Comadurán's record showed a total in back pay of $26.75 but he had no funds to retire the debt. He offered Pedro land instead and presented his kinsman with the deed to a *solar* bounded on the north by the old military plaza. This would be the last presidial grant in what soon became Arizona.[9]

Solomon Warner, who arrived in Tucson on February 29th, 1856, made his first land purchase four days later. This time Ensign Comadurán represented the seller. He stood in for his uncle, Eustaquio Ramírez, in transferring to Warner the land inside the presidio walls that Ramírez had earlier acquired from Clemente Telles. The price was 40 pesos, a good deal for the time and place. To avoid a conflict of interest, Comadurán made Sergeant Joaquín Morales acting post commander. Morales legalized the sale.

On March 8th, the ensign again supervised land transactions, approving the sale to Warner of the remaining piece of the old Telles grant. It lay next to Warner's earlier purchase. Apparently it had no dwelling on it and Clemente Telles let it go for 10 pesos.[10] It was on these two plots that Warner would establish a store operated in partnership with Mark Aldrich, who soon became the biggest landholder in the community.[11]

Population and Land

With the soldiers from Tucson and Tubac newly settled at Imuris and Santa Cruz and a few civilians also established on the Mexican side of the boundary, the Hispanic population of the area during the last half of 1856 dropped to its lowest point in a century. It would not be long, however, before Anglo mining activity dramatically revived Tubac—which had already risen from the dead several times. Impressive growth in the Yuma area was just around the corner as well. The Hispanic portion of Tucson's population, on the other hand, probably took another dip in 1857 as some people headed south to take advantage of the economic boom in the Tubac area. By the end of the decade, returnees and newcomers from Mexico would replace those who had gone elsewhere and the number of Hispanic Tucsonans counted in the 1860 census would again approach the total of 760 enumerated by Mexican officials in 1848.[12]

The departure of Tucson's Mexican forces left vacant many houses inside the fort.[13] Given the prevailing situation of land tenure, it is unlikely that many of the soldiers could prove ownership of the dwellings and small lots which they occupied. When they left the village, therefore, their former holdings were up for grabs. Both Anglos and other Mexicans soon claimed these and other vacant properties. In the six years that passed before a property record was compiled, Yankee newcomers staked claim to numerous lots within the old presidio walls and to the west between the fort and the fields. Mexicans from pioneer families continued to hold the fields and some of the lots within the walls but they claimed much more property to the south of the fort, where some had lived when not under fire from the Apaches. One might imagine that after having been confined so often to the limited acreage of the walled town, they welcomed the opportunity to live elsewhere.

On August 5th, 1862, Union Army Major David Fergusson published an order calling upon all persons living within three miles of Tucson to register their real estate.[14] Designated as registrar was

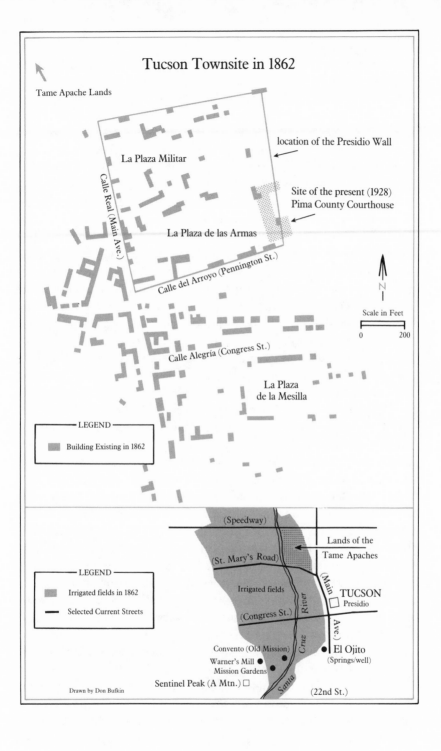

Tucson Townsite in 1862

Tame Apache Lands

La Plaza Militar

location of the Presidio Wall

Site of the present (1928)
Pima County Courthouse

Calle Real (Main Ave.)

La Plaza de las Armas

Calle del Arroyo (Pennington St.)

N

Scale in Feet

0   200

Calle Alegría (Congress St.)

La Plaza
de la Mesilla

LEGEND

Building Existing in 1862

(Speedway)

Lands of the
Tame Apaches

(St. Mary's Road)

LEGEND

Irrigated fields in 1862

Selected Current Streets

Irrigated fields

TUCSON
Presidio

(Congress St.)

Convento (Old Mission)

Warner's Mill
Mission Gardens

Sentinel Peak (A Mtn.)

El Ojito
(Springs/well)

(22nd St.)

Drawn by Don Bufkin

William S. Oury, one of the community's few bilingual residents. Between August 11th and January 31st, 1863, he registered 129 lots. Forty of these were claimed by Anglos, some of whom Oury reported to be absent from Tucson at the time.[15] In half of these forty cases, Oury shows Americans as the original owners, probably meaning that no Mexican claimants were around when the first Anglos landed on them. Also, twenty of the forty were registered in the names of just three persons—Mark Aldrich, Solomon Warner and Oury. Warner, who had begun acquiring his Tucson estate earlier than the others, was among those absent during the registration period.[16]

Although American immigrants had acquired considerable property in and around Tucson by 1862, they had made relatively little headway in gaining ownership of the nearby fields, a situation that would continue for another dozen or so years. When a map of the fields was prepared in 1876, it showed most of the irrigated land still in Mexican hands, although Anglos married to Mexicans—among them Sam Hughes and Hiram S. Stevens—had also become the owners of considerable acreage.[17]

Tubac was completely abandoned when Charles D. Poston and his companions reached it in September, 1856. The dwellings previously occupied by members of the small Mexican garrison were in "a fair state of preservation," according to Poston, although they lacked doors and windows, which had been carted away by the departing soldiers. In a relatively short time, the newcomers established themselves at the site of the fort, reconstructing old houses and building new ones. By late autumn, quarters sufficient to accommodate about three hundred men were ready. This activity attracted settlers from both Tucson and Sonora, and Poston estimated that a thousand "souls" were living in the Santa Cruz Valley near Tubac by Christmas.[18] Included were former presidial soldiers who "had little holdings of land in the valley, and returned to cultivate their farms, in many cases accompanied by their families."

Although Poston's population figures are unquestionably inflated, they do make clear that Tubac was undergoing a major, uninhibited renaissance. Written evidence of Mexican holdings at Tubac that antedate the 1856 resettlement are meager indeed,[19] and in his record book Poston entered only Anglo preemption claims.[20] Apparently the Americans did not challenge the right of Tubac's former Mexican residents to cultivate their fields lying along the river. Most Yankees seriously respected stories they had heard about land-grant rights although some squatted on grants pending a challenge to their occupancy.[21]

The Fate of the Haciendas

The first purchase by Anglos of a Mexican land grant was negotiated by Poston. In December, 1856, he persuaded Ignacio Ortiz to part with the Hacienda La Arivac (Arivaca) for $10,000. Shortly after, Sylvester Mowry acquired the Sópori ranch from a group of American and Mexican claimants, among them heirs of Joaquín Astiazarán, who maintained that their ancestor had received title to an extensive tract in 1838, including the holdings they sold.[22]

The record of the United States government in deciding the validity of Arizona land grants clearly affirms the truth of the old maxim that "justice delayed is justice denied." Final action on some of the claims did not come until after the turn of the twentieth century. The ultimate irony was the 1914 supreme court decision approving the location of Baca Float No. 3 on lands that had once been part of legitimate, historically earlier grants at Tumacácori-Calabazas and San José de Sonoita. The Court—in fact, if not in law—created a Mexican land grant in an area that had been detached from Mexico for more than half a century![23]

At the time the United States assumed jurisdiction over southern Arizona, the Spanish and Mexican grants in the Pimería Alta had been abandoned by their owners for fifteen years or more. Most of the owners, or their successors in interest, were Mexican citizens out of touch with developments to the north. Newcomers like Poston were initially interested only in acquiring properties with mining potential, and as long as the Apache menace continued they did not seek control of other lands within the grants.

Following the Treaty of Guadalupe Hidalgo in 1848, Congress established procedures for considering land claims in the Territory of New Mexico, which included present-day Arizona north of the Gila River. However, these procedures were not extended to the area acquired through the Gadsden Purchase until 1870 and never proved effective thereafter. Local surveyors had the initial responsibility for examining claims and arriving at decisions about both the extent and the validity of purported grants. They were then ex-

Sketch of Tubac in the 1860s (Browne, *Adventures in the Apache Country*)

Sabino Otero and Charles Poston (Arizona Historical Society)

pected to forward their recommendations, with supporting information, to the General Land Office in Washington. The head of that agency, after reviewing the work of the surveyors, was to advise the Secretary of the Interior on the appropriate action. The Secretary's decision was not final, however, until ratified by Congress.

By 1888, Congress had received recommendations concerning all except a handful of the Arizona claims, but had not acted on a single one! With very few exceptions, the claims were pressed by Anglo and Mexican speculators who had purchased the rights of original grantees, often for pitifully small amounts. To complicate matters, the issue had become deeply involved in territorial politics.

Finally driven into action (refusing, however, to assume responsibility for any decisions) Congress created a Court of Private Land Claims in 1891 to settle the matter in both Arizona and New Mexico. Thirteen more years would pass before it completed its work and appeals would go on for some time after.[24] When the task was finally finished, eight grants were confirmed, but the original owners and their descendants were not among the title holders. The court acknowledged the validity of several other grants but rejected confirmation on technicalities. One of these was the Tumacácori-Calabazas property which, according to the judges, had been illegally acquired by Francisco Aguilar in 1844.[25] Rejection of this claim should have opened the way for descendants of the original Pima owners to seek recovery of the land but no such effort was mounted. Instead, those who had acquired the interests of the Baca family of New Mexico pressed their claims for the establishment of a "floating grant" in the area.

Luis María Baca had acquired a very large grant in northern New Mexico in 1821 at about the time Mexico obtained its independence. He grazed his flocks in the region until his death but within a few years raids by hostile Indians made it impossible for his descendants to continue. In 1835, the land was re-granted to a group of citizens who proposed establishing a village in the area. That colony soon grew into the town of Las Vegas.

Baca heirs brought their original title to the attention of the U.S. Surveyor General. Satisfied of its legitimacy, the Secretary of the Interior laid the matter in the lap of Congress. Members of that body recognized both claims in 1860, but decided not to allow the family to disposses the townspeople. Instead, the legislators gave the Bacas three years to select alternate public-domain land within the Territory of New Mexico (which included all of Arizona and part of southeastern Colorado at the time). They could choose five grants of up to 100,000 acres each.

Among the tracts selected before 1863 was one in the central Santa Cruz Valley that included Tubac, Tumacácori and Calabazas. Because of Apache problems the acreage was not immediately surveyed and in 1866 the lawyer for the Baca heirs, contending that a mistake had been made in the location of the initial point, asked for a "corrected" site to the northeast of the first one. In 1908, the second choice was rejected because it contained minerals, which was contrary to the provisions of the legislation.

The attorneys for the Baca successors-in-interest then argued that their original 1863 selection should be approved since it was not mineral land and the only competing claims were those of the Tumacácori-Calabazas grant which had been denied ten years before. They won their case in the court of appeals and the decision was confirmed by the Supreme Court in 1914. Many homesteaders who had settled in the area after 1898 were forced to give up their holdings, creating bitter feelings that survived for more than half a century.[26]

The technicality that eliminated the Arivaca and Los Nogales de Elías grants was based on the fact that their boundaries had never been surveyed and, thus, never specifically defined. The court held this to be a violation of Article VI of the Gadsden Treaty which provided that in order to be respected, grants had to be "located and duly recorded in the Mexican archives." In the Nogales case, the decision was a great relief to the residents of the new American town with that name.[27]

Familiar Faces in New Surroundings

Teodoro Ramírez was one of the first Tucsonans to move his family to Sonora after the boundary survey was completed. Sometime in the fall or early winter of 1855, he and María de los Angeles Salazar took their four youngsters to Santa Cruz.[28] José Francisco de Paula, the oldest, was eleven at the time; Manuel was four. Teodoro was well acquainted with Santa Cruz, having passed through it many times when travelling to Arizpe. Furthermore, his

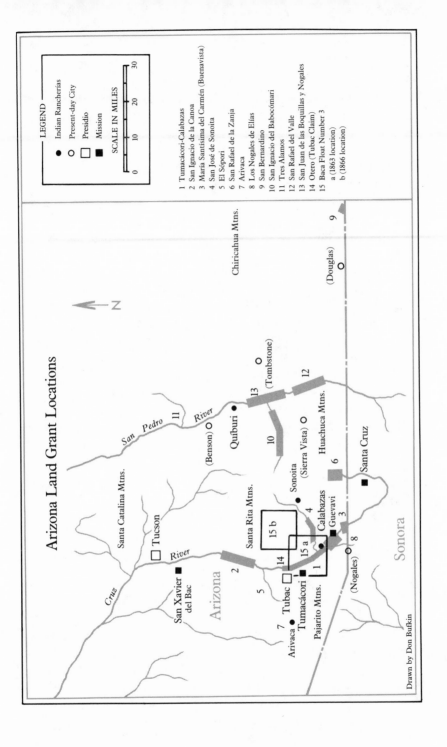

Arizona Land Grant Locations

LEGEND
• Indian Rancherías
○ Present-day City
□ Presidio
■ Mission

SCALE IN MILES
0   10   20   30

1 Tumacácori-Calabazas
2 San Ignacio de la Canoa
3 María Santísima del Carmén (Buenavista)
4 San José de Sonoita
5 El Sópori
6 San Rafael de la Zanja
7 Arivaca
8 Los Nogales de Elías
9 San Bernardino
10 San Ignacio del Babocómari
11 Tres Alamos
12 San Rafael del Valle
13 San Juan de las Boquillas y Nogales
14 Otero (Tubac Claim)
15 Baca Float Number 3
   a (1863 location)
   b (1866 location)

Drawn by Don Bufkin

brother Pedro had lived there with his family a quarter of a century before.[29]

Once the family settled in, Teodoro returned to Tucson from time to time to look after his property and affairs. He remained involved in the politics of both countries. On July 27th, 1856, for example, he signed a petition at Santa Cruz denouncing Manuel María Gándara's supporters for overthrowing Governor José de Aguilar, who had been appointed by President Ignacio Comonfort only two months before.[30] Native Tucsonan Manuel Ygnacio Elías, who had taken his family to live among his wife's relatives while awaiting the outcome of events farther north, also signed the petition.[31]

A month after lending his support at Santa Cruz, Ramírez was in Tucson long enough to add his signature to a memorial drafted by Anglo newcomers requesting territorial status for the area they now called Arizona. The names of many of Teodoro's fellow Mexicans appear on the memorial as well, but it is apparent that others signed the document for most of them.[32]

Late in December, 1856, Ramírez was named to the post of first justice of the peace in Santa Cruz; two weeks later, however, he turned down the appointment, stating that he had passed his sixty-fifth birthday and felt age might be an impediment to carrying out his duties. On the same day he wrote the San Ignacio prefect to reject the assignment, Teodoro composed another letter pointing out that many of the citizens of Santa Cruz were critically ill and the death rate was high. A deeply religious man, he lamented the lack of a priest to administer last rites and recommended that a chaplain be appointed for the military colony.[33]

Late in January, Teodoro travelled to the Gándara sheep ranch at Calabazas. On the return trip, he was joined by fourteen other persons from the hacienda and from Tucson. In the Patagonia Mountains, at a place known as San Antonio Pass, the party was ambushed on January 31st by a band of over fifty Apaches. Three Mexicans were killed, among them Luis Elías of Tucson, father of three children ranging in age from five to eleven.[34] The Apache attack was not the only event that made Teodoro's homecoming to Santa Cruz a sad occasion. On February 2nd, as he rode into town, his oldest child, José Francisco de Paula, died at the age of twelve years and ten months. When he could control his grief, the old man wrote another letter to the San Ignacio prefect about the epidemic at Santa Cruz, repeating his plea for a resident priest.[35]

Following his son's death, Teodoro Ramírez ceased for a time to be active in public life. Apparently he continued to live at Santa Cruz with his family for his name is absent from the New Mexico Territorial Census of 1860. In spite of his advanced age, however, he must have visited Tucson frequently to look after his property. His oldest daughter, Manuela, was married there on May 10th, 1863, to an Irish-American blacksmith named John William Sweeney.[36]

In December, 1864, Ramírez's distinctive handwriting reappears in the public record, this time from Tucson where, hale and hearty at seventy-three, he served as one of the town's justices of the peace.[37] He had decided to spend the rest of his days in the village to which he had devoted so much of his life. It was in Tucson during the hot summer of 1871 that he breathed his last. Writing of Teodoro's death, a reporter for the *Tucson Citizen* commented that "he was a man of scholarly accomplishments, and in the vigor of his life contributed to the literature of his country."[38]

Following the departure of the Mexican troops in 1856, Hispanic Arizonans younger than Teodoro also went on to new lives, some in the United States, others in Mexico. Among those remaining in Tucson was Juan Elías, married briefly to Teodoro's daughter Serafina.[39] He and his brother, Jesús María, found favor with the electorate, both serving in the territorial legislature. Juan was also a county supervisor.

Angel Elías, a relative of Juan and Jesús María, moved quickly up the ranks of the Mexican army after helping with the evacuation of civilians from Tucson. Eventually he was chosen to head the Tucson company and to lead the transfer from Imuris to Fronteras. Later, he fought against the French in Sonora and retired with the rank of colonel. Angel died in 1910, the year the Mexican Revolution began. His son, Manuel, afterward moved the family to Arizona. Half a century later, Angel's great-grandson, Arnold, became Tucson's postmaster.

Joaquín Comadurán, oldest son of Tucson's long-time *comandante* and Ana María Ramírez, held the rank of ensign (*alférez*) when he marched out of Tucson in the late winter of 1856. Within a year, he was promoted to first lieutenant. Early in 1859, when the Tucson troopers were scheduled for a transfer to Fronteras, Comadurán was assigned to Santa Cruz as commanding officer and a short time afterward received a promotion to his father's old rank of captain.

Although Joaquín's uncle, Teodoro Ramírez, lived in Santa

Cruz, the post was not a happy command for Joaquín at first. Since the fort had been converted to a military colony a decade before, the village old-timers had fought with every *comandante* and the situation proved no different for Captain Comadurán. In January, 1860, he was ordered to appear in Guaymas to defend himself against charges brought by some of the Santa Cruz residents. Refusing to do so, he defected to Tucson.[40]

In the first few months following Comadurán's defection, other military officers also grew restless. Lacking supplies, they appropriated what they needed from citizens of the frontier towns, but were reprimanded by higher authorities when the civilians complained. Fed up, many were ready to rebel. The Gandaristas, as always, were quick to take advantage of a new opportunity to regain the power they had lost to the Pesqueira faction three years before. Early in the fall of 1860, Comadurán joined several of his fellow officers in a revolt against the Pesqueira regime. This effort failed and among those losing their lives as a consequence was Captain Hilarión García, Comadurán's superior officer in Tucson. Early the following year, Pesqueira pardoned those who had taken part in the revolt.[41]

Apparently Comadurán did not return to a military career following the events of 1860. The 1864 Arizona territorial census shows him working as foreman at the Mowry mine in the Patagonia Mountains. He continued to make his home in Santa Cruz, however, and writer J. Ross Browne found him there a short time after the census was taken. Browne describes him as "an intelligent Mexican, whose friendship toward Americans travelling through the country has long been proverbial."[42]

There is no record that Joaquín Comadurán ever returned to the area where he was born, although all of his siblings remained in Arizona. Somewhat mysteriously, however, his name appears in the Pima County Book of Births and Deaths.[43] Dr. Joseph Pool prepared a certificate in 1890 attesting that he was the attending physician on February 18th when Comadurán died of pneumonia. There is no indication where the death occurred but it may have been in Benson at the home of Joaquín's brother Antonio. Dr. Pool had a ranch on the San Pedro River not far away.[44]

One of the Tucson soldiers who did come back to live in his home town was Francisco Solano León. Married to Ramona Elías, sister of Luis Elías who was killed by Indians in 1857,[45] León was a sergeant when he accompanied the Mexican forces to Imuris.[46] He

Gravestones of Teodoro Ramírez and María de los Angeles Salazar, Florence cemetery (courtesy of Ann Brady Padilla)

Juan Elías (Arizona Historical Society)

Jesús María Elías (Arizona Historical Society)

had been promoted to *alférez* by June, 1857, when he and other officers of the Mexican garrisons in Sonora swore their allegiance to Mexico's new liberal constitution.[47] Shortly afterward he retired from active military service and by 1859 again resided in Tucson.[48] Deeply respected by all Tucsonans, Francisco Solano León served three terms on the Arizona Territorial Council. He and his wife had thirteen children, eight of whom lived to maturity. When he died in 1891 at seventy-two, the *Arizona Daily Star* characterized him as "the soul of honor."[49] Nine years before, John Wasson, United States surveyor for Arizona, had referred to him as "a man of unblemished reputation."[50]

During the Mexican period in Arizona's history Manuel María Gándara was the most dominant political figure in the region. Never far from the seat of power and always ready to fight to regain control of Sonora's government, Gándara occupied the governor's chair ten times between 1837 and 1856. For the most part, Sonora's fighting forces were never able to mount a sustained effort to subdue the Apaches because of the numerous insurrections that the Gandaristas engineered.[51]

With his brother-in-law's acquisition of the Tumacácori-Calabazas property in 1844, Gándara began an association with southern Arizona that continued during the first decade of United States rule. One of Manuel María's sons and other followers were at Calabazas early in 1857 and Mexican officials feared they were seeking American help to regain power.[52] Poston favored Gándara and was one of those responsible for spreading the rumor that his principal opponent Ignacio Pesqueira was plotting with a group of Americans to oust Gándara, seize control of Sonora, and turn it over to the United States.[53]

Sonorans viewed the matter somewhat differently. For nearly a year, Mexican newspapers had linked Gándara—not Pesqueira—with a seditious movement being organized by Agustín Ainza, whose brother-in-law Henry A. Crabb was a prominent San Francisco adventurer. Both Ainza and Crabb were in Sonora during the late spring of 1856, shortly before the Gandaristas threw José de Aguilar out of the governor's office. Crabb returned to San Francisco early in June, and not long afterward, Ainza was arrested and charged with high treason by a court in Hermosillo. He was released before the end of July, however, and never came to trial.[54]

Ignacio Pesqueira's elevation to the post of interim governor

Henry A. Crabb (Arizona Historical
Society)

General Ignacio Pesqueira, governor
of Sonora (Arizona Historical
Society)

in August, 1856, proved devastating for Gándara's sheep ranch. Following the departure of the Mexican troops from Tucson, Frederick Hulsemann drove the livestock to Imuris, where they were grazing on August 28th when Pesqueira ordered the confiscation of Gándara's Sonora property. Hulsemann was not in Imuris the day the order came through but local authorities wasted no time in taking the sheep into custody. Lamb and mutton soon appeared on the tables of local Mexican soldiers. The Tucson garrison at Imuris received 433 of the animals; 496 were consigned to the two companies stationed at Santa Cruz.[55]

In the spring of 1857 a party of Americans, led by Henry A. Crabb, invaded Sonora. They crossed the border at Sonoita and by April 1st were in Caborca. Pesqueira rushed Mexican troops to the scene. After nearly a week of savage fighting, Crabb and his surviving companions surrendered. The Sonorans wasted no time in executing all except a sixteen-year-old boy.[56]

Gándara may have visited the Calabazas ranch after his sheep were confiscated but, if so, he did not stay in the area for more than a few days. By June, 1857, the main building of the ranch was occupied by William D. Mercer, deputy customs director for New Mexico. Agustín Ainza, who had escaped from Sonora following the Crabb fiasco, was Mercer's guest at Calabazas in September.[57]

Promulgation of a liberal constitution in 1857 sparked new revolutionary activity in Mexico. For the next three years, the country was caught in a struggle that has since been known as the War of the Reform. The Gandaristas, seeing another opportunity to seize power in Sonora, embraced the conservative Plan of Tacubaya and carried the civil war to their home state. As so often had been the case, they managed to persuade some Sonoran Indians—the Opatas this time—to join them. Their efforts were frustrated, however, by the armies of Governor Pesqueira and Jesús García Morales. In February, 1858, Jesús Gándara was killed in battle, and a short time later his brother, Manuel María, fled to Chihuahua. Gándara's stay in the neighboring state was brief. Not long after he arrived, General Félix Zuloaga, who had proclaimed himself Mexico's president after jailing Benito Juárez, chose Manuel María to replace Pesqueira as governor and military commander. Prevented by Pesqueira from returning to Sonora, Gándara went to Sinaloa where he allied himself with other conservatives. Pesqueira's army defeated them early in 1859, however, and Manuel María again sought safety in Arizona.[58]

With the aid of supporters still in Sonora, Gándara engineered rebellions against Pesqueira in mid-1859 and again in 1860. Killed in the 1859 action was Indian Juan Tánori, a leader of the Pimas and Opatas who had been a loyal Gándara follower since 1842.[59] The 1860 affair cost the life of Captain Hilarión García.[60]

Manuel María and other members of his family were living in Tucson when the territorial census of 1864 was taken.[61] Two years before, Sonoran newspapers had implied that he was seeking the help of the American Confederacy to get back into the governor's office,[62] and his popularity in his native state may have reached a low point shortly afterward. Still, he maintained contact with the wealthiest and most conservative members of Sonoran society and was aware of their support for the French-imposed administration of Emperor Maximilian that had been installed in Mexico City in June. The French intervention provided Gándara still another opportunity to further his political ambitions. When the Imperialists seized Sonora in 1865, he wasted no time in getting back into the thick of things. Pesqueira, meanwhile, was obliged to flee for his life and, ironically, found refuge at Calabazas.[63]

By the end of 1865, Gándara was again in Hermosillo, this time to reclaim property that had been stripped from him. In August, 1866, Maximilian named him Imperial Prefect of the Department of Sonora, but once more he was obliged to flee the state before he could assume the office. Pesqueira's armies, commanded by García Morales, routed the French and forced them to sail from Guaymas on September 14th.[64] Gándara accompanied them as far as Tepic, where he remained until taken into custody and imprisoned at San Luis Potosí. Late in 1869, he was moved to Mexico City and in June, 1870, he was declared innocent of all the treason charges that had been brought against him. He returned to Hermosillo where he died of apoplexy in 1878.[65]

Apaches!

When the Forty-Niners passed through the Pimería Alta, many were unabashedly critical of the Mexican soldiers whom they accused of cowardice in facing the Apaches. Even Commissioner Bartlett was scornful. But the first Anglo-Americans to reside in southern Arizona quickly came to realize that the Apaches were fierce and skilled warriors and they were glad that the Mexican troopers were able to remain in Tucson as long as they did. Poston, who had visited the region in 1854, knew perfectly well what kind of problem the hostile Indians could be and he took pains to negotiate a private treaty with some of them when he returned two years later.[66]

Knowing that the Mexican forces would not stay once the boundary survey was completed, late in 1855 Tucsonans petitioned to have American troops stationed in the area.[67] None had arrived when the last Mexican soldiers marched away on March 10th, 1856, however. Uncertain how long they might have to wait for U.S. dragoons, Tucson settlers invited Mexican soldiers and civilians to join them in an offensive against the Apaches.[68] Such an action, they felt, could keep Mexican troopers in the area a while longer.

The San Ignacio prefect endorsed the proposal and even suggested an early September date. In the meantime, however, New Mexico military authorities decided to transfer four companies of dragoons to southern Arizona. The move was delayed, and the soldiers did not reach the Tucson area until November 14th. Major Enoch Steen, the commanding officer, set up a temporary camp at San Xavier and rode into Tucson to investigate. Disappointed in the quality of available quarters, he decided to establish the post elsewhere. Poston may have been influential in persuading him to rent Gándara land at Calabazas and establish a camp there. The Americans named the post Camp Moore.[69]

Steen's first campaign against the Apaches was probably the 1857 action described by Teodoro Ramírez when Ramírez and his party were attacked in the Patagonia Mountains between Santa Cruz and Calabazas.[70] The American commander's initial problems were not with Apaches, however, but with local Mexicans and with his superior officers, both of whom were unhappy with him for not having chosen a post closer to Tucson.

Early in 1857, Mexican authorities began corresponding with Steen about Gandarista activities and about their concern of a possible invasion of Sonora by associates of Agustín Ainza. When Crabb and his filibusters arrived in April, Steen was caught in the middle. Wishing to maintain good relations with the Sonorans—essential for dealing with the Apache problem—he was also obliged to investigate and report on the embarrassing disaster at Caborca.[71]

The Crabb affair kicked off a period of tense relations between some of the Anglos in southern Arizona and elements of the Hispanic population—a situation that complicated Army efforts to control hostile Indians. In spite of the tension, some of Steen's dragoons (part of a force led by Colonel Benjamin L. E. Bonneville, departmental commander at Santa Fe) took the field against Mogollon, Gila and Coyotero Apaches shortly after the Crabb incident. The campaign accomplished little and Bonneville and his men quickly found that fighting Apaches was not as simple as they thought it would be. The colonel was criticized by some of his more experienced officers for the manner in which he organized and conducted the operation.[72]

Sometime early in June, 1857, shortly before the end of the Bonneville campaign, Major Steen moved the last members of his garrison to newly established Fort Buchanan on Sonoita Creek (near modern Patagonia). His superiors had not approved the Calabazas location and had suggested to him that he reconsider a location for a fort in the Tucson area. For reasons that are not clear, however, Steen was firmly against having his troops stationed anywhere near the old Mexican town. In selecting the Sonoita site, he managed to get them even farther from Tucson, much to the displeasure of its residents.[73]

The Apaches made occasional attacks against the settlers of southern Arizona during the late 1850s but concentrated most of their destructive raiding on Sonoran communities to the south. Such leaders as Mangas Coloradas and Cochise were particularly active and the towns of northeastern Sonora suffered extensive losses. To counter the depredations, Governor Pesqueira reorganized the northern line in 1858, placing his greatest strength at the old fort of Fronteras.[74] Beginning in 1860, however, the situation escalated. Initially, Cochise and his Chiricahua Apaches struck southern Arizona and New Mexico towns and the success of their attacks encouraged other Apache groups to step up their raiding.

The problems with Cochise began when a Mexican boy was kidnapped from his home on Sonoita Creek in January, 1861. The child's mother was María de Jesús Martínez, a native of Santa Cruz; his father was a man named Téllez from the same village. Following the death of Téllez, Jesús became the common law wife of John Ward, an Irish-American teamster, with whom she was living at the time her son was captured. Lieutenant George Bascom, stationed at Fort Buchanan, was ordered to take up the chase.[75] Believing that Cochise and his warriors were involved in the attack on Ward's ranch, Bascom invited the Indian leader to meet with him at Apache Pass (east of Tucson) on February 4th. At this parley, the lieutenant asked for the return of the child. Denying that he had been involved in the kidnapping, Cochise said he would try to find the boy and bring him to Bascom. The American officer then seized six Chiricahuas as hostages pending Cochise's return. The next day, the Apache leader captured stage-driver James Wallace as a hostage of his own.[76] When he could not negotiate the release of the Chiricahuas, Cochise led an attack on a wagon train that produced the torture-deaths of eleven persons. The Americans were now to experience what the Sonorans had endured for over a century.

With the outbreak of the Civil War, American troops were withdrawn from southern Arizona posts, leaving many settlers at the mercy of the hostile Indians.[77] In 1862, the presence of Union soldiers—the California Volunteers commanded by General James H. Carleton—helped to curtail some raiding but the situation remained desperate. Despite Carleton's Apache extermination policy,

Eskiminzin, leader of the Apaches at
Camp Grant (Arizona Historical
Society)

Pima Chief Antonio Azul (Arizona
Historical Society)

Cochise and his allies continued their depredations. The few victories American soldiers enjoyed could be credited to aid from experienced Mexican, Papago or Pima frontiersmen. In 1863, the year
Arizona gained territorial status, Jesús María Elías led Captain T.
T. Tidball and some of his soldiers—along with a few civilians, San
Xavier Papagos, and tame Apaches—in an attack on a Pinal Apache
camp in Arivaipa Canyon. Striking at dawn, a tactic long used by
Spanish and Mexican troopers, they killed fifty Pinals. They lost
just one soldier.[78]

In 1865, several companies of Arizona Volunteers were organized to replace soldiers who left the Territory at the end of the
Civil War. Although Anglo-Americans were technically in charge of
some of these units, the limited successes achieved in their campaigns can once again be largely attributed to the Mexicans and
Indians who made up most of the recruits. Lieutenant Manuel
Gallegos, a former Mexican soldier who belonged to one of Sonora's
important military families, was a member of Company E; Lieutenant Primitivo Cervantes headed Company A during most of its
existence; and Antonio Azul, son of the Pima leader often mentioned in these pages, was a lieutenant in Company C.

Some Anglo-Americans in the Volunteer units regarded their

Indian and Mexican comrades with scorn,[79] but officers such as Captain H. S. Washburn had words of praise for them. He concluded a lengthy report on the activities of Company E with the observation:

> the native troops are far superior to any others for field service in this Territory, and until this shall be taken as the basis of operations, no immediate good results can occur. Government may continue to spend its millions upon any other basis, and Apache raids will still continue, while 300 native troops, well officered, at an expense of less than $800 to the man per year, will, in less than two years, rid the Territory of its greatest bane and obstacle in the way of progress.[80]

Pioneer Hispanic families of the Pimería Alta continued to suffer losses of loved ones at Apache hands during the first twenty years of American rule, just as they had over the previous century. Ramón Comadurán, son of Tucson's old presidial captain, was ambushed and slain in 1861, shortly after the Chiricahuas resumed their attacks.[81] The following year, Jesús León and Jesús María Martínez were killed while cutting timber near the mouth of Madera Canyon. Five months later, Jesús María's father, old soldier José María Martínez, was shot twice by Apaches while looking after his stock at the foot of Black Mountain near San Xavier mission. Although he survived the incident, Martínez never completely recovered. Five years later, in the summer of 1868, his Apache adversaries finally finished him off.[82]

The Tucson and Tubac branches of the Elías family were perhaps the hardest hit during the 1850s and 1860s. First to fall victim to the Apaches was Luis, killed on a journey from Calabazas to Santa Cruz in January, 1857. Four years later, his cousin Ramón was slain in the Tortolita Mountains. Another cousin, Cornelio, died in 1863 of wounds received while trying to recover cattle which the Apaches had stolen from the Elías ranch. Ramón and Cornelio were the brothers of Jesús María and Juan Elías. It was shortly after Cornelio's death that Jesús María led Captain Tidball to Arivaipa Canyon, where his forces gained the important victory over the Apaches. Eight years later, Jesús María and Juan directed another expedition to the same location and this time the result made headlines in newspapers across the country.[83]

The 1871 raid on Apaches camped in Arivaipa Canyon resulted in the slaughter of a hundred or more Indians. Most of the dead, however, were women and children. Although from beginning to end the attack resembled many that had taken place before it, the "Camp Grant Massacre," as it was called, touched off a national scandal.

When many Anglo-Americans first came to Arizona, they expressed shock at the brutal aspects of Apache warfare. The anonymous diarist with Captain John Lewis Robards' Missouri party noted that Apache raiders characteristically killed men, women and children without discrimination, although sometimes women might be captured and made into concubines or slaves. In such cases they were "treated badly by the Indian women, who beat them, and make them labor very hard." Mexicans, on the other hand, were said to kill Apache women and children rather than make them prisoners. Captured men were taken to headquarters and burned or shot.[84] Papagos and Pimas often used war clubs to smash the Apaches' skulls. The Pimas in Company C of the Arizona Volunteers also placed the heads of wounded Apaches on flat rocks, then dropped large stones on their upturned faces. As mentioned often in this chronicle, both Pimas and Papagos also captured Apache children and enslaved them for their own use or for sale to Mexicans. The San Xavier Papagos who participated in the Camp Grant affair ran true to form, smashing Apache skulls and taking twenty-seven children as prisoners. Some of the captives were reportedly sold into slavery in Sonora.[85]

By the time of the Camp Grant Massacre, most of the Anglo-Americans in the southern part of territorial Arizona were so ill-disposed toward the Apaches that they applauded actions such as those of the veteran Papago, Pima and Mexican campaigners. Killing Apaches was the goal and one did not question the means employed to accomplish that task. Jesús María Elías, leader of the 1871 expedition, had just finished a term in the territorial house of representatives, and his brother Juan, also a member of the Camp Grant party, served in that same body at the time. Juan was re-elected to the legislature in 1873, his reputation enhanced rather than diminished by the massacre.

The general hostility toward Apaches seems not to have extended to the *Apaches mansos* who still lived at Tucson and Tubac. They

were a visible part of the population for well over a decade after
Major Steen and his dragoons marched into Tucson in 1856. Indian
Agent Charles D. Poston counted 100 at Tucson in 1863 and two
years later C. H. Lord distributed gifts and rations to twenty-five at
Tubac.[86]

Appointed to the Indian Bureau in 1865, M. O. Davidson carried the title "Special Agent for the Pimas, Maricopas, and Tame
Apaches, as well as for the Papagos of Arizona." Not long after
arriving at his Arizona post, Davidson cited the tame Apaches as
evidence that these hostile Indians were "capable of being re-
claimed." In a lengthy communication early in 1866, he reported on
a visit he had received from the head men of the *Apaches mansos*,
who told him of their previous association with lands in "the Valley
of the Sonoita." They expressed interest in having a reservation set
aside for them either on the Sonoita or the San Pedro. The agent
strongly endorsed locating them on the San Pedro River and promised to send a representative "to lay out a reservation 18 miles
square." Davidson closed with the comment that a reservation for
these Indians could serve as a "nursery wherein to place the women
and children of their wild brethren taken captive in the present
war."

The notion that tame and wild Apaches might be placed on the
same reservation continued to dominate the thinking of Indian
agents. In January, 1868, Davidson's successor, Levi Ruggles, presented his superiors with an ambitious argument that he believed
would solve the whole Apache problem. He suggested establishing
a large reservation on which the tame Apaches could settle. When a
wild band sought peace, the military leaders would insist they relocate immediately to the reservation. Here, they would be expected
to emulate the example set by their more civilized kinsmen and
grow the crops needed for subsistence. Quite plainly, the intention
was to pacify the hostile Indians, rather than to reward the peaceful
ones for all the help they had given the Americans and Mexicans as
scouts and militiamen. Creating a reservation for the tame Apaches
was to be no more than an excuse for setting aside a portion of the
public domain on which to imprison those who remained hostile!

Whether because of the Indian bureau's insistence on following a
plan such as Ruggles', or for some other reason, the tame Apaches
never received title to a reservation. As the years passed, they sim-

ply blended with other ethnic groups—both Indian and Mexican—
in southern Arizona, losing their identity as a separate element of
the population.[87]

The Acculturation Process

Most of the Anglo-Americans who came into the northern
Pimería Alta in the late 1840s and for some years after considered
the area to be an exotic, but primitive and dangerous place. Attitudes toward Mexicans and Indians reflected these ambiguities.
While viewed as contributors to the region's exotic attractiveness,
the natives were also considered responsible for both its dangers
and its primitiveness. The Anglo attitudes are well documented in
the comments of members of the Mormon Battalion and Major
Graham's detachment of dragoons, as well as those of the Forty-
Niners and later observers such as Bartlett, Bell, Cozzens, Browne,
Bourke and Hodge—to name but a few of the better known.[88]

Just as individuals of European ancestry had earlier considered
themselves *gente de razón*, the incoming Anglo-Americans viewed
themselves as the social and intellectual superiors of the native
population.[89] In 1858, Phocion R. Way wrote his sister about Tucson: "There are about forty Americans residing here who monopol-
ize all business and rule the place. The Mexicans fear them, ac-
knowledge them as a superior race, and submit without a mur-
mur." Way observed in his diary that native women "have a great
fancy for Americans and a greaser stands no chance with a white
man."[90]

If, indeed, the Mexicans were submissive in Tucson, they appear
to have been less so in the mining areas, especially in the years
immediately after the ill-fated Crabb expedition. Numerous writers
have commented on the violence that characterized this period,
some of it involving Sonorans who resented the superior attitudes of
the Americans and the way in which many chose to treat Mexican
workers, or who viewed Anglo capitalists as prime subjects for feats
of highway robbery.[91]

The need for Anglos to accommodate themselves to Mexican
lifestyles was not a problem in most of Arizona during the first
quarter century after the Gadsden Purchase. Only in the Santa Cruz
Valley had Hispanic culture really taken hold, and except for the

Tucson area most of what had been implanted had been uprooted. Poston and his associates reestablished Tubac to suit themselves; the Mexicans would have to make room. From its beginnings, Prescott was an Anglo community in appearance and in culture. Arizona City (later Yuma) had been laid out by Anglos and in spite of the prominence of such pioneers as José María Redondo the Mexicans never really established cultural dominance there. Phoenix, which was established under American rule was always an Anglo stronghold. Of the major Arizona towns in existence by 1875, the Mexican lifestyle was most influential in Tucson and Florence, with Yuma a distant third.

Phoenicians liked to call Tucson "a little Mexican town" until after the coming of the railroad in 1880.[92] Intermarriage between Anglos and Mexicans was common and Anglo men who were parties to these marriages—both formal and common law—were often the social, economic and political leaders of the community.[93] Mexican merchants prospered during the 1870s, sometimes in partnership with Anglos. Between 1868 and 1878, when the capital was in Tucson, Pima County was regularly represented in both houses of the territorial legislature by persons of Mexican descent, as well as by their Anglo in-laws.

Outside Tucson, in areas noted for antagonistic relations between Anglos and Mexicans during the late 1850s, the outbreak of a major war with the Apaches in 1860 brought these two groups closer together. They would remain comparatively close until the Apache struggle neared its end. Coinciding with that development would be the coming of the railroad in 1880, an event that brought many new Anglos into Arizona Territory. The pattern of intermarriage in Tucson would change dramatically, and the partnerships involving Anglo and Mexican merchants and teamsters would come to an end.[94]

Early in 1884, when the railroad was just beginning to make an impact on the area, don Manuel Ygnacio Elías died at the Tucson home where he had lived since his return from Santa Cruz many years before. He was considered Tucson's second oldest resident[95] and at the time of his death was one of very few individuals in the Territory with distinct memories of what the Pimería Alta was like when Spaniards ruled. Ironically, just one week to the day after Manuel Ygnacio died, Charles Debrille Poston called a meeting of old-timers at Tucson's Palace Hotel for the purpose of forming the

Portrait of Hiram S. Stevens and Samuel Hughes with their wives Petra and
Atanacia Santa Cruz (Arizona Historical Society)

Arizona Pioneers' Historical Society, an organization whose archives would have been greatly enriched by don Manuel's memoirs.

Poston had also been a principal figure at the celebration six
months earlier of General George Crook's return from Mexico after
what appeared to be a successful campaign against the Chiricahua
Apaches.[96] The general's visit brought a return to the community
for Crook's aide-de-camp, Captain John G. Bourke. Although little
impressed with the physical appearance of Tucson when he first
saw it in 1870, Bourke came to love the place and nothing fascinated him more about the town than its Hispanic aura. His words
of disappointment at seeing Tucson the "most changed" town in

the Southwest in 1884 provide an appropriate note on which to conclude this chronicle of Arizona's Hispanic years:

American energy and American capital had effected a wonderful transformation: the old garrison was gone; the railroad had arrived; where Jack Long and his pack train in the old times had merrily meandered, now puffed the locomotive. Muñoz's corral had been displaced by a round-house, and Muñoz himself by a one-lunged invalid from Boston. . . . American enterprise had moved to the front, and the Castilian with his "maromas" and "bailes" and saints' days and "funciones" had fallen to the rear; telephones and electric lights and Pullman cars had scared away the plodding burro and the creaking "carreta"; it was even impossible to get a meal cooked in the Mexican style with Mexican viands; our dreams had faded; the chariot of Cinderella had changed back into a pumpkin, and Sancho was no longer governor.[97]

Reference Material

Appendix A:
The Elías Family of Arizona and Sonora:
A Genealogical Essay

Forty minutes drive southward from Logroño, Spain, along the scenic Leza River one enters the quaint old town of Soto de Cameros. It is in the heart of the La Rioja district, the country's most famous wine producing region. Although Soto in recent times has suffered from a shortage of jobs and a surplus of housing, it was a major textile manufacturing center during the eighteenth century. The products of its looms were sold throughout Spain and even marketed in far-away America.[1]

It was from La Villa de Soto around 1720 that young Francisco Elías González de Zayas set out for La Nueva España, as Mexico was then known. His final destination was the mining town of Real de los Alamos[2] which lay in the far northern province of Sinaloa. Awaiting him at journey's end were close relatives of his mother.[3]

Church records confirm that Francisco had reached Alamos by 1729. On May 15th of that year, he married doña Agueda María Campoy, daughter of the wealthiest and most prominent family in the community. The Campoys were owners of the Hacienda de Thobaca where the bulk of the rich ore from the region was processed.[4] There is no record of any surviving children from this marriage which ended with Agueda's death sometime before 1740.[5] In that year, don Francisco Elías González de Zayas outfitted a militia force of 100 men at his own expense to combat an uprising of the Yaqui Indians. Because of his outstanding performance as the leader of this group, he was offered a commission in the Spanish army and assignment to the presidio of Janos.[6] Widowed and footloose, he accepted, and shortly after beginning a new career, he married doña María Ignacia Díaz del Carpio, daughter of his commanding officer.[7]

Lieutenant Elías González received his promotion to captain in 1751, and not long afterward replaced his father-in-law as commander of the Terrenate presidio. He remained at that Sonora post until his retirement in 1770.[8] By then members of his family were established in Arizpe and Captain Elías González undoubtedly spent many of his last years there. He may have visited relatives in Alamos but never again lived there. He died at El Paso del Norte (modern Ciudad Juárez, Chihuahua) in 1790.[9]

Such documents as the final will of Captain Elías, parish records at Arizpe, and papers associated with the ordination of Father Juan Chrisóstomo Elías González—a grandson of don Francisco—clearly identify the offspring of the latter and María Ignacia Díaz del Carpio. It is through these children and their descendants that the Elías name has become well known in Sonora and other parts of Mexico. A number of governors and state military commanders have belonged to this family and one of its members, Plutarco Elías Calles, attained Mexico's highest political office. The accompanying kinship diagrams identify some of the more prominent family members mentioned in the present volume as well as other notable personages associated with them.

Early Elías Contacts with Arizona

With his assignment as commanding officer of the Terrenate presidio, Captain Francisco Elías González became the first representative of his lineage to be involved in the affairs of the area that was later to be known as Arizona. Between 1753 and 1770, he often entered the region in forays against Apaches. He brought Indians from the San Pedro River to Tucson on March 19th, 1762, the date when he assigned the community the short-lived patronage of San José.

In 1788, a quarter century after his grandfather visited Tucson, young Simón Elías González began his military career as a distinguished soldier in the Tucson company. He remained at his post until 1793 when, boasting the new rank of cadet, he moved southward to the presidio of Buena-vista.[10] Four years later his first cousin, doña Gertrudis Elías González, joined her husband Lieutenant Mariano Urrea in Tucson where the couple remained until 1804. José Cosme Urrea Elías, oldest son of Mariano and Gertrudis, was born at the presidio in 1797, becoming the first representative of his mother's lineage to begin life in Arizona.[11]

Simón Elías González enjoyed two additional periods of military service that brought him into contact with people and events in Arizona history. In 1805, his superiors named him commander of the Pima Indian garrison at Tubac, a post he did not actively assume until 1807 and then for only a short time. He returned to the region in 1814, however, as commanding officer at Santa Cruz, a position he held until 1820.[12]

Another prominent member of the Elías González family, don Ignacio, became *comandante* at Tubac following the departure of his cousin Simón and stayed there until about 1823. His daughter, Josefa Clementa, married Tubac land-grant owner Tomás Ortiz prior to the transfer of her father.

During the period immediately following Mexican independence, members of the Elías family sought and received title to several land grants of their own, making them the largest property holders in the area. Because of the dangers of Apache attack, they did not live permanently on these grants, but continued to maintain their residences at Arizpe and other locations to the south.

The distinction of being the first Elías to make Arizona his permanent home belongs to Cornelio, a family member whose precise antecedents remain obscure. He apparently settled in Tucson about 1800. His name does not appear in the 1797 census, but he was in the community by 1801 when his wife gave birth to a son whom they named Juan Bautista. Later, both Cornelio and Juan became members of the Tucson presidial garrison.[13] In 1818, when a roster of Tucson soldiers was prepared, Cornelio was on detached service in New Mexico. His name is missing from the 1831 census and he may have died before that date.

The military career of Cornelio's son, Juan Bautista, seems to have been a short one. After independence, he moved to Tubac where he married Jesús Orozco. Sharing their household in 1831 were two other adults bearing the Elías surname, as well as a child who is listed as Juan María.[14]

Conclusive documentary evidence of a relationship between Cornelio and the main branch of the Elías family has not come to light, but family members in both Arizona and Sonora insist that a connection exists. Widely shared between the two branches of the family are certain male names, among them Francisco, Ignacio, Ramón, Alejandro, Juan, Antonio, Rafael, Miguel and Manuel; and female names such as Gertrudis, Juana, Ramona, Josefa, Jesús and Dolores. Shared, too, is a small set of compound names: Manuel Ignacio, Juan Bautista, Jesús María, José María and José Francisco.

Given Juan Bautista's birthdate of 1801, his father Cornelio was likely born shortly before 1780. This would have made him a member of the third Sonora generation of the family. His paternity, in such instance, would have been limited to one of the five sons of don Francisco Elías González de Zayas. Three of those sons—Fernando, Francisco and Simón—were married before 1780. A fourth, Miguel Gerónimo, was a priest; and no record has been found of the marriage of the fifth son, Juan Pablo. Simón and his wife had a son named Juan Bautista who may be the person for whom Cornelio named his first born. The oldest child of Fernando could have inspired the name for Manuel Ygnacio, another of Cornelio's sons.

Some differences between Cornelio and his Elías contemporaries deserve mention. During a period when others carrying that surname were members of the officer class, Cornelio and Juan served as common soldiers in the Tucson garrison. Furthermore, Cornelio seems to have preferred the simple form of the family surname, whereas the compound form "Elías González" was widely employed by the others of his generation. On Tucson's 1817 military roster, he appears as "Cornelio Elías," whereas the company's first ensign is carried as "José María Elías González."[15]

Because early Tucson church records are missing from the archives, genealogists are obliged to rely on family tradition and indirect documentary evidence for their conjectures about relationships within the Arizona branch of the Elías family. In the kinship diagram that accompanies this essay, a sibling relationship has been posited for Manuel Ygnacio and Luis based on the fact that they were sharing a Tucson household at the time of the 1831 census. In that same year, Juan Bautista, Teodoro and Gertrudis were living together in Tubac. Both Juan Bautista and Manuel Ygnacio had sons whom they named Cornelio and, according to descendants of Luis, he and Ramona were brother and sister.[16]

Of those persons listed in the accompanying diagram as children of Cornelio and Concepción, the evidence is flimsiest in the cases of Guadalupe and María Jesús. In fact, Guadalupe's relationship is based on conjecture alone. With respect to María Jesús, one document in the Magdalena (San Ignacio) parish archive strengthens the possibility that she was a sibling of Manuel Ygnacio. On September 2nd, 1844, her daughter Gertrudis became the godmother of José Francisco Adolfo, son of Manuel Ygnacio and his first wife Encarnación Durán. Selecting close relatives for godparent responsibilities was common in Mexican households then, as now.

Limited though it is, the kinship chart for the Arizona Elíases shows clearly the extent to which this lineage established early marriage relationships with such other deeply rooted Arizona families as the Gallegos, Pacheco, Herreras, Durán, Ramírez, Ruelas, León, Martínez, Saenz, Sosa and Romero. More recently, they have forged bonds with persons from other prominent families whose progenitors reached Arizona after 1850. Surnames represented include Carrillo, Aguirre, Moreno, Laos and Huerta.

In territorial Arizona, the best known representatives of the Elías family were brothers Juan and Jesús María, both of whom served in the legislature, as did their cousin-in-law Francisco Solano León. In the late 1920s, Perfecto M. Elías was a Tucson city councilman; Roy Laos, III—whose grandmother was an Elías—held a similar post in 1986. Arnold Elías, great grandson of Colonel Angel Elías, served in the Arizona legislature in the early 1960s; and Emilio Carrillo, great grandson of Manuel Ygnacio Elías, was a legislator from 1959 through 1961 and again in the 1970s.

One Tucson-born Elías who attained prominence without entering politics is known to the world of music as Richard Clark.[17] Early in the decade of the 1980s, he became a featured baritone with the Metropolitan Opera Company of New York.

Descendancy of Francisco Elías González de Zayas[1]

[1]Compiled from original documentary sources in the Alamos and Arizpe parish archives and files of the Elías family. No evidence has been uncovered to attest the birth of any children to Francisco and Agueda María Campoy, although Alamos priest José Joaquín Elías González de Zayas, who died in 1815, may have been a son. Agueda María died before 1740.

[2]Descendants of Fernando and José Francisco are shown on the pages that follow.

[3]The parentage of Juan Pablo has been confirmed by documents in the Arizpe Parish Archives. No information has been found concerning possible spouses or descendants.

[4]Simón died before his father and is not mentioned in the latter's will. He was married on April 28, 1777 to María Rossa Escalante, daughter of wealthy don Claudio Escalante and his equally wealthy wife, doña Juliana Herrera. The priest who performed the ceremony was his brother, Miguel Elías González. The only known child of Simón is a son, Juan Bautista Nepomuceno, but there may have been others.

[5]Arizpe parish records show that Gerónima Atilena Moradillas, a daughter of Juana and Francisco, was married in 1798 to Francisco Caxigas, nephew of María Francisca Caxigas who the preceding year had married José Florentino Rafael Elías González, Gerónima's first cousin. On October 30, 1791, Francisco Díaz de Moradillas and his wife baptized twin daughters, whom they named María Manuela Narcissa and María Guadalupe Narcissa. José Francisco Antonio and Fernando, brothers of the twins' mother, were godfathers for Manuela and Guadalupe respectively. Juana and Francisco may have had other children in addition to these three daughters.

Descendancy of Fernando Elías González[1]

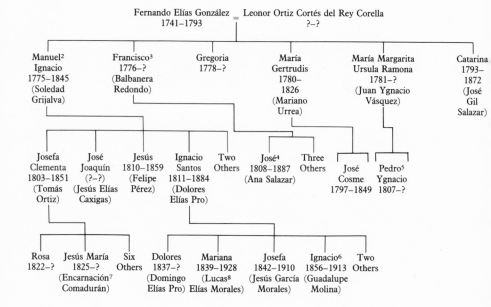

[1]Information from a variety of sources including the Arizpe and Oquitoa parish archives, Arizona land grant documents, Arizona territorial censuses, Elías family records, and *Compendio de Datos Históricos de la Familia Elías* by Armando Elías Chomina. An attempt has been made to include members of the Elías family listed in the text, as well as to illustrate commonality of intra-familial marriages and frequency of marriages with representatives of Sonoran elite families such as the Pérez, Ortiz, and Salazar. We have not attempted to show the names or number of progeny in all cases. The absence of this information on the chart does not mean there were no descendants.

[2]Together with Nepomuceno Félix, Manuel Ignacio Elías (known as Capitán Ignacio and also as "El Míchigo") was the owner of the San Juan de las Boquillas y Nogales grant on the San Pedro River south of St. David.

[3]Francisco may have been married also to Dominga Montaño and fathered a son named Joaquín Vicente.

[4]José Elías Redondo was the first owner of the Los Nogales de Elías land grant. Some of his descendants still reside in Nogales, Sonora.

[5]Margarita may have had other children in addition to Pedro Ygnacio who was born in Altar.

[6]Descendants of Ignacio Elías Elías constitute the most prominent branch of the family still residing in Arizpe.

[7]Encarnación Comadurán was the daughter of Antonio Comadurán, commanding officer of the Tucson presidio for many years.

[8]Lucas Elías Morales was a half-brother of General Jesús García Morales.

Descendancy of José Francisco Antonio Elías González[1]

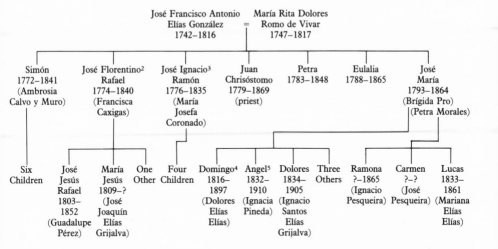

José Francisco Antonio Elías González 1742–1816 = María Rita Dolores Romo de Vivar 1747–1817

Simón 1772–1841 (Ambrosia Calvo y Muro)

José Florentino[2] Rafael 1774–1840 (Francisca Caxigas)

José Ignacio[3] Ramón 1776–1835 (María Josefa Coronado)

Juan Chrisóstomo 1779–1869 (priest)

Petra 1783–1848

Eulalia 1788–1865

José María 1793–1864 (Brígida Pro) (Petra Morales)

Six Children

José Jesús Rafael 1803–1852 (Guadalupe Pérez)

María Jesús 1809–? (José Joaquín Elías Grijalva)

One Other

Four Children

Domingo[4] 1816–1897 (Dolores Elías Elías)

Angel[5] 1832–1910 (Ignacia Pineda)

Dolores 1834–1905 (Ignacio Santos Elías Grijalva)

Three Others

Ramona ?–1865 (Ignacio Pesqueira)

Carmen ?–? (José Pesqueira)

Lucas 1833–1861 (Mariana Elías Elías)

[1]Information from a variety of sources including the Arizpe Parish Archives, Arizona land grant documents, and Elías family records. Compiled with the assistance of Armando Elías Chomina and Carmen Pellat Sotomayor. An attempt has been made to include members of the Elías family mentioned in the text, as well as demonstrate the commonality of intra-familial marriages and the frequency of marriage relationships with other elite lineages of Sonora. No attempt has been made to include the names of all descendants at the third generation level.

[2]This is the sub-lineage to which Mexican President Plutarco Elías Calles belonged. He was a great, great grandson of José Florentino Rafael, who went by the name of Rafael. In addition to the important San Pedro Palominas land grant in Sonora, Don Rafael was owner of the San Rafael del Valle grant stretching along the San Pedro River in Arizona. His descendants make up the San Pedro Palominas branch of the Elías family.

[3]Don Ignacio Elías Romo de Vivar and his sister Eulalia were owners of the Babocómari land grant in Arizona.

[4]The descendants of Domingo Elías Pro are the only family members in Sonora who have continued to use the double name "Elías González." Don Francisco Elías González, oldest surviving male member of this line, resided in Cananea in 1987.

[5]Don Angel Elías Pro eventually came to command the Tucson presidial garrison following its transfer to Imuris in 1856. His great grandson, Arnold Elías, was Tucson's postmaster in 1987.

324   Appendix A

The Elías Family of Tucson and Tubac[1]

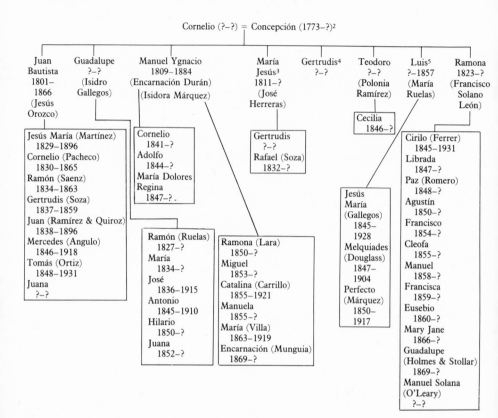

Cornelio (?–?) = Concepción (1773–?)[2]

Juan Bautista 1801–1866 (Jesús Orozco)

Jesús María (Martínez) 1829–1896
Cornelio (Pacheco) 1830–1865
Ramón (Saenz) 1834–1863
Gertrudis (Soza) 1837–1859
Juan (Ramírez & Quiroz) 1838–1896
Mercedes (Angulo) 1846–1918
Tomás (Ortiz) 1848–1931
Juana ?–?

Guadalupe ?–? (Isidro Gallegos)

Manuel Ygnacio 1809–1884 (Encarnación Durán) (Isidora Márquez)

Cornelio 1841–?
Adolfo 1844–?
María Dolores Regina 1847–? .

Ramón (Ruelas) 1827–?
María 1834–?
José 1836–1915
Antonio 1845–1910
Hilario 1850–?
Juana 1852–?

María Jesús[3] 1811–? (José Herreras)

Gertrudis ?–?
Rafael (Soza) 1832–?

Ramona (Lara) 1850–?
Miguel 1853–?
Catalina (Carrillo) 1855–1921
Manuela 1855–?
María (Villa) 1863–1919
Encarnación (Munguia) 1869–?

Gertrudis[4] ?–?

Teodoro ?–? (Polonia Ramírez)

Cecilia 1846–?

Jesús María (Gallegos) 1845–1928
Melquiades (Douglass) 1847–1904
Perfecto (Márquez) 1850–1917

Luis[5] ?–1857 (María Ruelas)

Ramona 1823–? (Francisco Solano León)

Cirilo (Ferrer) 1845–1931
Librada 1847–?
Paz (Romero) 1848–?
Agustín 1850–?
Francisco 1854–?
Cleofa 1855–?
Manuel 1858–?
Francisca 1859–?
Eusebio 1860–?
Mary Jane 1866–?
Guadalupe (Holmes & Stollar) 1869–?
Manuel Solana (O'Leary) ?–?

[1]Sibling relationships in the second generation have not been confirmed by documentation in all cases. See the text of Appendix A for further explanation. Because of the large number of progeny, the author has not attempted to expand the genealogical chart beyond three generations.

[2]The author has not been able to determine Concepción's family name. The date of her birth is from the 1860 U.S. Census of Tucson. If she is the mother of the children shown in the chart, this birth date is probably too early. She may have been born as late as 1785.

[3]The year of birth for María Jesús is based on information in the 1864 U.S. Census. The Census of 1860 shows her to be somewhat younger. Her name appears in the 1831 Mexican Census as Juana rather than María Jesús.

[4]Gertrudis appears in the 1831 census of Tubac as an adult woman living in the household of Juan Bautista Elías and Jesús Orozco, along with Teodoro Elías and a child identified as Juan María, but who was almost certainly Jesús María. The author could not locate any additional information concerning Gertrudis.

[5]The 1831 Mexican Census of Tucson shows Luis Elías as a boy living with bachelor soldier Manuel Ygnacio.

Appendix B

The Elías-Ortiz Kin Group and the Arizona Land Grants[1]

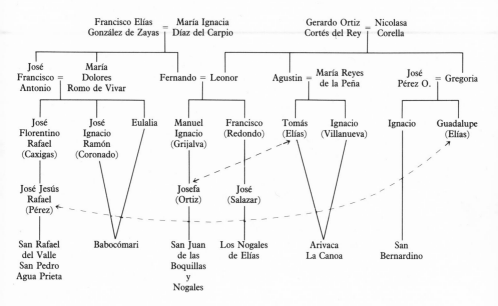

[1]The primary sources of information for this chart are the Arizpe Parish Archives and the "Journal of Private Land Grants" (microfilm 2174, University of Arizona Library, Tucson).

Appendix C

Comadurán Family Tree

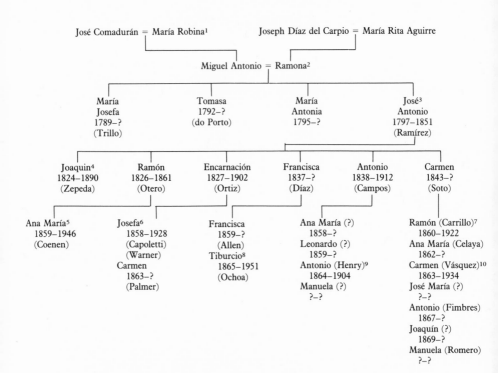

José Comadurán = María Robina[1]   Joseph Díaz del Carpio = María Rita Aguirre

Miguel Antonio = Ramona[2]

| María Josefa 1789–? (Trillo) | Tomasa 1792–? (do Porto) | María Antonia 1795–? | José[3] Antonio 1797–1851 (Ramírez) |

| Joaquin[4] 1824–1890 (Zepeda) | Ramón 1826–1861 (Otero) | Encarnación 1827–1902 (Ortiz) | Francisca 1837–? (Díaz) | Antonio 1838–1912 (Campos) | Carmen 1843–? (Soto) |

Ana María[5] 1859–1946 (Coenen)

Josefa[6] 1858–1928 (Capoletti) (Warner) Carmen 1863–? (Palmer)

Francisca 1859–? (Allen) Tiburcio[8] 1865–1951 (Ochoa)

Ana María (?) 1858–? Leonardo (?) 1859–? Antonio (Henry)[9] 1864–1904 Manuela (?) ?–?

Ramón (Carrillo)[7] 1860–1922 Ana María (Celaya) 1862–? Carmen (Vásquez)[10] 1863–1934 José María (?) ?–? Antonio (Fimbres) 1867–? Joaquín (?) 1869–? Manuela (Romero) ?–?

[1]José Comadurán was a native of Barcelona. His wife was from Gerona.

[2]Miguel Antonio, surgeon in the Spanish royal army, married Ramona on February 4, 1789 at the Villa de Chihuahua. Her parents were well-to-do Creoles from Chihuahua.

[3]José Antonio, Tucson's *comandante* during the Mexican period, was born in Arizpe on September 11, 1797. Several of his female descendants have been named for his wife, Ana María Ramírez.

[4]Joaquín, who lived in Santa Cruz, Sonora, had children but the author did not discover their names or number. One may have been Manuel Comadurán whose wife was Luisa Elías. At Santa Cruz on June 24, 1866, Manuel and Luisa baptized a daughter whom they named María Dolores.

[5]Ana María's granddaughter, Ana María Maldonado Fimbres, resided at Green Valley, Arizona in 1987.

[6]Josefa's granddaughter, Elva Warner Taylor, lived in Tucson in 1987.

[7]Ramón had four children, one of whom—María Soto Audelo—made her home in Tucson in 1987. The family historian—Martha Soto Green of Gilbert, Arizona—is a great granddaughter of Ramón.

[8]Two of Tiburcio's daughters, Hortensia and Amelia, were residents of Mesa, Arizona in 1987. A granddaughter, Dena Díaz Almazán, lived in Tucson.

[9]Two of Antonio's four children—Antonio and Mercedes—lived in California in 1987. Grandsons Alberto, Mariano, Juan, and Antonio resided in Benson. Grandsons José and Manuel lived in Globe and Douglas, Arizona.

[10]Carmen Soto Vásquez founded and operated the Teatro Carmen, an important site for Spanish-language plays and musical events between 1915 and 1922. See Sheridan, *Los Tucsonenses*, 200–202.

Appendix D

Ramírez Family Tree[1]

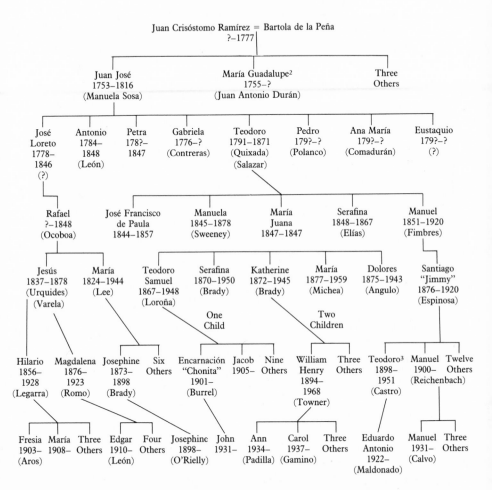

[1]This kinship chart identifies only a few of the many hundreds of descendants of Juan Crisóstomo and Bartola. Beginning with the second generation, it focuses on the sub-lineage of Juan José; and from the third generation, includes information only about descendants of José Loreto and Teodoro. In 1987, this family could claim residence in Arizona for ten generations. An effort has been made to include the names of persons mentioned in the text as well as names of those who helped compile the genealogy.

[2]A daughter of María Guadalupe Ramírez and Juan Antonio Durán married Ignacio Pacheco, founder of the principal line of Pachecos in southern Arizona.

[3]In 1987, Teodoro Ramírez and Esther Castro had a grandson named Teodoro Antonio Ramírez and a great grandson named Eusebio Teodoro Ramírez—both living in Tucson. The name Teodoro Ramírez thus continues in the city.

Appendix E
Agent Ruggles and the
Tame Apaches of Tucson

U.S. Indian Agency
Pima Villages
January 31, 1868

Sir,

In my annual report under date of June 20, 1867 I endeavored as explicitly as possible to call the attention of the Indian Bureau to the necessity of providing at an early day a reservation for the tame Apache Indians of this Territory, and as this is a matter in which I feel a deep interest, and one to which I am desirous of enlisting the attention of the Department, I have deemed it of sufficient importance to call your special attention to it, and would therefore most respectfully set forth the following facts for your information.

There are located at Tucson about 100 of these Indians (I estimated them at 70 in my annual report) who are willing and anxious to locate on a suitable reservation where they can be protected in the cultivation of the soil for subsistence. I have already suggested that they be located on such a reservation and protected by military force from the encroachment of the hostile Indians and that those of the hostile bands who from time to time should become willing to make treaties of peace, be required to live on their reservation, and by so doing, the hostile Apaches of this Territory would be rendered a peaceable, industrious and self-sustaining people in no great length of time.

At the hazard of being considered as attempting to foreshadow in this communication the proper course for the military authorities of this Territory to pursue in regard to these hostile bands, I would suggest that when hostile bands of Apaches come to military posts under the pretense (whether false or on good faith) of making peace treaties that they be *immediately* required to settle on the reservation, where they could be provided for and protected until they were enabled thereby to protect themselves and provide their own sustenance, and in the event of any band refusing to comply immmediately with this request, they should be ordered to leave the military post, and vigorous campaigns made against them at once.

The hostile Apaches of this Territory, as you are no doubt aware, are divided into small bands over each of which is a chief or headman, who seems to govern only those of his band; however it may have been years ago, there does not now appear to be an recognized head chief of the Apaches of this Territory and, consequently, treaties made with anyone claiming to speak for all would not be considered as binding by those not present. Therefore, it becomes necessary to make as many treaties as there are bands. This course, however, would be unnecessary if the head men of each band could be induced to treat at the same time, but here arizes [sic] the great difficulty; they are either purposely or accidentally never all ready to treat for peace at the same time, so that while one band is at a military post under the pretense of forming treaties, other bands are committing depredations in the vicinity of neighboring posts. Now the course in short that I would advise and I think it is the proper one to be pursued in regard to making treaties with these Indians, is, when any band comes to a military post, who are willing to make a treaty of peace, treat with them at once, and in the treaty make stipulations, and have them fully understand that they will be required to settle on the reservation and there remain under military protection with an agent to see that they are properly supplied with means necessary to enable them to cultivate the land on the reservation, on the products of which they should depend for their clothing and subsistence.

Since my arrival in this Territory there has scarcely been a time when there was not one or more of these bands at some one of the military posts under the pretense of making treaties, and at the same time being fed by the government. It is universally conceded, I believe, that it is more economical for the government to feed Indians than to fight them, and surely it is more honorable, but to a certain extent the Government has been, and is now, doing both with the Apaches of the Territory. I have no desire to censure in any degree the actions of the various military commanders in this Territory, for they have, as far as my knowledge extends, done as well as could have been expected under all the existing circumstances. I have, however, the utmost confidence in the feasibility of the plan of settling our Indian differences in this Territory.

Then let there be at once a suitable reservation set apart for them, on which, as I have already said, those Tame Apaches at Tucson would willingly locate and by so doing, would have a tendency to induce the hostile bands more readily to come and settle with them.

I am credibly informed that such a reservation can be had in the Sinoite [sic] valley near Tubac in this Territory, where there is an abundance of rich and fertile land, and plenty of wood and water, and in which valley the tame Apaches have in years past cultivated lands with some success, but which they were compelled for want of proper protection to abandon.

With this plan which I have sketched in the foregoing perfected and properly carried out, many valuable lives and hundreds of thousands of dollars in money would be saved to the Government annually, for not over one-fourth of the troops that are now doing duty in the Territory against the Apaches would form a sufficiently strong guard to protect them and prevent them from leaving the reservation.

If you deem the above view of sufficient importance, please forward this letter to the Indian Bureau. I have the honor to remain very respectfully your most obedient servant.

/s/ Levi Ruggles

Hon. G.W. Dent, Superintendent,
Indian Affairs, La Paz, Arizona

(Original in M-234 [10-46-5], Arizona Superintendencies, 1863–1869. U.S. National Archives, Washington, D.C.)

Appendix F
Last Register of
Mexican Soldiers in Tucson[1]

Name	Rank	Status
Hilarión García	Captain	Serving with boundary escort
Manuel Romero	Lieutenant	Serving with boundary escort
Joaquín Comadurán	2d Lieutenant	Present in camp
Antonio Comadurán	Armorer	Present in camp

Infantry

Joaquín Morales	Sergeant	Present in camp
Jesús Martínez	Drummer	Present in camp
Andrés Granillo	Private	Guard duty
Santos Santa Cruz	Private	Guard duty
Francisco Romero	Private	Sick
Francisco Grijalva	Private	Present in camp
Francisco Morales	Private	Guard duty
Juan Ochoa	Private	Present in camp
Juan Evangelista	Private	Present in camp
Mauricio Vásquez	Private	Guard duty

Cavalry

Santos Michelena	Sergeant	Detached service—Ures
Solano León	Sergeant	Serving with boundary escort
Pio Romero	Sergeant	Serving with boundary escort
Ramón Comadurán	Sergeant	Serving with boundary escort
Juan Bojorques	Corporal	Present in camp
Bautista Gallegos	Corporal	Serving with boundary escort
José María Peralta	Corporal	Serving with boundary escort
José María Márquez	Corporal	Serving with boundary escort
José María Quinteros	Corporal	Guard duty
Pedro Quijada	Trumpeter	Serving with boundary escort
Antonio Ramírez	Trumpeter	Serving with boundary escort

[1]Transcribed and translated from report by Joaquín Comadurán, Tucson, September 1, 1855. M-M 381, No. 153. Pinart Collection, BL.

Santiago Gonzales	Trumpeter	Present in camp
Ildefonso Márquez	Private	Present in camp
Fernando Galas	Private	Serving with boundary escort
Francisco Ramírez	Private	Serving with boundary escort
José Rodríguez	Private	Serving with boundary escort
Juan Gallardo	Private	Present in camp
Pascual Ochoa	Private	Detached service—Ures
Ramón Ortega	Private	Present in camp
Germán Morillo	Private	On duty with the mail
Buenaventura Ortega	Private	Present in camp
Vicente Calvadillo	Private	In the guard house[2]
Pedro Montaño	Private	Serving with boundary escort
Manuel Jácome	Private	Serving with boundary escort
Pedro Sotelo	Private	Detached service—Ures
Higinio Moreno	Private	On duty with the mail
Antonio Rodríguez	Private	Detached service—Ures
Jesús Núñez	Private	Serving with boundary escort
Matías Romero	Private	On duty with remount herd
Susano Ramírez	Private	Serving with boundary escort
Ramón Yescas	Private	Serving with boundary escort
Ramón Munguía	Private	Detached service—Ures
Bernardino Alvares	Private	Present in camp
Jesús Gallego	Private	On duty with remount herd
Rafael Ochoa	Private	Sick
Alejo Barragán	Private	Serving with boundary escort
Angel Munguía	Private	On duty with remount herd
Vitorino Acedo	Private	Serving with boundary escort

Total in the company—52[3]
On duty—49
Sick—2
In jail—1

[2]Private Calvadillo deserted while serving with the escort for the boundary commission. He turned himself in to Sergeant Joaquín Morales at Imuris on August 6. See Morales affidavit, M-M 381, No. 150, Pinart Collection, BL.

[3]Although the register clearly shows 52 men assigned to the Tucson company Comadurán reported only 49. He evidently did not count the two who were sick and Private Calvadillo who was in jail.

Notes

Chapter 1. Myth and Reality in the Upper Pimería

1. Bancroft, *History of Arizona and New Mexico, 1530–1888*.
2. Farish, *History of Arizona*, vol. 1, chap. 4. See Lockwood and Page, *Tucson, The Old Pueblo*, 7–10, for comments on some of these fanciful interpretations.
3. Hamilton, "Arizona—An Historical Outline."
4. *Hammond's World Atlas*, 207.
5. Polzer, "Legends of Lost Missions and Mines."
6. Park, "The History of Mexican Labor in Arizona during the Territorial Period."
7. Pitt, *The Decline of the Californios*, ix. Also, see Robinson, *Mexico and the Hispanic Southwest in American Literature*, chap. 5.
8. Meier and Rivera, *The Chicanos: A History of Mexican Americans*; Bancroft, *History of Arizona and New Mexico 1530–1882*, 382; and Velasco, *Noticias Estadísticas del Estado de Sonora*, 103–104.
9. Kessell, *Mission of Sorrows* and *Friars, Soldiers, and Reformers*. Also, see Dobyns, "Tubac Through Four Centuries: An Historical Resume and Analysis."
10. Herring, *A History of Latin America*, 144–145; Villamarín, *Indian Labor in Mainland Colonial Spanish America*, 95–96.
11. Spicer, *Cycles of Conquest*.
12. Polzer in his *Kino Guide II* provides a comprehensive bibliography of Kino and later Jesuits. Also, see Kessell, *Mission of Sorrows*.
13. Almada, *Diccionario de Historia, Geografía, y Biografía Sonorenses*, 65–67; Herring, "The Silver of El Real de Arizonac."
14. Wagoner, *Early Arizona: Prehistory to Civil War*, 108.
15. Dobyns, *Spanish Colonial Tucson*, 99–100.
16. Kessell, *Friars, Soldiers, and Reformers*, 261 ff.
17. Velasco, *Noticias Estadísticas del Estado de Sonora*, 103–104.
18. Hodge, *Handbook of American Indians North of Mexico*, vol. 2, 738–739.
19. McClintock, *Arizona*, vol. 1, 3.
20. Charles D. Poston credited himself with suggesting the name Arizona for the region. Feather, "Origin of the Name Arizona."
21. Douglass, "On the Naming of Arizona," 217–234.

22. Herbert E. Bolton's map of Pimería Alta 1687–1711, included in *Kino's Historical Memoir*, II, shows no site called Arizonac. However, in his book *On the Trail of a Spanish Pioneer*, Elliot Coues does show a Pima village of that name later in Jesuit times.

23. Almada, *Diccionario*, 65.

24. Barnes, *Arizona Place Names* (revised edition by Byrd H. Granger), 103.

25. Pearce (ed.), *New Mexico Place Names*, 63.

26. Bancroft, *History of Arizona and New Mexico, 1530–1888*, 163 fn. 41.

27. Corle, *The Gila, River of the Southwest*, 9.

28. Kessell, *Mission of Sorrows*, 46–47.

29. Barnes, *Arizona Place Names*.

30. Pearce (ed.), *New Mexico Place Names*, 102; Barnes, *Arizona Place Names*, 79.

31. Wormser, *Tubac*, 5.

32. Dobyns, *Spanish Colonial Tucson*, 4–33.

33. Fontana, "Biography of a Desert Church: The Story of Mission San Xavier del Bac."

34. Kessell, *Friars, Soldiers, and Reformers*, 202, 254.

35. Personal communications from Watson Smith and Emory Seka-quaptewa (author's files). Also, see Kay, "Hopis turn for help to fight looters."

36. Montgomery, Smith, and Brew, "Franciscan Awatovi."

37. *Ibid.*, 18–23.

38. Fontana, "Calabazas of the Rio Rico."

39. Kessell, *Friars, Soldiers, and Reformers*, 87–88.

40. Kessell, *Mission of Sorrows*, 119 fn. 50; Robinson, "Mission Gue-vavi: Excavations in the Convento," 135, 171; Wasley, "Ravaged Ruins: The Destruction of Our Cultural Heritage."

41. Kessell, *Friars, Soldiers, and Reformers*, 169; Thomas, *Teodoro de Croix*, 181–184; Navarro García, *Don José de Gálvez*, 242.

42. Munson, "Don Ignacio and Doña Eulalia Elías and the History of Their Hacienda on the Babocomari: Camp Wallen."

43. Brophy, "San Ignacio del Babocomari."

44. Anonymous, "The Changing Heart of Downtown Tucson."

45. The earliest roof beams dated from about 1876. See Laboratory of Tree-Ring Research, "Report on the CORDOVA HOUSE."

46. Kessell, *Friars, Soldiers, and Reformers*, 308.

47. Anonymous, "A Barrio Libre" (compiled from newspaper accounts).

48. Browne, *Adventures in the Apache Country*, 132–133.

49. Bourke, *On The Border With Crook*, 55–56.

50. Carpenter, "Architectural Development in Tucson."

51. Cataldo, "Evolution of Armory Park Architectural Expression."

52. *Ibid.*; Carpenter, "Architectural Development in Tucson." Also, see Sobin, "From Vigas to Rafters."

53. Stewart, "The Mansions of Main Street."

54. Cheek, "Tucson's architecture: The Spanish accent is here to stay," *Tucson Citizen*, January 16, 1982.

55. Simons, "Longtime team saves local old-time houses," *Arizona Daily Star*, July 15, 1979; García, "Barrio childhood spurred architect's pride, *Arizona Daily Star*, November 2, 1980."

56. Polzer, *Kino Guide II*, 9, 18; Bannon, *The Spanish Borderlands Frontier*, 70.

57. Kessell, *Mission of Sorrows*, 32, 74–75.

58. Wagoner, *Early Arizona*, 157–241.

59. Cooke, *The Conquest of New Mexico and California in 1846–1848*, 145–146; Bartlett, *Personal Narrative of Explorations and Incidents in Texas, California, Sonora, and Chihuahua*, vol. 1, 256–258.

60. Robinson, *The Story of Arizona*, 319–320.

61. McWilliams, "The Heritage of the Southwest"; Seibold, "Cattle Ranching and Spanish Speech in Southern Arizona."

62. Campa, *Hispanic Culture in the Southwest*, 68–71; Aguirre, "The Last of the Dons," and "Echoes of the Conquistadores: Stock Raising in Spanish-Mexican Times."

63. Hinton, *Handbook to Arizona*, 213; Park, "The History of Mexican Labor in Arizona," 169.

64. Farish, *History of Arizona*, vol. 6, 56–57; Wildman, "Great Days at Silver King"; Hinton, *Handbook to Arizona*, 278–279, 285–286.

65. Kessell, *Mission of Sorrows*, 106; Couts, *Hepah, California! The Journal of Cave Johnson Couts*, 58–59.

66. Hardy, *Travels in the Interior of Mexico, in Baja California, and Around the Sea of Cortes, 1825, 1826, 1827, and 1828*, 432; Poston, *Building a State in Apache Land*, 46.

67. Park, "The History of Mexican Labor in Arizona," 149–151, 155; Probert, "Bartolomé de la Medina: The Patio Process and the 16th Century Silver Crisis"; Young, "The Spanish Tradition in Gold and Silver Mining."

68. Almada, *Diccionario*, 74.

69. Encarnación Comadurán, daughter of Tucson's longtime presidial commander, signed her deposition with an "X" when she provided testimony in the Arivaca land grant hearings. See Arizona (Ter.) Surveyor General, "Journal of Private Land Grants," University of Arizona Microfilm, University of Arizona Library (hereafter, UAM) 2174, vol. 2, 185.

70. Using civil records, Janet Lecompte produced an excellent account

of women's statuses in frontier New Mexico. See Lecompte, "The Independent Women of Hispanic New Mexico, 1821–1846." Tucson's civil records of the Mexican period were purportedly burned after being carried to Imuris in 1856. See Page, "The Mexican troop's departure from Tucson, as recalled by Doña Atanacia Santa Cruz. . . ."

71. Arriquibar to the Bishop, January 4, 1804, Archivo de la Mitra de Sonora (hereafter, AMS). UAM 422, reel 2.

72. In "Reminiscences of an Arizona Pioneer," Hilario Gallego mentions the trade in rag dolls. Atanacia Santa Cruz helped make bullets for an expedition against the Apaches in 1863. See Santa Cruz, "Reminiscences of an Arizona pioneer. The personal experiences of Mrs. Samuel Hughes," ms. 881, Charles Morgan Wood papers (1923–1927), Arizona Historical Society, Tucson (hereafter, AHS).

73. Eaton, "Frontier Life in Southern Arizona, 1858–1861," 184; Poston, *Building a State in Apache Land*, 74–75. For a broader view of relations between Anglo men and Mexican women see Miller, "Cross-Cultural Marriages in the Southwest: The New Mexico Experience, 1846–1900."

74. Dobyns, *Spanish Colonial Tucson*, 146–148.

75. Simmons, "Spanish Attempts to Open a New Mexico-Sonora Road"; Thomas, *Forgotten Frontiers*, 195–205.

76. Dobyns, *Spanish Colonial Tucson*, 107; Hammond, "The Zúñiga Journal, Tucson to Santa Fe"; Holterman, "José Zúñiga, Commandant of Tucson." Zúñiga's forces killed one warrior and four other persons, while taking five prisoners. The *comandante* was disappointed at encountering so few Apaches.

77. Almada, *Diccionario*, 52–55.

78. Bee, *Crosscurrents Along the Colorado*, 1–2.

79. Bean and Mason (eds.), *Diaries and Accounts of the Romero Expeditions*, 4.

80. *Ibid.*, 3–26, 57–72.

81. *Ibid.*, 88–91.

82. Stagg, *The First Bishop of Sonora*. Although the Sonoran Diocese was authorized in 1779 and Reyes was appointed the following year, the bishop did not reach Sonora from Spain until 1783.

83. Kessell, *Friars, Soldiers, and Reformers*, 243.

84. *Ibid.*, 39.

85. Dobyns, *Spanish Colonial Tucson*, 113–114.

86. Stoner and Dobyns, "Fray Pedro de Arriquibar."

87. James G. Bell, a Tucson visitor in 1854, commmented on the heavy drinking habits of the local priests. Samuel L. Cozzens in 1860 observed that the San Xavier pastor owned fighting cocks. The area had no resident

clergy at either time and it is difficult to know to whom they referred. Father Machebeuf of Santa Fe, who visited Tucson in 1859, is not a likely candidate. See Bell, "A Log of the Texas-California Cattle Trail," pt. 2, 315–316; Cozzens, *The Marvelous Country*, 183; Howlett, *Life of the Right Reverend Joseph P. Machebeuf*; Horgan, *Lamy of Santa Fe*.

88. The Magdalena fiesta was originally held on December 3 in honor of St. Francis Xavier, a founder of the Jesuit order. The present Magdalena church was dedicated on that date in 1832. Not long afterward, the celebration was shifted to October 4, feast day of St. Francis of Assisi, founder of the Franciscans. The church dedication in 1832 is described on page 132 of a typescript prepared by Father E.Y. López and entitled "Artículos Históricos Sonorenses," UAM 811, roll 26. The original document is on page 155, Baptismal Register 4, Magdalena Parish Archive.

89. For information about Sonoran frontier epidemics see *Spanish Colonial Tucson*, "Tubac Through Four Centuries," and "Indian Extinction in the Middle Santa Cruz River Valley, Arizona"—all by Dobyns; and Jackson, "Causes of Indian Population Decline in the Pimería Alta Missions of Northern Sonora."

90. Report prepared by Justice of the Peace Miguel Pacheco, Tucson, December 31, 1851, *Carpetón* (hereafter, "folder") 242, file cabinet 11, drawer 3, Archivo Histórico del Estado de Sonora, Hermosillo (hereafter, AHES). Also, Fr. Lorenzo Vásquez, Altar, July 27, 1851, AMS, UAM 811, Roll 7, IIIJ 1d.

Chapter 2. Early Exploration and Settlement

1. Bancroft (*History of Arizona and New Mexico*, 17–19) was convinced that the Vaca party did not enter Arizona; Sauer ("The Road to Cibola," 16) believed they did. Similar arguments have raged over whether Fray Marcos de Niza ever set foot in what is today Arizona. See Hallenbeck, *The Journey of Fray Marcos de Niza*, 59; Bolton, *Knight of Pueblos and Plains*, 32–34; DiPeso, Rinaldo, and Fenner, *Casas Grandes, a Fallen Trading Center of the Gran Chichimeca*, vol. 4, 87; Sauer, "The Credibility of the Fray Marcos Account"; and Wagner, "Fr. Marcos de Niza."

2. The literature concerned with the Coronado expedition is abundant. All of the following are recommended: Winship, *The Coronado Expedition*; Hammond and Rey (eds.), *Narratives of the Coronado Expedition*; Bolton, *Coronado, Knight of Pueblos and Plains*; and Udall, "In Coronado's Footsteps."

3. Critical to the location of the Coronado route and those of other expeditions into the region are two sites—Corazones in Sonora and Chichilticale in Arizona. For differing views of where these sites lay, see

DiPeso *et al.*, *Casas Grandes*, vol. 4, 88–103; Haury, "The Search for Chichilticale"; and Hammond and Rey, "Obregón's Sixteenth Century Explorations," 162, fn. 241.

4. Bolton devotes a chapter to the fate of the martyred priests in *Coronado, Knight of Pueblos and Plains*, 335–342.

5. Accounts of the so-called Chamuscado Expedition of 1580 are provided in Hammond and Rey, *The Rediscovery of New Mexico*, 6–15, 51–150; and Bolton, *Spanish Explorations*, 137–160.

6. Hammond and Rey, *The Rediscovery of New Mexico*, 15–28, 153–242; Bolton, *Spanish Explorations*, 163–195; Kessell, *Kiva, Cross, and Crown*, 39–45.

7. Kessell, *Kiva, Cross, and Crown*, 45.

8. Hammond and Rey, *The Rediscovery of New Mexico*, 28–50, 245–320; and *Don Juan de Oñate, Colonizer of New Mexico*. Also, see Hammond, "Don Juan de Oñate and the Founding of New Mexico," 13–73; and Kessell, *Kiva, Cross, and Crown*, 45–73.

9. There is controversy as to whether the mineral deposits were in the Verde Valley or along the headwaters of the Bill Williams. Bolton, *Spanish Explorations*, 204, 239–240; Hammond, *Don Juan de Oñate*, 111–112, 165, fn. 634.

10. Bolton, *Spanish Explorations*, 268–280; Hammond, "Don Juan de Oñate and the Founding of New Mexico," 13–73.

11. Brew, "The History of Awatovi," 3–26; Bartlett, "Spanish Contacts With The Hopi, 1540–1823"; Holterman, "Mission San Bartolome de Xongopavi."

12. Bannon, *The Mission Frontier in Sonora*, 1–6.

13. Spicer, *The Yaquis: A Cultural History*, 16 ff.

14. Polzer, *Kino Guide II*, 5. Bolton's *Rim of Christendom* and Kino's *Historical Memoir of Pimería Alta* are the most widely consulted references concerned with this remarkable pioneer.

15. Kessell, *Mission of Sorrows*, 29–32.

16. Burrus (ed.), *Kino's Plan for the Development of Pimería Alta: Arizona and Upper California*, 30.

17. Kessell, *Mission of Sorrows*, 32.

18. Polzer, *Kino Guide II*, 23.

19. Hammond, "Pimería Alta After Kino's Time," 227–235; Kessell, *Mission of Sorrows*, 38–49.

20. Kessell, *Mission of Sorrows*, 51, fn. 12; Almada, *Diccionario*, 612.

21. Almada, *Diccionario*, 65–67; 557; Douglass, "On the Naming of Arizona"; Herring, "The Silver of El Real de Arizonac."

22. Kessell, *Mission of Sorrows*, 61–62; Barnes, Naylor, and Polzer, *Northern New Spain: A Research Guide*, 135.

23. Guevavi sacramental registers, Archive of the Diocese of Tucson

(hereafter, ADT); Hastings, "People of Reason and Others: The Colonization of Sonora to 1767."

24. Moorhead, *The Presidio*, 22–23; Almada, *Diccionario*, 250, 554. Although authorized in 1692, the Fronteras presidio may not have been established until somewhat later. Its garrison was initially a mobile detachment (*compañía volante*).

25. Wagoner, *Early Arizona*, 82–83; Spicer, *Cycles of Conquest*, 124–125. The Apaches and Sobaipuris may have enjoyed peaceful relations until disturbed by Spaniards in 1692. See Wyllys, "Father Luis Velarde: Relación of Pimería Alta," 138; and Forbes, *Apache, Navajo, and Spaniard*, 244–245.

26. Spicer, *Cycles of Conquest*, 232–238. New Mexico colonists contended with the Apaches earlier than the Sonorans. See Worcester, "The Beginnings of the Apache Menace of the Southwest."

27. The Terrenate company was formed on June 1, 1742. Captain Joseph Gómez de Silva, the first commander, died before assuming his post and Captain Bernardo Tagle y Bustamante actually founded the presidio. Kessell, "The Puzzling Presidio," 33–36; Navarro García, *Don José de Gálvez*, 84. The original garrison was variously called San Phelipe de Guevavi, San Phelipe de Gracia Real de Terrenate, and San Phelipe de Jesús de Terrenate.

28. Kessell, *Mission of Sorrows*, 55.

29. *Ibid.*, 79–82, 92.

30. Brew, "The History of Awatovi," 28; Dunne, *Jacobo Sedelmayr*, 5, 33–34.

31. Kessell, *Mission of Sorrows*, 24, 98; Dunne, *Jacobo Sedelmayr*, 55–64.

32. Brew, "The History of Awatovi," 29–34.

33. Kessell, *Mission of Sorrows*, 99–100.

34. *Ibid.*, 100–105.

35. Ewing ("The Pima Outbreak in November, 1751") and Dobyns ("Tubac Through Four Centuries," vol. 1, 111–123) have used original manuscript materials in writing of the Pima Revolt.

36. Dobyns, "Tubac Through Four Centuries," vol. 1, 120–123. Díaz del Carpio, longtime commander at Janos, had moved over to Terrenate in 1750, replacing Santiago Ruiz de Ael (see Navarro García, *José de Gálvez*, 111–112). He retired from Terrenate shortly after the Pima Revolt.

37. Sedelmayr dated his recommendation May 10; that of Segesser bears the date of May 25; and Stiger's comments are undated. Highly influential in the decision to establish new forts was Father Juan Antonio Balthasar, Jesuit provincial. His report of January 18, 1752, and the suggestions of the other priests are in Archivo General de Indias (hereafter, AGI), Guad., 419. Charles Polzer provided the author translated copies.

38. Dobyns, "Tubac Through Four Centuries," vol. 1, 156–159. The Ocuca detachment withdrew when another presidio was established at Altar in 1755. Almada, *Diccionario*, 43. Captain Juan Tomás de Belderrain was the first *comandante* at Tubac, and Captain Bernardo de Urrea was in charge at Altar.

39. Kessell, *Mission of Sorrows*, 132–143.

40. Treutlein, "Father Gottfried Bernhardt Middendorff, S.J., Pioneer of Tucson," 316–317; Kessell, *Mission of Sorrows*, 146–147.

41. Guevavi burial register, ADT.

42. Kessell, *Mission of Sorrows*, 156–157.

43. *Ibid.*, 160–162. Dobyns (*Spanish Colonial Tucson*, 20–21) has translated into English Elías' report to the governor concerning the Sobaipuri relocation. In it the Terrenate commander states, "I applied the name of Señor San José to Tucson, because the . . . settlement occurred on the Feast of the Holy Patriarch [March 19]."

44. Elías' La Rioja nativity is noted in "Diligencias de Legitimidad y Limpieza de Sangre de Dn. Juan Chrisóstomo Elías González," AMS, 1801 (copy on UAM 422, reel 1). Also, see Corbalá Acuña, *Rodolfo Elías Calles*, 50; and Appendix A of this volume for a genealogical essay on the Elías family of Arizona and Sonora.

45. Marriages between first cousins were common and occasionally an uncle might marry one of his nieces. An example of the latter occurred within the Elías family during the 19th century when Domingo Elías Pro, a great grandson of Captain Elías González de Zayas, married his niece, Dolores Elías Elías. Following the marriage his wife's full name became Dolores Elías Elías de Elías!

46. Dobyns, *Spanish Colonial Tucson*, 153. See Christiansen ("The Presidio and the Borderlands: a Case Study") for comments on the ethnic composition of the soldiers at Janos during this same period.

47. Pfefferkorn, *Description of the Province of Sonora*, 284.

48. A highly recommended compendium of Spanish racial terminology is that included by Barnes, Naylor, and Polzer in *Northern New Spain*, 90–93. They show four distinct meanings for *coyote* in addition to its use as a synonym for *mestizo blanco*.

49. Pfefferkorn, *Description of the Province*, 284.

50. *Ibid.*, 292–294.

51. Several members of the second and third generations of the Elías family became priests. Two of the best known were Miguel Gerónimo and Juan Chrisóstomo, both of whom served the Arizpe Parish. An 18th century Alamos priest was Joseph Joaquín Elías González de Zayas, whose relationship to Captain Francisco has not been determined.

52. Pfefferkorn, *Description of the Province of Sonora*, 286–290. Pfefferkorn's colleague, Juan Nentvig, also remarked on the heavy drinking habits of the Pimas. See Nentvig, *Rudo Ensayo*, 60–61.

53. Pfefferkorn, *Description of the Province of Sonora*, 195–197.

54. *Ibid.*, 290–295. For a detailed study of the presidial soldier of this period see Moorhead, "The Soldado de Cuera: Stalwart of the Spanish Borderlands." Brinckerhoff and Faulk include excellent photographs of the equipment used by frontier troopers in *Lancers for the King*.

55. Pfefferkorn, *Description of the Province of Sonora*, 152–157. Because of the combined actions of the Seris and others, many AltarValley locations were abandoned during these years. Nentvig, *Rudo Ensayo*, 127–128.

56. McCarty, *Desert Documentary*, 5–7; Kessell, *Mission of Sorrows*, 165; Almada, *Diccionario*, 408.

57. Almada, *Diccionario*, 231–232.

58. Kessell, *Mission of Sorrows*, 165–166.

59. *Ibid.*, 169.

60. *Ibid.*, 174–175, citing the Rubí extract of December 21, 1766 in AGI, Guad., 511; Kinnaird, *The Frontiers of New Spain*, 175–176; Bannon, *The Spanish Borderlands Frontier*, 172–180; Thomas, *Teodoro de Croix*, 166–167.

61. Kessell, *Mission of Sorrows*, 181–190; McCarty, *A Spanish Frontier in the Enlightened Age*, 5–6.

62. Kessell, *Friars, Soldiers, and Reformers*, 36.

63. Garcés to Anza, San Xavier del Bac, July 29, 1768, Spanish American Manuscript 1093, Ayer Collection, Newberry Library. For an English translation see McCarty, *Desert Documentary*, 9–10.

64. Pineda to Marqués de Croix, June 17, 1768, Archivo General de la Nación (hereafter, AGN), Provincias Internas (hereafter, PI), 47.

65. Pineda to Marqués de Croix, Horcasitas, October 17, 1768, AGN, PI, 47; McCarty, *A Spanish Frontier in the Enlightened Age*, 86–88.

66. Garcés to Pineda, San Xavier del Bac, February 21, 1769, Spanish Manuscript 1094, Ayer Collection, Newberry Library. See Kessell, *Friars, Soldiers, and Reformers*, 48–50; also, McCarty, *A Spanish Frontier*, 91–92.

67. Kessell, *Friars, Soldiers, and Reformers*, 39.

68. *Ibid.*, 56; McCarty, *A Spanish Frontier*, 66.

69. McCarty, *Desert Documentary*, 16–18.

70. Ximeno to Guardian, March 5, 1773, AGN, PI, 81; Kessell, *Friars, Soldiers, and Reformers*, 56–57.

71. Kessell, *Friars, Soldiers, and Reformers*, 78–79.

72. Baldonado, "Missions of San José de Tumacácori and San Xavier del Bac in 1774"; Mission registers from Tumacácori and Calabazas, ADT; Kessell, *Friars, Soldiers, and Reformers*, 87–88; Robinson, "Mission Guevavi," 171.

73. For a record of the travels of Father Garcés in 1775–76, see Coues (ed.), *On the Trail of a Spanish Pioneer*.

74. Kessell, *Friars, Soldiers, and Reformers*, 93–96.

75. An English translation of the 1772 regulations is found in Brincker-hoff and Faulk, *Lancers for the King*. Also, see Vigness, "Don Hugo Oconor"; and Dobyns, *Spanish Colonial Tucson*, 58.

76. The various views concerning relocation of Sonoran forts are sum-marized by Thomas in *Teodoro de Croix*, 132–230. After moving to the San Pedro, the Terrenate garrison took its new name from the old Sobaipuri village of Santa Cruz de Gaybanipitea which had been located nearby. See Manje, *Luz de Tierra Incógnita*, 77, 97, 221, 247–248. DiPeso apparently misread the Thomas reference cited above, and identified the Terrenate site with the Sobaipuri village of Quíburi, rather than that of Gaybanipitea (DiPeso, *The Sobaipuri Indians*, 42 ff). Williams has provided the most complete account of the ill-fated San Pedro garrison in "The Presidio of Santa Cruz de Terrenate: A Forgotten Fortress of Southern Arizona."

77. Anza to Bucareli, Horcasitas, September 23, 1775, AGN, PI, 88.

78. Roque de Medina, May 3, 1779 review of the Tucson garrison, AGI, Guad. 271; Dobyns, *Spanish Colonial Tucson*, 59.

79. Bolton, *Anza's California Expeditions*, vol. 4, 392. In his report on the realignment of the northern presidios, Oconor indicated that the Tubac troopers were to be at their new location in Tucson by December 10, 1775. However, there is no documentary evidence from any other source to confirm that they made the move prior to mid-1776. See Moore and Beene, "The Report of Hugo O'Conor, January 30, 1776," 271. The Fronteras and Terrenate garrisons were apparently at their new locations before June of 1776. Navarro García, *Don José de Gálvez*, 262.

80. McCarty, *Desert Documentary*, 43; Dobyns, *Spanish Colonial Tuc-son*, 63. Allande actually reached Tucson in June. See Allande to Teodoro de Croix, Tucson, June 15, 1777, AGI, Guad., 515.

Chapter 3. The Provincias Internas of New Spain

1. Almada, *Diccionario*, 148, 57. For a description of Arizpe at this time, see Carlisle and Fontana, "Sonora in 1773."

2. Almada, *Diccionario*, 164. During the existence of the Interior Prov-inces, there was often considerable confusion as to who was in charge of what. See Loomis, "Commandants-General of the Interior Provinces, a Preliminary List."

3. Allande to Croix, Tucson, June 15, 1777, AGI, Guad., 515.

4. Manuel Barragán, Francisco Castro, and Antonio Romero, Report to Captain Pedro de Allande, San Agustín del Tucson, November 24, 1777, translated as Appendix C in Parke, *Report of Explorations for Rail-road Routes from San Francisco Bay to Los Angeles . . . and from the Pimas Villages on the Gila to the Rio Grande*. (Barragán's name appears in this document as Barragua.)

5. Kessell, *Friars, Soldiers, and Reformers*, 128. Information about the death of Juan Crisóstomo Ramírez is taken from the burial register of San José de Tumacácori, November 17, 1777, ADT and UAM 3431.

6. Kessell, *Friars, Soldiers, and Reformers*, 130–131; Navarro García, *Don Jose de Gálvez*, 327; Thomas, *Forgotten Frontiers*, 115–117.

7. Santa Cruz *comandantes* slain by Apaches were Francisco Tovar and Francisco Ygnacio Trespalacios. Thomas, *Teodoro de Croix*, 144, 151; Navarro García, *Don José de Gálvez*, 242, 260, 331; Williams, "The Presidio of Santa Cruz de Terrenate." Dobyns describes Allende's plight in *Spanish Colonial Tucson*, 60–61.

8. Navarro García, *Don José de Gálvez*, 359; Almada, *Diccionario*, 309. Manuel Augustín Mascaró provided a detailed description of Arizpe in 1781 that Fireman translated for *The Spanish Royal Corps of Engineers* (216–226). According to Pradeau (*Sonora y Sus Casas de Moneda*, 22–23), Croix directed the construction of a mint building at Arizpe in 1782, but it was never equipped and used. For at least a decade thereafter, Arizpe remained a small settlement with few public buildings. See Salmón, "A 1791 Report on the Villa de Arizpe." Shortly after reaching Sonora, Croix ordered the return of the San Bernardino garrison to Fronteras and relocation of the Santa Cruz troop to Las Nutrias. Thomas, *Teodoro de Croix*, 184, 189; Williams, "The Presidio of Santa Cruz," 16–20.

9. Perdigón's ambush occurred June 26. It and the Apache attack on the Pimans are described in Morfi, *Diario y Derrotero*, 279, 285, 299–302. Croix mentions Miguel de Urrea's death in his report of March 26, 1780, AGI, Guad. 271. (See Kessell, *Friars, Soldiers, and Reformers*, 135). Apaches also apparently killed a close relative of Miguel's named Mariano during this period (Morfi, *Diario*, 418, n. 749). Tucson's Captain Allende described the attack on the Pimans while in Arizpe on April 26. Not long afterward, according to Morfi (324), Allende requested that Croix permit him to leave his post and go to Mexico City to rest and await his reincorporation into the Spanish army with the rank of lieutenant colonel. Croix responded that if he was too sick to continue at his post, he should retire permanently. Eight years later, he would finally make it to Mexico City. McCarty, *Desert Documentary*, 57–59. Meanwhile, the Pimas—badly shaken by the 1780 disaster and another six years earlier—designed new defense strategies that would prove more successful. Ezell, *Hispanic Acculturation of the Gila River Pimas*, 119.

10. Matson and Fontana, *Friar Bringas Reports to the King*, 84–87, 96–111; McCarty, *Desert Documentary*, 35–40; McCarty, "The Colorado Massacre of 1781: María Montelo's Report"; Kessell, *Friars, Soldiers, and Reformers*, 138–146; Garcés, *On the Trail*, vol. 1, 14–24. Yates, "Locating the Colorado Mission of San Pedro y San Pablo de Bicuñer"; Ives, "Retracing the Route of the Fages Expedition of 1781."

11. Kessell, *Friars, Soldiers, and Reformers*, 144, 154, fn. 18. Barragán

and Castro were two of those who had reported to Captain Allande in 1777 concerning conditions at Tubac.

12. Dobyns, *Spanish Colonial Tucson*, 71–81; Navarro García, *Don José de Gálvez*, 438–439, fn. 29. By the time word of the King's action reached Tucson, Carrillo was dead. The Apaches killed him in a new attack on August 1, 1784.

13. Stagg, *The Almadas and Alamos*, 3–4. During the 18th century it was a common practice for recently immigrated Spaniards (*peninsulares*) to marry the daughters of wealthy mine owners. D. A. Brading has dealt at length with this subject in his description of the Guanajuato mining elite (see Brading, *Miners and Merchants in Bourbon Mexico*, 306, 312). Julian de Alvarado, Luz's father, was a native-born Spaniard who had also married a wealthy *criolla* (Spanish woman born in Mexico). Her mother was Petra González de Zayas y Quirós, daughter of wealthy Juan Chrisóstomo González de Zayas who was probably a first cousin of Captain Francisco Elías González de Zayas. See, also, Appendix A.

14. Kessell, *Friars, Soldiers, and Reformers*, 154–160.

15. Croix to Reyes, June 25, 1783, AMS, UAM 811, roll 2, IIIA-2c. Also, see Morfi, *Diario*, 253; and Villa, *Historia*, 127–128.

16. Stagg, *The First Bishop of Sonora*, 81–95; Fireman, *The Spanish Corps of Engineers*, 224.

17. Moorhead, *The Presidio*, 97; Almada, *Diccionario*, 442.

18. Galindo Navarro to José Rengel, Chihuahua, April 30, 1785, AMS, UAM 811, roll 2, IIIA-3.

19. Almada, *Diccionario*, 139.

20. By 1810 when Mexico's quest for independence began, the *afromestizo* population stood at almost 625,000, about ten percent of the total. See Meyer and Sherman, *The Course of Mexican History*, 218 (quoting from Agustín Cue Cánovas, *Historia social y económica de México*, 134). For a comparison of the racial situation in different areas of northern New Spain, see Weber, *The Mexican Frontier*, 214–215. Forbes ("Black Pioneers") discusses Negro admixture in California, and Tjarks ("Comparative Demographic Analysis") in Texas.

21. Historical Society of Los Angeles, "First Census of Los Angeles."

22. Dobyns, *Spanish Colonial Tucson*, 65, 153. In his remarks about racial classifications, Dobyns relies on Gregorio Torres Quintero, *México hacia el fin del Virreinato español: Antecedentes sociológicos del pueblo mexicano*. The Tubac troop roster for 1775 includes an unusually high percentage of individuals whose racial status is listed as "Spaniard." Of twenty-seven soldiers assigned to various categories, twelve or nearly half were so identified. None of the twelve, however, appears to have been born in the Iberian peninsula. Apart from those classified as Spaniards, *mulatos* and *moriscos*, ten troopers were placed in the *coyote* category, indicating a

mixture of Indian and European ancestry. Had the native percentage been less than a quarter, they would likely have been classified as *españoles* or *castizos*.

23. In some areas, offspring of Indian fathers and Negro mothers were called *zambos*, a term not used on the Sonora frontier. See Barnes, Naylor, and Polzer, *Northern New Spain*, 91; Pfefferkorn, *Sonora, a Description of the Province*, 284.

24. Pfefferkorn, *Sonora, a Description of the Province*, 284.

25. Moorhead, *The Presidio*, 97–99; Almada, *Diccionario*, 588–589.

26. McCarty, *Desert Documentary*, 42–46.

27. Moorhead, *The Apache Frontier*, 22. After 1787, Ugarte commanded only the western sector of the Interior Provinces.

28. Moorhead, *The Presidio*, 100–101.

29. Kessell, *Friars, Soldiers, and Reformers*, 164.

30. Almada, *Diccionario*, 727; Dobyns, "Tubac Through Four Centuries," vol. 3, 446.

31. Like his father, Juan José became a soldier. He was an ensign (*alférez*) in 1811 when he married Petra Morales of Arizpe. See Banamichi Parish Archives, "Marriage solicitation, Juan José Villaescusa, 26 November, 1810"; and "Copy of Certificate of Baptism, 9 June 1799, Mission of San José de Tumacácori, as entered in the book of baptisms of the Pima Company at Tubac on 21 July 1783," UAM 811, roll 10, VI: I, 1–2.

32. The author follows Dobyns ("Tubac Through Four Centuries," vol. 3, 448) in crediting Villaescusa with transferring the San Rafael garrison to Tubac. Kessell (*Friars, Soldiers, and Reformers*, 171) concluded that Errán was in charge at that time. The exact date of the transfer has not been established.

33. Kessell, "The Puzzling Presidio," 38–39. The river that flowed by the old Pima town of Soamca had since Kino's time been known as the Santa María. Following the establishment of the presidio, a few people started calling it the Santa Cruz. It took some time for the new name to become generally popular. As late as 1826, the governor of Occidente used the name Santa María in an official document. (Circular signed by Simón Elías exempting inhabitants of the presidios from certain taxes, Print 32, June 18, 1826, Pinart Papers, BL, UAM 563, reel 1.)

34. Moorhead, *The Apache Frontier*, 193–195.

35. Almada (*Diccionario*, 55) calls Anza "one of the most distinguished explorers in the history of the state." He ranks him on the same level of importance as Pedro de Perea, founder of the first Spanish colony in Sonora.

36. Almada, *Diccionario*, 612; Dobyns, *Spanish Colonial Tucson*, 94. Romero left behind a widow, Luisa Bohórquez, and at least two sons, one of whom was destined to be Tucson's *comandante* just as his father had

been. The other son was probably the Juan Romero who was an early mayor of Tucson.

37. Dobyns, "Tubac Through Four Centuries," vol. 3, 478–482; Kessell, *Friars, Soldiers, and Reformers*, 171; Ray H. Mattison, "Early Spanish and Mexican Settlements in Arizona," 282.

38. Dobyns, "Tubac Through Four Centuries," 482–483. The first Otero in Sonora was Dos Santos Antonio de Otero y Peón, who accompanied Captain General Juan Agustín de Iriarte to Alamos in 1745. (See Almada, *Diccionario*, 357–358). Although descendants of Dos Santos later lived in Alamos, it is not clear whether he made his home there. Joseph de Otero, father of land grantee Toribio and possibly a son of Dos Santos, was a resident of Cucurpe at the time of his son's marriage in 1779 (Dobyns, "Tubac Through Four Centuries," vol. 3, 482). In 1749, four years after reaching Alamos, Dos Santos Antonio was at Guevavi, where he served as godfather at the baptism of an infant daughter of frontiersman Nicolás Romero (Baptismal register from Guevavi, March 6, 1749, ADT and UAM 3431). His godchild was named María del Carmen and sometime after 1775, she became the second wife of Joseph Pacheco, founder of that family line in southern Arizona. See Baptismal register for San José de Tumacácori, January 8, 1775, ADT and UAM 3431. Ygnacio (Ignacio) Pacheco, an early Tucson mayor, was her son. The original Otero may have been a relative of Pedro Luciano de Otero, one of the owners of Guanajuato's famous La Valenciana silver mine (Brading, *Miners and Merchants*, 307 ff). According to Carlota Miles (*Almada of Alamos*, 47, 97, fn. 186), the Oteros owned an elegant mansion in Alamos around the middle of the 19th century. A standard reference on Spanish surnames lists the Oteros as a Castilian family with longstanding claims to nobility. See Atienza, *Nobiliario Español*, 1045.

39. McCarty, *Desert Documentary*, 61; Dobyns, *Spanish Colonial Tucson*, 94–101, 106–107. Wagoner (*Early Arizona*, 151) states that Soler, like Romero, was killed by Apaches.

40. Dobyns, *Spanish Colonial Tucson*, 96.

41. Echeagaray to Nava, January 21, 1793, F. 527–528, AGN, PI, 171; Dobyns, *Spanish Colonial Tucson*, 98–102; McCarty, *Desert Documentary*, 61–63. In 1796, Adjutant Inspector Roque de Medina assigned land to the Tucson Apaches at a location north of the *presidio*. Comadurán affidavit, Pima County Book of Deeds no. 3, 448 ff.

42. Service record of Salvador Moraga, AGN, PI, 243. Partially translated by McCarty in *Desert Documentary*, 115–116.

43. Almada, *Diccionario*, 149.

44. Nava directive of October 14, 1791, entitled "Ynstruccion que han de observar los Comandantes de los Puestos encargados de tratar con los Indios Apaches que actualmente se hallan de Paz en varios Parages de la

Nueva Vizcaya y con los que en lo Subcesivo la soliciten," included with letter, Nava to Campo Alange, May 2, 1793, Villa de Chihuahua, AGI, Guad. (103–5–8), Bancroft Library copy. The author thanks Jack S. Williams for calling this document to his attention. In the May 2, 1793 letter, Nava wrongly dates the original set of instructions "14 de octubre de *1793.*"

45. Nava to Real Audiencia, April 1, 1794, AMS, UAM 811, roll 2, IIIB, 1a.

46. Hammond, "The Zúñiga Journal: Tucson to Santa Fe," 40–65; Dobyns, *Spanish Colonial Tucson*, 107; Kessell, *Friars Soldiers, and Reformers*, 185–186. Zúñiga used friendly Apache scouts on his New Mexico expedition, a practice followed thereafter by other Tucson *comandantes.*

47. Matson and Fontana, *Friar Bringas Reports to the King*; Kessell, *Friars, Soldiers, and Reformers*, 183–187; Meyer, *Water in the Hispanic Southwest*, 56–57.

48. Whiting, "The Tumacácori Census of 1796."

49. Rouset Edict, September 28, 1796, AMS, UAM 811, roll 2, IIIC 1a.

50. Collins, "Fray Pedro de Arriquibar's Census of Tucson, 1820." Collins and others misdated this census because of accompanying documents. Dobyns, who in one of his articles had accepted the 1820 date, later caught the error and corrected it (see Dobyns, "The 1797 Population of the Presidio of Tucson: A Reconsideration").

51. Almada, *Diccionario*, 660; Hastings, "People of Reason and Others."

52. McCarty, *Desert Documentary*, 122–123, 137.

53. Dobyns, *Spanish Colonial Tucson*, 108; Arizpe Parish Archives, "Marriage Presentations, 1793–1801," UAM 811, roll 11, VII D5. Gertrudis was the daughter of Fernando Elías González, oldest son of Captain Francisco Elías González de Zayas, and Leonor Ortiz Cortés y Corella. Her maternal grandfather was Gerardo Ortiz Cortés del Rey, owner of the Hacienda Santísimo Nombre de Jesús in Bacanuchi (Carlisle and Fontana, "Sonora in 1773") and a descendant of Sargento Mayor Valerio Cortés del Rey, who in 1679 was awarded the largest *mayorazgo* (entailed estate) in Chihuahua (Almada, *Resumen de la Historia del Estado de Chihuahua*, 78–79.) The Corellas, too, were a family of note (Almada, *Diccionario*, 165–168). The wedding of Gertrudis and Mariano must have been the social highlight of the year in Arizpe. The diagram in Appendix B indicates the various relationships between the Elías and Ortiz families, and shows how, together, they controlled most of the land grants in Arizona.

54. Almada, *Diccionario*, 709

55. Ignacio Zúñiga is best known today for a book he authored in 1835 while serving as auditor of the customs house in Guaymas. It is called

Rápida Ojeada de Sonora and includes important information about Tucson in the last years of Spanish rule and the period following Mexican independence. Ignacio had a younger brother who was named Mariano in honor of Mariano Urrea, a close friend of their father. Information about the birthdates of the Zúñiga brothers is from their 1817 service records in AGI, PI, 233. At that time, Ignacio was an ensign and Mariano a cadet. Both were serving in the presidio at Horcasitas.

56. Matson and Fontana, *Friar Bringas Reports to the King*, 65–66.

57. These documents have not been located. However, the settlement alluded to by Galindo may be the one referred to thirty years later when another dispute broke out over water. Writing to Acting Governor Gaxiola in December of 1828, Manuel Escalante y Arvizu, political chief of the Arizpe district, makes reference to a "treaty" with the Indians that allotted them three fourths and the Spanish one quarter of the waters from an important spring upon which all agriculture in the immediate area was dependent. Escalante to Acting Governor Gaxiola, December 9, 1828, Apache file AHES; Meyer, *Water in the Hispanic Southwest*, 56–57.

58. Matson and Fontana, *Friar Bringas Reports to the King*, 72–73.

59. Fontana, "Biography of a Desert Church," 7–9; McCarty, *Desert Documentary*, 87–88.

60. Hard and Doelle, *The San Agustín Mission Site, Tucson, Arizona*; Greenleaf and Wallace, "Tucson: Pueblo, Presidio, and American City," 21; Brinckerhoff, "The Last Days of Spanish Arizona 1786–1821," 15; Dobyns, *Spanish Colonial Tucson*, 42; Lockwood and Page, *Tucson—The Old Pueblo*, 21–22; Williams, "San Agustín del Tucson: A Vanished Mission Community in the Pimería Alta."

61. Dobyns, *The Apache People (Coyoteros)*, 18–19.

62. McCarty, *Desert Documentary*, 87–88.

63. Nava to Rouset, November 18, 1797; and Royal Cedula, Aranjuez, March 18, 1797, AMS, UAM 811, roll 2, IIIC, 2b, i and iii.

64. Fr. Juan Felipe Martínez to Bishop Rouset, Pitic, May 21, 1799, AMS, UAM 811, roll 2, IIID, 1a.

65. Testimony at Pitic, August, 1799, AMS, UAM 811, roll 2, IIID, 1b.

66. "Padrón de la ciudad de Arizpe y sus anexos Chinapa, Bacanuchi, Huepaverachi en este año de 1798," Municipal Archive, Arizpe. For information about Spanish policy on captured Apaches, see Moorhead, "Spanish Deportation of Hostile Apaches," 209; Dobyns, Ezell, *et al.*, "Who Were Nixoras?"; and Bailey, *Indian Slave Trade in the Southwest*.

67. Matson and Fontana, *Friar Bringas Reports to the King*, 67. Indian household servants, acquired through capture or purchase, were common throughout the area from California to Texas in both Spanish and Mexican times. Weber, *The Mexican Frontier*, 212–213.

68. Arizpe Parish Archives: Baptisms, 1783–1794, UAM 811, roll 11, VII D4.

Chapter 4. The Last Years of Spanish Rule

1. "Census, Pimería Alta, 1801," AMS, UAM 811, roll 3, IIID, 2f.

2. For the baptism of María del Carmen Romero, see Baptismal register from Guevavi, March 6, 1749, ADT and UAM 3431.

3. We know of the literacy of both Pacheco and León through letters signed and presumably written by them in the late 1820s.

4. Kessell, *Friars, Soldiers, and Reformers*, 201.

5. Pacheco sold his grant to Pedro Villaescusa, whose adopted daughter failed in her effort to have it confirmed by the Court of Private Land Claims. See Bradfute, *The Court of Private Land Claims*, 150; and "Reyes Pacheco Grant," reel 10.1.22, microfilm section, Arizona State Library and Archives, Phoenix. The 1767 register of civilian males at Tubac is in the Biblioteca Nacional de México, Franciscan Archives, 233. The death of María de los Santos Gómez is recorded in the Guevavi burial register, October 22, 1764, ADT and UAM 3431. Pacheco's survival in the Yuma incident is mentioned in Garcés, *On the Trail of a Spanish Pioneer*, vol. 1, 23.

6. Kessell, *Friars, Soldiers, and Reformers*, 202. Gutiérrez apparently brought in laborers, including Spaniards.

7. "Circular of August 4, 1803," AMS, UAM 811, roll 3, IIID, 3b; Dobyns, *Spanish Colonial Tucson*, 117 ff.

8. Paz y Goicochea to Rouset, Cieneguilla, November, 13 1803, AMS, UAM 811, roll 3, IID, 3a.

9. McCarty provides translations of the Tucson and Tubac reports of 1804 in *Desert Documentary*, 82–92. The originals are in folder 819, box 36, Franciscan Archives, Biblioteca Nacional de México.

10. Kessell, *Friars, Soldiers, and Reformers*, 203.

11. McCarty, *Desert Documentary*, 87.

12. Arizona (Ter.) Surveyor General, "Journal of Private Land Grants," UAM 2174; Wagoner, *Early Arizona*, 218–222; Kessell, *Friars, Soldiers, and Reformers*, 206–214. Kessell quite correctly points out that much confusion about the Tumacácori-Calabazas property comes from reliance on copied and translated documents rather than the original sources.

13. María Reyes Peña had been married earlier to José Pedro Quixada, who died sometime after 1790. Serafina and Carmen, two daughters from this marriage, later married prominent citizens of Tucson and Tubac. Also, Serafina and an older sister, Leonor, began referring to themselves as Ortiz following their mother's remarriage. See testimony of Gertrudis Herreras in Arizona (Ter.) Surveyor General, "Journal of Private Land

Grants," vol. 2, 87, UAM 2174. Also, Teodoro Ramírez, "Notebook," translated copy at Special Collections, University of Arizona Library (hereafter, UAL), orignal in the possession of Manuel Ramírez (Eloy, Arizona).

14. The marriage of Agustín Ortiz and María Reyes Peña took place sometime between 1790—when she gave birth to Serafina, her last child by Pedro Quixada—and 1796, when Tomás Ortiz was born. See the baptismal register of the Arizpe Parish Archive, entry of August 27, 1790; and the will of Tomás Ortiz prepared in 1876, copy included among the documents associated with the Arivaca land claim, Arizona (Ter.) Surveyor General, "Journal of Private Land Grants," vol. 2, UAM 2174. Tomás's younger brother, Ignacio, was born either in 1800 or 1801. See Kessell, *Friars, Soldiers, and Reformers,* 291. Kessell is a good general source on the Arivaca land grant, but Wagoner provides more details in *Early Arizona,* 210–214.

15. Villa, *Historia del Estado de Sonora,* 154–155.

16. Dobyns, "Tubac Through Four Centuries," vol. 3, 446–447.

17. McCarty, *Desert Documentary,* 115–124. One of the first Tucson soldiers to go south with Villaescusa was José Domingo Granillo whose father had been a sergeant in the Tucson company. Granillo left Tucson for the Sinaloa front on November 23, 1810.

18. Rosario was to Mazatlán what Hermosillo was to Guaymas. It served as a trade center for all goods entering Mexico through the important Pacific port. It was a strategic location to defend against the insurgents. See Voss, *On The Periphery of Nineteenth Century Mexico,* 45.

19. This description of the 1810–1811 fighting in Sinaloa is taken primarily from three sources: Almada's *Diccionario,* 280; Villa's *Historia del Estado de Sonora,* 153–159; and Calvo Berber's *Nociones de la Historia de Sonora,* 127–132. These authors do not always agree. Villa, for example, considers Hermosillo's action in releasing Villaescusa following the Battle of Rosario to have been a generous but foolish act. Calvo Berber portrays Villaescusa as a coward "crying for his life."

20. San Ignacio Piaxtla received attention in American newspapers in 1982 because of the murder of an American college professor there. Boudreaux, "Highway 15's history worries U.S. tourists," *Arizona Daily Star,* July 27, 1982.

21. Almada, *Diccionario,* 215–217; Villa, *Galería de Sonorenses Ilustres,* 56. Elías González began his military career at Tucson in 1788. He was *comandante* at Tubac in 1805.

22. On September 5, 1828, the town of Pitic was renamed Hermosillo in honor of the insurgent leader. See Print no. 103, September 5, 1828, Pinart Collection, BL, UAM 563, reel 2.

23. McCarty, *Desert Documentary,* 111–132.

24. Service record of Ignacio Zúñiga, 1817, AGI, PI, 233.

25. Zúñiga's comments about the effects of the independence movement on the frontier communities are found in *Rápida Ojeada de Sonora*, 71 ff.

26. José Miguel Borboa was killed by Apaches at Tumacácori in April of 1819. Kessell, *Friars, Soldiers, and Reformers*, 238.

27. Dobyns, *Spanish Colonial Tucson*, 101–104.

28. *Ibid.*, 139.

29. Kessell, *Friars, Soldiers, and Reformers*, 203, 238; Dobyns, *Spanish Colonial Tucson*, 139. Well before the end of the 18th century, the terms *vecino* and *gente de razón* had come to include Christian Indians not associated with missions, as well as persons of European descent.

30. Kessell, *Friars, Soldiers, and Reformers*, 239.

31. McCarty, *Desert Documentary*, 32; Kessell, *Friars, Soldiers and Reformers*, 97, 123, 154.

32. Kessell, *Friars, Soldiers, and Reformers*, 247.

33. Almada, *Diccionario*, 74; Villa, *Historia del Estado de Sonora*, 163–164.

34. Dobyns, *Spanish Colonial Tucson*, 108.

35. Cevallos to Sr. Comandante General, Durango, December 23, 1814, Cartas de Sonora, Archivo del Colegio de Santa Cruz de Querétaro, Celaya, Guanajuato. Differences between civil and religious authorities, as well as Franciscan in-fighting, prevented Father Cevallos from carrying out many of his plans for the Sonora missions. See Kessell, *Friars, Soldiers, and Reformers*, 220–233. Cevallos was at San Xavier in July, 1814, after visiting Tumacácori. See Auto de Visita, San Xavier del Bac, July 7, 1814, Cartas de Sonora, Archivo del Colegio de Santa Cruz de Querétaro, Celaya, Guanajuato.

36. Arizpe Parish Archives, Baptismal Records, 1757–1801, UAM 811, reel 11, VII, Dl.

37. On January 12, 1814, Arvizu became the commanding officer of the Fourth Flying Company of Nueva Vizcaya, but he was in Tucson as its interim commander during the preceding fall. He officially became the presidio's *comandante* in June, 1816, and still held that post in December, 1818. Dobyns, *Spanish Colonial Tucson*, 109; McCarty, *Desert Documentary*, 136–137.

38. The instability of the presidial garrisons during the Mexican war of independence was one of the factors that Ignacio Zúñiga would later blame for the decline of the Apache peace establishments. See Zúñiga, *Rápida Ojeada de Sonora*, 71 ff.

39. Almada, *Diccionario*, 69.

40. Dobyns, *Spanish Colonial Tucson*, 109.

41. Dobyns, "Tubac Through Four Centuries," vol. 3, 451.

42. León Service Record, December 1817, AGN, PI, 233. Manuel began his military service in his home town of Bacoachi.

43. Dobyns, "Tubac Through Four Centuries," vol. 3, 454. Sotelo may have died in the epidemic of 1816 that killed many Indians.

44. Service Record of Ignacio Elías González, December, 1817, AGN, PI, 233.

45. Elías was probably in Tubac by April, 1815, when Sotelo was briefly assigned as commander at Tucson. Later in that same year, León returned to Tubac. McCarty, *Desert Documentary*, 130, 132.

46. Among the soldiers associated with the Tucson and Tubac presidios who went on to play prominent roles in Mexican politics, the most notable were Mariano and José de Urrea, Ignacio Zúñiga, Antonio Narbona, and Simón, José María, and Ignacio Elías González.

47. Dobyns, "Tubac Through Four Centuries," vol. 3, 454.

48. José Soto service record, Santa Cruz, December, 1817, AGN, PI, 233.

49. Tumacácori marriage records in the closing years of the 18th century clearly establish the presence of Ocoboas described as Yaquis. Juan Ocoboa (Ocovoa) and Alvino Ocoboa, Tucson soldiers in 1783 and 1831, may have belonged to this family. Shortly before the end of Mexican rule, Alvino's daughters, Victoriana and Petra, married into Tucson's prominent Romero and Ramírez lineages. (The Francisco Romero file in the Arizona Historical Society contains an unsupported assertion that Alvino was born in Spain.) Juan's name is listed in the 1783 inspection report of the Tucson Company (Dobyns, *Spanish Colonial Tucson*, 157) and Alvino's is in the 1831 census (McCarty, "Tucson Census," pt. 2, 42).

50. All of these small settlements were populated, abandoned and repopulated several times between 1740 and 1820. The process would continue in the Mexican and early Anglo periods.

51. Kessell, *Friars, Soldiers, and Reformers*, 225; Dobyns, *Spanish Colonial Tucson*, 120.

52. Circular from Bishop Rouset, August 4, 1803, AMS, UAM 811, Roll 3, IIID 3b.

53. This and the following reports from Arriquibar to the Bishop of Sonora are taken from AMS, UAM 422, Rolls 1 and 2. Dobyns has summarized them in *Spanish Colonial Tucson*, 117–120.

54. Tumacácori baptismal register, March 20, 1776, ADT and UAM 3431.

55. Officer and Dobyns, "Teodoro Ramírez, Early Citizen of Tucson," 222.

56. Dobyns, *Spanish Colonial Tucson*, 108.

57. Stoner and Dobyns, "Fray Pedro Antonio de Arriquibar," 77.

58. AMS, UAM 811, roll 4, IIIE 1f; McCarty, *Desert Documentary*, 93–110.

59. Dobyns, *Spanish Colonial Tucson*, 101.

60. Kessell, *Friars, Soldiers, and Reformers*, 239.

Chapter 5. The Sonoran Frontier After Independence

1. Meyer and Sherman, *The Course of Mexican History*, 294–296.

2. Almada, *Diccionario*, 262.

3. Villa, *Historia del Estado de Sonora*, 161; Almada, *Diccionario*, 69. The author has not been able to ascertain when Ignacio Elías González and José Romero, commanding officers at Tubac and Tucson, swore allegiance to the Plan of Iguala.

4. Villa, *Historia del Estado de Sonora*, 162.

5. Almada, *Diccionario*, 444.

6. *Ibid.*, 712–714. Iturbide removed Urrea as governor of Nueva Vizcaya in August, 1822.

7. *Ibid.*, 664.

8. *Ibid.*, 713.

9. Villa, *Historia del Estado de Sonora*, 163; Calvo Berber, *Nociones de Historia de Sonora*, 137; Almada, *Diccionario*, 713.

10. Villa, *Historia del Estado de Sonora*, 163.

11. Almada, *Diccionario*, 713–714. Urrea's wife, Gertrudis Elías González, remained in Arizpe where she died on March 23, 1826, register of burials, Arizpe Parish Archives. Information provided the author by Arizpe archivist Carmen Pellat Sotomayor.

12. Sources differ as to why Elías González resigned. Both Villa (*Historia del Estado de Sonora*, 164) and Calvo Berber (*Nociones de Historia de Sonora*, 138) state that he resigned because he could not serve concurrently as governor and military commander. But Almada (*Diccionario*, 216) says it was the governorship of Chihuahua, not Occidente, that he resigned because of the conflict over his military and civilian roles. In any event, he did leave his Chihuahua post also a month after assuming it. In succeeding years he occupied both political and military positions in northwest Mexico, including the military command of New Mexico and Chihuahua and, again, the governorship of the latter state. According to Almada (*Diccionario*), his death in 1841 was "keenly felt by members of all social classes . . . for he was by nature humble. . . . His private life was exemplary, and he distinguished himself by his integrity."

13. Kessell, *Friars, Soldiers, and Reformers*, 243.

14. Teodoro's paternal grandmother was Bartola de la Peña. Serafina's mother was María Reyes Peña. See Baptisms 1757–1795, Arizpe Parish Archives, UAM 811, roll 11, VII-D1.

15. Ortiz died in Tubac in 1817, four years before his son's wedding. See fragmentary Tubac burial register in M-M 411, Pinart Collection, BL, entry of January 9, 1817.

16. Leonor Ortiz Cortés del Rey Corella, a paternal aunt of Tomás, was the wife of Josefa Clementa's grandfather, Fernando Elías González. There were probably other ties between these members of old elite lineages. See the Elías family genealogy charts, Appendix A.

17. María Reyes Peña, mother of Tomás Ortiz, was first married to don Joseph Pedro Quixada, by whom she had several children, one of whom— Serafina—was baptized August 27, 1790. See Arizpe Parish Archives, Baptismal Register 1757–1795, UAM 811, Roll 11, VII D1.Following the death of Joseph Pedro, she married Agustín Ortiz, father of Tomás and Ignacio. See testimony of Gertrudis Herreras, Arizona (Ter.) Surveyor General, "Journal of Private Land Grants," vol. 2, 87, UAM 2174.

18. In his "Notebook" (Special Collections, UAL), Teodoro Ramírez comments that the bishop did not charge him for the dispensation required for his marriage. He refers to his bride as Serafina Ortiz because she was reared in the household of her stepfather, Agustín Ortiz. See previous footnote.

19. José Romero, not to be confused with the Tucson presidial commander of the same name, was the son of veteran frontier soldier Juan Bautista Romero and his wife María del Loreto Cota. Juan retired at Tubac in 1818 with the rank of ensign. See Dobyns, "Tubac Through Four Centuries," vol. 3, 458; Kessell, *Friars, Soldiers, and Reformers*, 234.

20. Romero Road in Tucson was named for Francisco, who owned property near there as well as in the downtown area to the west of the presidio. Some of the land formerly in the Romero Ranch north of Tucson became part of a state park in 1983. See Francisco Romero files in the Hayden Collection (AHS).

21. Bean and Mason (eds.), *Diaries and Accounts of the Romero Expeditions in Arizona and California.*

22. Matrimonios o Casamientos, rollo 55, Libro 5 (beginning July 27, 1789), Archive of the Cathedral of Chihuahua (copy supplied the author by Martha T. Green of Gilbert, Arizona). The completion date for construction of the Arizpe hospital is unknown. A document purportedly written in 1791 does not mention it. See Salmón and Naylor, "A 1791 Report on the Villa de Arizpe"; also, Pellat "El Hospital Militar de Arizpe, Sonora (1786–1862)."

23. The second wife of Francisco Elías González de Zayas was María Ignacia Díaz del Carpio. See Appendix A.

24. Almada, *Diccionario*, 69.

25. Bean and Mason (eds.), *Diaries and Accounts of the Romero Expeditions in Arizona and California*, 78.

26. *Ibid.*, 82.

27. The exact date of Romero's return to Tucson has not been discovered. Nor do we know what happened to him afterward for his name does not appear in the Tucson census of 1831. He should have been about fifty

years old in 1826 and would have had enough years of service to retire with full pension benefits.

28. Villa, *Historia del Estado de Sonora*, 163. We know of León's election as mayor of Tucson from documents in the Apache file, AHES. Tubac's first mayor was don León Herreros, owner of the San José de Sonoita land grant. See documents pertaining to the Ygnacio Cruz land grant, reel 10.1.22, microfilm section, Arizona State Library and Archives, Phoenix.

29. Fontana ("Biography of a Desert Church," 12) states that Díaz was the last resident priest at San Xavier during the Mexican period, but Antonio González served after him between 1834 and 1837. See Kessell, *Friars, Soldiers, and Reformers*, 292–293.

30. *Ibid.*, 251.

31. González to Bishop of Sonora, Caborca, December 9, 1822, AMS, UAM 811, roll 5, IIIF, 2n.

32. Kessell, *Friars, Soldiers, and Reformers*, 251.

33. Elías' departure date from Tubac is not known. He and his wife baptized a child there in October, 1822. Baptismal registry of Tumacácori, ADT.

34. Kessell, *Friars, Soldiers, and Reformers*, 261.

35. Villa, *Historia del Estado de Sonora*, 163. A copy of León's letter of protest over the tax exemption can be found in the Apache file, AHES. See, also, Print 33, Pinart Collection, BL.

36. During the first three decades of the 19th century there were several members of the León family, in addition to Mayor José and Lieutenant Manuel, living in Tucson. One was Leonardo León, probably a son of Manuel, who had a distinguished military career before being killed by Apaches. (Almada, *Diccionario*, 46.) Another was Juan, possibly a brother of José, who was a soldier at the end of the Spanish period. Juan appears to have been the father of Francisco Solano León, one of the most prominent Hispanic residents of southern Arizona during territorial days. In 1831, a boy named Francisco Solano was living in Juan's household. See McCarty, "Tucson Census of 1831," pt. 2 "Military Households," 42.

37. Pattie, *Personal Narrative*, 46–65 (dates are revised from those shown by Pattie). See Weber, *The Taos Trappers*, 93, fn. 37.

38. Circular, Governor Simón Elías González to the Alcalde of Santa Cruz, Arizpe, May 17, 1826, Print 27, Pinart Collection, BL (UAM 563, roll 1); Weber, *The Taos Trappers*, 112 ff.

39. The Americans referred to were probably members of an expedition headed by W. S. ("Old Bill") Williams and Cerain St. Vrain. See Weber, *The Taos Trappers*, 120–122.

40. Pacheco to Governor Gaxiola, Tucson, November 4, 1826, typescript M-A 19, pt. I, 0002, Pinart Collection, BL.

41. Throughout this volume the author has assumed that Alcalde Juan

Romero was the son of Pablo Romero and the brother of José Romero, both commanders of the Tucson presidio. However, the name Juan was so common among the Romeros that Tucson's mayor could have belonged to an altogether different branch of the family.

42. Romero to Iriarte, Tucson, January 4, 1827, Apache file, AHES. The author has not been able to establish the identity of the first American visitors to Tucson.

43. Pattie, *Personal Narrative*, 76–83; Weber, *The Taos Trappers*, 123–124.

44. Kessell (*Friars, Soldiers, and Reformers*, 247, fn. 11) notes that Agustín Ortiz was buried beneath the floor of the Tubac military chapel "near the chancel." Also, see Tubac burial register, M-M 411, Pinart Collection, BL, entry of January 9, 1817.

45. General information about the Arizona land grants is from Wagoner, *Early Arizona*, 159–241; Ray H. Mattison, "Early Spanish Settlements in Arizona"; and microfilm copies of the reports of the Surveyor General in the University of Arizona Library and the Arizona Department of Library and Archives, Phoenix. The Canoa grant is treated separately by Willey in "La Canoa: Spanish Land Grant Lost and Found."

46. The only extant title to the Canoa grant was issued in 1849.

47. Wagoner, *Early Arizona*, 185; Print 4, May 20, 1825, Pinart Collection, BL (UAM 563, roll 1).

48. The Pérez family owned the Cananea mines (Almada, *Diccionario*, 122). They were intermarried with the Ortiz, who, along with members of the Elías family, owned most of the Arizona land grants. The diagram in Appendix B elucidates these relationships.

49. Kessell, *Friars, Soldiers, and Reformers*, 245–251. Also, see M-M 379, nos. 71, 72, 75 of the Pinart Collection, BL. The Rafael Elías González referred to was one of Sonora's most prosperous ranchers. Kessell incorrectly identifies him as a brother of Ignacio Elías González, Tubac's commanding officer. (They were first cousins.) At about the time Rafael assumed responsibility for paying the Tumacácori debt, his son married Lieutenant Pérez' sister, Guadalupe.

50. The extensive testimony submitted in connection with confirmation of the San Rafael de la Zanja grant suggests that the identity of the *parcioneros* was once known. One witness, José María Montoya, stated that the list of twenty or thirty names had been lost. See Arizona (Ter.) Surveyor General, "Journal of Private Land Grants," vol. 1, UAM 2174.

51. Published references invariably refer to Juvera as Tuvera. This error was first made by someone copying the original Mexican documents and carried forward by other copiers and translators.

52. Descendants of Rafael Elías do not include Joaquín among his brothers. The exact relationship remains obscure.

53. Ignacio's residence in the Altar Valley in the closing years of Spanish rule is attested in the sacramental registers of the Oquitoa Mission Church (copies in the author's possession). However, he is regarded by Elías descendants as the founder of the Rayón branch of the Elías family.

54. Title to the Babocómari grant was awarded on December 25, 1832.

55. The San Bernardino grant was larger in overall extent than the Babocómari, but only a small part of it lay north of the present border between the United States and Mexico. The author has not mentioned the Agua Prieta and San Pedro grants because neither, as originally constituted, apparently included any land within the present boundaries of Arizona. The petition for the San Pedro grant was filed in 1821 and that for the Agua Prieta grant in 1831. The elder Rafael Elías González had an interest in both and was sole owner of the San Pedro. His descendants today constitute the San Pedro Palominas branch of the Elías family.

56. Wagoner, *Early Arizona*, 229; Almada, *Diccionario*, 219–220.

57. Almada, *Diccionario*, 463. An excellent secondary source about the fight over dividing Occidente is Voss, *On the Periphery of Nineteenth-Century Mexico*, 52–61. Also, see Villa, *Historia del Estado de Sonora*, 164–182.

58. Pedro Villaescusa was a son of Pedro Sebastián Villaescusa, the first commander of Tubac's San Rafael Company. He was born in Cucurpe, home of his mother, María Ygnacia Otero. Pedro's younger brother, José María, would later command the Tubac garrison (Kessell, *Friars, Soldiers, and Reformers*, 270–283).

59. *Ibid.*, 270, 293–295; Fontana, "Biography of a Desert Church," 12. Father Rafael Díaz was permitted to remain in Sonora. Kessell states that he came back to Tucson late in 1828 and stayed there until 1830 (*Friars, Soldiers, and Reformers*, 277, 278 fn. 2). His only evidence for this conclusion is a statement by Father José María Pérez Llera that "being a Spaniard, Fray Rafael resolved to live in the most remote of the villages—that of Tucson—until the fervor that still burned against [the Spaniards] subsided." (See Pérez Llera, "Apuntes sobre los acontecimientos acaecidos en este colegio de la Santa Cruz de Querétaro desde el año de 1821 y sus misiones haste el mes de diciembre de 1844," Archivo del Colegio de Santa Cruz de Querétaro, Celaya, Guanajuato.) No other documents have come to light to confirm Díaz' residence in Tucson between 1828 and 1830. It is clear that after 1830 he resided at Cocóspera. Regardless of his home base, however, he unquestionably served southern Arizona settlements between 1828 and 1834 when Father Antonio González was assigned to San Xavier. Between 1837 and his death in 1841, Díaz attended Arizonans from San Ignacio.

60. Romero to Gobernador, Tucson, March 4, 1827, Apache file, AHES.

61. Santiago Redondo to Excelentísimo Gobernador del Estado de Occidente, Altar, April 1, 1828, Apache file, AHES.

62. Ignacio Sardina was probably a son of one of the soldiers of that surname listed in the 1797 census of Tucson.

63. Sardina to Excelentísimo Sr. Gobernador, Tucson, May 4, 1828, Apache file, AHES.

64. A copy of the militia proclamation is in the Aguiar Collection, AHS. Militias were of great importance along the entire northern frontier of Mexico during this period. See Weber, *The Mexican Frontier*, 115 ff.

65. Escalante to Gobernador, Arizpe, November 22, 1828, Apache file, AHES.

66. The author has not located a copy of Sardina's report or the governor's request for comment on it.

67. Escalante to Gobernador, Arizpe, December 9, 1828, Apache file, AHES.

68. Almada, *Diccionario*, 69. Arvizu died at Arizpe early in 1832 at the age of seventy-one.

69. Kessell, *Friars, Soldiers, and Reformers*, 279–281. It is not clear whether Ortiz was dismissed because of the "inequities" mentioned by Escalante or for other reasons.

70. Saenz, *et al.*, to Governor Aguilar, Tucson, May 6, 1852, folder 242, file cabinet 11, drawer 3, AHES. The expulsion of the Franciscan priests was followed by an action of the Occidente legislature to convert mission lands to private property owned by the Indians, and to restore to the indigenous population lands taken from them illegally after 1811. See "Ley Para El Repartimiento de Tierras de Los Pueblos de Indígenas, Reduciéndolas a Propiedad p.ticular," September 13, 1828, folder 55, file cabinet 6, drawer 2, AHES.

71. On March 16, 1834, Tucson's justice of the peace, don Juan González, wrote Governor Manuel Escalante y Arvizu seeking relief from conditions imposed by Grande concerning use of El Pueblito lands. Escalante forwarded a copy of the letter to Fray José María Pérez Llera, by then the custodian of mission property. He recommended approval of the petition. Escalante to Pérez Llera, Arizpe, April 12, 1834, Documento no. 63, Asuntos de Misiones, Gobierno Eclesiástico, Gobierno Civil, Archivo del Colegio de Santa Cruz de Querétaro, Celaya, Guanajuato.

72. Pima County Book of Deeds no. 3, 448 ff.

73. See White's 1876 map of the Tucson fields (AHS).

Chapter 6. Sonora Becomes a Separate State

1. Voss, *On The Periphery of Nineteenth-Century Mexico*, 59–61; Almada, *Diccionario*, 463–465.

2. Almada, *Diccionario*, 464.

3. Voss, *On the Periphery of Nineteenth-Century Mexico*, 60, fn. 88.

4. Villa, *Historia del Estado de Sonora*, 184–185; Voss, *On the Periphery of Nineteenth-Century Mexico*, 64–65.

5. Villa, *Historia del Estado de Sonora*, 184. Villa refers to "Commanding General Elías González" as the circulator of the petitions. It is more likely, however, that this was done for him by his younger brother who was in close contact with presidial officers. Lieutenant Colonel José María Elías first entered politics in 1827, when he was named Adjutant Inspector of the Occidente military command. He continued to be a factor in Sonoran politics almost until his death in 1864. He was acting governor of the state in 1843, and served various times as military commander. One of his sons named Angel became commanding officer of the Tucson presidial garrison after it was transferred to Imuris in March, 1856. Almada has a biography of José María in his *Diccionario*, 213–214. His death was reported in *La Estrella de Occidente*, May 27, 1864. Information about his birth is from the Arizpe Parish Archives, Baptisms 1783–1794, UAM 811, reel 11, VII D4.

6. Ramón Morales was the son of Rafael Morales, owner of the Motepori mines. For a short time in 1823, the elder Morales was acting governor of Sonora. See Almada, *Diccionario*, 430. Morales replaced Colonel Elías González in June, 1831.

7. According to Villa (*Historia del Estado de Sonora*, 185), the citizens of Santa Cruz threatened violence if the capital was not placed in Arizpe.

8. The document that includes information about municipal officers and their election is Print 243, Pinart Collection, BL (UAM 563, reel 2.)

9. Villa, *Historia del Estado de Sonora*, 186–187; Voss, *On The Periphery of Nineteenth-Century Mexico*, 64–65.

10. C. Gobernador to C. Comandante General, Alamos, February 15, 1830, Apache file, AHES; also, M-M 380, no. 55, Pinart Collection, BL.

11. The Arizpe political chief at the time of Ortega's letter was Manuel Escalante y Arvizu, who was replaced during 1830 by Rafael Elías González (Almada, *Diccionario*, 215, 220).

12. Francisco Ortega to Jefe Político de Arizpe, Tucson, April 8, 1830, Apache file, AHES. José Romero's name appears on the list of those volunteering to campaign against the Apaches. This is almost certainly the José Romero who was a common soldier at the presidio in 1818, and not the *comandante* of the early 1820s.

13. Escalante to Gobernador, Arizpe, Dec. 9, 1828, Apache file, AHES.

14. Fernando María Grande to Gobernador Constitucional, Cucurpe, May 25, 1830, item 149, drawer 1, file cabinet 1, AHES.

15. Dobyns, *From Fire to Flood*, 16–26.

16. In the 1831 census, Jesús María, a child of just over one year old, is incorrectly listed as Juan María.

17. Soldiers named Jácome (also spelled Xácome) served earlier at the

Santa Cruz fort. See the Santa Cruz presidial register of December, 1817, AGN, PI 233.

18. The contemporary Jácome family of Tucson is descended from Carlos Jácome who came to the United States in the 1880s.

19. The Pedro living with Teodoro at this time was probably a nephew. His brother with that first name was a resident of Santa Cruz when the 1831 census was taken. Copies of census registers are in the archive of the Franciscan College of Santa Cruz de Querétaro in Celaya, Guanajuato. McCarty translated them for *Copper State Bulletin* (published in 5 parts, 1981–1982).

20. Potash, "Notes and Documents," 332–335.

21. See the September monthly report of Tucson's last mayor, José Grijalva, and letter from the Political Chief of Arizpe to the Governor of Sonora. Arizpe, October 25, 1831, Apache file, AHES.

22. The Jackson party was back in Tucson in June, 1832, but no information has been found on what transpired during that visit. See Hays, "David E. Jackson," 214–244.

23. Calvo Berber (*Nociones de Historia de Sonora*, 142) implies that the defections at Fronteras, Bacoachi and Tucson were more serious than seems to have been the case. He does not cite a source.

24. Juan José Tovar led a rebellion against the Sonoran government in 1832 that was part of a more general revolt against President Bustamante orchestrated by López de Santa Anna. After sacking the port of Guaymas, Tovar prevailed upon some of the Yaquis to join his forces. See Almada, *Diccionario*, 699.

25. Irigoyen's letter, dated June 10, 1832, and Villaescusa's comments on the military situation at Tubac are included with correspondence dated June 18, 1832, from Lieutenant Colonel José María Elías González to Governor Manuel Escalante y Arvizu, Apache file, AHES.

26. Zubia to Escalante, Tubac, October 4, 1832, Apache file, AHES.

27. Information about the operations of the *Sección Patriótica* is found in the Apache files, for May and June 1832, AHES. Kessell has summarized various items from the file that relate particularly to southern Arizona (*Friars, Soldiers, and Reformers*, 282–286). The remarkable achievements of the militiamen, many of whom had probably served formerly as presidial soldiers, were later applauded by Ignacio Zúñiga in *Rápida Ojeada de Sonora*, 85–86. New Mexico militias had some success in fighting Navajos, as did those from Texas and California in contests with smaller tribes. See Weber, *The Mexican Frontier*, 118–120.

28. The author has been unable to determine the precise relationship between Joaquín Vicente Elías and other prominent members of that family. The register of marriage presentations in the Arizpe Parish Archives shows that on July 5, 1821, a man of that name married Dominga

Rodríguez. The parents of the groom were Francisco Elías González and Perfecta Montaño. Documents associated with the San Rafael del Valle land grant identify Joaquín as a brother of Rafael, a relationship Rafael's descendants could not confirm. Beginning in 1834, Joaquín was secretary for the Sonora legislature and *junta*. See prints of government documents in the Pinart Collection, BL, during the years 1834–1852, UAM 563, reels 2 and 3.

29. In April, 1871—in the same area—there would be another slaughter of Apaches involving a civilian party headed by members of the Elías family. Most of the victims were women and children. That incident has since become known as the Camp Grant Massacre. See Hastings, "The Tragedy at Camp Grant in 1871"; and Schellie, *Vast Domain of Blood*.

30. Spicer, *The Yaquis, A Cultural History*, 131; Voss, *On The Periphery of Nineteenth-Century Mexico*, 66–67.

31. Simpson, *Many Mexicos*, 209.

32. Almada, *Diccionario*, 665.

33. Calvo Berber, *Nociones de Historia de Sonora*, 143–144.

34. *Ibid.*, 145.

35. Villa, *Historia del Estado de Sonora*, 187–188; Calvo Berber, *Nociones de Historia de Sonora*, 145. Among the signers of the petition calling for the removal of Arregui were officers from the Arizona presidios: Antonio Comadurán, Salvador Moraga, Antonio Ramírez and José María Villaescusa. See "Contestaciones Habidos entre el Gobierno del Estado de Sonora y el Comandante de Armas Interino," M-M 288, vol. 1, 242–48, September 30, 1832, Pinart Collection, BL.

36. A description of the Sosa trial is found in the Archive of the College of Santa Cruz de Querétaro in Celaya, Guanajuato. For a summary translation, see Kessell, *Friars, Soldiers, and Reformers*, 290–291.

37. Elías González to Escalante, Arizpe, January 29, 1834, Apache file, AHES. Problems with turning settlers into Indian fighters were common throughout the frontier area. See Weber, *The Mexican Frontier*, 117–120.

38. Almada (*Diccionario*, 375) says that Leonardo León, who had once served in the Tucson garrison, was killed in January, 1834, during an Apache attack on Santa Cruz. Either Almada was wrong about the date of León's death, or Elías had not heard about it more than two months later.

39. Elías to Escalante, Tubac, April 3, 1834, Apache file, AHES. The main house on the Babocómari ranch was built in 1833 and may have been occupied by Ignacio Elías and his sister Eulalia when the Apaches attacked on March 30, 1834. See Munson, "Don Ignacio and Doña Eulalia Elías and the History of Their Hacienda on the Babocómari: Camp Wallen," 5.

40. González to Escalante, Tucson, April 9, 1834, Apache file, AHES.

41. Proclamation signed by Juan González, Tucson, April 20, 1834, M-M 380, no. 60, Pinart Collection, BL.

42. Elías to Escalante, Tubac, April 21, 1834, Apache file, AHES. Tubac's commander at the time of Elías' letter was Lieutenant Salvador Moraga. Not everybody agreed with Elías about him. In August, Tubac citizen Valentín Sotelo wrote Escalante to complain about Moraga's rumored transfer to Altar, describing him as "respected" by the residents of Tubac. See Sotelo to Escalante, Tubac, August 17, 1834, Apache file, AHES.

43. Ramírez to Elías González, Tucson, July 3, 1834, Apache file, AHES. Ramírez was acting for his brother-in-law, Antonio Comadurán, who may have been in Arizpe lobbying the legislature to approve the proposed campaign against the Apaches.

44. Elías to Escalante, Tubac, July 4, 1834, Apache file, AHES.

45. González to Escalante, Tucson, September 1, 1834, Apache file, AHES.

46. Antonio Narbona was the son of the man who had been Tucson's commanding officer and later governor of both Occidente and New Mexico. The elder Narbona died in Arizpe in 1830. His son would go on to reach the rank of colonel before being killed by Apaches in December, 1848. See Almada, *Diccionario*, 441. Ramón Urrea was one of many descendants of Captain Bernardo de Urrea who chose military careers.

47. Escalante to Bustamante, Division Headquarters on the Babocómari, September 29, 1834, Apache file, AHES.

48. José María Elías González to Vice-Governor Bustamante, Arizpe, October 8, 1834, Apache file, AHES. Elías reproduced for the vice-governor's benefit a letter from Justice of the Peace González, written on October 1, in which information about the foray against the Pinal Apaches is included. On the same date, Escalante sent Bustamante the original. Ten horses were lost on the journey, four of them apparently taken by the Gila River Pimas.

49. Escalante to Bustamante, Campaign Division Headquarters on the Hacienda de San Pedro, November 2, 1834, Apache file, AHES. Sometime in October, Escalante shifted his headquarters to the San Pedro ranch of Rafael Elías, brother of the owners of the Babocómari grant. Being closer to the presidios of Santa Cruz, Bacoachi and Fronteras, it was safer. It also placed Escalante nearer the seat of his government in Arizpe.

50. Those who took part in the 1834 offensive were civilians, some of whom undoubtedly had military experience. The operation was under the direction of the Sonoran government, whereas the soldiers of the presidial garrisons were part of the federal establishment.

51. Nava to Real Audience, April 1, 1794, AMS, UAM 811, Roll 2, IIIB 1a. Also, Royal Cedula, Aranjuez, March 18, 1797, AMS, UAM 811, Roll 2, IIIC, 2b, i and iii.

52. Francisco Neblina to Friar José María Pérez Llera, Caborca, February 28, 1835, cabinet 1, drawer 1, AHES.

53. Antonio Urrea to Escalante, Altar, March 4, 1835, Papago file, *cuaderno* (hereafter, "notebook") 6, AHES.

54. Elías to the governor of Sonora, Arizpe, June 23, 1835, folder 67, file cabinet 6, drawer 3, AHES.

55. Bustamante to deputies of Sonoran Congress, Arizpe, June 25, 1835, folder 67, file cabinet 6, drawer 3, AHES.

56. Secretariat of the Sonoran Congress to the Governor of Sonora, Arizpe, July 11, 1835 (signed by deputies José Joaquín García Herreras and Jose Francisco Talavera), folder 67, file cabinet 6, drawer 3, AHES.

57. Undated draft letter signed "E. Arvizu," included in Sonoita proposal file, folder 67, file cabinet 6, drawer 3, AHES.

58. According to evidence submitted to the Surveyor General of Arizona Territory in the Sonoita land grant hearing, the actual price that Elías paid to León Herreras for the property was 200 *fanegas* (320 bushels) of wheat which was to be delivered to Father Rafael Díaz "of the Pimería Alta missions." See Sonoita file, Arizona (Ter.) Surveyor General's Office, "Journal of Private Land Grants," vol. 1, 297 ff, UAM 2174.

59. Letter (apparently from Escalante y Arvizu) to the Sonoran Congress, September 7, 1835, folder 67, file cabinet 6, drawer 3, AHES. All correspondence regarding the "new town" for the Tucson Apaches is included in a file entitled "Espediente que comprehende el establecimiento que va a darse a un pueblo nuebo en el Estado para residencia fija de los Yndigenas Apaches del presidio del Tucson. . . ."

60. "Establecimiento de Apaches del Tucson: Padrón de los Apaches de Paz de este establecimiento, y sus familias . . ." signed by Antonio Comadurán, Arizpe, July 16, 1835, original in M-M 380, no. 62, Pinart Collection, BL (copy provided the author by Kieran McCarty). By the time of the 1835 census, the monthly wheat rations to the peaceful Apaches had been reduced by half over former years. The total of each month's allocation was a little over eighty bushels. Given the population of 486 Apaches, an individual share was about 3 1/3 quarts.

61. See Sonoita file, Arizona (Ter.) Surveyor General's Office, "Journal of Private Land Grants," vol. 1, 363, UAM 2174.

Chapter 7. Power Struggles Leave the Frontier Helpless

1. Weber, *The Mexican Frontier*, 243–244; Herring, *A History of Latin America*, 313–316.

2. Calvo Berber, *Nociones de Historia de Sonora*, 146–147; Almada, *Diccionario*, 758. In March, 1835, Mexico's government ordered reductions in the size of the state militias, further inhibiting the frontier areas in their efforts to cope with the hostile Indian tribes. See Weber, *The Mexican Frontier*, 244.

3. Weber, *The Mexican Frontier*, 250.

4. Herring, *A History of Latin America*, 317, fn. 9; Weber, *The Mexican Frontier*, 250–251.

5. Meyer and Sherman, *The Course of Mexican History*, 339–340.

6. Almada, *Diccionario*, 710.

7. *Ibid.*, 213–214.

8. Originals of the 1836 Pinal peace treaty and a covering letter from Elías González transmitting it to Governor Escalante are manuscripts 13 and 14, Documentos del Gobierno Civil, Asuntos de Misiones de Sonora, Archive of the Francisco College of Santa Cruz de Querétaro, Celaya, Guanajuato (translated copies provided by Kieran McCarty).

9. Dobyns, "Tubac Through Four Centuries," vol. 3, 457.

10. McCarty, *Desert Documentary*, 139, 142. As early as 1747, a Martínez family was prominent in Tubac. On June 21 of that year Joseph Alberto Martínez married Antonia de Luques. Pioneer settler Nicolás Romero and his wife, María Ifigenía Perea, were the godparents (Guevavi marriages, ADT, copy on UAM 3431). In 1774, Juan Vicente Martínez served as godfather for a daughter of Joseph Ramírez and Manuela Sosa. On October 30 of the same year, Joseph María Martínez and María Ygnacia Medina baptized a daughter whose godparents were don Phelipe Belderrain, son of Tubac's first commanding officer, and doña María Ygnacia Peñuelas (Guevavi and Tumacácori baptismal registers, ADT, copy on UAM 3431). In all these cases, the names of Martínez family members are linked with those of the frontier elite. María Clara Martínez, wife of Manuel Otero and mother of Sabino and Teófilo, may have belonged to the same family as José María, although the author has not been able to document the relationship. In any event, José María Martínez, an important Arizonan of the Mexican years, unquestionably had very deep roots in the Pimería Alta.

11. From the time of Martínez' appointment as Tucson's commanding officer until his death at the hands of the Apaches in 1868, the career of this unusual man can be followed in documents printed in both Spanish and English. Should the sacramental registers of Tucson's presidio ever be found, the mystery concerning his birth and parentage will likely be cleared up.

12. González to Excelentísimo Señor Governador, Tucson, April 27, 1836, folder 74, cabinet 6, drawer 4, AHES.

13. Martínez to Ignacio Elías González, Interim Commander General, November 4, 1837, folder 86, cabinet 7, drawer 1, AHES.

14. Herring, *A History of Latin America*, 318–319; Meyer and Sherman, *The Course of Mexican History*, 327–328.

15. Almada, *Diccionario*, 553. After 1837, Tucson and Tubac justices of the peace in their communications with higher authorities dealt almost entirely with prefects and sub-prefects. Direct correspondence with governors and other state officials became less common.

16. Almada, *Diccionario*, 215, 220–221. Both born in Arizpe, Elías and Escalante y Arvizu were almost certainly relatives, as well as close friends. In 1830, President Bustamante named Escalante to the national senate; Elías became his replacement in Arizpe.

17. Martínez to José María Elías González, Tucson, February 6, 1837, Apache file, AHES.

18. Almada, *Diccionario*, 60.

19. Voss, *On the Periphery of Nineteenth Century Mexico*, 95–96; Calvo Berber, *Nociones de Historia de Sonora*, 148–149; Print 470, Pinart Collection, BL, UAM 563, reel 2.

20. Ramírez to Elías González, Tucson, September 6, 1837, notebook 9, Papago file, AHES.

21. Elías González to Interior Minister; Arizpe, September 20, 1837, notebook 9, Papago file, AHES.

22. Kessell, *Friars, Soldiers, and Reformers*, 292–293.

23. Ramírez, "Notebook," Special Collections, UAL. Teodoro's second wife, by whom he had four children, was a daughter of Leonor Quixada (also called Ortiz after her stepfather) and Francisco Salazar of Santa Ana.

24. Almada, *Diccionario*, 221.

25. Calvo Berber, *Nociones de Historia de Sonora*, 143–144.

26. Almada, *Diccionario*, 288–294; Voss, *On the Periphery of Nineteenth Century Mexico*, 92–94.

27. Francisco Xavier Redondo, to whom this prominent Altar Valley family traces its ancestry, married Ana María Gortari. Juan Martín de Gortari was a Croix deputy in Arizpe in 1782; and Miguel de Gortari died there in 1787. See Navarro García, *Don José de Gálvez*, 393, fn. 155; Morfi, *Diario*, 417, fn. 729.

28. Voss, *On the Periphery of Nineteenth Century Mexico*, 97–98; Almada, *Diccionario*, 710; Calvo Berber, *Nociones*, 149–150.

29. Calvo Berber, *Nociones*, 149–150. Escalante's selection as vice-governor represented a compromise between the Arizpe and Hermosillo factions. Although born in Arizpe, he resided in Hermosillo and favored having the capital there. Weber, in *The Mexican Frontier* (chap. 12), provides a comprehensive discussion of north Mexican separatist movements in the late 1830s and early 1840s. Sonoran references are on pages 260–261 and 270.

30. Villa, *Galería de Sonorenses Ilustres*, 181–182.

31. Calvo Berber, *Nociones de Historia de Sonora*, 150–152; Almada, *Diccionario*, 571–574. Gándara began his campaign to regain the governor's post on May 16, 1838 in San Miguel de Horcasitas. One of his early accomplishments was to reach an accord with José María Elías González, relative and supporter of General Urrea. In trouble later with the federalists for what he had done, Elías wrote a letter to the public in July, 1838,

explaining the reason for his action. See Print 527, July 20, 1838, Pinart Collection, BL, UAM 563, reel 2.

32. Redondo to José Urrea, Altar, April 28 and May 14, 1838, folder 92, cabinet 7, drawer 2, AHES.

33. The closing pages of Chapter VI provide information about earlier events causing problems in the Papaguería.

34. Manuel María Gándara to Juan Cancio Carreras, Native Captain General of Pimería Alta, Hermosillo, October 1, 1838, Pima file, AHES. Among the alleged supporters of Urrea to whom Gándara refers in this letter to the Indian leader is Rafael Moraga, whose diary had been sent to Urrea by Santiago Redondo.

35. Villa, *Historia del Estado de Sonora*, 187–188; Calvo Berber, *Nociones de Historia de Sonora*, 145; proclamation signed by Juan González, Tucson, April 20, 1834, M-M 380, no. 60, Pinart Collection, BL.

36. Print 433, August 28, 1835, Pinart Collection, BL (UAM 563, reel 2).

37. Print 494, August 10, 1837, Pinart Collection, BL (UAM 563, reel 2).

38. In his "Reminiscences of an Arizona Pioneer," Hilario Gallego describes such houses for the period of the 1850s.

39. García, "The Story of Jesús García," ms., AHS; Gallego, "Reminiscences of an Arizona Pioneer." *Tagua* comes from an expression in Mexican Spanish that means "common" or "of poor quality." See Santamaría, *Diccionario de Mexicanismos*, 996. Some of the cotton cloth used for garments may have been made locally, but most of it came from Hermosillo.

40. Hispanic Arizonans enjoyed betting on Indian kick-ball races in which both Indians and Mexicans participated. See José León report, Tucson, February 1, 1825, Apache file, AHES. Also, North, *Samuel Peter Heintzleman*, 154. San Juan's day celebrations are common throughout the Spanish speaking world. The fiesta of San Agustín was held in Tucson to commemorate the patron saint of that community. Magdalena's fiesta, begun in the 18th century, remains Sonora's most noted religious celebration.

41. Pfefferkorn, *Description of the Province of Sonora*, 195–200; Gallego, "Reminiscences of an Arizona Pioneer." Jesús García ("The Story of Jesús García") states that coffee was introduced into Tucson by the Oury brothers in the 1850s and the Mexican women of the town—unfamiliar with the beans—tried to cook them without roasting and grinding them.

42. Safford and Hughes, "The Story of Mariana Días."

43. In an affidavit prepared for the hearings on the Arizona land grants in 1886, Francisco Solano León stated that he first visited the Tres Alamos site in 1838 and found evidence of cultivation there, but no settlers. Elsewhere in the document, he noted that "the commander of the presidio sent

troops to escort the laborers to Tres Alamos and guard them while cultivating the crops. . . ." See "Affidavit" in the Francisco Solano León biographical file, AHS. Francisco Romero, a contemporary of León, provided similar testimony concerning a later time period. Romero first visited the Tres Alamos site in 1851 and observed that "the commander of the presidio sent troops to escort laborers . . . to cultivate crops for the subsistence of the soldiers at Tucson. This was done in the spring of the year, and after the crops were raised . . . the troops and laborers returned to Tucson and spent the winter." ("Affidavit" in Francisco Romero biographical file, AHS.)

44. See Gallego "Reminiscences of an Arizona Pioneer."

45. As early as 1830 cowboys working on the land grants were losing their lives in Apache raids. See M-M 380, no. 55, Pinart Collection, BL.

46. Much of this testimony is found in, Arizona (Ter.) Surveyor General, "Journal of Private Land Grants," UAM 2174.

47. According to the baptismal register of the Arizpe Parish Archives, Rosa was born in 1822. Her full name was María Rosa Anacleta.

48. In his article on the Babocómari ranch, Munson implies that Eulalia Elías continued to reside there after her brother's death in 1835. This is highly unlikely in view of the Indian situation. See Munson, "Don Ignacio and Doña Eulalia Elías and their Hacienda on the Babocómari: Camp Wallen."

Chapter 8. Sonoran Politics and Indian Affairs

1. The account of the Johnson incident is primarily based on Strickland's "The Birth and Death of a Legend: The Johnson 'Massacre' of 1837." According to one source cited by Strickland Chief Juan José was reared in the Elías household in Arizpe. In his biography of the Compá family, William B. Griffen makes no reference to any such upbringing. See "The Compás: A Chiricahua Apache Family of the Late 18th and Early 19th Centuries." Luis Encinas Johnson, great-grandson of John, was Sonora's governor in the 1960s.

2. Brandes, "Don Santiago Kirker, King of the Scalp Hunters," 3–4; Smith, "The Scalp Hunter in the Borderlands, 1835–1850."

3. According to some authors, the decision of José María Elías González and his brother Simón (then governor of Chihuahua) not to do more to frustrate Gándara's quest for power related to a September appeal from the central government for unity in the face of a threatened invasion by the French. See Voss, *On the Periphery of Nineteenth-Century Mexico*, 100; and Almada, *Diccionario*, 572. The incident with the French is described in Meyer and Sherman, *The Course of Mexican History*, 328–331.

4. Almada, *Diccionario*, 652–653.

5. See M-M 380, no. 543, August 13, 1839, Pinart Collection, BL. The Apache file of the Sonora Historical Archive indicates comparatively little warfare with the Apaches in 1839.

6. González and Moraga reports, April 31 and May 11, 1840, notebook 15, Papago file, AHES.

7. Papago campaign reports for January, 1841, notebook 18, Papago file, AHES.

8. García to Manuel María Gándara, January 9–16, 1841, notebook 26, Papago file, AHES. García would later become the last military commander of Tucson prior to the transfer of the garrison to Imuris in 1856.

9. The account of the Arizpe incident, as well as the subsequent break between Gándara and Ignacio Elías González, is taken from correspondence included in Prints 572–576 of the Pinart Collection, BL, UAM 563, reel 2. Supplementary sources include Almada, *Diccionario*, 653, 809.

10. Urrea's mother, Gertrudis Elías González, was a younger sister of Ignacio.

11. Almada, *Diccionario*, 183.

12. *El Voto de Sonora*, December 20, 1841. The public career of Ignacio Elías González apparently ended with the defeat of Urrea's supporters in the early summer of 1841. He died four years later at his home in Arizpe.

13. *El Voto de Sonora*, February 15, 1842.

14. *Ibid.*, March 15, 1842.

15. Almada, *Diccionario*, 711.

16. *El Voto de Sonora*, January 15, 1842.

17. *Ibid.*, March 1, 1842.

18. Almada, *Diccionario*, 574–575.

19. Print 613, July 12, 1842, Pinart Collection, BL, UAM 563, reel 3.

20. The figure of "more than six-hundred" is taken from Calvo Berber, *Nociones de Historia de Sonora*, 153. Almada (*Diccionario*, 575) offers the somewhat more conservative estimate of 500.

21. *El Voto de Sonora*, December 21, 1842. Apparently, those who launched the attack on Ures were Gándara partisans from his old stronghold of San Miguel de Horcasitas.

22. At the time of the 1842 Apache campaign, José María Elías González was an elected deputy to the Mexican national congress. However, he also was apparently commanding officer of the northern line. A few months later, Urrea would name him "second chief" of all the department's military forces. See Almada, *Diccionario*, 214.

23. M-M 381, no. 1, Ibarra to Elías González, October 28, 1842, Pinart Collection, BL.

24. Comadurán to Elías González, Tucson, December 1, 1842, M-M 381, no. 38, Pinart Collection, BL. At this time, Comadurán was both

commanding officer at Tucson and general commander of the second section of the northern line which included the other three nearby forts.

25. Martínez to Urrea, Altar, December 21, 1842, notebook 127, file cabinet 8, drawer 1, AHES.

26. Ignacio Zúñiga and José Urrea were both Tucson natives. Anselmo, Ignacio's younger brother, was born at his mother's home in Arizpe in 1802, but spent his infancy at the Tucson presidio.

27. The activities of the Zúñiga brothers and Gaxiola are reported in *El Voto de Sonora*, December 14 and December 21, 1842.

28. M-M 381, no. 41, January 16, 1843, Pinart Collection, BL.

29. The exact date and place of González' death are not known. By 1844, Trinidad García Rojas was ministering to the spiritual needs of the residents of the northern presidios and missions. See Kessell, *Friars, Soldiers, and Reformers*, 302, fn. 47.

30. We learn of the purpose of Comadurán's Arizpe mission from a later communication to Elías González. See Comadurán to Elías, March 5, 1843, M-M 381, nos. 47, 48, Pinart Collection, BL.

31. Monthly report of Lieutenant Roque Ibarra for February 1843. Dated March 1 at Tubac. See M-M 381, no. 45, Pinart Collection, BL.

32. Comadurán to Elías, March 5, 1843, M-M 381, nos. 47, 48, Pinart Collection, BL. Also, see Almada, *Diccionario*, 214. During 1843, Elías had his headquarters at Rayón, a Gándara stronghold in the lower San Miguel Valley.

33. Translated into English, Culo Azul means "Blue Anus." Henry Dobyns, however, believes that "Culo" in this case may be a Spanish perversion of the Pima word "kerli" that means "old man." On the other hand, in view of the fact that personal names referring to the human posterior and genitalia are fairly common among Piman-speakers, it is plausible that Culo Azul is an actual translation of the man's name. Bernard L. Fontana, another student of Pima naming patterns, reports that Culo Azul's son had an Indian name that translates into English as "Blue Vagina." (Letters in the author's files.)

34. Comadurán to Elías, March 12, 1843, M-M 381, no. 49, Pinart Collection, BL. The Indian apprehended at El Pueblito could not have expected to recruit many Papagos there. According to a contemporary report of the San Ignacio sub-prefect, only six Indians were cultivating land at that location. See Joaquín Quiroga report to the Secretary of the Department, Cucurpe, 31 May 1831, folder 121, cabinet 8, drawer 1, AHES. A transcript is included as Appendix I of Hard and Doelle, *The San Agustín Mission Site*.

35. The interpreter was probably Teodoro Ramírez, although Comadurán does not identify him by name.

36. Voss, *On The Periphery of Nineteenth Century Mexico*, 101.

37. Almada, *Diccionario*, 357.

38. The Elías circular is Print 647, March 13, 1843, Pinart Collection, BL, UAM 563, reel 3. Comadurán's response of March 28 is M-M 381, no. 50 of the same collection.

39. Papago file, notebook 28, AHES.

40. Flores to Elías González, April 24, 1843, in special supplement to *El Voto de Sonora*, June 1, 1843. Lorenzo Rodríguez was a young soldier in the Tucson garrison at the time of the census of 1831. Married to Francisca Soto, he had a daughter named María de la Luz. Following the Papago War, Rodríguez rose to the rank of captain. He commanded the Mexican force that first engaged members of the Crabb expedition at Caborca in April of 1857. In that clash, he was badly wounded and died shortly thereafter. See McCarty, "Tucson Census of 1831," pt. 2, "Military Households," 41; and Villa, *Historia del Estado de Sonora*, 251–253.

41. Information about the peace offer to the Pimas, Papagos and Maricopas is found in three letters: Ensign Manuel Orozco to Comadurán, Tucson, May 3, 1843; Comadurán to Elías, Tubac, May 5, 1843; and Elías to Urrea, Ures, May 11, 1843. All were published in the special supplement to issue number 50 of *El Voto de Sonora*, June 1, 1843, 1–3.

42. Comadurán's recommendation for a show of force is mentioned in *El Voto de Sonora*, May 3, 1843, 120.

43. The reports from the Tucson and Tubac justices are in folder 121, cabinet 8, drawer 1, AHES. See letters of May 31, 1843, Joaquín Quiroga, Cucurpe, to Secretary of the Department.

44. The statue of Our Savior of Esquipulas ("the Black Christ") can today be seen at the church in Imuris, Sonora. Mexican troops from the Tucson garrison took it there in 1856.

45. Mexicans alive during the 1830s and 1840s who survived into the American period do not mention any production or consumption of wine by Tucsonans in those earlier years. Furthermore, it is difficult from the 1843 report of Tucson's *juez* to date the indiscretions which he accuses Father Díaz of committing. The priest resided at San Xavier until 1828; between 1837 and 1841, he served Tucson area residents from his headquarters in San Ignacio. Since he did not collect any rents from the El Pueblito fields after 1839, he must have developed his winery (*vinitería*) before that time. The Tucson justice of the peace states that Father Díaz took the output of his winery to San Ignacio (*"Sus products se le remitieron a San Ygnacio."*) This may explain the absence of references to wine making or drinking in the reminiscences of early Mexican residents of Tucson.

46. *El Voto de Sonora*, May 25, 1843, 184–185.

47. Urrea's dealings with the Apache chiefs is reported in *El Voto de Sonora*, June 15, 1843, 193–195.

48. Narbona's plans for his offensive are set out in a letter to the Santa Cruz justice of the peace on June 6, 1843. See M-M 381, no. 54, Pinart

Collection, BL. The Pinal treaty of 1836 did not result in the permanent peace Tucson residents had hoped for when they negotiated and signed it.

49. Comadurán to Elías González, Tucson, October 17, 1844, M-M 381, no. 70, Pinart Collection, BL.

50. Narbona to Elías González, Tucson, July 8, 1843; *El Voto de Sonora*, August 10, 1843, 224–226.

51. The Tubac post reports are found in the Pinart collection, BL, mss. 39, 45, 58, 60, and 61 in the M-M 381 series.

52. Testimony about the San Rafael grant is in vol. 1, Arizona (Ter.) Surveyor General, "Journal of Private Land Grants," UAM 2174. In June of 1843, Apaches killed three residents of Cucurpe and the Santa Cruz raid may have come at that time. See letter from Loreto Elías, Magdalena justice of the peace, June 6, 1843, M-M 381, no. 55, Pinart Collection, BL.

Chapter 9. Urrea Wins in Sonora, Gándara in Mexico City

1. Calvo Berber, *Nociones de Historia de Sonora*, 154. Criticized for not playing a role in defeating the Yaquis, in late September Colonel Elías González again appealed for unity in the face of a continuing threat of French invasion; and once more insisted he was not a Gandarista. Print 677, September 25, 1843, Pinart Collection, BL, UAM 563, reel 3.

2. Calvo Berber (*Nociones de Historia de Sonora*, 154–155) states that Aguayo was beaten to death with clubs, riddled with bullets, and his body dragged behind a horse. Almada (*Diccionario*, 13) says only that he died defending Ures from attack by Gandaristas.

3. Calvo Berber (*Nociones de Historia de Sonora*, 155) writes at some length on the execution of the hostages, whereas Almada (*Diccionario*, 575) fails to mention it. Although not sympathetic to Gándara, Almada is more critical of Urrea than other Mexican historians, perhaps because much of the Almada fortune was lost in Urrea's cause. Calvo Berber is an unabashed Urrea partisan.

4. Almada, *Diccionario*, 575–576.

5. Kessell, *Friars, Soldiers, and Reformers*, 302, fn. 49.

6. Gándara did not officially acquire title from Aguilar until 1869. After paying $499 for it, he sold it nine years later for $12,500 in gold coin. Since Aguilar never settled on or developed the grant, it has been assumed that he acted as Gándara's agent in buying it in the first place. See Tumacácori file in Arizona (Ter.) Surveyor General, "Journal of Private Land Grants," UAM 2174; also, Kessell, *Friars, Soldiers, and Reformers*, 302.

7. 1844 baptismal registers of the Magdalena Parish Archives. Tame Apaches, possibly transferred from Tucson, were common in Tubac by the 1840s.

8. Later, Juana María Martínez would marry Manuel Smith; after his

death she wed Thomas Berger. The Martínez land grant near San Xavier Mission was for many years referred to as the Berger Ranch (see José María Martínez files, AHS). Manuel Otero was a son of Atanasio and a grandson of land grantee Toribio Otero. He was also the father of Sabino and Teófilo Otero. His wife, María Clara Martínez, may have been a sister of José María.

9. Tragically, the Ramírez first-born did not live to become an adult. According to an entry in his father's notebook, he died on February 2, 1857.

10. In his "Notebook" (Special Collections, UAL) Teodoro Ramírez incorrectly records the name of José Francisco's godmother as Rosa Ortiz de Elías. She was the eldest child of Tomás Ortiz and Josefa Clementa Elías, daughter of Tubac presidial commander Ignacio Elías González.

11. Rafael was the son of Teodoro's older brother, José Loreto. He was also the great grandfather of María Urquides, a prominent Tucson educator for whom one of that community's schools is named.

12. Comadurán to Elías González, Tucson, September 17, 1844, M-M 381, no. 64, Pinart Collection, BL.

13. Comadurán's account of the 1844 battle is the first mention the author has encountered of the military career of Francisco Solano León who, in the early American period, was one of Arizona's most prominent and highly respected citizens. After 1844, León's name appears with increasing frequency in accounts of affairs involving the soldiers and civilians of Tucson. When his military career ended, he was an *alférez* (ensign or second lieutenant) in the Tucson company stationed in Imuris.

14. Comadurán to Elías González, Tucson, September 29–October 1, 1844, M-M 381, no. 66, Pinart Collection, BL.

15. A policy very similar to this was followed by Americans such as Charles Poston when they first came into Arizona in 1854 and somewhat later. The Sonorans liked it even less when practiced by Americans than when practiced by their compatriots in Chihuahua.

16. Calvo Berber (*Nociones de Historia de Sonora*, 156) reports twenty-nine Mexicans killed, whereas Almada (*Resumen de Historia del Estado de Chihuahua*, 217) places the number at thirty-three.

17. *El Voto de Sonora*, September 5, 1844, 262. One of the junior officers with Elías was a German-born Mexican named Frederick A. Ronstadt, founder of the Ronstadt family of Tucson.

18. Almada (*Resumen de Historia del Estado de Chihuahua*, 217) mistakenly reports the attack on the Janos settlement as taking place in April rather than August. He and Calvo Berber (*Nociones de Historia de Sonora*, 156) agree that fifteen Apaches were slain in that onslaught.

19. Elías González to Francisco Durazo, Arizpe, October 3, 1844, M-M 381, no. 67, Pinart Collection, BL.

20. M-M 381, nos. 68–69, 71-78, Pinart Collection, BL. Among the towns responding to Elías's request were Fronteras, Moctezuma, Bacoachi, Bavispe, Bacerac and Sahuaripa. Especially lengthy was the communication signed by Captain Teodoro Aros, acting commander at Fronteras. Altar was Aros' regular post, but he had also served at Tubac. Descendants of Captain Aros—whose full name was López de Aros—were important ranchers in southern Arizona during the Anglo period. In Spain, the López de Aros (Haro) family was of the highest Basque nobility. King Felipe II of Spain on January 20, 1559, conferred on don Diego López de Haro y Sotomayor the title Marqués de Carpio. Don Diego López de Haro y Sotomayor y de la Cueva, Fifth Marqués de Carpio, was named Grandeza de España ("Grandee of Spain") on May 10, 1640. See Atienza, *Nobiliaro Español*, 769, 1414.

21. Narbona to Elías, Fronteras, December 3, 1844, M-M 381, no. 72, Pinart Collection, BL.

22. Almada, *Diccionario*, 548.

23. Urrea to Elías, Hermosillo, January 1, 1845, M-M 381, no. 80, Pinart Collection, BL.

24. Herring, *A History of Latin America*, 319–320.

25. The San Ignacio sub-prefect requested the information from the towns under his jurisdiction on January 9, 1845. Captain Comadurán responded later that month, as also did Leonardo Orozco, *segundo juez de paz* of Tubac. See folder 50, file cabinet 8, drawer 5, AHES.

26. The Urrea plan for dominating the Apaches was published in *El Voto de Sonora* on May 8, 1845. The author is grateful to Kieran McCarty for supplying information about its contents.

27. Almada, *Diccionario*, 507. The ties between the Pesqueiras and the family of Urrea's mother were very close and have remained so. Within twenty years, Pesqueira would also be a general.

28. *Ibid.*, 223, 576.

29. The editor of *El Voto de Sonora*, in the edition of March 27, 1845 (283), reflected on this anxiety, closing his article with the prayer that Duque not encourage "the faction of darkness and of such tragic memories for Sonora" to regain control of the government.

30. Almada, *Diccionario*, 49.

31. *Ibid.*, 576. Since Urrea made no effort to get his Apache offensive underway in the spring of 1845, it seems likely that he used this excuse to remain in Sonora so that he could mount another effort to regain control. Had he succeeded in getting back into power, he might have administered a sound defeat to the Apaches. None of his critics ever contended that he lacked ability as a military leader and tactician.

32. Herrera undoubtedly considered Gaxiola to be a neutral figure in the Urrea-Gándara conflict.

33. Almada, *Diccionario*, 271.

34. *Ibid.*, 183. Cuesta's appointment meant a demotion for Colonel Elías González. Duque may have felt this change necessary because of the close relationship between Elías and Urrea. However, he did not want to lose the advantage of Elías' experience on the Apache frontier and, therefore, left him in charge of that area.

35. Elías to Duque, Ures, April 30, 1845, M-M 381, no. 81, Pinart Collection, BL. On July 19, Elías forwarded details of his plan to Minister of War García Conde with a copy to the commanding general of Sonora and Sinaloa. In this document, he mentions important roles for Lieutenant Colonel José María Martínez and for Captain Hilarión García who would later be the *comandante* of the Tucson presidio. See vol. 3, Apache file, AHES.

36. Almada is one of few historians to mention Cuesta's implication in the 1845 effort to overthrow Gaxiola. If he was involved, it did not affect his career. He was later both governor and military commander of Sonora. See Almada, *Diccionario*, 183, 712.

Chapter 10. No Matter How Bad, Things Can Always Get Worse

1. Comadurán to Elías, Tucson, August 17, 1845, M-M 381, no. 82, Pinart Collection, BL. The author has found no documents that reveal what happened later to this Athapascan Mata Hari.

2. Kessell, *Friars, Soldiers, and Reformers*, 296. The 1843 grant was the one that later came to be known as Los Nogales de Elías. Further research is needed to establish the identity of González. Because the petition for the grant shows him as the husband of Balbanera Redondo and the father of José Elías, the author had assumed he was Francisco *Elías* González in spite of the fact that throughout the petition, his name appears as González only. The fact is, he may have been Francisco González Forano, who was prefect at San Ignacio during the 1850s. If such is true, he was Balbanera Redondo's second husband with a name remarkably like that of her first. The title to the Los Nogales de Elías property was awarded to José Elías, who served as the prefect of the San Ignacio district in the late 1850s and whose descendants still live in Nogales, Sonora. See Barnett, "La Reclamación del Rancho 'Los Nogales de Elías' Ante la Suprema Corte de Justicia de Estados Unidos."

3. León Herreras (also spelled Herreros and Herrera) should be regarded as the founder of the family with that surname in Arizona, although others with the name were also in the area quite early. Don Antonio Herreros loaned money to build the San Xavier church (Fontana, "Biography of a Desert Church," 9); and don Ramón García Herreras was an early resident of Tubac (Kessell, *Friars, Soldiers, and Reformers*, 171-

172). Originally from the Arizpe area, the Herreras were known as *ricos* ("rich people").

4. A report of the Tucson meeting and manifesto appeared in *El Centinela de Sonora* (Ures), October 10, 1845.

5. Antonio Culo Azul to Segundo Cabo de la Comandancia General, Tucson, October 20, 1845, M-M 381, no. 83, Pinart Collection, BL. The Pima leader does not say in his letter whether the deserters were Indians but they may well have been. According to the manifesto published in *El Centinela de Sonora* (October 10, 1845), the Gila River people had agreed to join Colonel Elías' great Apache offensive. The author has not been able to locate any documents that reveal whether Culo Azul's appeal was successful.

6. Comadurán to Elías (two letters), Tucson, December 7, 1845, M-M 381, nos. 84 and 85, Pinart Collection, BL.

7. Comadurán to Elías González, Tucson, February 3, 1846, M-M 381, no. 86, Pinart Collection, BL.

8. Cuesta report from Hermosillo, December 21, 1845, Print no. 772, Pinart Collection, BL, UAM 563, reel 3.

9. Almada, *Diccionario*, 183, 577; Voss, *On The Periphery of Nineteenth Century Mexico*, 104. Voss implies that Gándara was allied with Cuesta in overthrowing Gaxiola, which is not consistent with Almada's statement that Cuesta subdued the Gandaristas after becoming governor. More than anything else, Cuesta appears to have been an opportunist. He supported Gándara in refusing to recognize Ignacio Elías González as Sonora's military commander in 1841 but apparently backed Urrea in trying to unseat Gaxiola in the summer of 1845. According to Almada, Urrea viewed Cuesta as a Gandarista.

10. Slidell was instructed to seek the purchase of California and that part of New Mexico not claimed by Texas. See Meyer and Sherman, *The Course of Mexican History*, 343.

11. Comadurán's wife was Ana María Ramírez, sister of Teodoro.

12. Juan Bautista Elías was justice of the peace at Tubac in the 1830s. His presence in Tucson in 1846 is further evidence of the population shift to that presidio.

13. While unable to account for this most unusual state of affairs, the author is satisfied that it represents a high degree of social disruption at the Tubac presidio. Dobyns attributes the situation to a decline in morality in the absence of a resident priest. See "Tubac Through Four Centuries," vol. 3, 595–596.

14. Simpson, *Many Mexicos*, 221–222; Meyer and Sherman, *The Course of Mexican History*, 345–346.

15. Almada, *Diccionario*, 183; Voss, *On the Periphery of Nineteenth Century Mexico*, 104–105.

16. Meyer and Sherman, *The Course of Mexican History*, 346; Emory, *Lieutenant Emory Reports*. Kearny left Santa Fe on September 26 and struck the headquarters of the Gila on October 20. He and his men crossed the Colorado River on November 25.

17. Farish, *History of Arizona*, vol. 1, 136–137. Cooke, *The Conquest of New Mexico and California in 1846–1848*, i (Preface).

18. Cooke said he sent back fifty-five men. Henry Bigler, one of the soldiers, said there were "60–odd" in the group. See Cooke, *The Conquest*, 106–107; Bigler, "Journal Extracts from Henry W. Bigler," 42.

19. Cooke, *The Conquest*, 143.

20. Golder, *The March of the Mormon Battalion*, 190; Bliss, "The Journal of Robert S. Bliss," 79; Bigler, "Journal Extracts," 47. The exemplary Mrs. Hunter, who accompanied the battalion all the way to San Diego, died there on April 13, 1847, apparently from complications resulting from the birth of a child two weeks earlier. She was about six months pregnant when at the Rancho San Bernardino in December. See Jones, "The Journal of Nathaniel V. Jones," 16.

21. Cooke, *The Conquest*, 140–141; Bigler, "Journal Extracts," 47. Allen was the name of the man whom the Apaches robbed. He had been away from the rest of the battalion on a hunting expedition when he lost his way.

22. Cooke, *The Conquest*, 140. Englishman Robert Whitworth was one soldier who admired the appearance of the Apache women, calling them "very good looking, plump pieces of baggage." He was impressed at the amount of beef and mescal they could consume. See "Robert Whitworth's Diary," 49. Kearny earlier in the year had traded mules to the Apaches, apparently in exchange for horses. See Farish, *History of Arizona*, vol. 1, 135–136.

23. Whitworth, "Diary," 150.

24. Bigler, "Journal Extracts," 48.

25. Cooke, *The Conquest*, 146. According to Cooke, the battle of the bulls took place on December 11, which is also the day mentioned by Robert S. Bliss ("The Journal," 80). Regardless of when it occurred, it made a considerable impression on all and the event was celebrated in song by one of the members of the battalion. See Layton, *Christopher Layton*, 56–58.

26. Cooke, *The Conquest*, 146–147.

27. According to Nathaniel V. Jones ("The Journal," 8), the march westward from the San Pedro was along a sandy plain. This may indicate they left the river at Galleta Flat on the northern outskirts of modern Benson. A march of twenty to twenty-five miles would have taken them to water at Cienega Wash or Davidson Canyon.

28. Bigler, "Journal Extracts," 48.

29. Cooke, *The Conquest*, 147.

30. *Ibid.*, 148. The corporal was undoubtedly Joaquín Comadurán, who had begun his military career as a cadet in the Tucson company the preceding year. See Comadurán to Elías González, Tucson, December 7, 1845, M-M 381, no. 85, Pinart Collection, BL.

31. Cooke described the conference with the two Mexican officers as "tedious" and lasting two hours. See Gardner (ed.), "Cooke Report," 24.

32. Cooke, *The Conquest*, 149. According to Gardner ("Cooke Report," 27), two carbines and three lances were to serve as the tokens of surrender, and the members of Cooke's battalion were to be allowed to enter the town and trade with the inhabitants.

33. Cooke prepared the battalion to march at daybreak but some of the mules wandered away during the night and it took time to recover them. See Gardner, "Cooke Report," 27.

34. Cooke, *The Conquest*, 149.

35. *El Sonorense*, January 1, 1847, 2–3. It is not clear why Cuesta was travelling to Tubac.

36. The American camp was about a half mile from town. See Cooke, *The Conquest*, 150.

37. Layton, *Christopher Layton*, 61; Cooke, *The Conquest*, 150.

38. Whitworth, "Diary," 151; Golder, *The March of the Mormon Battalion*, 195; Bliss, "The Journal," 80.

39. Bigler, "Journal Extracts," 49.

40. Golder, *The March*, 195–196. Although the Tucsonans seem willingly to have given or sold food to the Americans, members of Cooke's company also appropriated supplies without being invited to do so. James Van Nostrand Williams wrote in his diary that, "There was a quantity of public wheat stored of which our Colonel ordered to be taken to camp what he thought the mules could pull for feeding them. We also took some beans and shelled corn." Williams and others commented, however, that Cooke ordered them not to molest civilians or their property. See Williams, "Life Sketch," 40.

41. Bliss, "The Journal," 81.

42. "Samuel Hollister Rogers Visited Arizona 130 Years Ago (Excerpts From His Journal 1846–47)," 2, Snowflake Historical Society, Snowflake, Arizona.

43. Jones, "The Journal of Nathaniel V. Jones with the Mormon Battalion," 9.

44. Bigler, "Journal Extracts," 49.

45. Gardner, "Cooke's Report," 27.

46. Cooke, *The Conquest*, 151.

47. Golder, *The March*, 196. In mentioning "the cause of our being here in the United States Service," Standage may have been referring to

the hope many Mormons had that their display of patriotism would elimi-
nate some of the prejudice directed against them by other Americans.

48. Whitworth, "Diary," 151.

49. Cooke, *The Conquest*, 153–154. The midnight scare is reported in
the diaries and journals of other soldiers also.

50. Leroux and other guides called the peak "the great horn."

51. Bigler, "Journal Extracts," 49–50.

52. *Ibid.*, 52.

53. Cooke, *The Conquest*, 168.

54. Bigler, "Journal Extracts," 51; Cooke, *The Conquest*, 150.

55. Farish, *History of Arizona*, vol. 1, 142.

56. The editor of *El Sonorense* reported on January 8, 1847, that ten
days before, Colonel Elías and his detachment had passed through Santa
Cruz on their way to join the troops at Tucson. He guessed that there was
little possibility of Elías overtaking the Americans. Almada (*Diccionario*,
214, 239) states that Elías remained in Tucson for some time as commander of the garrison.

57. The information from Father García Rojas' registers is in the archive
of the parish of Santa María Magdalena in Magdalena, Sonora.

58. Almada, *Diccionario*, 588. The founder of the prominent Redondo
family of Sonora was don Francisco Xavier Redondo. According to some
of his Tucson descendants, he arrived in Sonora with the original Altar
presidial garrison in the 1750s. If so, he must have lived a very long life.
Dobyns reports that, although born in Spain, he was permitted to remain
in Mexico when other Spaniards were expelled in the late 1820s. See
Dobyns, "Some Spanish pioneers in Upper Pimería," 20.

Chapter 11. The War Years, 1847–1848

1. Bancroft, *North Mexican States and Texas*, vol. 2, 604–612.

2. Almada, *Diccionario*, 339.

3. *El Sonorense*, April 13, April 23, 1847.

4. *Ibid.*, April 30, 1847.

5. *Ibid.*, June 25, 1847.

6. Almada, *Diccionario*, 258–259.

7. Print no. 909, Pinart Collection, BL; *El Sonorense*, September 10,
1847.

8. Pedro Ruelas appears to have been a brother of Francisco Ruelas,
prominent in Tucson during the early Anglo years and a Pima County
supervisor in the 1870s. A sister, María, was married to Luis Elías and was
the mother of pioneer Tucson jeweler Perfecto R. Elías.

9. *El Sonorense*, October 8, 1847.

10. Villa, *Historia del Estado de Sonora*, 203–208.

11. *Arizona Weekly Citizen*, June 15, 1889; also, see *The Arizona Historical Review*, vol. 1, no. 4 (January, 1929).

12. The author has never encountered any Mexican documents to confirm the Adams story. In the original article, the judge reported that he was back in Tucson some years later and found it much changed.

13. Dobyns ("Tubac Through Four Centuries," vol. 3, 600–604) reports a very high death rate for the Mexican residents of Tubac in 1847–1848. His statistics are from a Santa Cruz burial register misfiled with Tubac material. M-M 411, Pinart Collection (BL).

14. Meyer and Sherman, *The Course of Mexican History*, 351. News of the treaty signing did not reach the northern frontier until several weeks had passed. The last battle of the war ended with surrender of Mexican forces at Chihuahua City on March 16. See Bancroft, *North Mexican States and Texas*, 611–612.

15. Comadurán's stay in Ures may have been prolonged by the fact that he was assigned as prosecutor in a military trial involving a fellow officer named Juan Villela. See *El Sonorense*, May 15, 1848. The April mutiny and Comadurán's trip to Ures are described in a letter he wrote to Colonel José María Elías González on January 26, 1849, file cabinet 2, drawer 3, Apache file, AHES (reel 15, Hermosillo archive microfilm, AHS).

16. Dobyns ("Tubac Through Four Centuries," vol. 3, 610) reported that the massacre occurred in 1847. He also wrote that Tubac's commander, Saturnino Limón, led soldiers and settlers from that fort to recover the bodies and buried them there on July 7. However, Limón himself—who was *comandante* at Santa Cruz rather than Tubac—wrote Comadurán on July 6 that he had recovered the bodies and was interring them at Santa Cruz. The confusion stems from a misplaced burial register in the Pimería Alta (Pinart) Collection of the Bancroft Library. This document is filed with the Tubac records whereas it belongs with those of Santa Cruz. See burial register 1847–1848, Tubac documents, M-M 411, Pinart Collection, BL; and letter, Limón to Comadurán, Santa Cruz, July 6, 1848, Apache file, AHES. In his letter, Limón refers to "twenty bodies," but the burial record mentions only fifteen, none identified. Comadurán, in a report sent to the Sonoran General Command, tells of an effort to recover the bodies that José Ramírez made prior to Comadurán's return from Ures. See Comadurán to Comandancia General, Tucson, August 8, 1848, Apache file, AHES.

17. Comadurán to Gándara, July 6, 1848, with enclosures, Apache file, AHES. Particularly hard hit by the massacre was the Ocoboa family. In addition to losing Tomás, they suffered the death of in-law Rafael Ramírez, husband of Petra Ocoboa. Sharing their grief were the Romeros. Mariano Romero lost her husband, Juan Martínez, and Francisco Romero, who was married to Victoriana Ocoboa, lost his brother-in-law, Tomás.

18. *El Sonorense*, October 6, 1848.

19. Bancroft, *North Mexican States and Texas*, 671, fn. 72; Roske, "The World Impact of the California Gold Rush, 1849–1857," 198–199.

20. Cave Johnson Couts, *Hepah, California!*, 50–55.

21. *Ibid.*, 55–59. The gold deposits near Guevavi, first mentioned in documents of the mid-18th century, may be the oldest in Arizona to be worked by Spaniards or under their direction. Beginning about 1814, Yaquis were employed as laborers at Guevavi. Anglo-Americans knew of the deposits and worked them as early as the 1860s. See Kessell, *Mission of Sorrows*, 106; and *Friars, Soldiers, and Reformers*, 239, 305. At the time the Graham party came through southern Arizona, the Guevavi mines and those in the Papaguería were the only ones being worked. No Spanish documents confirm any mining activity during the 1840s in the Superstition Mountains, in spite of what novelists have written about the matter. (See, for example, Allen, *The Story of Superstition Mountain and the Lost Dutchman Gold Mine*, 5–7.) The Peralta family, some of whose members were reported to have been in the Superstititons in the 1840s, later did some mining in Arizona, but in a different region. See Blair, *Tales of the Superstitions*, 80 ff.

22. Couts, *Hepah, California!*, 59. There had been no resident priest at Tumacácori for twenty years when the Americans came through.

23. *Ibid.*, 61-62; Samuel Chamberlain, *My Confession*, 257–258.

24. Couts, *Hepah, California!*, 62. In October of 1848, Comadurán would have been fifty-one; but thirty of those years had been spent on the frontier. Given what he had endured he deserved to look older than he was and probably did.

25. *Tasajo* is a regional term specifically associated with Veracruz, but apparently diffused to other areas. See Santamaría, *Diccionario de Mexicanismos*, 1014.

26. Chamberlain's story after he encountered Hitchcock is a confusing jumble of times and places; and the reader is wise to be wary of his description of events also. To begin with, Urrea had not been Sonora's governor for more than three years. Also, Glanton's band was not organized until the early summer of 1849, more than six months after Graham's troopers were in Tucson. See Chamberlain, *My Confession*, 258–260; Smith, "John Joel Glanton, Lord of the Scalp Range," 15. Urrea died of cholera in Durango on August 1, 1849. See Almada, *Diccionario*, 712.

27. Couts, *Hepah, California!*, 63.

28. The Charco de las Yumas was near the modern town of Rillito.

29. The Mexican government ratified the Treaty of Guadalupe Hidalgo at Querétaro on May 21, 1848.

30. *El Sonorense*, May 12, 1848.

31. The 1848 census report is an enclosure to the election notice dated September 27, 1848. See Print 980, Pinart Collection, BL.

32. Print 977, September 18, 1848, Pinart Collection, BL.

33. Almada, *Diccionario*, 12–15. Aguilar did not take office for several months after being elected; Juan Gándara served as interim governor.

34. Some of Teodoro's descendants are of the opinion that he studied at the Franciscan college of Santa Cruz de Querétaro.

35. Ramírez, "Notebook," Special Collections, UAL. Manuela grew up to marry John W. Sweeney, a Pima County supervisor and territorial legislator. Teodoro and María de los Angeles had another daughter, Serafina, who was born in December, 1848.

36. Comadurán to Comandancia General, Tucson, December 14, 1848, file cabinet 2, drawer 3, Apache file, AHES (reel 15, Hermosillo archive microfilm, AHS). The death toll at Tubac in the December 9 raid was reported to be nine persons. See *El Sonorense*, February 21, 1849. Tumacácori was also attacked at this time and abandoned shortly afterward. See Kessell, *Friars, Soldiers, and Reformers*, 308.

37. Comadurán to Colonel José María Elías González, Tucson, January 26, 1849, File cabinet 2, drawer 3, Apache file, AHES (reel 15, Hermosillo archive microfilm, AHS). By the time of Comadurán's January letter, Elías González had replaced Gándara as Sonora's military commander.

Chapter 12. The Yanqui Forty-Niners

1. Teodoro Ramírez commented in his "Notebook," Special Collections, UAL, on the status change. For an evaluation of the effectiveness of presidios, see Faulk, "The Presidio: Fortress or Farce?"

2. Stevens, "The Apache Menace in Sonora, 1831–1849," 221–222.

3. Faulk, "Projected Military Colonies for the Borderlands, 1848," 39.

4. In his "Notebook," Special Collections, UAL, Teodoro Ramírez reported that on December 29, 1848, his daughter Serafina was baptized by Vázquez, which pinpoints one of the dates when the priest was in Tucson. He must have laid over several days because of the heavy workload.

5. Vázquez report, Villa de Guadalupe del Altar, January 16, 1849, AMS, UAM 811, roll 7, IIIH 2e.

6. The Gándara-Elías exchange was carried in *El Sonorense* on February 21, 1849, 2–4. Since the beginning of the Urrea-Gándara feud, Elías had tried to maintain a neutral position, but it had gained him nothing from Manuel María Gándara; the February letter from Gándara's brother was the straw that broke the camel's back.

7. Lieutenant Couts in his diary of the Graham expedition mentioned

encountering some returning Mexicans on November 25, 1848, who were headed back to Sonora to get their families. "News of California favorable," he wrote. See Couts, *Hepah, California!*, 82.

8. Vázquez to the Bishop, Altar, March 23, 1849, AMS, UAM 811, roll 7, IIIH 2f.

9. Bieber (ed.), *Southern Trails to California*, 20–25.

10. Nevins, *Fremont, The West's Greatest Adventurer*, vol. 2, 417–418.

11. Wood, *Personal Recollections*, 11.

12. *Ibid.*, 11. Although Wood himself provides no information about Tucson, John G. Goodman, III, editor of his diary, presents a dismal portrait of the community, commenting that "Tucson was an ancient adobe town of roughly 500 inhabitants . . . so unimpressive that the overlanders mentioned it primarily as a place where they could obtain a small amount of food. More important than the town, in the eyes of one diarist, was a wretched creature assuming the attitude of a woman, but said to be a hermaphrodite, who was showing her deformity for presents." His reference to the hermaphrodite is from an account by Charles Pancoast, a traveler with the Peoria party, who was in Sonora during October. Contrary to what Goodman says, Pancoast did not place the encounter with the hermaphrodite in Tucson, but at an Indian camp through which he passed later. The incident may, in fact, have occurred at the settlement of tame Apaches northwest of town. See Pancoast, *A Quaker Forty-Niner*, 242.

13. These charges grow dimmer as Americans experience more trouble at the hands of the Apaches and Yumas.

14. Wood, *Personal Recollections*, 12.

15. Couts, *Hepah, California!*, 59.

16. Wood, *Personal Recollections*, 13–14.

17. *El Sonorense*, April 27, 1849, 1–2.

18. Aguilar to Commanding Officer, Santa Cruz, Ures, April 30, 1849, M-M 381, no. 113, Pinart Collection, BL.

19. According to later observers, the Santa Cruz went underground at about the site of La Canoa.

20. Bieber (ed.), *Southern Trails to California*, 203–226.

21. Clarke, *Travels in Mexico and California*, 76–108.

22. Robinson, *Mexico and the Hispanic Southwest in American Literature*, 31.

23. Governor José de Aguilar to Bishop Garza y Ballesteros, Ures, June 8, 1849, AMS, UAM 811, roll 7, IIIH 2g; Consuelo Boyd, "Forgotten Filibuster," 7–15.

24. Bustamante to Aguilar, Caborca, June 5, 1849; *El Sonorense*, June 15, 1849, pp. 2–3. According to Bustamante, the Americans attacked Cieneguilla on June 1 and reached Caborca two days later. However,

Governor Aguilar informed the Bishop that the raid on Cieneguilla occurred on June 3. Boyd ("Forgotten Filibuster," 7–8) also cites June 3 as the date for the assault, pointing out that the Americans had been in Cieneguilla since May 21 and had been kindly treated by the local populace. Father Lorenzo Vásquez, parish priest at Altar,wrote the governor on the same day as Bustamante, advising that he and eight other men were going to the relief of the people of Cieneguilla. He seemed to believe there were as many as 500 Americans—members of several different parties—in the region. According to *El Sonorense*, Aguilar received these letters on June 8 and immediately gave orders that the Americans be pursued. To this day it has not been determined who was responsible for sacking Cieneguilla. They may have been outlaws, rather than Forty-Niners.

25. Harris, *The Gila Trail*, 74–79. The *alcalde* that Harris mentions at Santa Cruz was, in fact, the presidial commander, José María Villaescusa, the same individual Durivage had lauded for his kindness and beautiful manners. The highest civil official at both Tucson and Santa Cruz was not an *alcalde* but a *juez de paz*.

26. Bachman, "Audubon's Ill-Fated Western Journey," 297–300.

27. Harris, *The Gila Trail*, 67–71. Three years earlier, the soldiers with General Kearny had also heard from Mangas Coloradas and his chiefs that the Apaches regarded the Americans as their friends in driving Mexicans from the region. One Indian remarked, "You have taken New Mexico, and will soon take California; go, then, and take Chihuahua, Durango, and Sonora. We will help you. . . . " See Emory, *Lieutenant Emory Reports*, 100.

28. All the accounts of Apache attacks during July and August are taken from *El Sonorense* for August 24, 1849 (2–3). By this time, the Apache situation had become so desperate that the official state newspaper was carrying a regular column on the subject.

29. In four pages of the published version of his diary, Evans spells Tucson three different ways: Tupison, Tucson and Teusson. Other spellings favored by Forty-Niners were Tuscan and Teuson.

30. Evans, *Mexican Gold Trail*, 147–151. Evans made some sketches for his diary, including one of Indian houses at San Xavier.

31. Bieber (ed.), *Southern Trails to California*, 319–320.

32. The members of the Harris party learned later that the sick woman had died on the way back to Texas.

33. Cox, "From Texas to California in 1849," 142–143. Cox greatly exaggerated the size of Santa Cruz, which probably at no time in 1849 had more than about five hundred inhabitants.

34. *Ibid.*, 206–207.

35. Hunter, "Transcript of a Diary-Journal of Events, Etc. on a Journey from Missouri to California in 1849," 110; Anonymous, "Transcript

of a Diary of a Member of the Robards' Company," 58. The Mexican officer referred to was Lieutenant Colonel José Ignacio Terán y Tato who later served as Mexican consul in Liverpool and who died in Cannes, France, in 1868. Almada, *Diccionario*, 688–689; also, Hadley, "Nuevas Perspectivas Sobre el Contacto Interétnico: La Campaña Apache del Coronel Don José María Elías González Durante la Gran Migración a los Placeres de California."

36. Pancoast, *A Quaker Forty-Niner*, 233.

37. Powell, *The Santa Fe Trail to California*, 133–137.

38. The Luques were in the Santa Cruz Valley as early as the 1740s. María Josepha de Luque, wife of the owner of the Arivaca stock ranch, became the godmother of a male child at the Guevavi mission on January 7, 1742. Three years later, on October 20, 1745, Juan Pascual Luque and his wife baptized a daughter there. Luques served in the Tubac garrison, and soldiers of that surname were at the Tucson fort during all its existence. Guadalupe, who led the Papagos to Arivaipa Canyon, was a member of the Tucson garrison in 1831. See Guevavi baptismal registers, ADT; McCarty, "Tucson Census of 1831," pt. 2: "Military Households," 43. During the early Anglo period, some Luques apparently changed their surname to Lucas.

39. Luis Burruel, Tucson's justice of the peace, reported the Arivaipa raid to the San Ignacio prefect on October 9, 1849. The item was later picked up and published on November 16 in the Apache column of *El Sonorense*. A copy of Burruel's report is in file cabinet 2, drawer 3 of the Apache file, AHES (reel 15 of the Hermosillo archive microfilm, AHS). Tucson's justice stated that the only compensation Luque received for his efforts was the good opinion and respect of his superiors.

40. Hunter, "Transcript of a Diary-Journal," 120–121.

41. Pancoast, *A Quaker Forty-Niner*, 238–239. The anonymous diarist with the Robards' company identified the child as a boy, leaving Pancoast in the minority on this issue. See Anonymous, "Transcript of a Diary of a Member of the Robards' Company," 65–66.

42. Hunter, "Transcript of a Diary-Journal," 123.

43. Pancoast, *A Quaker Forty-Niner*, 241–242.

44. Hunter, "Transcript of a Diary-Journal," 124–125.

45. Again, the writer refers to the highest civil official as *alcalde* rather than as *juez*. The former title may have been used as a casual term of reference by the local Mexican population.

46. Powell, *The Santa Fe Trail to California*, 144–147.

47. *Ibid.*, 153–155.

48. Elías' campaign diary is in file cabinet 2, drawer 3, Apache file, AHES (reel 15 of the Hermosillo archive microfilm, AHS). Captain Comadurán and sixty soldiers from Tucson took part in the expedition. There were many problems with deserters, including some from the Tucson

company. A brief account of the campaign appeared in *El Sonorense* on November 16. Also, see Eccleston, *Overland to California on the Santa Fe Trail*, 175–176; Greer, *Colonel Jack Hays*, 240–246; and Hadley, "Nuevas Perspectivas Sobre el Contacto Interétnico."

49. Eccleston, *Overland to California*, 184–186. Colonel John C. Hays, Fremont Association leader, made the decision to go through Apache Pass, called Puerto del Dado by the Mexicans.

50. *Ibid.*, 201–203.

51. General Urrea was serving as Durango's military commander at the time of his death. Despite having led a full life, he was only fifty-one years old. See Almada, *Diccionario*, 712.

Chapter 13. California Sours for Sonorans

1. Doris Marion Wright estimated that 8,000 Mexicans, most from Sonora and Sinaloa, reached California in 1849. See "The Making of Cosmopolitan California."

2. Velasco, *Noticias Estadísticas del Estado de Sonora*, 242.

3. Pitt, *The Decline of the Californios*, 54–55.

4. See *El Sonorense*, February 1, 1850, 4. The Tucson troopers always seem to have been short of mounts and the civilian population may also have been low at this time because of selling livestock to the Forty-Niners. Louisiana Strentzel, who passed through Tucson in August, 1849, reported that the citizens had for sale, mules, oxen, cattle, calves and sheep. Strentzel, "A Letter from California, 1849," 255–256.

5. Letter from Antonio Sotelo to San Ignacio Prefect, Tucson, February 6, 1850, AMS, UAM 811, roll 7, IIIJ 1b. Other petitioners were Gerónimo González, José María Orozco, Manuel de Soto, Ramón and Luis Burruel, Ramón Castro, and Juan José Azedo. Tucson's request for a resident priest was not met although it was approved by a special commission appointed by the bishop of Sonora. See Kessell, *Friars, Soldiers, and Reformers*, 311.

6. *El Sonorense*, April 26, 1850, 3. Based on information from the 1848 census, it would appear that nearly twenty percent of the people of Hermosillo sought their fortunes in California, whereas the proportion of migrants from Tucson and the Altar Valley was under ten percent.

7. Pitt, *The Decline of the Californios*, 46–68.

8. *El Sonorense*, September 13, 1850.

9. Bancroft, *History of Arizona and New Mexico*, 486–487; Pitt, *The Decline of the Californios*, 64; Pancoast, *A Quaker Forty-Niner*, 254–258.

10. Eccleston, *Overland to California*, 231–233; Hayes, *Pioneer Notes From The Diaries of Judge Benjamin Hayes*, 45; Almada, *Diccionario*, 128; Greer, *Colonel Jack Hays*, 249–250.

11. Bancroft, *History of Arizona and New Mexico*, 487–488; Wagoner,

Early Arizona, 305–306; Smith, "John Joel Glanton, Lord of the Scalp Range," 14; Chamberlain, *My Confession*, 287–291; Martin, *Yuma Crossing*, 138–152.

12. Lockwood, *Pioneer Portraits*, 11–13. In one instance, Pancoast observed American soldiers crossing over to Mexican soil to collect duty from the returning Sonorans. See Pancoast, *A Quaker Forty-Niner*, 254–258; Couts, *From San Diego to the Colorado in 1849*, 47–48.

13. *El Sonorense*, November 22, 1850, 3–4.

14. *Ibid.*, November 29, 1850, 4; January 31, 1851, 1.

15. Comadurán's report was published in *El Sonorense*, January 10, 1851, 1–3. It was part of a communication from Colonel Elías to the Governor of Sonora. Elías closed his letter to the governor with words of high praise for Corporal Tomás Gastelo and Sergeant Solano León, as well as for the citizens of Tucson and the Papagos of San Xavier. In 1893, elderly Tucsonan Juan B. Elías, in a newspaper interview, recalled from personal experience the Apache attack of December, 1850, as well as a similar one that occurred in June, 1852. See *Arizona Daily Citizen*, August 3, 1893.

16. *El Sonorense*, December 27, 1850, 1.

17. *Ibid.*, January 31, 1851, 3–4. Corella, member of a pioneer Arizpe family, went on from the defeat at Ojo Hediondo to become one of Sonora's most renowned fighting men. He reached the rank of major general and in 1888 was honored with a special citation by the Sonora state legislature. See Almada, *Diccionario*, 167–168.

18. *El Sonorense*, January 31, 1851, 1–2; Almada, *Diccionario*, 552. Almada refers to the battle site near Cumpas as Pozo Hediondo ("stinking well"), but Pesqueira in his January 23 account of the fighting called it Ojo Hediondo and thus it was described in *El Sonorense*.

19. Comadurán to Carrasco, Tucson, March 3, 1851, folder 231, file cabinet 11, drawer 2, AHES. Mexican fears about Americans fighting alongside the Apaches were not far-fetched. An Englishman in the Fremont Association party joined the Indians in combat against Colonel Elías's forces in October 1849. It was not a new experience for this individual who boasted that he hated Mexicans. See Greer, *Colonel Jack Hays*, 240–244.

20. Almada, *Diccionario*, 128.

21. Carrasco to Comadurán, Ures, March 28, 1851, folder 231, file cabinet 11, drawer 2, AHES.

22. *El Sonorense*, April 4, 1851, 3.

23. *Ibid.*, June 27, 1851, 2–3.

24. Arizona (Ter.) Surveyor General, "Journal of Private Land Grants," vol. 4, 80–130, UAM 2174. The courts confirmed the Martínez grant even through it lay within the boundaries of an Indian reservation created in 1874. For many years after the death of Martínez, the grant was occupied

by one of his daughters and her second husband, a man named Berger. Tucsonans began referring to it as the Berger Ranch and so it has been known ever since. The Martínez name has been preserved, however. It is still applied to the hill across the Santa Cruz River from the grant.

25. Almada, *Diccionario*, 65–67 and 557; Douglass, "On the Naming of Arizona;" Herring, "The Silver of El Real de Arizonac."

26. *El Sonorense* published the Flores report on August 1 (4). At the end of 1851, Tucson Justice of the Peace Miguel Pacheco reported 122 deaths during the year, a figure close to a quarter of the total population of the town. Only nineteen children were born. See Pacheco report, December 31, 1851, folder 242, file cabinet 11, drawer 3, AHES.

27. Surita to the Inspector General of Military Colonies, Tucson, April 28, 1851 (two letters), file cabinet 2, drawer 3, Apache file, AHES (reel 17, Hermosillo microfilm, AHS). In his report, Surita stated that the few horses available to the Tucson soldiers were all in use by troopers escorting the paymaster and he could not send any soldiers to the rescue of the supply train. With the aid of the Tucson justice of the peace, Surita recruited a few *vecinos* and Indians from San Xavier, who were placed under the command of National Guard Captain Guadalupe Luque. Once again, Luque and his recruits came through. They intercepted the raiders, killed several and recovered all the stolen goods. In addition, they freed several captives the Indians had taken in Caborca and confiscated other booty, including livestock which Luque was permitted to distribute among his followers.

28. Fr. Lorenzo Vásquez, Altar, July 27, 1851, AMS, UAM 811, roll 7, IIIJ ld.

29. Calvo Berber, *Nociones de Historia de Sonora*, 167.

30. *El Sonorense*, October 24, 1851, 4.

31. Bartlett, *Personal Narrative*, vol. 1, 388–392; Graham, *Report*, 41–42.

32. *El Sonorense*, October 14, 1851, 4. The San Ignacio prefect wrote the governor on September 30; he may have meant to date the Apache attack September 27, instead of a month earlier. The soldiers were escorting a herd of horses northward and it is possible they were at that very time on their way to resettle Tubac. They surrendered some of the horses to the Indians and their sergeant and another soldier were wounded.

33. Bartlett, *Personal Narrative*, vol. 2, 117–119, 304–305. The Mormons did not linger for long in Tubac. Sometime in the spring of 1852, they moved on to the San Bernardino area of California where members of the U.S.-Mexico Boundary Commission found them in May.

34. Almada, *Diccionario*, 249.

35. The letters from the justices of the peace at Santa Cruz and Tucson are found in folder 242, file cabinet 11, drawer 3, AHES.

36. Bartlett, *Personal Narrative*, vol. 1, 269.

37. *Ibid.*, vol. 1, 272–299.

38. The Santa Cruz captives were brought to the vicinity of Tucson by the Apaches who attacked the presidio on December 15, 1860. See Comadurán's report in *El Sonorense*, January 10, 1851.

39. Bartlett, *Personal Narrative*, vol. 1, 303–317.

40. Bartlett (*ibid.*, vol. 1, 307) states that Inez González was the daughter of Jesús González. However, in a footnote on page 405, he corrects himself. She was apparently the step-daughter of a man named Jesús Ortiz.

41. *Ibid.*, vol. 1, 319–405.

42. *Ibid.*, vol. 1, 410.

43. Kessell, *Friars Soldiers, and Reformers*, 312; Ramírez, "Notebook," Special Collections, UAL. As godparents for Juan Manuel—their last child—Teodoro and María de los Angeles chose Jesús María and Teresa Martínez, son and daughter of José María. Teresa later married Jesús María Elías. Her brother, father, and two brothers-in-law were all killed by Apaches.

44. Bartlett, *Personal Narrative*, vol. 1, 422–424. Bartlett and his party were in Magdalena during the San Francisco fiesta and his description of the event is an ethnographer's delight.

45. The Mexican boundary commissioner was a son of Alejo García Conde, governor of Sonora and Sinaloa when the movement for Mexican independence began in 1810. He defeated the insurgents at the battle of San Ignacio Piaxtla on January 8, 1811. His son Pedro was but forty-five years old when he died in Arizpe. In spite of his youth, he had held many important positions in the Mexican government. He was secretary of the war and the navy in the cabinet of President Herrera. In terms of accomplishment, the García Conde family was one of the most important in Sonoran history. See Almada, *Diccionario*, 298.

46. Bartlett, *Personal Narrative*, vol. 1, 264–265.

Chapter 14. The End of Mexican Rule

1. Sheep were the first livestock to be brought to California in large numbers. See Woodward (ed.), *Journal of Thomas W. Sweeny*, fn. 70, 248–249; Bartlett, *Personal Narrative*, vol. 2, 293. Texas cattle drives came later, reaching a peak in 1853–54. See Bell, "A Log of the Texas-California Cattle Drive, 1854," pt. 1, 208–209.

2. Hargett, "Pioneering at Yuma Crossing," 334; Woodward (ed.), *Journal Of Thomas W. Sweeny*, 150–159; Lockwood, *Pioneer Portraits*.

3. Faulk, "Projected Mexican Military Colonies for the Borderlands, 1848," 44 (especially Article 20); *El Sonorense*, June 27, 1851, 2–3.

4. According to the 1831 census, Herrán and his wife Trinidad Noriega

had a son named Dolores, through whom the family line continued in Tucson. See McCarty, "Tucson Census of 1831," pt. 2, "Military Households," 42.

5. Francisco Herrán to Señor Prefecto del Partido, Tucson, April 26, 1852; and González to Gobernador del Estado, San Ignacio, June 18, 1852, folder 242, file cabinet 11, drawer 3, AHES.

6. The letter states that the citizens of the town had been using the Pueblito lands since the expulsion of the Spanish Franciscans in 1828. Although some Indians remained at El Pueblito into the 1840s, the mission *visita* did not effectively exist after about 1845, and Tucsonenses felt its lands should be officially declared vacant and made available for their purchase and use.

7. Saenz, *et al.*, to Governor Aguilar, Tucson, May 6, 1852, folder 242, file cabinet 11, drawer 3, AHES.

8. Romero's certificate, attesting the success of the Papago action, was transmitted along with a report for the governor prepared by Captain Luque. Both were dated May 10. See *El Sonorense*, May 28, 1852, 2–3.

9. The Tucson French colony was short lived. Before the end of the summer of 1852, its members went overland to California or south to join a larger group of their countrymen at Cocóspera. See Wyllys, *The French in Sonora*, 64–65.

10. Ramón Comadurán was married to Francisca Otero, whose grandfather, Atanasio, served various times as the *juez de paz* in Tubac. She was the oldest sister of Sabino Otero, well-known southern Arizona rancher during the late 19th and early 20th centuries.

11. Romanos' report on the Tucson attack was published along with other items of Apache correspondence forwarded to the governor of Sonora by General Blanco on June 27 in *El Sonorense*, July 23, 1852, 2–4.

12. Bartlett's description of the trip from the Colorado River to Tucson is found in *Personal Narrative*, vol. 2, 185–292. A good account of the murder of Craig is provided in Woodward's *Journal of Thomas W. Sweeny*, 159–164.

13. Since the middle of the 19th century, Mexicans have often referred to Anglo-Americans as *patones* ("big-feet").

14. Bartlett's is the oldest known drawing of Tucson and San Agustín del Pueblito. The modern St. John's Church on Ajo Road in Tucson is said to be a copy of the chapel that once stood at the foot of Sentinel Peak.

15. Bartlett, *Personal Narrative*, vol. 2, 295–296. The boundary commissioner was under the impression that El Pueblito was an abandoned hacienda, rather than a former Indian village. On the last night of their stay in Tucson, the commission's Mexican muledrivers got drunk and painted the town red, much to Bartlett's distress. They repeated the performance later in Santa Cruz.

16. *Ibid.*, vol. 2, 302–317. The commissioner's efforts to obtain Inez' release from Captain Gómez did not succeed. Later, however, the two parted company and when J. Ross Browne visited Santa Cruz in 1864, he found Inez married to another man. See Browne, *Travels in the Apache Country*, 179.

17. In his report on the Gila expedition of General Kearny in 1846 Emory wrote, "[Mexican] Women, when captured, are taken as wives by those who capture them, but they are treated by the Indian wives . . . as slaves, and made to carry wood and water; if they chance to be pretty, or receive too much attention from their lords and masters . . . they are . . . unmercifully beaten and otherwise maltreated. . . ." See Emory, *Lieutenant Emory Reports*, 84.

18. Bartlett, *Personal Narrative*, vol. 1, 399; and vol. 2, 328–329. Although the boundary commissioner states that García was commanding "200 Mexican troops from Tucson" at the time of the San Bernardino encounter, it is unlikely than more than a handful of these soldiers were members of the Tucson military colony which never seems to have been garrisoned with even half that number. García did not officially become Tucson's commanding officer until some time after Bartlett's visit.

19. Woodward (ed.), *Journal of Thomas W. Sweeny*, 170.

20. Bartlett, *Personal Narrative*, vol. 2, 292–293.

21. Calvo Berber, *Nociones de Historia de Sonora*, 170–173.

22. *El Sonorense*, February 18, 1853, 2.

23. The United States Court of Private Land Claims later ruled that Aguilar's purchase of the Calabazas lands was illegal; those who bought the title from Gándara were left holding the bag.

24. A translation of the Gándara contract appears in Fontana, "Calabazas of the Rio Rico," 77. Among those signing the document was a Frenchman named Luis Pierre Chambón, who remained in southern Arizona after its transfer to the United States. His name appears in the 1864 territorial census. He died shortly afterward and his Mexican-born widow took as her second husband Augustus Brichta, who adopted her children and gave them his name. Bernabé Brichta, one of Tucson's most prominent Hispanic citizens around the turn of the 20th century, was Chambón's son.

25. Almada, *Diccionario*, 150 and 275. Fontana ("Calabazas of the Rio Rico") states that Calabazas was reoccupied early in 1853, but this assertion is based on a misunderstanding about the date of a battle with the Apaches witnessed by Peter R. Brady of the A. B. Gray survey team. The surveyors were at Calabazas in 1854, rather than 1853. Kessell (*Friars, Soldiers, and Reformers*, 313), citing Fontana, also shows 1853 as the date for the founding of the Gándara ranch at Calabazas. The year is probably correct, but the Brady account cannot serve as proof of that fact.

26. Cota to General Commander, Tubac, June 17, 1853, M-M 381, no. 117, Pinart Collection, BL.

27. Zenteno to Gándara, Tubac, July 18, 1853; and Gándara to Zenteno, Ures, July 18, 1853, M-M 381, nos. 118–120, Pinart Collection, BL.

28. See correspondence, Zenteno to Gándara, July 30–August 11, 1853, M-M 381, nos. 121–125, Pinart Collection, BL.

29. Dobyns, "Tubac Through Four Centuries," vol. 3, 631.

30. Correspondence concerning conditions in the Santa Cruz colony was particularly heavy during November, 1852. See the San Ignacio file for that month, folder 242, cabinet 11, drawer 3, AHES.

31. Jesús María Ortiz was married to Encarnación Comadurán, oldest daughter of Captain Antonio Comadurán and Ana María Ramírez.

32. Flores ceased to be commander in January, 1852, and Blanco, a year later. For a list of Sonoran military commanders, see Almada, *Diccionario*, 148–150.

33. San Ignacio Prefect González forwarded Ortiz' letter to Gándara on September 15, 1853. See the file for the San Ignacio District, folder 261, file cabinet 12, drawer 1, AHES.

34. Circular, Gándara to commanders of the military colonies, Ures, September 13, 1853, M-M 381, no. 126, Pinart Collection, BL.

35. Gándara draft order, Ures, September 28, 1853, M-M 381, no. 129, Pinart Collection, BL; Draft notes, Gándara to González, September 28 and 29, 1853, folder 261, cabinet 12, drawer 1, AHES; also, see Oury property file, 51, 62, 67, AHS.

36. The author could find no documentary record of Romanos' presence at Tucson after July, 1852, nor of García's arrival before 1854.

37. Gándara to Zenteno, Ures, November 9, 1853, M-M 381, nos. 131–132, 135–136, Pinart Collection, BL.

38. Zenteno to Bernabé Gómez, Tubac, January 18 and January 21, 1854, M-M 381, nos. 138–139, Pinart Collection, BL.

39. Fort Defiance had been established in 1852–53 and American troops were stationed there at the time of the Gadsden Purchase. The Yuma settlement was on the California side of the river.

40. Ratification by the Mexican government occurred in June, 1854, and the U.S. Congress voted a treaty appropriation on the 30th. President Pierce formally published the agreement on the latter date and President Santa Anna did so three weeks later. See Bancroft, *Arizona and New Mexico*, 491–492.

41. Section XI of the Guadalupe Hidalgo Treaty obligated the American government to control invasions of Mexican territory, punish the offenders, and compensate Mexicans for property losses. The resources needed for this effort were never provided. See Park, "The Apaches in Mexican-American Relations."

42. Wagoner, *Early Arizona*, 323–324; Parke, *Report on Explorations for Railroad Routes from San Francisco.* . . . The Gadsden Treaty and what lay behind it are discussed in Coffey, "Some General Aspects of the Gadsden Treaty"; Faulk, "The Controversial Boundary Survey and the Gadsden Treaty"; Lockwood, "The Gadsden Treaty"; Schmidt, "Manifest Opportunity and the Gadsden Purchase"; and Park, "The Apaches in Mexican-American Relations."

43. In his reminiscences, Brady stated that the survey party came to Calabazas in May, but contemporary Mexican sources placed the date somewhat earlier. See *El Nacional*, May 12, 1854, 4.

44. Gray and Brady, *The A. B. Gray Report*, 209–213. Brady reported the leaders of the Mexican forces were don "Gilanin" García and Lieutenant "Commodoran."

45. Gallegos was not killed at Calabazas as Zenteno reported, and three years later returned to his family in Sonora. See San Ignacio district file for June, 1857, folder 303, file cabinet 13, drawer 2, AHES.

46. Zenteno's description was carried in *El Nacional*, May 12, 1854, 4. García, in his account of the Calabazas battle, reported learning of the planned attack from a woman whom the Pinals had abducted from the Tucson Apache village. He also noted the death of José María Orozco, whose horse fell on him while he was on a scouting mission with Luque. Although a Mexican, Orozco—like Luque—lived at San Xavier. See García Campaign Diary, April 28, 1854, folder 7, file cabinet 2, drawer 3, AHES. The Brady commentary mentions Orozco's fall from his horse and adds that the Apaches afterward lanced him many times. Brady refers to Luque (whom he calls "Lucas") as "an old Mexican with one eye who lived at San Xavier." See Gray and Brady, *The A. B. Gray Report*, 210.

47. Almada, *Diccionario*, 567.

48. The Imuris petition, dated July 18, 1854, and related correspondence are in folder 267, file cabinet 12, drawer 2, AHES. Manuel María Gándara, who was Sonora's second ranking military officer, wrote to Governor and General Commander Yañez on August 2, 1854, concerning the Apache peace offer. He included with his letter correspondence from García, dated July 17, and a copy of his response dated July 31. See Gándara to Governor and Commanding General, Topahue, August 2, 1854, folder 7, file cabinet 2, drawer 3, AHES (reel 17, Hermosillo Archive microfilm, AHS). García apparently took no further action with respect to the Apache treaties. By the time he received Gándara's response, he was undoubtedly aware that the Arivaipas had become residents of the United States.

49. García to Segundo Cabo, Tucson, September 16, 1854, in *El Nacional*, October 6, 1854, 3. Also, see Bell, "A Log of the Texas-California Cattle Trail, 1854," pt. 2, 308, fn. 34. Angel Elías was the nineteen-year-

old son of Colonel José María Elías González. Before retirement from the Mexican army, he would reach the same high rank as his father.

50. The purported survey is described by Love in "Poston and the Birth of Yuma," 403–405. First mentioned by Poston in 1891, the story has its apocryphal aspects.

51. Bartlett, *Personal Narrative*, vol. 1, 459–462.

52. Farish, *History of Arizona*, vol. 1, 278–279.

53. Bell, "A Log of the Texas-California Cattle Trail," pt. 2, 311–316. The same cattle train later passed through Tucson, where one of its members reported the presence of two Mexican priests.

54. Tubac was abandoned when Poston returned there in 1856.

55. Froebel, *Seven Years' Travel in Central America, Northern Mexico, and the Far West of the United States*, 496.

56. Fontana, "Calabazas of the Rio Rico," 79.

57. There was no town at the present site of Ambos Nogales in 1855.

58. Bennett, "A Dragoon in New Mexico," 164.

59. Emory, *Report on the United States and Mexican Boundary Survey*. Michler's description of his activities is found in vol. 1, 101–125; Emory tells of the Nogales meeting with the Indians on 95–96. Antonio Azul was among the Pimas in attendance.

60. Comadurán to Ayudante Inspector, Tucson, May 15–16, 1855, M-M 381, no. 146, Pinart Collection, BL.

61. Compañía Presidial de Cavallería de Tucson, Lista Para La Revista, September 1, 1855, M-M 381, no. 153, Pinart Collection, BL. The author has transcribed and translated a portion of Comadurán's report in Appendix F.

62. The Tucson petition and accompanying letters are in the file of Letters Received, 1822–1860, Office of the Adjutant General, Record Group 94, National Archives, Washington, D.C. Pinkston's letter of transmittal is dated September 19, although the petition itself bears the date of September 10. Goerlitz had been a member of the Poston party that visited Sonora in 1854. See Sacks, "The Origins of Fort Buchanan, Myth and Fact," 209, fn. 9. Neither he nor Pinkston is listed in the 1860 Arizona census but Pinkston is reported to have been at Gila City in 1859 and later to have sold property in Tucson to Solomon Warner. See Hayden files, AHS. Mexican signatories to the 1855 petition included Ygnacio Saenz. Missing, however, is the signature of Teodoro Ramírez, who had already moved his wife and children to Santa Cruz.

63. Biographical files, AHS; Poston, "Old Record Book 'A,'" Pima County Recorder's Office, Tucson; Wagoner, *Early Arizona*, 215.

64. Brady, "Portrait of a Pioneer," 179–180.

65. Altar Valley settlers wanted the Tucson garrison in Búsani. Altar file, February 2, 1856, folder 288, cabinet 12, drawer 5, AHES.

66. The primary English-language source about the January departure is a letter from Goerlitz in the *California Chronicle* (San Francisco), May 8, 1856. See Sacks, "Origins of Fort Buchanan," 210–211. Sonoran archives include a copy of a letter written by García stating that the soldiers arrived in Imuris on January 2. See Ignacio Pesqueira to Sonora's General Commander, Santa Cruz, January 12, 1856, correspondence of the San Ignacio Prefecture, file cabinet 2, drawer 3, AHES (reel 18, Hermosillo microfilm, AHS).

67. Well documented information about the final departure of Mexican soldiers and civilians from Tucson has yet to come to light. The Elías account is found in Sandomingo's *Historia de Agua Prieta*, 50. It does not mention Captain García or the transfer of the Tucson company to Imuris, although it is known from documents in the Sonora Historical Archive that the soldiers did go there. Statements from Anglos in Tucson at the time agree that the departure occurred on March 10. Most published descriptions of the flag raising incident are based on an account by William H. Kirkland ("Kirkland" Hayden file, AHS). Some of the tame Apaches apparently accompanied the Mexicans to Imuris and Santa Cruz but returned to the community a short time later. See copy of a letter from Thomas F. M. McLean to Sylvester Mowry, December 25, 1859 ("McLean" Hayden file, AHS).

Chapter 15. Epilogue

1. Bartlett, *Personal Narrative*, vol. 2, 296.

2. Copies (in Spanish) of the documents obtained by Teodoro Ramírez in 1855 are in Pima County Book of Deeds no. 2, 448 ff. Teodoro's son, Manuel, filed them in 1874. A map of the Tucson fields prepared in 1876 shows Teodoro's holdings north of St. Mary's Road to be the most extensive in the area. Manuel Ramírez sold some of this land in 1879 for railroad right-of-way. See Pima County Book of Deeds no. 6, 32.

3. An untranslated copy of Comadurán's record of the September 15 transaction is found in the Pima County Book of Deeds no. 1, 23–24. José Telles, father of Clemente, was a Tucson soldier (McCarty, *Desert Documentary*, 138) and he may have acquired the *solar* as a presidial grant. A downtown street is named for the Telles family, prominent in the town since colonial times.

4. Americans who reached Tucson before January, 1856, were occupying land but it is not recorded whether they settled on unclaimed plots or acquired them from Mexicans in transactions that were not documented.

5. A map of the Tucson fields prepared in 1862 does not show any land claimed by Juana Rosario or George Leach; nor is there a record of sale by

either party in the Pima County Book of Deeds. An untranslated copy of Comadurán's report on the granting of the deed and subsequent sale to Leach is in the Book of Deeds no. 1, 3–5.

6. Pima County Book of Deeds no. 1 records the Galas transactions on pages 2 and 3. Later, on March 8, Leach acquired a third parcel of land from Manuel Burruel. For a short time thereafter he was the biggest American property holder of record in the Tucson community.

7. A copy of Oury's 1862 Property Record is in the archive of the Arizona Historical Society, Tucson. The original is at the Pima County Recorder's Office.

8. Oury Property Record, 36. A few days after registering the property with William S. Oury, the widow Solares apparently sold a small piece of it to Francisco Solano León. See page 45 of the Oury Property Record. Lacking original documents, it is impossible to tell whether the grant was made by Lieutenant Colonel Pedro de Allande y Saabedra, Tucson's *comandante* from 1777 to 1786; or by his son, Pedro María, who was also an army officer. Oury says that the title of the granting official was "assistant inspector" (possibly a mistranslation of *ayudante inspector*), a title that the older Allande never had. However, Oury reports the officer's name to have been Pedro Allande y Saabedra, whereas the son of the old *comandante* was always referred to in military records as Pedro María Allande. If the grant was made by the Tucson commander, it was one of the oldest in the presidio. If it was made by his son, the date could have been as late as the early 1820s.

9. Oury Property Record, 59. There were several persons named Pedro Ramírez living in Tucson at this time and the land records do not show which one received the grant. All were part of the same family and all related to Comadurán. The Ramírez lot was located north of Alameda Street near the intersection with Meyer.

10. Pima County Book of Deeds no. 1, 24–25. Translations of these documents are in the Warner file, AHS.

11. Warner bought his first two pieces of property in the name of Solomon Warner and Company, listing his partners as George F. Hooper and F. Hinton. It was from Hinton's storehouse at Yuma that he obtained the consignment of goods that he carried with him on his first visit to Tucson.

12. According to the official census report of 1860, Tucson had a population of 820 "white" persons, and Tubac, 310 (U.S. Bureau of the Census, "Population of the United States in 1860," 568). Only 620 Tucsonans of all racial and ethnic groups are listed in the excerpt of the 1860 census of Arizona County, New Mexico, reproduced at the request of Senator Carl Hayden and published as Senate Document 13, 89th Congress, 1st session. No explanation is provided for this discrepancy. For additional com-

ment on the matter, see North, "'A Real Class of People' in Arizona," fn. 7, 265.

13. An elderly man from one of Tucson's oldest Hispanic families told an interviewer in 1926, shortly before his death, that "There was a connected chain of little one-room houses all around the inside of the wall that had been built for the soldiers and their families and a few other people." See Hilario Gallego, "Reminiscences of an Arizona Pioneer."

14. Byars, "Documents of Arizona History: The First Map of Tucson," 189.

15. Confederate troops occupied Tucson from February until May, 1862, and those not sympathetic to the Southern cause left town. Although a Confederate supporter, Oury sought to protect the interests of some of these persons by entering their names in his book. Between January 31, 1863, and January 10, 1864, he registered four additional lots, making a total of 133. He had been away from his books for so long when he added the first of the latter group that he assigned it a number he had used earlier. In addition to the 133 town lots, Oury also recorded the ownership of fields and other property.

16. Warner throughout his life was a close friend of Oury, perhaps in part because of his gratitude for Oury having protected his property interests while he was away. See Smith, *William Sanders Oury*, 87.

17. Stevens and Hughes were married to the Santa Cruz sisters, Petra and Atanacia. Property registered in the Santa Cruz family name dated from the eighteenth century. Pima County Book of Deeds no. 1, 238–244. To some degree, these two men owed their success to fortunate marriages.

18. Poston, *Building a State in Apache Land*, 64–74.

19. The Otero *solar* acquired in 1789 and held by descendants of the grantee until 1938 is an exception to the general pattern.

20. Poston, "Old Record Book 'A,'" 179 ff, Pima County Recorder's Office, Tucson. James Lucas, clerk of the Probate Court for Doña Ana County, New Mexico, appointed Poston a deputy clerk on July 15, 1856.

21. Pete Kitchen was living on lands of the Canoa grant before the 1855 boundary survey was completed and William Kirkland began ranching there in 1857. At nearby Sópori, Colonel James W. Douglass and C. C. Dodsen may have been ranching and farming as early as 1854. See Wagoner, *Early Arizona*, 169, 215. Also, see biographical files of the Arizona Historical Society, Tucson.

22. Wagoner, *Early Arizona*, 210–218. Copies of several Spanish and Mexican documents related to Sópori and Arivaca are found in Poston's "Old Record Book 'A.'" Among the Sópori Ranch owners in Spanish times were Bernardo de Urrea, founder of the presidio at Altar, and Captain Juan Bautista de Anza. Kessell, *Mission of Sorrows*, 74; and Sópori documents, "Old Record Book 'A,'" 19–33 (see especially the

report of Teodoro de Islas, Arizpe, July 18, 1810). The U.S. Court of Private Land Claims rejected confirmation of both the Arivaca and Sópori grants. See Bradfute, *The Court of Private Land Claims*, 163, 166–167.

23. Mattison, "The Tangled Web: The Controversy over the Tumacácori and Baca Land Grants"; Wagoner, *Early Arizona*, 200–208.

24. Wagoner, *Early Arizona*, 165. Jane Wayland Brewster has documented the political maneuvering of the 1880s in connection with one Arizona grant. See "The San Rafael Cattle Company," 143–145, 150–151. According to Acuña (*Occupied America*, 57–60), the New Mexico grants were even more involved in politics than were those of Arizona. Bradfute (*The Court of Private Land Claims*) provides the best published account of events leading up to the creation of the land claims tribunal.

25. The Court ruled that the Sonoran official who approved the sale of the grant lacked the authority. The question of whether the Pima Indians had abandoned the land, making it available for sale, was not considered. Wagoner, *Early Arizona*, 222.

26. Mattison, "The Tangled Web"; Wagoner, *Early Arizona*, 200–208; Laumbach, "Las Vegas Before 1850," 244–247. In addition to Baca Float No. 3 in southern Arizona, a smaller tract, known as Baca Float No. 5, was approved in Yavapai County northwest of Prescott.

27. Ready, *Open Range and Hidden Silver*, 49–50.

28. In a communication prepared in January, 1857, while he was serving as first justice of the peace in Santa Cruz, Ramírez stated that he had been living in that community for more than a year. See Ramírez to San Ignacio Prefect, Santa Cruz, January 12, 1857, folder 303, file cabinet 13, drawer 2, AHES.

29. Pedro Ramírez and his family are listed on the Santa Cruz census of 1831. See McCarty, "Santa Cruz Census of 1831," 65.

30. The action by the Gandaristas resulted in the installation of Ramón Encinas as Sonora's provisional governor. It also kicked off a feud between Gándara and Ignacio Pesqueira that would dominate Sonora politics for the next decade. Almada, *Diccionario*, 217, 258, 507.

31. Following the death of his first wife, Encarnación Durán, Manuel Ygnacio married Isidora Márquez, daughter of Don Pedro Márquez and Rosalía Montiel. McCarty, "Santa Cruz Census of 1831," 64; Manuel Ygnacio Elías file (AHS).

32. The names of some of the signatories are included in Appendix A (2) of Sacks, *Be It Enacted*, 118–119. Several Mexican signatures appear in the same handwriting and a few are badly misspelled. There is no question, however, about the validity of Teodoro's distinctive script.

33. Teodoro Ramírez to José Elías. Santa Cruz, January 12, 1857 (two letters), files of the San Ignacio Prefecture, folder 303, file cabinet 13, drawer 2, AHES.

34. Teodoro Ramírez to José Elías, Santa Cruz, February 10, 1857, files of the San Ignacio Prefecture, folder 303, file cabinet 13, drawer 2, AHES. Following the ambush, Teodoro and his companions reported the incident to Major Enoch Steen who had arrived at Calabazas with his dragoons just two months before. The American soldiers pursued the Apaches unsuccessfully and Teodoro, writing of the incident shortly after, observed that the dragoons were untrained in Indian fighting and did not know the countryside. He recommended that a Mexican sergeant and a small squad of soldiers be assigned to serve as guides for them. Luis Elías, at the time of his death, may have been on his way to Santa Cruz to see Manuel Ygnacio Elías, a close relative with whom he was living when Tucson's 1831 census was taken. Perfecto, the youngest of Luis's sons, would later marry Juana Márques who was related to Manuel Ygnacio's second wife.

35. Teodoro Ramírez to José Elías, Santa Cruz, February 10, 1857; and José Elías to Governor Gándara, San Ignacio, February 20, 1857. Both are in the file of the San Ignacio Prefecture, folder 303, file cabinet 13, drawer 2, AHES.

36. Sweeney obituary, *Arizona Weekly Citizen* (Florence), January 18, 1878.

37. On December 22, 1864, Teodoro Ramírez recorded the purchase by Francisco Romero of a Tucson house and lot previously owned by Fernando Urquides. The price was 1,000 gold pesos. See Pima County Book of Deeds no. 1, 475.

38. *Tucson Citizen*, July 8, 1871. Following Teodoro's death, John Sweeney moved the family to Florence, where they remained until well into the 20th century. Teodoro's son, Manuel, operated a ranch near Picacho and also was the town postmaster. Following his mother's death in 1885, Manuel arranged to have her and his father buried side-by-side in the Sweeney family plot at Florence. Their graves and those of John and Manuela Sweeney are enclosed by a wrought iron fence and are conspicuous for the dates on the headstones. Teodoro's birth is recorded as taking place at San Ignacio on November 1, 1791. For information about other Ramírez descendants in Arizona, see Appendix D; and Officer and Dobyns, "Teodoro Ramírez, Citizen of Tucson."

39. Serafina Ramírez de Elías died in childbirth in 1867. Juan later married Antonia Quiroz with whom he had seven children.

40. The files of the San Ignacio Prefecture for 1857 through 1860 are the primary source of information concerning the careers of the Tucson soldiers transferred to Imuris. See folders 303, 322, 327, 329, 330, 343, 345, 355, and 356, in file cabinets 13–15, AHES. Microfilm copies are on reels 49–51 of the Hermosillo files, AHS.

41. Villa, *Historia del Estado de Sonora*, 274–275; Calvo Berber, *Nociones de Historia de Sonora*, 214–218. Major Frederick A. Ronstadt,

founder of the Arizona family, commanded a battalion of Pesqueira's forces in the crucial battle against the rebels. In his service record, Ronstadt mentions the death of García. The author is grateful to Edward Ronstadt, grandson of the major, for a copy of this document.

42. Browne, *Adventures in the Apache Country*, 212. The writer misspelled Joaquín's name as Commodoran.

43. Pima County Book of Births and Deaths, no. 1, page 15. A copy of the entry is in the "Comadurán" Hayden file, AHS.

44. Although he resided for a time in Benson and some of his descendants continued to live there, Antonio Comadurán moved to Tucson where he died in 1912. He is buried in Holy Hope Cemetery. Ramón, the other Comadurán brother and husband of Francisca Otero, met death at the hands of the Apaches in 1861. A sister, Encarnación, married Jesús María Ortiz, son of one of the co-owners of the La Canoa land grant. She died in Tucson in 1902 and is buried in the Solomon Warner plot of Holy Hope Cemetery. Her daughter was the wife of Warner's adopted son. Carmen, another sister, married José María Soto; and the remaining sister, Francisca, was the wife of Jesús Díaz. The author was able to locate descendants of all these persons living in Arizona in 1987.

45. Elías was killed by Apaches in the Patagonia Mountain ambush.

46. Compañía Presidial de Cavallería de Tucson, Lista Para La Revista, September 1, 1855, M-M 381, no. 153, Pinart Collection, BL. See partial translation in Appendix F.

47. Affidavit in the files of the San Ignacio Prefecture, June 1, 1857, folder 303, file cabinet 13, drawer 2, AHES.

48. A document in the León biographical file of the Arizona Historical Society states that Francisco Solano in 1859 turned over to Father Machebeuf one of his houses to be used as a church. León himself testified in the Martínez land grant case that he had been a lieutenant in the Mexican army. See Martínez file, Arizona (Ter.) Surveyor General, "Journal of Private Land Grants," vol. 4, UAM 2174.

49. *Arizona Daily Star*, March 3, 1891. The *Arizona Citizen*, in an article carried the preceding day, mistakenly reported León's age as eighty-five. It said also that his funeral in the Catholic Church "was very largely attended." A partial listing of León's descendants is included in the genealogy chart "The Elías family of Tucson and Tubac." See Appendix A.

50. See Wasson's report on the Rancho de Martínez, Arizona (Ter.) Surveyor General, "Journal of Private Land Grants," vol. 4, UAM 2174.

51. In spite of the many times he was in office, Gándara usually held the governor's post for periods of less than a year. His longest term was from May, 1847, to February, 1849. In several cases when others served, he was the power behind the throne. See Almada, *Diccionario*, 288–294, 310–311.

52. San Ignacio Prefect to Governor of Sonora, February 18, 1857,

folder 303, file cabinet 13, drawer 2, AHES. In his report on activities at Calabazas, the San Ignacio prefect mentioned the presence there of Antonio Gándara and Ygnacio Loaiza, who were felt to be conspiring with a local judge to repossess some of the livestock previously confiscated by order of Pesqueira. Poston may have been the judge.

53. According to Poston, "Pesquiera [sic] was in desperate straits, and agreed to whatever was necessary; the substance of which was that the Americans should come with five hundred men, well armed, and assist him in ousting Guadara [sic]. . . . " Poston, *Building a State in Apache Land*, 86.

54. Sonoran historians such as Calvo Berber and Villa have been reluctant to link either Gándara or Pesqueira with the Ainza conspiracy, whereas Americans have tended to implicate Pesqueira. See Farish, *History of Arizona*, vol. 1, 327–332; Acuña, *Sonoran Strongman*, 32–35. Somewhat provocative, but overlooked by historians on both sides of the line, is the fact that Agustín Ainza was married to a daughter of Manuel Iñigo, longtime patron and friend of Gándara. See Voss, *On the Periphery*, 93 ff; also, Farish, *History of Arizona*, vol. 1, 330.

55. San Ignacio Prefect to Governor Pesqueira, June 4, 1857, folder 303, file cabinet 13, drawer 2, AHES. Also, see affidavits by Henry Alfing and John C. Clark[e], "Old Record Book 'A,'" Pima County Recorder's Office, 209–212. In all, 1,782 of the Gándara sheep were confiscated.

56. Acuña, *Sonoran Strongman*, 35–37. Villa, *Historia*, 249–265.

57. In June, 1857, the San Ignacio prefect recommended putting a Mexican customs station near one that the Americans had established at Calabazas. See San Ignacio Prefect to Governor Pesqueira, June 19, 1857, correspondence of the San Ignacio Prefecture, AHES. Ainza's September stopover at Calabazas is mentioned in Fontana, "Calabazas of the Rio Rico," 83.

58. Almada, *Diccionario*, 258–259, 508.

59. *Ibid.*, 679.

60. Acuña (*Sonoran Strongman*, 66–69) feels that Pesqueira behaved in tyrannical fashion after gaining power in 1856. As a result, he alienated persons such as García, Comadurán, Remigio Rivera and Hilario Gabilondo—all men of excellent reputation. The discontent of such individuals was exploited by the Gandaristas who were always alert to such opportunities.

61. While in Tucson in 1864, Gándara sold a Tubac lot to the firm of Tully and Ochoa. His sons, Francisco and Antonio, had built a house on the property and lived there. See Pima County Book of Deeds no. 1, 473–474.

62. Almada, *Diccionario*, 259.

63. Acuña, *Sonoran Strongman*, 86–87; Fontana, "Calabazas of the Rio

Rico," 85. In October of 1865, while Pesqueira and his family were at Calabazas, his wife died. She was Ramona Elías Morales, daughter of Colonel José María Elías González. Angel Elías and Jesús García Morales were both half-brothers of Ramona.

64. Acuña, *Sonoran Strongman*, 91–92.

65. Almada, *Diccionario*, 259–261. In March, 1869, while his father was still in custody, Gándara's son, Miguel, purchased the Tumacácori-Calabazas property from his uncle, Francisco Aguilar. The transaction took place in Guaymas and the purchase price was 499 pesos. Miguel had gone to San Luis Potosí to obtain a power of attorney from Manuel María, in whose name the title was recorded at Tucson on July 23, 1869. See Pima County Book of Deeds no. 1, 348–351. In 1877, the year before Gándara's death, Charles P. Sykes of San Francisco purchased the old grant from the Gándara family for $12,500 in gold coin.

66. Poston, *Building a State in Apache Land*, 66–68.

67. Office of the Adjutant General, Letters Received, 1822–1860, Record Group 94, National Archives, Washington, D.C.

68. José Elías to Gobernador, San Ignacio, July 11, 1856, Apache material, file cabinet 2, drawer 3, AHES.

69. Sacks, "Origins of Fort Buchanan," 213–218. Steen's decision to locate the camp on Gándara's property probably compromised the major somewhat in his dealings with the Sonoran government which was aware that Manuel María's son, Antonio, was using the Calabazas ranch as a headquarters from which to plot his father's return to power. On the other hand, the border location stimulated trade with Sonora and provided the Mexicans protection against the Apaches.

70. Ramírez to José Elías, Santa Cruz, February 10, 1857, files of the San Ignacio Prefecture, folder 303, file cabinet 13, drawer 2, AHES.

71. Sacks, "Origins of Fort Buchanan," 219–220.

72. Wagoner, *Early Arizona*, 410–414; Walker (ed.), "Colonel Bonneville's Report: The Department of New Mexico in 1859," 345. Bonneville's principal critic was Captain Richard S. Ewell of the First Dragoons, one of the units under Major Steen's command. In spite of the fact that it did not produce any major victories over the Apaches, the 1857 campaign may have intimidated them into refraining from raids on the principal settlements. The Apache front was relatively quiet during 1858 and 1859 at a time when tensions between Anglos and Mexicans were mounting as a result of the Crabb expedition and other developments.

73. Wagoner, *Early Arizona*, 410. Although the documentary record does not confirm it, Steen probably chose Calabazas in the first place because of Poston's influence, and felt obliged thereafter to rationalize the choice by calling Tucson an unacceptable location. After moving to the the Sonoita site, he informed his superiors that Tucson was not a mining or

manufacturing center; therefore, its need for military protection was less urgent than that of the Sonoita Valley. Unhappy Tucsonans protested his decision, stating, among other charges, that Steen was attempting to make farmers of the soldiers, rather than using them to protect the populace— charges remarkably reminiscent of those made by the San Ignacio prefect against the commander of the Tucson military colony in 1852. See Sacks, "Origins of Fort Buchanan," 220–225.

74. See correspondence of Governor Pesqueira in folder 322, file cabinet 13, drawer 5, AHES.

75. Santiago Ward, a son of John Ward and Jesús Martínez, told a representative of the Arizona Pioneers' Historical Society in 1934 that the father of the child carried off by Apaches in 1861 was not an Apache, as some had claimed, but a man named Téllez. He was likely the Santiago Téllez, listed in the Santa Cruz census of 1831, and Jesús Martínez named her son by John Ward after him. Félix Téllez, the kidnapped boy, was reared by Apaches and, under the name of Mickey Free, served as a scout for American forces in later Apache wars. See Santiago Ward biographical file, AHS; also Fontana and Greenleaf, "Johnny Ward's Ranch"; Mulligan, "Apache Pass and old Fort Bowie"; McCarty, "Santa Cruz Census of 1831," 64.

76. Wagoner, *Early Arizona*, 418–424; Wallace (ed.), *Pumpelly's Arizona*, 129–130; Altshuler, *Chains of Command*, 15–16.

77. Serven, "The Military Posts on Sonoita Creek." The Gila River Pimas and Maricopas continued to keep the Apaches at bay during this time and their villages were safer than elsewhere.

78. Wagoner, *Early Arizona*, 465; Jesús María Elías biographical file, AHS; Santa Cruz, "Reminiscences of an Arizona Pioneer," 7–8; Lockwood, *The Apache Indians*, 147.

79. Underhill (ed.), "Dr. Edward Palmer's Experiences With The Arizona Volunteers," 51. Underhill has also provided biographical information about the Arizona Volunteers. See *Genealogy Records of the First Arizona Volunteer Infantry Regiment*. Among the more complete accounts of the actions of the Volunteers are those of Thrapp, *The Conquest of Apacheria*; Farish, *History of Arizona*, Volume 4; and Lockwood, *The Apache Indians*.

80. Farish, *History of Arizona*, vol. 4, 98–110. General George C. Crook preferred Indians to Mexicans as scouts, but his aide, Captain John G. Bourke, was high in his praise of Mexicans as scouts and fighters. See Crook, *General George Crook: His Autobiography*, 163; Bourke, *On The Border With Crook*, 98; and Lockwood *The Apache Indians*.

81. Personal communication, 1958, from Anita Coenen de Maldonado, Comadurán's granddaughter, to the author (author's files).

82. José María Martínez biographical file, AHS.

83. Elías family files (AHS). Jesús María Elías was married to a daughter of José María Martínez, so he lost a father-in-law and brother-in-law to the Apaches, as well as siblings and a cousin.

84. Anonymous, *Transcript of a Diary of a Member of the Robards' Company*, 58.

85. Thrapp, *The Conquest of Apacheria*, 35, 90. R. A. Wilbur, special agent for Papago Affairs, reported that six of the captive Apache children were in the homes of Hispanic Tucsonans Jesús Mendoza, Nicolás Martínez, José Lucas, Leopoldo Carrillo, Manuel Martínez and Francisco Romero. See letter from Wilbur to Lieutenant Royal Whitman, U.S.A., Tucson, October 25, 1871, National Archives, microfilm file M-734(5), Records of the Arizona Superintendency of Indian Affairs, 1863–1873, Letters Received, 1871.

86. Poston to Acting Commissioner of Indian Affairs, April 18, 1863, National Archives microfilm file M-234 (3), Letters Received by the Office of Indian Affairs 1824–1860, Arizona Superintendency, 1863–1869. Also, Department of the Interior, *Annual Report of the Commissioner of Indian Affairs for the Year 1866*, 112.

87. M. O. Davidson to Hon. D. N. Cooley, Commissioner of Indian Affairs, November 8, 1865; Davidson to Cooley, January 23, 1866; Levi Ruggles to Superintendent G. W. Dent, January 31, 1868; Dent to Commissioner of Indian Affairs Taylor, April 1, 1868. All these documents are in National Archives microfilm file M-234 (3), Letters Received by the Office of Indian Affairs 1824–1860, Arizona Superintendency, 1863–1869. After 1869, references to the tame Apaches in government documents are hard to come by and include little information about them. One of these Indians who was an important scout for the American soldiers during Crook's early campaigns was Manuel Durán, who may also have taken part in the Camp Grant Massacre. Papago Agent Wilbur mentions that Durán was reported to have sold a six-year-old Pinal girl taken in that raid. Tucson's 1870 census shows Durán married to a woman named Dolores and occupying a household with two children, Francisco and Agustina. Durán's involvement in the Apache campaigns of the early 1870s is mentioned in Bourke's *On The Border With Crook*. Levi Ruggles' 1868 letter proposing a reservation for the tame Apaches is reproduced in full in Appendix E.

88. Bartlett, *Personal Narrative*; Bell, "A Log of the Texas-California Cattle Trail"; Cozzens, *The Marvelous Country*; Browne, *Adventures in the Apache Country*; Bourke, *On the Border With Crook*; Hodge, *1877 Arizona As It Was*. Also, see Cremony, *Life Among The Apaches*; Way, "Overland Via Jackass Mail in 1858"; Mowry, *Arizona and Sonora*; and Tevis, *Arizona in the 50s*.

89. Hastings, "People of Reason and Others."

90. Way, "Overland Via 'Jackass Mail' in 1858," pt. 2, 161. Also, see Eaton, "Frontier Life in Southern Arizona, 1858–1861," 182, fn. 31, 184. For a different view of how Mexican women regarded Anglo males, see Myres, "Mexican-Americans and Westerning Anglos: A Feminine Perspective."

91. Park ("The History of Mexican Labor in Arizona During the Territorial Period," 39–45) has provided one of the most comprehensive discussions of the stereotype of the "treacherous" Mexican worker that came into being in Arizona at this time. Also, see North, "'A Real Class of People' in Arizona"; and Acuña, *Occupied America*, chap. 4. Perhaps in part as a carryover from the California experience, Anglos in Arizona's mining camps treated Mexicans worse than those in other situations, both through exploiting their labor and through trying to exclude them from participating in the ownership of mines. Also, see Spude, "The Walker-Weaver Diggings and the Mexican Placero, 1863–1864."

92. When the author was living in Phoenix in 1944, some of his friends from that community still viewed Tucson as a "mostly Mexican" town, although fewer than a third of its residents were Hispanic.

93. Hodge, *1877 Arizona As It Was*, 155. For information about intermarriage in other towns, see Dysart, "Mexican Women in San Antonio, 1830–1860"; Trulio, "Anglo-American Attitudes Toward New Mexican Women"; Griswold del Castillo, "Tucsonenses and Angelenos"; and Miller, "Cross-Cultural Marriages in the Southwest: The New Mexico Experience, 1846–1900."

94. Officer, "Historical Factors in Inter-Ethnic Relations in Tucson"; Sheridan, *Los Tucsonenses*, 55–57.

95. He is reported to have been seventy-five when he died, but he was probably older. *El Fronterizo*, February 1, 1884. The town's oldest resident was probably José Herreras, brother-in-law of Manuel Ygnacio, who lived until 1887.

96. Thrapp, *The Conquest of Apachería*, 295.

97. Bourke, *On The Border With Crook*, 55–56, 450. In writing that "Sancho is no longer governor" Bourke is referring to Anson Peacely-Killen Safford, a close friend of his, who was governor during Crook's first campaign in the territory. Of the many outsiders appointed to the post of territorial chief executive, Safford was by far the most popular among the Hispanic residents of the state. Two of his three wives were of Mexican descent.

Appendix A

1. Information about the town of Soto de Cameros was provided by Spanish anthropologist Luis Vicente Elías who has written extensively

about the history of the La Rioja district (interview with J. E. O., spring 1986). Elías' grandfather, Lorenzo Luis Elías Romero, was born in Soto de Cameros. In 1763, when Soto was at the height of its prominence, the weavers consumed 320,000 pounds (12,800 *arrobas*) of wool. By 1816, that consumption had slumped to 40,000 pounds. See Agustín González Enciso, "La Industria Dispersa en la Sierra de Cameros, 1700–1840," 43–46 (copy provided the author by Luis Vicente Elías).

2. The formal name for Alamos was La Real de Minas de la Purísima Concepción de los Alamos.

3. Francisco González de Zayas, probably an uncle of Francisco Elías, was in Alamos at least by January, 1720, when he served as a witness at the wedding of don Cristobal de Góngara and doña Juana de Araujo. His name appears on the register as "Cap. [Captain] don Francisco de Sayas." See Primer Libro de Información Matrimonial, Alamos Parish Archive, reverse side of 29. His wife was doña María Gertrudis de Burboa and Andrés was one of his sons. See marriage presentation of Andrés Gonzales de Sayas, October 22, 1745 (loose pages in the unnumbered Libro de Información Matrimonial, Alamos Parish Archive). According to oral tradition among the Mexican Elíases, don Francisco was fourteen years old when he reached Mexico in 1721 accompanied by two older brothers. See Elías Chomina, *Compendio de Datos Históricos de la Familia Elías*, 83.

4. The wedding of Francisco and Agueda is recorded in the Primer Libro de Información Matrimonial, Alamos Parish Archive. Also, see Acosta, *Apuntes Históricos Sonorenses: La Hacienda de Beneficio de Santa María de Guadalupe de Thobaca y sus Fundadores: La Familia Campoy*; and Elías Chomina, *Compendio*, 84–85.

5. Many writers, including the present author, have attributed various offspring to Francisco and Agueda, but intensive research in the Alamos Archive fails to confirm the birth of any. Rather, it appears that members of the González de Zayas family have been wrongly listed as descendants of their close kinsman, Francisco Elías. This author has abandoned his earlier opinion that the prominent Almada, Salido and Palomares families of Sonora are linked ancestrally to the Elíases. They are, instead, descended through maternal lines from the González de Zayas. See the entry for Francisco Elías González de Zayas in Almada's *Diccionario* (213). Also, Officer, Elías Chomina and Pellat Sotomayor, "Los Hijos de Pancho: La Familia Elías, Guerreros Sonorenses." Apart from don Francisco, the only other person with the surname Elías mentioned in the Alamos parish archive during the eighteenth century was a priest named Joseph Joaquín. Although he was undoubtedly a close relative of don Francisco, the exact nature of that relationship is not clear. Confounding the picture additionally in the Alamos archival materials dating from 1730 to 1760 are references to a "don Elías de Zayas." Elías, in this case, appears to be a

personal name. The individual in question was certainly a relative of the others, however. See the entry concerning the baptism of twins born to Andrés Armenta and Antonia Coronado, "servants of Dn. Juan de Zayas in the capacity of administrator of the estate of Dn. Elías de Zayas standing in for Dn. Joseph de Tavelo." Chapel of San Antonio de Padua, Hacienda de Thovaca, 29 June 1760. Loose pages in the unnumbered Libro de Informaciones Matrimoniales, 1762 [sic] a 1794, Alamos Parish Archive. This entry is signed by Father Pedro Joaquín Campoy.

6. Acosta, "La Ciudad de Alamos," 142. In order to receive a commission in the Spanish army, Francisco would have been required to prove his *pureza de sangre* ("purity of blood"). This exercise would also have revealed the nobility of his birth. It is not known when the first members of the lineage received titles, but by 1800 they were comparatively common and several of the holders were natives of Soto. Oral tradition within both the Spanish and Mexican branches of the family maintains the Elías surname was originally Jewish, although as early as the 12th century an individual named Pedro Elías was an archbishop in Santiago de Compostela. In Spanish documents, the name has been attributed to Galician, Basque, and Catalan origins. It appears in varied forms such as Elia and Elio, in addition to Elías. See Elías Chomina, *Compendio*, 19–23.

7. The exact date of don Francisco's second marriage has not been established but a number of documents confirm that it did take place. See particularly "Testimonio de las Diligencias de Ynformacion de Legitimidad y Limpieza de Sangre de Dn. Juan Chrisóstomo Elías González, actual Colegial en el Tridentino de la Ciudad de Durango" (AMS, 1801).

8. Almada, *Diccionario*, 213.

9. Although by the end of the 18th century it was often called "El Paso," the town's formal name was El Pueblo de Nuestra Señora de Guadalupe del Paso del Norte. It is Francisco's will that tells us of his residence there in 1790. A portion of this document is reproduced in Elías Chomina (*Compendio*, 89–91).

10. Almada, *Diccionario*, 215.

11. Almada (*Diccionario*, 709) credits Tucson with being the birthplace of José Cosme, whereas Villa (*Galería de Sonorenses Ilustres*, 177) assigns that honor to Altar. Almada is probably correct, for the boy was baptized in Tucson on September 30, 1797.

12. Dobyns, *Spanish Colonial Tucson*, 129.

13. McCarty, *Desert Documentary*, 139, 142.

14. The child's name is incorrect. It should be Jesús María, born in 1829. Neither Cornelio nor his wife appears in the 1831 Mexican censuses of Tucson and Tubac; but an elderly woman named Concepción was residing in the home of Juan Bautista Elías in 1860 at the time of the first U.S. Census. She must have died shortly thereafter for she is not listed on subsequent registers.

15. Although assigned to the Tucson presidio in 1817, José María never actually served there.

16. In the Francisco Solano León biographical files of the Arizona Historical Society, Mary Jane León, Ramona's granddaughter, is quoted as saying that Luis Elías was Ramona's father. Given the fact that both were identified as children in the 1831 Mexican Census, this would not have been possible. They were probably siblings who were very close to the same age.

17. Richard is the son of Richard Clark, Sr., and Manuela "Nellie" Elías. His mother is a great granddaughter of Luis Elías and María Ruelas.

Bibliography

Archives and Collections Cited

ADT—Archive of the Diocese of Tucson (Baptismal, marriage, and death registers: Guevavi; Tumacácori)
AGI—Archivo General de Indias
AGN—Archivo General de la Nación PI (Provincias Internas)
    Aguiar Collection (Arizona Historical Society, Tucson)
AHES—Archivo Histórico del Estado de Sonora, Hermosillo
AHS—Arizona Historical Society, Tucson
Alamos (Sonora) Church Archive
AMS—Archivo de la Mitra de Sonora
Archive of the Cathedral of Chihuahua
Archive of the Franciscan College of Santa Cruz de Querétaro, Celaya, Guanajuato, Mexico
Arizona Department of Library and Archives, Phoenix
Arizona (Ter.) Surveyor General "Journal of Private Land Grants"
Arizpe (Sonora) Municipal Archive
Arizpe (Sonora) Parish Archives
Banamichi (Sonora) Parish Archives
Biblioteca Nacional de México (Franciscan Archives)
BL—Bancroft Library, University of California, Berkeley (Pinart Collection)
Magdalena (Sonora) Parish Archives
National Archives, Washington, D.C.
Newberry Library (Chicago Ayer Collection)
Oquitoa (Sonora) Mission Archives
Pima County (Arizona) Book of Deeds, Tucson
Pima County (Arizona) Recorder's Office, Tucson
UAL—University of Arizona Library, Tucson
UAM—University of Arizona Microfilm, University Library, Tucson

Newspapers Cited

Arizona Citizen (Tucson)
Arizona Daily Star (Tucson)
Arizona Weekly Citizen (Florence)
California Chronicle (Sacramento)
El Fronterizo (Tucson)

El Nacional (Ures, Sonora, 1853–1855)
El Sonorense (Ures, Sonora, 1840; 1846–1853)
El Voto de Sonora (Ures, Sonora, 1842–43; 1844–45)
La Estrella de Occidente (Ures, Sonora, 1859–1865; 1866–1876)
Tucson Citizen (Tucson)

Books, Journals, and Miscellaneous Works

Acosta, Roberto
  1949   "La Ciudad de Alamos en la Epoca de las Guerras de Reforma y del Imperio," *Memorias de la Academia de Historia Mexicana.* Tomo VIII.
  1953   *Apuntes Históricos Sonorenses: La Hacienda de Beneficio de Santa María de Guadalupe de Thobaca y sus Fundadores: La Familia Campoy. México, D.F.: Talleres Gráficos de la Editorial Comeval.*
Acuña, Rodolfo F.
  1974   *Sonoran Strongman: Ignacio Pesqueira and His Times.* Tucson: The University of Arizona Press.
  1981   *Occupied America: A History of Chicanos.* Harper & Row.
Aguirre, Yjinio
  1969   "The Last of the Dons," *Journal of Arizona History,* vol. 10, no. 4. "Echoes of the Conquistadores," *Journal of Arizona History,* vol. 16, no. 3.
Allen, Robert Joseph
  1971   *The Story of Superstition Mountain and the Lost Dutchman Gold Mine.* New York: Pocket Books.
Almada, Francisco
  1952   *Diccionario de Historia, Geografía, y Biografía Sonorenses.* Chihuahua: Ruiz Sandoval.
  1955   *Resumen de Historia del Estado de Chihuahua.* México, D.F.: Libros Mexicanos.
Altshuler, Constance Wynn
  1981   *Chains of Command: Arizona and the Army, 1856–1875.* Tucson: The Arizona Historical Society.
Anonymous
  1962   "A Barrio Libre," (compiled from newspaper accounts), *Journal of Arizona History,* vol. 3, no. 2.
  1977   "The Changing Heart of Downtown Tucson," *Sunset* (magazine), January.
  n.d.   "Transcript of a Diary of a Member of the Robards' Company," John Lewis Robards' Hannibal, Mo. Collection. Joint Collection University of Missouri Western Historical Manuscript Collection, Columbia, and State Historical Society of Missouri Manuscripts.

Arizona (Ter.) Surveyor General
  n.d.   "Journal of Private Land Grants." Microfilm copy at the University of Arizona Library, Tucson.
Atienza, Julio de
  1948 *Nobiliario Español: Diccionario Heráldico de Apellidos Españoles y de Títulos Nobiliarios. Madrid, Spain: Industrias Gráficas, México 49.*
Aubry, Francois Xavier
  1938 "Diaries of Francois Aubry, 1834–1854," in *Exploring Southern Trails, 1846–1854,* ed. by Ralph P. Bieber and Averam Bender. Glendale, California: The Arthur H. Clark, Co.
Bachman, Jacob Henry
  1942 "Aububon's Ill-Fated Western Journey: Recalled by the Diary of J.H. Bachman," ed. by Jeanne Skinner Van Nostrand. *California Historical Quarterly,* vol. 21, no. 4.
Bailey, Lynn R.
  1966 *Indian Slave Trade in the Southwest: A Study of Slave Taking and the Traffic of Indian Captives.* Los Angeles: Westernlore Press.
Baldonado, Luis
  1959 "Missions San José de Tumacácori and San Xavier del Bac in 1774," *The Kiva,* vol. 24, no. 4.
Bancroft, Hubert Howe
  1889 *History of Arizona and New Mexico, 1530–1888.* San Francisco: The History Company.
         History of the North Mexican States and Texas. Vol. II, 1801–1889. San Francisco: The History Company.
Bandelier, Adolph
  1883 *Historical Introduction to Studies Among the Sedentary Indians of New Mexico.* Boston: Papers of the Archaeological Institute of America, American Series 1, 2d edition.
Bannon, John Francis
  1955 *The Mission Frontier in Sonora, 1620–1687.* New York: The United States Catholic Historical Society.
  1974 *The Spanish Borderlands Frontier, 1513–1821.* Albuquerque: University of New Mexico Press.
Barnes, Thomas C., Thomas H. Naylor, and Charles W. Polzer
  1981 *Northern New Spain: A Research Guide.* Tucson: The University of Arizona Press.
Barnes, Will C.
  1960 *Arizona Place Names.* Edition revised and enlarged by Byrd H. Granger. Tucson: The University of Arizona Prress.
Bartlett, John Russell
  1854 *Personal Narrative of Explorations and Incidents in Texas, New Mexico, California, Sonora, and Chihuahua.* Two volumes. New York: D. Appleton and Company.

Bartlett, Katherine
   1934   "Spanish Contacts With The Hopi, 1540–1823," *Museum Notes*, Museum of Northern Arizona, vol. 6, no. 12.
Bean, Lowell John and William Marvin Mason (eds.)
   1962   *Diaries and Accounts of the Romero Expeditions in Arizona and California, 1823–1826*. Los Angeles: Ward Ritchie Press.
Bee, Robert L.
   1981   *Crosscurrents Along the Colorado: The Impact of Government Policy on the Quechan Indians*. Tucson: The University of Arizona Press.
Bell, James G.
   1932   "A Log of the Texas-California Cattle Trail," ed. by J. Evetts Haley. In three parts. *Southwestern Historical Quarterly*, vol. 35, nos. 3–4, and vol. 36, no. 1.
Bennett, James A.
   1947   "James A. Bennett, a Dragoon in New Mexico," *New Mexico Historical Review*, vol. 22, no. 2.
Bieber, Ralph P. (ed.)
   1937   *Southern Trails to California in 1849*. Vol. 5, The Southwest Historical Series. Glendale, California: The Arthur H. Clark Co.
Bigler, Henry W.
   1932   "Extracts from the Journal of Henry W. Bigler," *Utah Historical Quarterly*, vol. 5, no. 2.
Blair, Robert
   1975   *Tales of the Superstitions*. Tempe, Arizona: Arizona Historical Foundation.
Bliss, Robert S.
   1931   "The Journal of Robert S. Bliss," *Utah Historical Quarterly*, vol. 4, no. 3.
Bolton, Herbert Eugene
   1930   *Anza's California Expeditions*. Five volumes. Berkeley: University of California Press.
   1931   *Font's Complete Diary: A Chronicle of the Founding of San Francisco*. Berkeley: University of California Press.
   1949   *Coronado, Knight of Pueblos and Plains*. Albuquerque: The University of New Mexico Press.
   1952   *Spanish Explorations in the Southwest, 1542–1706*. New York: Barnes and Noble Publications.
   1960   *Rim of Christendom: A Biography of Eusebio Francisco Kino, Pacific Coast Pioneer*. New York: Russell and Russell.
Boudreaux, Richard
   1982   "Highway 15's history worries U.S. tourists," *Arizona Daily Star*, July 27.

Bourke, John Gregory

1971 *On the Border With Crook.* Glorieta, New Mexico: The Rio Grande Press. (First printing by Charles Scribner's Sons, 1891.)

Boyd, Consuelo

1979 "Forgotten Filibuster," *The Journal of Arizona History*, vol. 20, no. 1.

Bradfute, Richard Wells

1975 *The Court of Private Land Claims: The Adjudication of Spanish and Mexican Land Grant Titles, 1891–1904.* Albuquerque: University of New Mexico Press.

Brading, D.A.

1971 *Miners and Merchants in Bourbon Mexico: 1763–1810.* Cambridge: Cambridge University Press.

Brady, Francis P.

1975 "Portrait of a Pioneer," *The Journal of Arizona History*, vol. 16, no. 2.

Brandes, Ray

1962 "Don Santiago Kirker, King of the Scalp Hunters," *The Smoke Signal*, no. 6. Tucson Corral of the Westerners.

Brew, J.O.

1949 "The History of Awatovi," in *Franciscan Awatovi* by Ross Gordon Montgomery, Watson Smith, and John Otis Brew. Report no. 3 of the Awatovi Expedition, *Papers of the Peabody Museum of Archaeology and Ethnology*, vol. XXXVI. Harvard University.

Brewster, Jane Wayland

1966 "The San Rafael Cattle Company: A Pennsylvania Enterprise in Arizona," *Arizona and the West*, vol. 8, no. 2.

Brinckerhoff, Sidney

1967 "The Last Years of Spanish Arizona," *Arizona and the West*, vol. 9, no. 1.

Brinckerhoff, Sidney B. and Odie B. Faulk

1965 *Lancers for the King.* Phoenix: Arizona Historical Foundation.

Brophy, Frank Cullen

1966 "San Ignacio del Babocómari," *Arizona Highways*, September.

Browne, J. Ross

1974 *Adventures in the Apache Country: A Tour Through Arizona and Sonora.* Introduction, annotations, and index by Donald M. Powell. Tucson: The University of Arizona Press.

Burrus, Ernest J.

1961 *Kino's Plan for the Development of Pimería Alta, Arizona, and Upper California.* Tucson: Arizona Pioneers' Historical Society.

Byars, Charles

1966 "Documents of Arizona History: The First Map of Tucson," *The Journal of Arizona History*, vol. 7, no. 4.

Calvo Berber, Laureano
  1958   *Nociones de Historia de Sonora*. México, D.F.: Librería de Manuel Porrua, S.A.
Campa, Arthur L.
  1979   *Hispanic Culture in the Southwest*. Norman: University of Oklahoma Press.
Carlisle, Charles R. and Bernard L. Fontana
  1969   "Sonora in 1773: Reports by Five Jaliscan Friars," *Arizona and the West*, vol. 11, nos. 1–2.
Carpenter, Philip R.
  1979   "Architectural Development in Tucson," in *Tucson Preservation Primer*, ed. by Robert C. Giebner. Tucson: College of Architecture, University of Arizona.
Cataldo, John
  1974   "Evolution of Armory Park Architectural Expression," in *Tucson Preservation Primer*, ed. by Robert C. Giebner. Tucson: College of Architecture, University of Arizona.
Chamberlain, Samuel
  1956   *My Confession*. New York: Harper and Brothers.
Cheek, Lawrence W.
  1982   "Tucson's architecture: The Spanish accent is here to stay," *Tucson Citizen*, January 16.
Christiansen, Paige W.
  1969   "The Presidio and the Borderlands: A Case Study," *Journal of the West*, vol. 8, no. 1.
Clarke, Asa Bement
  1852   *Travels in Mexico and California*. Boston: Wright and Hasty.
Coffey, Frederic A.
  1933   "Some General Aspects of the Gadsden Treaty," *New Mexico Historical Review*, vol. 8, no. 3.
Collins, Karen Sikes
  1970   "Fray Pedro de Arriquibar's Census of Tucson, 1820," *The Journal of Arizona History*, vol. 11, no. 1.
Cooke, Philip St. George
  1964   *The Conquest of New Mexico and California in 1846–1848*. Albuquerque: Horn and Wallace.
Corbalá Acuña, Manuel
  1970   *Rodolfo Elías Calles: Perfiles de un Sonorense*. Hermosillo.
Corle, Edwin
  1951   *The Gila, River of the Southwest*. Rivers of the Southwest Series. Rinehart and Company.
Cosulich, Bernice
  1953   *Tucson*. Tucson: Arizona Silhouettes.

Coues, Elliot (ed.)
    1900   *On the Trail of a Spanish Pioneer.* Two volumes. New York: Francis P. Harper.

Couts, Cave Johnson
    1932   *From San Diego to the Colorado in 1849: The Journal and Maps of Cave J. Couts,* ed. by William McPherson. Los Angeles, California: Arthur M. Ellis.
    1961   *Hepah, California! The Journal of Cave Johnson Couts from Monterrey, Nuevo León, Mexico to Los Angeles During the Years 1848–49,* ed. by Henry F. Dobyns. Tucson: Arizona Pioneers' Historical Society.

Cox, Cornelius C.
    1902   "Reminiscences of C.C. Cox," *Southwestern Historical Quarterly,* vol. 6, no. 2.
    1925   "From Texas to California in 1849," ed. by Mabelle Eppart Martin. *Southwestern Historical Quarterly,* vol. 29, nos. 1–3.

Cozzens, Samuel W.
    1967   *The Marvelous Country or, Three Years in Arizona and New Mexico, The Apaches' Home.* Minneapolis: Ross & Haines, Inc.

Cremony, John C.
    1954   *Life Among the Apaches.* Tucson: Reprinted by Arizona Silhouettes.

Crook, George
    1960   *General George Crook: His Autobiography,* ed. by Martin F. Schmitt. Norman: University of Oklahoma Press.

Cue Canovas, Agustín
    1972   *Historia Social y Económica de México (1521–1854).* Mexico.

Department of the Interior
    1866   *Report of the Commissioner of Indian Affairs for the Year 1866.* Washington: U.S. Government Printing Office.
          Annual Report on Indian Affairs by the Acting Commissioner, 1867. Washington: U.S. Government Printing Office.

DiPeso, Charles C.
    1953   *The Sobaipuri Indians of the Upper San Pedro River Valley, Southeastern Arizona.* Dragoon, Arizona: The Amerind Foundation.

DiPeso, Charles C., John B. Rinaldo, and Gloria J. Fenner
    1974   *Casas Grandes, A Fallen Trading Center of the Gran Chichimeca.* Vol. 4. The Amerind Foundation, Inc., Dragoon, Arizona. Flagstaff, Arizona: Northland Press.

Dobyns, Henry F.
    1959   "Some Spanish Pioneers in Upper Pimeria," *The Kiva,* vol. 25, no. 1.

n.d. "Tubac Through Four Centuries: An Historical Resume and Analysis." Three volumes. Commissioned by the Arizona State Parks Board, 1959. Copy in the Arizona State Museum Library, Tucson.

1963 "Indian Extinction in the Middle Santa Cruz River Valley, Arizona," *New Mexico Historical Review*, vol. 38, no. 2.

1971 *The Apache People: Coyoteros*. Phoenix: Indian Tribal Series.

1972 "The 1797 Population of the Presidio of Tucson: A Reconsideration," *The Journal of Arizona History*, vol. 13, no. 3.

1976 *Spanish Colonial Tucson: A Demographic History*. Tucson: The University of Arizona Press.

1981 *From Fire to Flood: Historic Destruction of Sonoran Desert Riverine Oases*. Socorro, New Mexico: Ballena Press.

Dobyns, Henry F., Paul H. Ezell, Alden W. Jones, and Greta S. Ezell
1960 "Who Were Nixoras?", *Southwestern Journal of Anthropology*, vol. 16, no. 2.

Douglass, William A.
1979 "On the Naming of Arizona," *Names*, vol. 27, no. 4.

Dunne, Peter Masten (editor and translator)
1955 *Jacobo Sedelmayr, Missionary, Frontiersman, Explorer in Arizona and Sonora*. Tucson: Arizona Pioneers' Historical Society.

Dysart, Jane
1956 "Mexican Women in San Antonio: The Assimilation Process," *Western Historical Quarterly*, vol. 7, no. 4.

Eaton, W. Clement
1933 "Frontier Life in Southern Arizona, 1858–1861," *The Southwestern Historical Quarterly*, vol. 36, no. 3.

Eccleston, Robert
1950 *Overland to California on the Southwestern Trail, 1849*, ed. by George P. Hammond and Edward H. Howes. Berkeley and Los Angeles: University of California Press.

Elías Chomina, Armando
1986 *Compendio de Datos Históricos de la Familia Elías*. Hermosillo, Sonora, México. Privately printed.

Emory, W.H.
1857 *Report on the United States and Mexican Boundary Survey Made Under the Direction of the Secretary of the Interior By William H. Emory, Major First Cavalry, and United States Commissioner*. Two volumes. Washington: A.O.P. Nicholson, Printer.

1951 *Lieutenant Emory Reports: A Reprint of Lieutenant W.H. Emory's Notes of a Military Reconnaissance*. Introduction and Notes by Ross Calvin. Albuquerque: The University of New Mexico Press.

Evans, George W.B.
    1945   *Mexican Gold Trail: The Journal of a Forty-Niner*, ed. by Glen S.
            Dumke. San Marino, California: Huntington Library.
Ewing, Russell C.
    1938   "The Pima Outbreak in November, 1751," *New Mexico Histor-
            ical Review*, vol. XIII, no. 4.
Ezell, Paul H.
    1961   *The Hispanic Acculturation of the Gila River Pimas*. Memoir 90,
            American Anthropological Association, vol. 63, no. 5, part 2.
Farish, Thomas Edwin
    1915–18 *History of Arizona*. Eight volumes. San Francisco: The Filmer
            Brothers Electrotype Company, Typographers and Stereo-
            typers.
Faulk, Odie B.
    1962   "The Controversial Boundary Survey and the Gadsden Treaty,"
            Arizona and the West, vol. 4, no. 3.
    1968   "Projected Military Colonies for the Borderlands," *The Journal
            of Arizona History*, vol. 9, no. 1.
    1969   "Projected Military Colonies in the Borderlands," *The Journal of
            Arizona History*, vol. 10, no. 2.
    1969   "The Presidio: Fortress or Farce?" *Journal of the West*, vol. 8,
            no. 1.
Feather, Adlai
    1964   "Origin of the Name Arizona," *New Mexico Historical Review*,
            vo. 39, no. 2.
Fireman, Janet R.
    1977   *The Spanish Royal Corps of Engineers in the Western Borderlands.
            Instrument of Bourbon Reform, 1764 to 1815*. Glendale, Califor-
            nia: The Arthur H. Clark Co.
Fontana, Bernard L.
    1961   "Biography of a Desert Church," *The Smoke Signal*, no. 3. Tuc-
            son Corral of the Westerners.
    1971   "Calabazas of the Rio Rico," *The Smoke Signal*, no. 24. Tucson
            Corral of the Westerners.
Fontana, Bernard L. and J. Cameron Greenleaf
    1962   "Johnny Ward's Ranch: A Study in Historic Archaeology," *The
            Kiva*, vol. 28, nos. 1–2.
Forbes, Jack D.
    1960   *Apache, Navajo, and Spaniard*. Norman: University of Okla-
            homa Press.
    1971   "Black Pioneers: The Spanish-Speaking Afroamericans of the
            Southwest," in *Minorities in California History*, ed. by George E.
            Frakes and Curtis B. Solberg. New York: Random House.

Forbes, Robert H.
1952 *Crabb's Filibustering Expedition Into Sonora.* Tucson: Arizona Silhouettes.

Froebel, Julius
1859 *Seven Years' Travel in Central America, Northern Mexico and the Far West of the United States.* London: Richard Bentley.

Gallego, Hilario
1935 "Reminiscences of an Arizona Pioneer," *Arizona Historical Review,* vol. 6, no. 1. (Manuscript copy in the library of the Arizona Historical Society, Tucson.)

Garcés, Francisco
1900 *On the Trail of a Spanish Pioneer: The Diary and Itinerary of Francisco Garcés (Missionary Priest) in His Travels Through Sonora, Arizona, and California, 1775-1776,* ed. by Elliot Coues. Two volumes. New York: Francis P. Harper.

García, Jesús
n.d. "The Story of Jesús García as told to Arturo Carrillo and Mrs. George F. Kitt, August 23, 1933." Unpublished manuscript in the library of the Arizona Historical Society, Tucson.

García, Philip
1980 "Barrio childhood spurred architect's pride in area's buildings," *Arizona Daily Star,* November 2.

García Valencia, Jesús
n.d. "Reminiscences of Jesús V. García as told to Mrs. George F. Kitt, February 12, 1934." Unpublished manuscript in the library of the Arizona Historical Society, Tucson.

Gardner, Hamilton
1954 "Cooke's Report," *Utah Historical Quarterly,* vol. 22, no. 1.

Gerald, Rex E.
1968 *Spanish Presidios of the Late Eighteenth Century in Northern New Spain.* Santa Fe: Museum of New Mexico Research Records, no. 7.

Giebner, Robert C. (ed.)
1974 *Armory Park.* Tucson: College of Architecture, University of Arizona.
1979 *Preservation Primer.* Tucson: College of Architecture, University of Arizona.

Golder, Frank Alfred
1928 *The March of the Mormon Battalion.* New York and London: The Century Company.

Graham, James Duncan
1853 *Report of Lt. Col. Graham on the Subject of the Boundary Line Between the United States and Mexico.* Senate Executive Document 121, 32d Congress, 1st Session.

Gray, Andrew B. and Peter R. Brady
  1963 *The A.B. Gray Report, and Including the Reminiscences of Peter R. Brady*, ed. by L.R. Bailey. Los Angeles: Westernlore Press.

Greenleaf, Cameron and Andrew Wallace
  1962 "Tucson: Pueblo, Presidio, and American City," *Arizoniana*, vol. 3, no. 2.

Greer, James Kimmins
  1952 *Colonel Jack Hays, The Texas Frontier Leader and California Builder*. E.P. Dutton Company.

Griffen, William B.
  1983 "The Compás: A Chiricahua Apache Family of the Late 18th and Early 19th Centuries," *The American Indian Quarterly*, vol. VII, no. 2.
  1985 "Apache Indians and the Northern Mexican Peace Establishments," in *Southwestern Culture History: Collected Papers in Honor of Albert H. Schroeder*, ed. by Charles H. Lange. Santa Fe: The Archaeological Society of New Mexico, 10.

Griswold del Castillo, Richard
  1979 "Tucsonenses and Angelenos: A Socioeconomic Study of Two Mexican Barrios, 1860–1880," *Journal of the West*, vol. 18, no. 1.
  1984 *La Familia: Chicano Families in the Urban Southwest, 1848 to the Present*. University of Notre Dame Press.

Hadley, Diana W.
  1986 "Nuevas Perspectivas Sobre el Contacto Interétnico: La Campaña Apache del Coronel José María Elías González Durante la Gran Migración a los Placeres de California." Paper read at the XI Simposio de Historia y Antropología de Sonora. Hermosillo, Sonora, México.

Hallenbeck, Cleve
  1940 *Alvar Nuñez Cabeza de Vaca: The Journey and Route of the First European to Cross the Continent of North America, 1534–1536*. Glendale, California: The Arthur H. Clark Co.
  1949 *The Journey of Fray Marcos de Niza*. University Press in Dallas.

Hamilton, Patrick
  1884 *Resources of Arizona*, 3d edition. San Francisco: A.L. Bancroft and Company, Printers.
  1928 "Arizona - An Historical Outline," *Arizona Historical Review*, vol. 1, no. 1.

Hammond, George P.
  1927 "Don Juan de Oñate and the Founding of New Mexico." *Historical Society of New Mexico Publications in History*, vol. II, October. Santa Fe: El Palacio Press.

1929   "Pimería Alta After Kino's Time," *New Mexico Historical Review*, vol. 4, no. 3.

1931   "The Zúñiga Journal, Tucson to Santa Fe: The Opening of a Spanish Trade Route, 1788–1795," *New Mexico Historical Review*, vol. 6, no. 1.

Hammond, George P. and Agapito Rey

1928   *Obregón's History of 16th Century Explorations in Western America.* Los Angeles: Wetzel Publications Company.

1940   *Narratives of the Coronado Expedition, 1540–1542.* Albuquerque: The University of New Mexico Press.

1966   *The Rediscovery of New Mexico, 1580–1594.* Albuquerque: The University of New Mexico Press.

Hammond Publishers

1958   *World Atlas.* Classics Edition.

Hard, Robert J. and William H. Doelle

1978   *The San Agustín Mission Site, Tucson, Arizona.* Cultural Resource Management Section, Arizona State Museum, The University of Arizona. Archaeological Series No. 118.

Hardy, Robert W.H.

1829   *Travels in the Interior of Mexico.* London.

Hargett, Janet L.

1983   "Pioneering at Yuma Crossing: The Business Career of L.J.F. Jaeger," *The Journal of Arizona History*, vol. 25, no. 4.

Harris, Benjamin Butler

1960   *The Gila Trail. The Texas Argonauts and the California Gold Rush.* Norman: University of Oklahoma Press.

Hastings, James R.

1959   "The Tragedy at Camp Grant in 1871," *Arizona and the West*, vol. 1, no. 2.

1961   "People of Reason and Others: The Colonization of Sonora to 1767," *Arizona and the West*, vol. 3, no. 4.

Haury, Emil W.

1984   "The Search for Chichilticale," *Arizona Highways*, April.

Hayes, Benjamin T.

1929   *Pioneer Notes from the Diaries of Judge Benjamin Hayes, 1849–1875*, ed. by Marjorie Tisdale Wolcott. Privately printed in Los Angeles.

Hays, Carl D.W.

1972   "David E. Jackson," in *The Mountain Men and the Fur Trade of the Far West*, vol. IX, ed. by Leroy R. Hafen. Glendale, California: The Arthur H. Clark Co.

Herring, Hubert

1965   *A History of Latin-America from the Beginning to the Present.* New York: Alfred A. Knopf.

Herring, Patricia R.
  1969 "A Plan for the Colonization of Sonora's Northern Frontier:
        The Paredes Proyectos of 1850," *The Journal of Arizona History*,
        vol. 10, no. 2.
  1978 "The Silver of El Real de Arizonac," *Arizona and the West*, vol.
        20, no. 2.
Hinton, Richard J.
  1970 *The Hand-Book to Arizona: Its Resources, History, Towns, Mines,
        Ruins and Scenery*. Glorieta, New Mexico: The Rio Grande
        Press.
Historical Society of Southern California
  1931 "First Census of Los Angeles," *Annual Publications*.
Hodge, Frederick Webb (ed.)
  1960 *Handbook of American Indians North of Mexico*. Two volumes.
        New York: Pageant Books.
Hodge, Hiram C.
  1965 *Arizona As It Was*. Chicago: Reprinted by the Rio Grande Press.
Holmes, Kenneth L. (ed.)
  1983 *Covered Wagon Women. Diaries & Letters from the Western Trails,
        1840–1890*, vol. I, 1840–1849. Glendale, California: The Arthur
        H. Clark Co.
Holterman, Jack
  1955 "Mission San Bartolome de Xongopavi," *Plateau* (Museum of
        Northern Arizona), vol. 28, no. 2.
  1956 "José Zúñiga, Commandant of Tucson," *The Kiva*, vol. 22,
        November.
Horgan, Paul
  1975 *Lamy of Santa Fe*. New York: Farrar, Straus, and Giroux.
Howlett, William Joseph
  1908 *Life of the Right Reverend Joseph P. Machebeuf*. Pueblo, Col-
        orado: The Franklin Press Company.
Hunter, William H.
  n.d. "Transcript of a Diary-Journal of Events, Etc. on a Journey
        from Missouri to California in 1849." Manuscripot concerned
        with the adventures of the Missouri Company of Captain Samuel
        W. Berry. Special Collections, University of Arizona Library,
        Tucson.
Ives, Ronald L.
  1959 "The Grave of Melchior Díaz: A Problem in Historical Sleuth-
        ing," *The Kiva*, vol. 25, no. 2.
  1966 "Retracing the Route of the Fages Expedition of 1781," *Arizona
        and the West*, vol. 8, nos. 1–2.
Jackson, Robert H.
  1983 "Causes of Indian Population Decline in the Pimería Alta

Missions of Northern Sonora," *The Journal of Arizona History*, vol. 24, no. 4.

Jones, Nathaniel V.

1931 "The Journal of Nathaniel V. Jones with the Mormon Battalion," *Utah Historical Quarterly*, vol. 4, no. 1.

Kay, Jane

1980 "Hopis turn for help to fight looters," *Arizona Daily Star*, November 28.

Kenny, William Robert

1967 "Mexican-American Conflict on the Mining Frontier, 1848–1852," *Journal of the West*, vol. 6, no. 4.

Kessell, John L.

1965 "Documents of Arizona History: A Personal Note from Tumacácori, 1825," *The Journal of Arizona History*, vol. 6, no. 3.

1966 "The Puzzling Presidio: San Felipe de Guevavi, alias Terrenate," *New Mexico Historical Review*, vol. 41, no. 1.

1970 *Mission of Sorrows: Jesuit Guevavi and the Pimas, 1691–1767.* Tucson: The University of Arizona Press.

1976 *Friars, Soldiers, and Reformers: Hispanic Arizona and the Sonora Mission Frontier 1767–1856.* Tucson: The University of Arizona Press.

1979 *Kiva, Cross, and Crown: The Pecos Indians and New Mexico: 1540–1840.* Washington: National Park Service.

Kinnaird, Lawrence

1958 *The Frontiers of New Spain. Nicolás LaFora's Description, 1766–1768.* Berkeley, California: The Quivara Society.

Kino, Eusebio Francisco, S.J.

1948 *Historical Memoir of the Pimería Alta*, trans. by Herbert E. Bolton. Two volumes in one. Berkeley: University of California Press.

Laboratory of Tree-Ring Research (University of Arizona)

n.d. "Report on CORDOBA HOUSE, 173–177 North Meyer, Tucson, Arizona," October 25, 1973.

Laumbach, Verna

1933 "Las Vegas Before 1850," *New Mexico Historical Review*, vol. 8, no. 4.

Layton, Christopher

1966 *Christopher Layton*, ed. by Myron W. McIntyre and Noel R. Barton. 2d edition. Kaysville, Utah: Christopher Layton Family Organization.

Lecompte, Janet

1981 "The Independent Women of Hispanic New Mexico, 1821–1846," *Western Historical Quarterly*, vol. 12, no. 1.

Lockwood, Frank C.
1938   *The Apache Indians.* New York: The Macmillan Company.
1943   *Life in Old Tucson, 1854–1864.* Los Angeles: The Ward Ritchie Press.
1946   "The Gadsden Treaty," *Arizona Quarterly,* vol. 2, no. 2.
1968   *Pioneer Portraits.* Tucson: The University of Arizona Press.
Lockwood, Frank C. and Donald W. Page
1930   *Tucson—The Old Pueblo.* Phoenix: The Manufacturing Stationers.
Lomnitz, Larisa Adler and Marisol Pérez Lizaur
1978   "The History of a Mexican Urban Family," *The Journal of Family History,* vol. 3, no. 4.
Loomis, Noel M.
1969   "Commandants-General of the Interior Provinces, A Preliminary List," *Arizona and the West,* vol. 11, no. 3.
Love, Frank
1978   "Poston and the Birth of Yuma," *The Journal of Arizona History,* vol. 19, no. 4.
Manje, Juan Mateo
1954   *Luz de Tierra Incógnita,* trans. of Part II by Harry J. Karns and associates. Tucson: Arizona Silhouettes.
Martin, Douglas D.
1954   *Yuma Crossing.* Albuquerque: The University of New Mexiico Press.
Matson, Daniel S. and Bernard L. Fontana (eds.)
1977   *Friar Bringas Reports to the King.* Tucson: The University of Arizona Press.
Mattison, Ray H.
1946   "Early Spanish and Mexican Settlements in Arizona," *New Mexico Historical Review,* vol. 21, no. 4.
1967   "The Tangled Web: The Controversy Over the Tumacácori and Baca Land Grants," *The Journal of Arizona History,* vol. 8, no. 2.
McCarty, Kieran
1975   "The Colorado Massacre of 1781: María Montielo's Report," *The Journal of Arizona History,* vol. 16, no. 3.
1976   *Desert Documentary: The Spanish Years, 1767–1821.* Historical Monograph no. 4. Tucson: The Arizona Historical Society.
1981   *A Spanish Frontier in the Enlightened Age: Franciscan Beginnings in Sonora and Arizona, 1767–1770.* Washington: Academy of Franciscan History.
1981   "Tucson Census of 1831," *Copper State Bulletin* (Arizona State Genealogical Society), vol. XVI, nos. 1 and 2.
1982   "Tubac Census of 1831," *Copper State Bulletin* (Arizona State Genealogical Society), vol. XVII, no. 1.

1982 "Santa Cruz Census of 1831," *Copper State Bulletin* (Arizona State Genealogical Society), vol. XVII, nos. 2–4.

McClintock, James H.

1916 *Arizona: Prehistoric, Aboriginal, Pioneer, Modern.* Three volumes. Chicago: The S.J. Clarke Publishing Company.

McWilliams, Carey

1973 "The Heritage of the Southwest," in *Chicano: The Evolution of a People*, ed. by Renato Rosaldo, Robert A. Calvert, and Gustav L. Seligmann. Minneapolis: Winston Press.

Meier, Matt S. and Feliciano Rivera

1972 *The Chicanos: A History of Mexican-Americans.* American Century Series. New York: Hill and Wang.

Meyer, Michael C.

1984 *Water in the Hispanic Southwest, A Social and Legal History, 1550–1580.* Tucson: The University of Arizona Press.

Meyer, Michael C. and William L. Sherman

1983 *The Course of Mexican History.* 2d edition. New York and Oxford: Oxford University Press.

Miles, Carlota

1962 *Almada of Alamos.* Tucson: Arizona Silhouettes.

Miller, Darlis A.

1982 "Cross-Cultural Marriages in the Southwest: The New Mexico Experience, 1846–1900," *New Mexico Historical Review*, vol. 57, no. 4.

Montgomery, Ross Gordon, Watson Smith, and John Otis Brew

1949 *Franciscan Awatovi: The Excavations and Conjectural Reconstruction of a 17th-century Spanish Mission Establishment at a Hopi Indian Town in Northeastern Arizona.* Report no. 3 of the Awatovi Expedition. *Papers of the Peabody Museum of Archaeology and Ethnology*, vol. XXXVI. Harvard University.

Moorhead, Max L.

1968 *The Apache Frontier: Jacobo Ugarte and Spanish-Indian Relations in Northern New Spain, 1769–1791.* Norman: University of Oklahoma Press.

1969 "The Soldado de Cuera, Stalwart of the Borderlands," *Journal of the West*, vol. 8, no. 1.

1975 "Spanish Deportation of Hostile Apaches: The Policy and the Practice," *Arizona and the West*, vol. 17, no. 3.

1975 *The Presidio.* Norman: University of Oklahoma Press.

Moore, Mary Lu and Delmar L. Beene

1971 "The Interior Provinces of New Spain: The Report of Hugo O'Conor, January 30, 1776," *Arizona and the West*, vol. 13, no. 3.

Morfi, Juan Agustín
　1967　*Diario y Derretero (1777–1781)*, ed. by Eugenio del Hoyo and Malcolm D. McLean. Monterrey, Nuevo León, México: Publicaciones del Instituto Tecnológico y de Estudios Superiores.

Mowry, Sylvester
　1864　*Arizona and Sonora: The Geography, History, and Resources of the Silver Regions of North America.* New York.

Mulligan, R.A.
　1965　"Apache Pass and Old Fort Bowie," *The Smoke Signal*, no. 11. Tucson Corral of the Westerners.

Munson, Robert W.
　1976　"Don Ignacio and Doña Eulalia Elías and the History of Their Hacienda on the Babocómari: Camp Wallen," *The Cochise Quarterly*, vol. 6, no. 1.

Myres, Sandra L.
　1982　"Mexican Americans and Westering Anglos: A Feminine Perspective," *New Mexico Historical Review*, vol. 57, no. 4.

Navarro García, Luis
　1964　*Don José de Gálvez y la Comandancia General de las Provincias Internas del Norte de Nueva España.* Publicaciones de la Escuela de Estudios Hispano-Americanos de Sevilla.

Nentvig, Juan, S.J.
　1980　*Rudo Ensayo, A Description of Sonora and Arizona in 1764*, translated, clarified, and annotated by Alberto Francisco Pradeau and Robert R. Rasmussen. Tucson: The University of Arizona Press.

Nevins, Allan
　1928　*Fremont, The West's Greatest Adventurer.* Two volumes. New York and London: Harper and Brothers.

North, Diane
　1980　*Samuel Peter Heintzelman and the Sonora Exploring and Mining Company.* Tucson: The University of Arizona Press.
　1984　" 'A Real Class of People' in Arizona: A Biographical Analysis of the Sonora Exploring and Mining Company, 1856–1863," *Arizona and the West*, vol. 26, no. 3.

Office of the Adjutant General
　n.d.　File of Letters Received, 1822–1860. Record Group 94. Washington: U.S. National Archives.

Officer, James E.
　1960　"Historical Factors in Interethnic Relations in the Community of Tucson," *Arizoniana*, vol. 1, no. 3.
　n.d.　"Sodalities and Systemic Linkage: The Joining Habits of Urban Mexican-Americans." Unpublished doctoral dissertation, University of Arizona, 1964.

Officer, James E. and Henry F. Dobyns
1984   "Teodoro Ramírez, Citizen of Tucson," *The Journal of Arizona History*, vol. 15, no. 3.

Officer, James E., Armando Elías Chomina, and Carmen Pellat Sotomayor
1983   "Los Hijos de Pancho: La Familia Elías, Guerreros Sonorenses," in *Memorias*, Octavo Simposio de Historia de Sonora. Hermosillo, Sonora, México: Instituto de Investigaciones Históricas.

Oury, William S.
n.d.   "Tucson Property Record, 1862–64." Pima County Recorder's Office, Tucson. Copy in the library of the Arizona Historical Society.

Page, Donald W.
n.d.   "The Mexican troop's departure from Tucson, as recalled by Doña Atanacia Santa Cruz de Hughes and told to Donald W. Page, May 12, 1929." Unpublished manuscript in the library of the Arizona Historical Society, Tucson.

Pancoast, Charles
1930   *A Quaker Forty-Niner: The Adventures of Charles Edward Pancoast on the American Frontier*, ed. by Anna Paschall Hannum. Philadelphia: University of Pennsylvania Press.

Park, Joseph F.
n.d.   "The History of Mexican Labor in Arizona During the Territorial Period." Unpublished MA thesis in the Department of History, University of Arizona, 1964.

1961   "The Apaches in Mexican-American Relations, 1848–1861: A Footnote to the Gadsden Treaty," *Arizona and the West*, vol. 3, no. 2.

Parke, John G.
1857   *Report on Explorations for Railroad Routes from San Francisco Bay to Los Angeles, California, west of the coast range and From the Pimas Villages on the Gila to the Rio Grande Near the 32d parallel of North Latitude*, vol. VII of the Reports of Explorations and Surveys to Ascertain the Most Practicable and Economical Route for a Railroad from the Mississippi River to the Pacific Ocean. Made under the direction of the Secretary of War in 1853–56. Washington: Beverley Tucker, Printer.

Pattie, James O.
1962   *The Personal Narrative of James O. Pattie*. The 1831 Edition, Unabridged, with Introduction by William H. Goetzmann. Philadelphia and New York: J.B. Lippincott Co.

Pearce, T.M. (ed.)
1965 *New Mexico Place Names*. Albuquerque: The University of New Mexico Press.

Pellat S., Carmen
1979 "El Hospital Militar Real de Arizpe, Sonora (1786–1862)," *El Imparcial* (Hermosillo, Sonora, México), 22 de Abril.

Pfefferkorn, Ignaz
1949 *Sonora: A Description of the Province*, trans. by Theodore E. Treutlein, vol. XII, Coronado Historical Series. Albuquerque: The University of New Mexico Press.

Pitt, Leonard
1971 *The Decline of the Californios*. Berkeley, Los Angeles, London: University of California Press.

Polzer, Charles W.
1968 "Legends of Lost Missions and Mines," *The Smoke Signal*, no. 18. Tucson Corral of the Westerners.
1982 *Kino Guide II*. Tucson: Southwestern Mission Research Center, Arizona State Museum.

Poston, Charles D.
n.d. "Old Record Book 'A'." Pima County Recorder's Office, Tucson.
1963 *Building a State in Apache Land*, preface and notes by John Myers Myers. Tempe, Arizona: Aztec Press.

Potash, Robert A.
1949 "Notes and Documents," *New Mexico Historical Review*, vol. XXIV, no. 4.

Powell, H.M.T.
1931 *The Santa Fe Trail to California 1849–1852. The Journal and Drawings of H.M.T. Powell*, ed. by Douglas S. Watson. San Francisco: Book Club of California.

Pradeau, Alberto Francisco
1983 *Sonora y Sus Casas de Moneda*, 2d edition. Hermosillo: Gobierno del Estado de Sonora.

Probert, Alan
1969 "Bartolomé de Medina: The Patio Process and the 16th Century Silver Crisis," *Journal of the West*, vol. 8, no. 1.

Ramírez, Teodoro
n.d. "Notebook," trans. by Kieran McCarty. Special Collections, University of Arizona Library, Tucson.

Ready, Alma
1973 *Open Range and Hidden Silver: Arizona's Santa Cruz County*. Nogales, Arizona: Alto Press.

1980   *Nogales, Arizona 1880–1980 Centennial Anniversary.* Nogales Centennial Committee.

Real Academic Española
1970   *Diccionario de la Lengua Española*, 19th edition. Madrid.

Robinson, Cecil
1977   *Mexico and the Hispanic Southwest in American Literature.* Tucson: The University of Arizona Press.

Robinson, Will H.
1919   *The Story of Arizona.* Phoenix: The Berryhill Company.

Robinson, William J.
1976   "Mission Guevavi: Excavations in the Convento." *The Kiva*, vol. 42, no. 2, 1976.

Roske, Ralph J.
1963   "The World Impact of the California Gold Rush, 1849–1857," *Arizona and the West*, vol. 5, no. 4.

Russell, Frank
1908   "The Pima Indians," *Twenty-Sixth Annual Report.* Washington: Bureau of American Ethnology.

Sacks, Benjamin
1964   *Be It Enacted: The Creation of the Territory of Arizona.* Phoenix: Arizona Historical Foundation.
1965   "The Origins of Fort Buchanan," *Arizona and the West*, vol. 7, no. 3.

Safford, A.P.K. and Samuel Hughes
1873   "The Story of Mariana Dias," *Arizona Citizen*, June 21. Manuscript copy in the library of the Arizona Historical Society, Tucson.

Salmón, Roberto Mario
1983   "A 1791 Report on the Villa de Arizpe," ed. by Thomas H. Naylor. *The Journal of Arizona History*, vol. 24, no. 1.

Sandomingo, Manuel
1951   *Historia de Agua Prieta.* Agua Prieta, Sonora, México: Imprenta Sandomingo.

Santa Cruz, Atanacia (Mrs. Samuel Hughes)
n.d.   "Reminiscences of an Arizona Pioneer. Personal Experiences of Mrs. Samuel Hughes (Atanacia Santa Cruz), 1926." Manuscript 881, Charles Morgan Wood Papers, 1923–1927. Library of the Arizona Historical Society, Tucson.

Santamaría, Francisco J.
1974   *Diccionario de Mexicanismos.* México, D.F.: Editorial Porrua.

Sauer, Carl O.
1932   "The Road to Cíbola," *Ibero-Americana: 3*. Berkeley: University of California Press.

1941   "The Credibility of the Fray Marcos Account," *New Mexico Historical Review*, vol. 16, no. 2.

Schellie, Don

1968   *Vast Domain of Blood: The Story of the Camp Grant Massacre.* Los Angeles: Westernlore Press.

Schmidt, Louis Bernard

1961   "Manifest Opportunity and the Gadsden Purchase," *Arizona and the West*, vol. 3, no. 3.

Seibold, Doris K.

1946   "Cattle Raising and Spanish Speech in Southern Arizona," *Arizona Quarterly*, vol. 2, no. 2.

Serven, James E.

1965   "The Military Posts on Sonoita Creek," *The Smoke Signal*, no. 12. Tucson Corral of the Westerners.

Sheridan, Thomas E.

1986   *Los Tucsonenses: The Mexican Community in Tucson, 1854–1941.* Tucson: The University of Arizona Press.

Simmons, Marc

1975   "Spanish Attempts to Open a New Mexico-Sonora Road," *Arizona and the West*, vol. 17, no. 1.

Simons, Anna

1979   "Longtime team saves local old-time houses," *Arizona Daily Star*, July 15.

Simpson, Lesley Bird

1966   *Many Mexicos.* Berkeley and Los Angeles: University of California Press.

Smith, Cornelius C., Jr.

1967   *William Sanders Oury, The History-Maker of the Southwest.* Tucson: The University of Arizona Press.

Smith, Ralph A.

1962   "Apache Plunder Trails Southward, 1831–1840," *New Mexico Historical Review*, vol. 37, no. 1.

1962   "John Joel Glanton, Lord of the Scalp Range," *The Smoke Signal*, no. 6. Tucson Corral of the Westerners.

1964   "The Scalp Hunter in the Borderlands, 1835–1850," *Arizona and the West*, vol. 6, no. 1.

Smith, Watson

1957   "Victor Rose Stoner, 1893–1957," *The Kiva*, vol. 23, no. 2.

1970   "Seventeenth-Century Spanish Missions of the Western Pueblo Area," *The Smoke Signal*, no. 21. Tucson Corral of the Westerners.

Snowflake (Arizona) Historical Society

1977   "Samuel Hollister Rogers Visited Arizona 130 Years Ago (Excerpts From His Journal 1846–47)." *Wagon Trails*, no. 19.

Sobin, Harris J.
   1975   "From Vigas to Rafters: Architectural Evolution in Florence,
          Arizona," *The Journal of Arizona History*, vol. 16, no. 4.
Spicer, Edward H.
   1967   *Cycles of Conquest*. Tucson: The University of Arizona Press.
   1980   *The Yaquis: A Cultural History*. Tucson: The University of Ari-
          zona Press.
Spude, Robert L.
   1975   "The Walker-Weaver Diggings and the Mexican Placero, 1863–
          1864," *Journal of the West*, vol. 14, no. 4.
Stagg, Albert
   1976   *The First Bishop of Sonora Antonio de los Reyes, O.F.M.* Tucson:
          The University of Arizona Press.
   1978   *The Almadas and Alamos, 1783–1867*. Tucson: The University
          of Arizona Press.
Stevens, Robert C.
   n.d.   "Mexico's Forgotten Frontier: A History of Sonora, 1821–
          1846." Unpublished doctoral dissertation, University of Califor-
          nia at Berkeley, 1963.
   1964   "The Apache Menace in Sonora, 1831–1849," *Arizona and the
          West*, vol. 6, no. 3.
Stewart, Janet Ann
   1979   "The Mansions of Main Street," *The Journal of Arizona History*,
          vol. 20, no. 2.
Stoner, Victor R.
   1959   "Fray Pedro de Arriquivar, Chaplain of the Royal Fort at
          Tucson," ed. by Henry F. Dobyns, *Arizona and the West*, vol. 1,
          no. 1.
Strentzel, Louisiana
   1983   "A Letter from California, 1849," in *Covered Wagon Women*, ed.
          by Kenneth L. Holmes. Glendale, California: The Arthur H.
          Clark Co.
Strickland, Rex
   1976   "The Birth and Death of a Legend—The Johnson Massacre of
          1837," *Arizona and the West*, vol. 18, no. 3.
Suárez Barnett, Alberto
   1983   "La Reclamación del Rancho Los Nogales de Elías Ante la Su-
          prema Corte de Justicia de Estados Unidos," *Boletín de la So-
          ciedad Sonorense de Historia en Nogales*, vol. 1, no. 1.
Tevis, James H.
   1954   *Arizona in the '50s*. Albuquerque: The University of New Mex-
          ico Press.
Thomas, Alfred Barnaby
   1941   *Teodoro de Croix and the Northern Frontier of New Spain, 1776–*

1783. Norman: University of Oklahoma Press.

1969 *Forgotten Frontiers, A Study of the Spanish Indian Policy of Juan Bautista de Anza, Governor of New Mexico 1777–1787*. Norman: University of Oklahoma Press.

Thrapp, Dan L.

1967 *The Conquest of Apachería*. Norman: University of Oklahoma Press.

Tjark, Alicia Vidaurreta

1979 "Comparative Demographic Analysis of Texas, 1777–1793," in *New Spain's Far Northern Frontier. Essays on Spain in the American West, 1540–1821*, ed. by David J. Weber. Albuquerque: The University of New Mexico Press.

Torres Quintero, Gregorio

1921 *México hacia el fin del Verreinato español: Antecedentes sociológicos del pueblo mexicano*. México: El Pensamiento Vivo de América.

Treutlein, Theodore E.

1957 "Father Gottfried Bernhardt Middendorf, S.J., Pioneer of Tucson," *New Mexico Historical Review*, vol. 32, no. 4.

Trulio, Beverly

1973 "Anglo-American Attitudes Toward New Mexican Women," *Journal of the West*, vol. 12, no. 2.

Tyler, Sergeant Daniel

1969 *A Concise History of the Mormon Battalion in the Mexican War*. The Rio Grande Press.

Udall, Stewart L.

1984 "In Coronado's Footsteps," *Arizona Highways*, April.

Underhill, Lonnie E.

1980 *Genealogy Records of the First Arizona Volunteer Infantry Regiment*. Pueblo, Colorado: Roan Horse Press.

1984 "Dr. Edward Palmer's Experiences With The Arizona Volunteers, 1865–1866," *The Journal of Arizona History*, vol. 26, no. 1.

Velasco, Francisco

1985 *Noticias Estadísticas del Estado de Sonora*. Hermosillo: Gobierno del Estado de Sonora.

Vélez Ibáñez, Carlos G.

1983 *Rituals of Marginality: Politics, Process, and Culture Change in Urban Central Mexico, 1969–1974*. Berkeley, Los Angeles, London: University of California Press.

Vigness, David M.

1967 "Don Hugo Oconor and New Spain's Northeastern Frontier, 1764–1766," *Journal of the West*, vol. 6, no. 1.

Villa, Eduardo W.

1948 *Galería de Sonorenses Ilustres*. Hermosillo, Sonora, México: Impulsora de Artes Gráficas.

1951 *Historia del Estado de Sonora*. 2d edition. Hermosillo, Sonora, México: Editorial Sonora.

Villamarín, Juan A. and Judith E.

1975 *Indian Labor in Mainland Colonial Spanish America*. Occasional Papers and Monographs, no. 1. Latin American Studies Program, University of Delaware.

Voss, Stuart F.

1982 *On the Periphery of Nineteenth-Century Mexico*. Tucson: The University of Arizona Press.

Wagner, Henry R.

1934 "Fr. Marcos de Niza," *New Mexico Historical Review*, vol. 9, no. 2.

Wagoner, Jay J.

1970 *Arizona Territory 1863–1912: A Political History*. Tucson: The University of Arizona Press.

1975 *Early Arizona: Prehistory to Civil War*. Tucson: The University of Arizona Press.

Walker, Henry P.

1980 "Colonel Bonneville's Report. The Department of New Mexico in 1859," *Arizona and the West*, vol. 22, no. 4.

Wallace, Andrew (ed.)

1965 *Pumpelly's Arizona*. Tucson: The Palo Verde Press.

Wasley, William W.

1971 "Ravaged Ruins: The Destruction of Our Cultural Heritage," *Brand Book 2*. Tucson Corral of the Westerners.

Way, Phocion R.

1960 "Overland Via 'Jackass Mail' in 1858: The Diary of Phocion R. Way," part 2, ed. by William A. Duffen, *Arizona and the West*, vol. 2, no. 2.

Weber, David J.

1971 *The Taos Trappers: The Fur Trade in the Far Southwest, 1540–1846*. Norman: University of Oklahoma Press.

1982 *The Mexican Frontier, 1821–1846. The American Southwest Under Mexico*. Albuquerque: The University of New Mexico Press.

Weber, David J. (ed.)

1973 *Foreigners in their Native Land*. Albuquerque: The University of New Mexico Press.

1976 *Northern Mexico on the Eve of the United States Invasion. Rare Imprints Concerning California, Arizona, New Mexico, and Texas, 1821–1846*. New York: Arno Press.

1979 *New Spain's Far Northern Frontier. Essays on Spain in the American West, 1540–1821*. Albuquerque: The University of New Mexico Press.

Whiting, Alfred F.
1953 "The Tumacácori Cenus of 1796," *The Kiva*, vol. 19, no. 1.
Whitworth, Robert
1965 "Robert Whitworth's Diary," *Arizona and the West*, vol. 7, no. 2.
Wildman, Perry
1977 "Great Days at Silver King," *The Journal of Arizona History*, vol. 18, no. 4.
Willey, Richard R.
1979 "La Canoa: A Spanish Land Grant Lost and Found," *The Smoke Signal*, no. 38. Tucson Corral of the Westerners.
Williams, Jack S.
1986 "San Agustín del Tucson: A Vanished Mission Community of the Pimería Alta," and "The Presidio of Santa Cruz de Terrenate: A Forgotten Fortress of Southern Arizona," *The Smoke Signal*, nos. 47 and 48 (combined), Tucson Corral of the Westerners.
Williams, James Van Nostrand
n.d. "Life Sketch of James Van Nostrand Williams." Manuscript 869, Arizona Historical Society, Tucson.
Winship, George Parker
1896 *The Coronado Expedition, 1540–1542*. Washington: Fourteenth Annual Report of the Bureau of American Ethnology, 1892–93, part I.
Wood, Harvey
1955 *Personal Recollections of Harvey Wood*. Pasadena, California.
Woodward, Arthur (ed.)
1956 *Journal of Lt. Thomas W. Sweeny, 1849–1853*. Los Angeles: Westernlore Press.
Worcester, Donald E.
1941 "The Beginnings of the Apache Menace of the Southwest." *New Mexico Historical Review*, vol. 16, no. 1.
Wormser, Richard
1975 *Tubac*. The Tubac Historical Society Bicentennial Project.
Wright, Doris Marion
1940–41 "The Making of Cosmopolitan California: An Analysis of Immigration, 1848–1870," *California Historical Society Quarterly*, vol. 19 (December) and vol. 20 (March).
Wyllys, Rufus Kay
1931 "Padre Luis Velarde: Relación of Pimería Alta," *New Mexico Historical Review*, vol. 6, no. 2.
1932 *The French in Sonora, 1850–1854. The Story of French Adventurers From California Into Mexico*. Volume 21, University of

California Publications in History. Berkeley: University of California Press.

1950 *Arizona: The History of a Frontier State.* Phoenix: Hobson and Herr.

Yates, Richard

1972 "Locating the Colorado Mission of San Pedro y San Pablo," *The Journal of Arizona History*, vol. 13, no. 2.

Young, Otis E.

1955 *The West of Philip St. George Cooke, 1809–1895.* Glendale, California: The Arthur H. Clark, Co.

1965 "The Spanish Tradition in Gold and Silver Mining," *Arizona and the West*, vol. 7, no. 4.

Zúñiga, Ignacio

1985 *Rápida Ojeada al Estado de Sonora.* 3d edition. Hermosillo: Gobierno de Sonora.

Index

Index

About the Author

JAMES E. OFFICER served with the diplomatic corps in Chile during the early 1950s and returned in 1979 as a Fulbright professor. He has also been a consultant on Indian affairs for the Organization of American States and the government of Panama, represented the United States on the governing board of the Interamerican Indian Institute in Mexico City, and directed the University of Arizona Summer School in Guadalajara. During the 1960s, he was Associate Commissioner of Indian Affairs and Administrative Assistant to Secretary of the Interior Stewart L. Udall. Since 1969, Officer has been a professor of anthropology at the University of Arizona. He publishes in both Spanish and English and is a recipient of the Creative Teaching Award presented by the University Foundation and of the Tucson Trade Bureau's Mexico Goodwill Award.